Introduction to
Data Structures

Introduction to Data Structures

Bhagat Singh
University of Wisconsin Center System

Thomas L. Naps
Lawrence University

WEST PUBLISHING COMPANY
St. Paul   New York   San Francisco   Los Angeles

Copyediting: Lyn Dupré
Design: Rick Chafian
Artwork: Reproduction Drawings Ltd.
Typesetting: Graphic Typesetting Service
Production Management: Greg Hubit Bookworks
Cover Photographs: Floyd Rollefstad, Laser Fantasy Production

Library of Congress Cataloging in Publication Data
Singh, Bhagat, 1940–
    Introduction to data structures.

    Includes index.
    1. Data structures (Computer science)   I. Naps,
Thomas L.   II. Title.
QA76.9.D35S58   1985   001.64'2   84-23695
ISBN 0-314-85299-9

To
Joan Pauline Young
and
Keith D. Naps

Contents

3

String and Character Manipulation 39

4

Queues and Stacks 62

5

Applications of Stacks 82

8
Multidimensional Arrays and Sparse Matrices   176

9
Graphs and Networks   196

Preface

With the rapid evolution of computer science, the study of data structures has found its way into the undergraduate curriculum as early as the sophomore year. Moreover, an increasingly diverse collection of students is studying this subject. Once solely the domain of hard-core computer science majors, data structures now often is taken by business, economics, engineering, and mathematics majors who wish to enhance their chosen discipline with a strong background in computer science. Texts that emphasize a highly rigorous mathematical approach to data structures no longer are appropriate for this growing number of heterogeneous students. In *Introduction to Data Structures*, we attempt to satisfy the needs of this new group of students by providing a text that emphasizes implementing and evaluating data structures in practical situations and avoids relying on an overly theoretical approach. The text is appropriate for anyone who has had a solid programming course in any language. No mathematics background beyond college-level algebra is assumed.

We have chosen to make the text language independent for an obvious reason—data structures are language independent! Although we certainly commend the current trend toward teaching Pascal in undergraduate curriculums, it is important for the student to realize that data structures can be implemented in any language. Pascal, with its dynamic memory allocation and record description capabilities, offers many features that are convenient for but not essential to data structures. All that is really necessary to implement data structures is a directly accessible address space, such as an array or random access file.

For these reasons, we have chosen to present algorithms in a pseudocode (called PSEUDO), which can be translated into any high level language. The student translating PSEUDO algorithms into Pascal may have an easier task than the student using FORTRAN or COBOL because certain aspects of algorithms that involve data structures are "automatic" in Pascal; for example, the supplied NEW and DISPOSE procedures to allocate and reclaim memory space. Recognizing that Pascal will be the language chosen by many students to implement data structures, we have included Pascal supplements entitled *If you work in Pascal* at the end of each chapter, and a PSEUDO/Pascal appendix. The Pascal supplements provide verifications of many of the algorithms discussed in the chapter, whereas the appendix highlights the essential differences and similarities between PSEUDO and Pascal.

The two main goals of the text are language independent: (1) the student must acquire an understanding of the algorithms that manipulate various data structures; (2) the student must learn to select from among the data structures available for a given application. Relative to this second goal, data structures could be considered the toolbox of the computer scientist or data processor. Many jobs can be accomplished in more than one way.

The student who understands data structures thoroughly is able to match the tool to the job most effectively.

Understanding of data structures is enhanced by pictures. For this reason, we have made this a graphically oriented book. Algorithms stated in PSEUDO are complemented by documentation in graphic form to clarify for what various segments of code are responsible. Never has the old saying, "One picture is worth a thousand words," been more true than it is in the study of data structures. Data structures are, after all, the programmer's way of implementing certain types of mental images within the computer. Every segment of a program is in some sense responsible for maintaining or altering that structural image. What better way to document what a program segment does than to picture it?

The order of topics presented in the book is relatively flexible, although the first seven chapters represent a core of fundamental material that should be covered before moving on to any of the topics in Chapters 8 through 12. Chapter 1 lays the groundwork for the rest of the book by specifying the small core of rules for PSEUDO. We assume that the reader has already encountered one-dimensional arrays in a previous programming course, so the first data structure discussed in detail is the linked list, presented in Chapter 2. Implementation of linked lists in this chapter is achieved through the use of parallel data and link arrays, with a full discussion of algorithms to maintain dynamically an available space pool. The Pascal supplement for this chapter illustrates how the NEW and DISPOSE procedures remove this particular worry. In Chapter 3, we consider strings in detail as an example of an application in which pointers, indices, and linked lists can be used effectively. Chapter 4 presents two special types of lists: queues and stacks, and Chapter 5 follows up on this theme by looking at two critically important applications of stacks: the parsing of arithmetic expressions and recursion. Chapters 6 and 7 cover in detail what we believe to be the most versatile of all data structures—the tree. We discuss both binary and general trees, and discuss variations such as threading and height-balancing.

Although the first seven chapters of the book should be studied consecutively, there is considerable leeway in the order in which the remaining topics of the book may be covered. Some instructors may find it possible to cover only selected topics from Chapters 8 through 12, and these chapters are connected loosely enough to allow picking and choosing. Chapter 8 fully describes multidimensional and sparse matrices, which serves as a convenient introduction to the adjacency matrix representation of graphs and networks, the topic of Chapter 9: Chapters 8 and 9 thus form a cohesive unit. However, it is possible to proceed directly from Chapter 7 to either Chapter 10 (Sorting) or Chapter 11 (Search Methods). Chapter 12, Data Structures and Data Management, presents a nice wrapup for a data structures course by describing how a variety of data structures can be applied in the areas of memory management and database management. Because not all instructors will find time in a semester to cover the material in Chapter 12, we have written it such that it lends itself to independent study. For those students going on to systems programming, the material in Chapter 12 on memory management algorithms used by operating systems should prove particularly valuable. For the more business-oriented student, the database management section is more suitable. The flowchart summarizes the possible sequences in which chapters can be covered.

Additional features of the book include "In the world of applications" boxes, which emphasize how data structures are used in a variety of settings; chapter exercises and programming problems; and an appendix of solutions to odd-numbered exercises. The Instructor's Manual provides useful hints on how to present the material in each chapter,

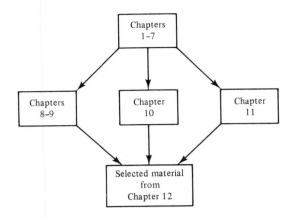

solutions to even-numbered exercises, and Pascal verifications of virtually all algorithms presented. Transparency masters that can be used to illustrate key concepts graphically in lectures also will be available for about 70 key figures in the text.

Acknowledgments

The text has come a long way from the version we first started to develop in 1981. It has progressed because of the contributions of a large number of people. The book has been classroom tested several times, and we owe a great deal to the perceptive feedback we received from our students. Jerry Westby, our editor, always had another fresh idea to try. Working with production editor Sharon Stanton and the rest of the staff at West Publishing proved to be a pleasure. Greg Hubit Bookworks developed the figures and graphic documentation that are so essential to the presentation of material in the book. Special thanks go to Susan Silton, who proofread the entire text more times than she cares to remember, and to the large group of skilled reviewers who offered constructive criticism on our efforts:

Gordon Bailes, East Tennessee State University
Rodney Bates, Kansas State University
Bruce Croft, University of Massachusetts, Amherst
Donald Epley, University of Iowa
Leonard Fisk, California State University, Chico
Thomas Gerasch, George Mason University
Robert Holloway, University of Wisconsin, Madison
Stephen Huang, University of Houston
Donald Kraft, Louisiana State University
Joseph M. Lambert, Pennsylvania State University
Sheau-Dong Lang, University of Central Florida
Dominic Magno, William Rainey Harper College
Steven Morgan, Texas A & M University
John Remmers, Eastern Michigan University
Sol Shatz, University of Illinois, Chicago

Jerrold Siegel, University of Missouri, St. Louis
John Todd, Northern Illinois University
Robert Trueblood, University of South Carolina
Karen Van Houten, University of Idaho
Vicki Walker, Arizona State University
Charles Williams, Georgia State University

Finally, of course, our *most* sincere appreciation goes to our wives and families. At times when it seemed as if the lists and trees in our minds were about to lose a crucial pointer, they were always there.

1

Data Structures—
An Overview

1-1   Introductory Considerations

The essence of programming and contemporary data processing requires **efficient algorithms** for accessing the data both in main memory and on secondary storage devices. This efficiency is directly linked to the structure of the data being processed. You do not have to progress far into the study of computers before realizing that only the most trivial applications allow data items to exist independently of each other. A data item that can be effectively linked to other data items takes on meaning that transcends its individual contents. For instance, a grade of "A" standing alone says very little. But a grade of "A" linked to a course title "Computer Science 480," which is in turn linked to the student "Mary Smith," takes on a much more significant meaning. A **data structure** is a way of organizing data that considers not only the items stored but also their relationship to each other.

A natural example is that of a **one-dimensional array** declared in a language like FORTRAN:

```
        INTEGER  I,M(20)
        READ (1,50)  (M(I),I=1,20)
  50    FORMAT (20I4)
```

We are told by these statements that the structure M contains 20 elements, each one integer word in length. The first element is M(1), the 10th element is M(10), and so on. The segment of the FORTRAN program given above will read numbers from an input medium

1

(specified by the unit number 1) and store them consecutively in M(1), M(2), . . . , M(20). The 20 words of memory associated with the structure M are contiguous. Thus, the way that data are accessed in M is a function of how it is organized.

The **record** is another common type of data structure used in languages such as PL/1, COBOL, and Pascal. In this structure, logically related data items of different types are grouped together under one name. An example of a record as it may be coded in COBOL is:

```
01      STUDENT-REC.
        02    NAME                 PIC  X(20).
        02    SEMESTER             PIC  99.
        02    EXAM-SCORE                PIC  9(3).
        02    GRADE                     PIC  X.
```

Its equivalent in Pascal is:

```
Studentrec   =   RECORD
                     Name : ARRAY [1..20] OF CHAR;
                     Semester : INTEGER;
                     Examscore : INTEGER;
                     Grade : CHAR
                 END;
```

These languages contain sufficient data description techniques to allow algorithms to access all or part of such a record structure. The concept of a record is essential to numerous applications in computer science and data processing, and we assume you have a basic familiarity with it.

Other more complex data structures such as stacks, queues, linked lists, trees, and graphs will be introduced as we progress.

A general understanding of data structures is essential to developing efficient algorithms in virtually all phases of advanced data processing and computer science. For example, in the implementation of a database management system, the two most commonly used techniques are the **linked list** (chain pointer) and **inverted file** methods. A clear notion of the relative advantages and disadvantages of each technique is obviously crucial to those designing such a system. However, as the advertisement reproduced in Figure 1-1 indicates, the buyer of a database management system also must be aware of the data structures involved in its design to avoid the risk of making a costly wrong decision.

The ability to make correct decisions is vital to anyone involved with computers. Such decisions typically involve the following general issues:

- The efficiency of a program with respect to its **run time.** Does it perform its task in a time allotment that does not detract from overall system performance?

- The efficiency of a program with respect to its **utilization of main memory and secondary storage** devices. Does it consume such resources in a fashion that makes its use impractical?

- The **developmental costs** of a program (or system of programs). Could a different approach to the problem significantly reduce the total person-hours invested in it?

Thorough knowledge of a programming language is *not* a sufficient base upon which to make these decisions. The study of data structures will expose you to a vast collection of

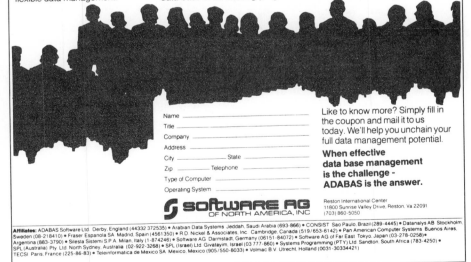

Figure 1-1   ADABAS database management advertisement
appealing to the buyer's knowledge of inverted file and chain
pointer data structures. (Reproduced courtesy of Software AG.)

In the world of applications . . .

Daniel D. McCracken, well-known computer author and consultant, identified five commandments for program developers in an article entitled "Software in the 80's," which appeared in *Computerworld* on September 17th, 1980.*

McCracken's 5 Commandments for Developers

1. Don't solve any problem that has already been solved.

2. Don't solve any problem twice yourself.

3. Don't solve any problem that someone else can solve better and more efficiently.

4. Don't "solve" any "problem" that results in a net loss of time and resources in completing the application.

5. Summary of above: Don't work any harder than you have to, don't do any useless work, and don't do any work that has negative value.

How do McCracken's commandments relate to the subject of data structures? The techniques you will learn in this book represent a collection of "problems that have already been solved." At one time they were part of a general computer folklore that one learned only by time-consuming, on-the-job experience. Today this *folklore* has come to be part of the documented knowledge we call **computer science.** It has become an essential part of what a prospective computer scientist is expected to know. Learn the techniques well! They can help you follow McCracken's commandments and devote your future efforts to solving new problems.

*Courtesy of Computerworld.

tried and proven methods used in designing efficient programs. Thus, as you develop an awareness of data structures, you will begin to realize the considerations involved in large-scale software projects. Later chapters and their exercises will illustrate applications of various data structures in such diverse areas as:

- Compiler design

- Operating systems

- Database management systems

- Statistical analysis packages

- Numerical analysis

- Graphics

- Artificial intelligence

- Simulation

- Network analysis

When you examine the relative advantages and disadvantages of different types of data structures in such applications, you become acutely aware of an old computer adage: *You get nothing for nothing*. That is, in many applications, different types of data structures could be used to achieve the same end. In such situations, the designer plays a game of tradeoffs. One data structure sacrifices memory compactness for speed; another utilizes memory efficiently but results in a slow run time. For each positive there is seemingly a corresponding negative. No absolute best data structure exists. Instead, designers must rely on their knowledge of the strong and weak points of various data structures to choose the one that best fits each application. These strengths and weaknesses will be fully discussed for each of the data structures we study.

1-2 Algorithms for Data Structures

Once a data structure has been chosen for a particular application, it is given life by the logical instructions that manipulate the related data items stored in it. Thus, a study of data structures is also necessarily a study of the **algorithms** that control them. Certain traits can be clearly identified as desirable in all such algorithms.

First, the algorithms must be expressed in a fashion that is completely *free of ambiguity*. Toward this end, the method we use to express algorithms must be formal enough to avoid the imprecision inherent in a natural language and yet flexible enough to allow us to focus on problem-oriented issues instead of syntactical considerations. In other words, an algorithm is best expressed as a happy medium between a natural language and a programming language.

Second, algorithms should be *efficient*. They should not unnecessarily use memory locations nor should they require an excessive number of logical operations. To analyze the efficiency of our algorithms, we will have to describe numerically the memory and logical operations that they require. Such a numerical analysis may tell us whether or not the algorithm is practical.

Third, algorithms should be *concise and compact* to facilitate verification of their correctness. **Verification** involves observing the performance of the algorithm with a carefully selected set of test cases. These test cases should attempt to cover all of the exceptional circumstances likely to be encountered by the algorithm. Just what these exceptional circumstances are will depend upon the data structure being manipulated. However, certain generic circumstances must be verified for *all* algorithms manipulating data structures:

- Does the algorithm work when the data structure is empty? For instance, does the logic of the algorithm correctly allow data to be added to a structure that presently contains no data? Is an attempt to delete data from such a structure appropriately trapped?

- Does the algorithm work when the data structure is full?

- Does the algorithm work for all the possibilities that can occur between an empty structure and a full structure?

The need for conciseness in algorithms becomes obvious when you consider the problem of verifying their correctness. The more an algorithm attempts to do, the more possibilities must be considered in its verification. Hence, we will take the view that *an algorithm should concern itself with one specific problem*. Each algorithm is a logical

module designed to handle a specific problem relative to a particular data structure. Such modules could be tied together by higher-level algorithms, which focus upon the connections between modules rather than the underlying data structures. However, our primary concern in this text will be with those algorithms that access the data structures. The interfacing of such modules into a complete system is appropriately studied in a course on systems analysis and design.

To express algorithms dealing with data structures, we will use a PSEUDO language. For the reader working in Pascal, we then offer many fully coded Pascal examples in supplements at the end of selected chapters. However, it is important to emphasize that data structures are language independent, and that PSEUDO is a general tool that allows adaptation to any high-level language.

Features such as **statement labels, variables** or **expressions,** and **assignment statements** are conceptually very similar in languages such as FORTRAN, PL/1, BASIC, COBOL, and Pascal. In addition to these broad categories, all high-level languages accept data in various forms, so that the notion of **data type** must be considered. Statements in such languages are further subdivided into **executable** and **nonexecutable.** For example, all languages will treat input/output instructions as executable, whereas statements specifying data type will generally be nonexecutable. A recent trend in the development of high-level languages has been minimization of the use of unconditional transfer instructions such as GOTO. This trend has led to constructs such as IF-THEN, IF-THEN-ELSE, CASE, WHILE-DO, and REPEAT-UNTIL, which lend further versatility to implementing refined and sophisticated data structures. Our goal in the description of PSEUDO that follows is to incorporate such considerations into a compact language capable of expressing efficient algorithms. The advantages of working in PSEUDO are that it communicates well and is free from the syntax considerations of a compiled language.

1-3 Specifics of PSEUDO

Data Types—Constants, Variables, and Expressions

All data described in PSEUDO must fit into one of five categories:

1. INTEGER

2. REAL

3. BOOLEAN

4. CHARACTER

5. LABEL

Both INTEGER and REAL data types are numeric. **INTEGER** data consist only of whole numbers, whereas **REAL** data have an appropriate exponential notation. For example, 18 is INTEGER but 1.8E1 and 0.92E-2 are REAL. In this text, REAL data will be used rarely.

BOOLEAN refers to logical data that have true and false as their only possible values. **CHARACTER** data are strings enclosed in quotes, such as "Simpson's Rule." In defining a **LABEL** data type, we are following the convention of languages such as Pascal and PL/1 in which labels assigned to procedural statements within a program are grouped under LABEL type. In PSEUDO, keywords associated with a particular statement are always underlined. Labels appear to the left of the statement they identify and are followed by a colon. As an example of these conventions, consider the PSEUDO segment:

```
GOTO PRINT-IT
       .
       .
       .
PRINT-IT: WRITE   SOC-SEC-NUM,NAME
```

Variables, or identifiers, are essentially memory addresses and must be declared to be one of the 5 data types via a nonexecutable VAR statement. Thus, we could have:

```
VAR   C1,C2,C3 :     INTEGER
VAR   EOF-FLAG :      BOOLEAN
VAR   STATUS-CODE :  CHARACTER
```

Data items may be compared using the relations:

$=$	equal to
$<$	less than
$>$	greater than
$<=$	less than or equal to
$>=$	greater than or equal to
$<>$	not equal to

We assume the standard arithmetic and logical operators $+$, $-$, $*$, $/$, *and, or,* and *not.* These operators can be applied to variables or constants to build up expressions that in turn belong to the same data type as their components. Note that *no mixing of data types within an expression is allowed.* As an example consider:

```
C3 := C1 + C2
```

Here C3 is assigned the integer sum of C1 plus C2 ($:=$ indicates assignment of a value to a particular variable).

Variables that are array names are followed by their size in the declaratory VAR statement:

```
VAR  MAN(15), JOB(5,4) : INTEGER
```

Because a CHARACTER variable contains a string of characters as a value, it is necessary to indicate the largest string it can hold by a parenthetical value following "CHARACTER" in the corresponding VAR statement. Hence:

```
VAR  NAME(10)  :  CHARACTER(8)
```

declares NAME to be a character array of extent 10. Each of the 10 locations NAME(1), NAME(2), . . . , NAME(10) is further declared to be of CHARACTER type with the capacity to hold a maximum of 8 characters. NAME(5,6) allows us to refer to the 6th character of the 5th name.

Finally, in PSEUDO we have no formal file-handling statements. Instead, when we discuss file structures, files will be viewed as arrays that exist on permanent storage devices. We will designate a particular record in a (direct access) file by referring to a subscript position in parallel arrays. Hence, given a file with records containing fields for social security number, name, and salary, we could refer to the *I*th record in the file merely via the combination of array entries:

```
SSN(I), NAME(I), SALARY(I)
```

This will allow us to describe file-handling algorithms in PSEUDO without the cumbersome OPENs, CLOSEs, READs and WRITEs necessary in compiled or interpreted languages.

Program Modules in PSEUDO

Program modules used in a description of an algorithm in PSEUDO may be the main program itself, procedures (subroutines), or functions. The general form of such a module is

```
⎧PROGRAM  ⎫
⎨PROCEDURE⎬ module-name [(argl,arg2,...)]
⎩FUNCTION ⎭
                .
                .
                .

[RETURN]
END           module-name
```

Here the list of arguments is used only for those modules that are subroutines and functions. For functions, the computed value is returned in the name of the function (as in Pascal or FORTRAN). Subroutine procedures are invoked by a CALL statement, whereas functions are invoked merely by their appearance in an expression. The RETURN entry in procedures and functions triggers a transfer of control back to the calling module. For instance, consider the following PSEUDO program, which calls for input of 2 numbers, interchanges them (via the procedure FLIP), and then outputs their sum (as computed by the function SUM).

```
PROGRAM MAIN-PROG

      (*Sample main program*)
      (*Declarations first*)

      VAR A,B: INTEGER

      (*Executable statements follow*)

      READ A,B
      CALL FLIP (A,B)
      WRITE SUM (A,B)
END MAIN-PROG

PROCEDURE FLIP(C,D)

      (*Procedure to interchange C and D *)

      VAR C,D, TEMP: INTEGER
      TEMP:=C
      C:=D
      D:=TEMP
      RETURN
END FLIP
```

```
FUNCTION SUM (X,Y)

    (*Function to sum up X and Y *)

    VAR X,Y : INTEGER
    SUM := X + Y
    RETURN
END SUM
```

In all PSEUDO procedures, it is assumed that arguments are passed *by reference;* that is, the called procedure receives the actual memory addresses of the calling program's variables. Hence, any changes made to these arguments in the called procedure are in fact affecting variables from the calling module. The only exceptions to this rule are arguments that are constants, expressions, or passed to a routine recursively. In such cases, the arguments are passed by their actual *value.* The need for this convention when recursion is used will be discussed in Chapter 5. Lengthy argument lists can at times be shortened by declaring certain variables GLOBAL to all modules. Such a GLOBAL declaration should appear in each of the modules. Thus, in PSEUDO, *variables are either local to one individual program module or globally known to all program modules.* To illustrate this concept, we can rewrite the preceding program using global variable names:

```
PROGRAM  MAIN-PROG

    (* Sample main program *)
    (* Declarations first *)

    GLOBAL VAR    A,B : INTEGER

    (* Executable statements *)

    READ A,B
    CALL FLIP

    (* No arguments needed because
     of global parameters *)

    WRITE SUM
END   MAIN-PROG

PROCEDURE FLIP

    (* Procedure to interchange A and B *)
    (* Local variable TEMP used
    for intermediate storage. *)

    GLOBAL VAR A,B : INTEGER
    VAR TEMP : INTEGER
    TEMP := A
    A := B
    B := TEMP
    RETURN
END FLIP
```

```
FUNCTION SUM

    (* Function to sum up A and B *)

    GLOBAL VAR A,B : INTEGER
    SUM := A + B
    RETURN
END SUM
```

Some additional remarks concerning the statements in these modules are in order. The statement

```
READ List of variables
```

is PSEUDO's basic **input** statement. Conversely,

```
WRITE List of variables
```

is used for **output,** with no consideration of formatting. Any text enclosed by (* . . . *) is viewed as a *comment*. Should a READ or WRITE list (or any PSEUDO statement) be so long as not to fit on one line, it may be continued by using *arrows* (→) at the end of the first line and the beginning of the continuation line, which should be *indented:*

```
WRITE     NAME, SOC—SEC—NUMBER, SALARY, --->
        ---> DEDUCTIONS
```

Logic and Control Structures in PSEUDO

Essential to PSEUDO's descriptions of logic and looping constructs is the idea that *no more than one instruction* (or part of one instruction in the case of continuation statements) *can appear on a given line.* PSEUDO uses this, with appropriate indentation and bracketing, to give a graphical (as opposed to syntactical) presentation of an algorithm.

Control Construct I—IF-THEN.

General Form:

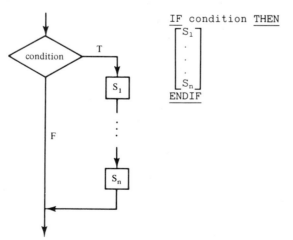

```
IF condition THEN
   ⌈S₁⌉
   │ . │
   │ . │
   │ . │
   ⌊Sₙ⌋
ENDIF
```

Example:

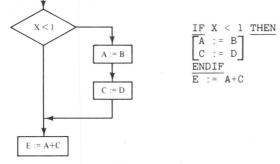

```
IF X < 1 THEN
 ⌈A := B⌉
 ⌊C := D⌋
ENDIF
E := A+C
```

Notice that square brackets [ ] are used to enclose the range of statements that are to be executed when the condition following IF is true. The indentation of these bracketed statements and the ENDIF delimiter serve to further highlight this range. Thus, in PSEUDO, we have a visual presentation of a program's logic instead of the syntax-dependent logic required of a formal compiled or interpreted language, such as Pascal's dependence on the careful placement of semicolons.

Control Construct II—IF-THEN-ELSE.

General Form:

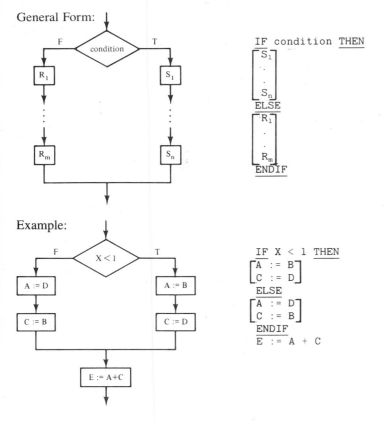

```
IF condition THEN
 ⌈S₁⌉
 | . |
 | . |
 ⌊Sₙ⌋
ELSE
 ⌈R₁⌉
 | . |
 | . |
 ⌊Rₘ⌋
ENDIF
```

Example:

```
IF X < 1 THEN
 ⌈A := B⌉
 ⌊C := D⌋
ELSE
 ⌈A := D⌉
 ⌊C := B⌋
ENDIF
E := A + C
```

Control Construct III—WHILE Loop.

General Form:

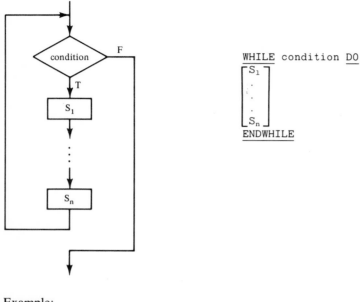

```
WHILE condition DO
⎡S₁ ⎤
⎢ .  ⎥
⎢ .  ⎥
⎢ .  ⎥
⎣Sₙ ⎦
ENDWHILE
```

Example:

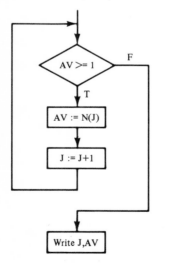

```
WHILE AV >= 1 DO
⎡AV := N(J)⎤
⎣ J := J+1 ⎦
ENDWHILE
WRITE J,AV
```

As in control constructs I and II, brackets, indentation, and the ENDWHILE clearly indicate the range of statements to be executed when the condition following WHILE is true.

Control Construct IV—REPEAT Loop.

General Form:

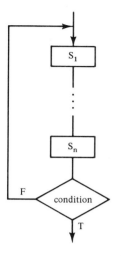

```
REPEAT
┌ S₁ ┐
│ .  │
│ .  │
│ .  │
└ Sₙ ┘
UNTIL condition
```

Example:

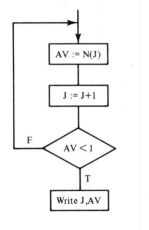

```
REPEAT
┌ AV := N(J) ┐
└ J  := J+1  ┘
UNTIL AV < 1
WRITE J,AV
```

Note that a REPEAT loop essentially uses the logically opposite condition to perform the same sequence of actions that could be achieved with a WHILE loop. There is, however, one fundamental difference: if the condition in a WHILE loop is false, the body of the loop will not be executed *at all*. In a REPEAT loop, the body is executed once prior to the testing of the condition and hence always will be executed *at least once*. It is always possible to exchange the function of a REPEAT or WHILE loop by making minor changes in a program.

Control Construct V—INCREMENTAL Loop.

General Form:

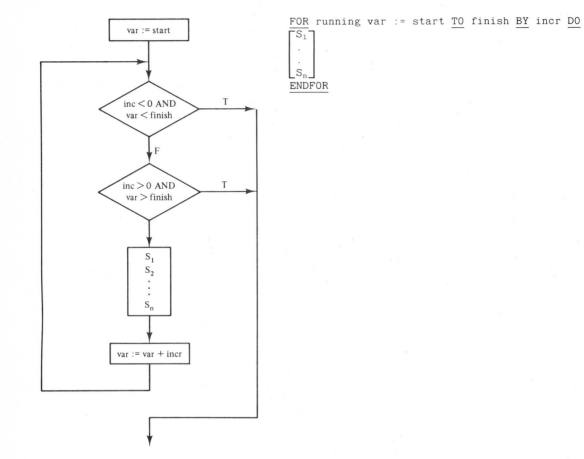

```
FOR running var := start TO finish BY incr DO
  ⌈S₁⌉
  │ . │
  │ . │
  ⌊Sₙ⌋
ENDFOR
```

Example:

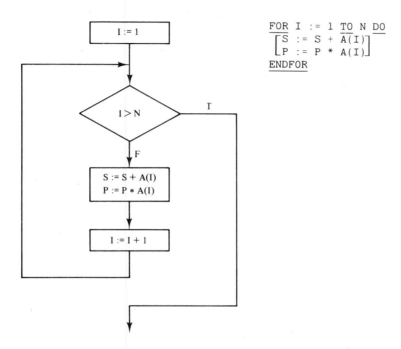

```
FOR I := 1 TO N DO
┌S := S + A(I)┐
└P := P * A(I)┘
ENDFOR
```

This control construct is just PSEUDO's version of the automatic looping mechanism found in all high-level languages; for example, FORTRAN's DO loop or Pascal's FOR loop. As do most of these high-level languages, we follow the convention that, if the increment is omitted, it is assumed to be +1. Note that the incremental loop is actually a luxury, because it can always be replaced by an equivalent WHILE loop. For instance, the incremental loop in the example is equivalent to:

```
I:=1
WHILE I<= N DO
  S:= S + A(I)
  P:= P * A(I)
  I:= I + 1
ENDWHILE
```

To illustrate the ease with which algorithms can be described in PSEUDO, we give below a POINTER SORT procedure to produce an alphabetized list of names, none of which exceed 20 characters. To highlight the action of the algorithm, marginal diagrams called "graphic documentation" are used.

```
PROGRAM  PSEUDO-DEMO
     GLOBAL VAR  POINTER(100) : INTEGER
     GLOBAL VAR  NAME(100) : CHARACTER(20)
     VAR  I,N : INTEGER
     (*The pointer sort method rearranges "pointers" to the*)
     (*various data elements without ever having to move any*)
     (*data itself*)
```

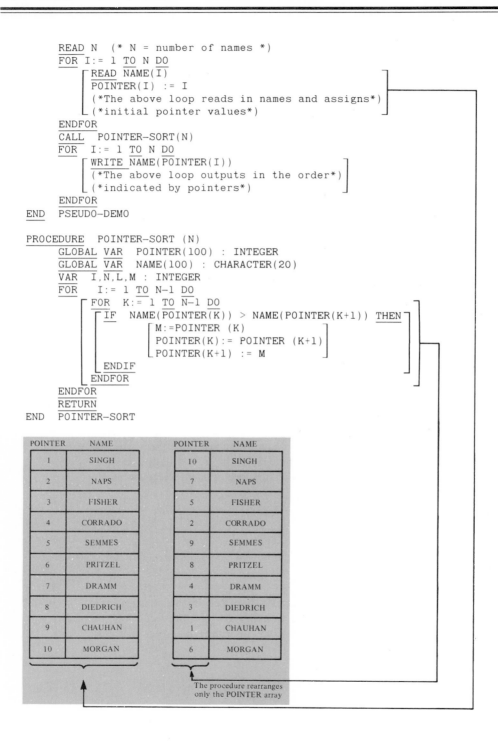

```
READ N  (* N = number of names *)
FOR I:= 1 TO N DO
      ┌ READ NAME(I)
      │ POINTER(I) := I
      │ (*The above loop reads in names and assigns*)
      └ (*initial pointer values*)
ENDFOR
CALL  POINTER-SORT(N)
FOR  I:= 1 TO N DO
      ┌ WRITE NAME(POINTER(I))
      │ (*The above loop outputs in the order*)
      └ (*indicated by pointers*)
ENDFOR
END  PSEUDO-DEMO

PROCEDURE  POINTER-SORT (N)
      GLOBAL VAR  POINTER(100) : INTEGER
      GLOBAL VAR  NAME(100) : CHARACTER(20)
      VAR  I,N,L,M : INTEGER
      FOR   I:= 1 TO N-1 DO
            ┌ FOR  K:= 1 TO N-1 DO
            │   ┌ IF  NAME(POINTER(K)) > NAME(POINTER(K+1)) THEN ┐
            │   │     ┌ M:=POINTER (K)
            │   │     │ POINTER(K):= POINTER (K+1)
            │   │     └ POINTER(K+1) := M
            │   └ ENDIF
            └ ENDFOR
      ENDFOR
      RETURN
END  POINTER-SORT
```

POINTER	NAME	POINTER	NAME
1	SINGH	10	SINGH
2	NAPS	7	NAPS
3	FISHER	5	FISHER
4	CORRADO	2	CORRADO
5	SEMMES	9	SEMMES
6	PRITZEL	8	PRITZEL
7	DRAMM	4	DRAMM
8	DIEDRICH	3	DIEDRICH
9	CHAUHAN	1	CHAUHAN
10	MORGAN	6	MORGAN

The procedure rearranges only the POINTER array

It is essential that you trace through and understand the POINTER SORT algorithm; we will be referring to it again in Chapter 2. Suppose, for example, that after the READ loop given in the PSEUDO-DEMO procedure, we had arrays of names and corresponding pointer values as follows:

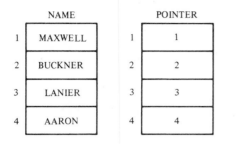

After a return from the procedure POINTER-SORT, the NAME array would be left untouched, but the POINTER array would be altered to appear:

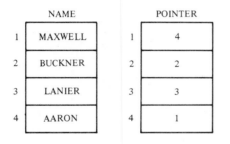

Notice that if we follow in order the NAME subscripts given in the POINTER array, we obtain an alphabetical listing of the names.

SUMMARY

A data structure is a way of organizing data that considers not only the items stored but also their relationship to each other. Advance knowledge about the relationship between data items allows design of efficient algorithms for the manipulation of data. Diverse applications such as compiler design, operating systems, database management systems, statistical analysis packages, numerical analysis, graphics, artificial intelligence, and simulation (to mention a few) use data structures heavily.

PSEUDO is a convenient vehicle we have designed to study data structures. You should become familiar with the language, because all algorithms in this text will be described in PSEUDO.

KEY TERMS

Data structure	IF-THEN-ELSE	CHARACTER
Array	REPEAT UNTIL	LABEL
Algorithm	INTEGER	GLOBAL
Variable	REAL	FUNCTION
Executable	BOOLEAN	IF

EXERCISES

1. Write a procedure in PSEUDO that will check for the largest and smallest entries in an integer array.

2. Write a procedure in PSEUDO that will sum the entries in a real array.

3. Write a procedure in PSEUDO that will reverse the order of the entries in an integer array.

4. Translate the PSEUDO POINTER SORT procedure from the end of this chapter into a high-level language of your choice.

If you work in Pascal . . .

The following program is a Pascal version of the PSEUDO POINTER SORT given at the end of the chapter. Note that, except for PSEUDO's freedom from syntactical considerations, a fairly direct mapping exists from PSEUDO to Pascal. One key difference, however, is that in PSEUDO subroutine procedures and functions generally appear below the modules that call on them. We believe that this positioning better reflects the subordinate nature of such modules.

```
    program pseudodemo(input,output);
  (*Illustrate mapping of PSEUDO to Pascal *)
  TYPE
    strings = ARRAY [1..100] OF ARRAY [1..80] OF char;
  VAR
    i,n : integer;
    name : strings;
    pointer : ARRAY [1..100] OF integer;
    PROCEDURE pointersort(VAR n : integer);
  (*Apply pointersort to array of  n  names*)
  VAR
    i,k,m : integer;
  BEGIN
    FOR i:=1 TO n-1 DO
    FOR k:=1 TO n-i DO
    (*Exchange adjacent names that are out of order*)
    IF name[pointer[k]] > name[pointer[k+1]]
      THEN
        BEGIN
          m:=pointer[k];
          pointer[k]:=pointer[k+1];
          pointer[k+1]:=m
        END
  END(*POINTERSORT*);
```

```
      BEGIN
       readln(n);
       FOR i := 1 TO n DO
        BEGIN
          readln(name[i]);
          pointer[i] := i
        END;
       pointersort(n);
       writeln;writeln;writeln('**NOW PRINT IN ORDER**');writeln;
       FOR i:=1 TO n DO writeln(name[pointer[i]])
      END(*PSEUDODEMO*).
```

Results of a demonstration run follow:

```
4
MAXWELL
BUCKNER
LANIER
AARON




**NOW PRINT IN ORDER**

AARON
BUCKNER
LANIER
MAXWELL


Ready
```

2

Linked Lists

A chain is only as strong as its weakest link.

OLD PROVERB

2-1   Introductory Considerations

We are all familiar with the dynamics of waiting in a long line. When someone cuts into the middle of the line, there is a dominolike effect that forces everyone behind that person to move back. When someone in the middle of the line decides to leave the line, the reverse effect occurs; everyone behind the departed person is able to move ahead one slot. It is possible to draw an analogy between people waiting in a line and data items stored next to each other in computer memory. If the data items are arranged in some type of order and it becomes necessary to insert into or delete from the middle of the line, a considerable amount of **data movement** is involved. This data movement requires computer time and decreases program efficiency. The central motivation behind the **linked list** data structure is *to eliminate the data movement associated with insertions into and deletions from the middle of the list.*

2-2   Arrays

One of the most commonly used data structures is an **array.** Although we shall say a great deal about multidimensional arrays in a later chapter, we assume that you are familiar with the concept of a one-dimensional array. Also termed a **vector,** this type of array simply refers to a specific number of consecutive memory locations. This number is the size of the vector. A one-dimensional array of data items is thus the computer equivalent of the densely packed line of people. Note that in an array we have the ability to access *directly* any item in the list merely by specifying its position. Two-, three-, or higher-dimensional arrays can be viewed for the time being as arrays of one-dimensional arrays.

   Arrays are often used for contiguous storage of data. For example, the FORTRAN array

DIMENSION M(10,15)

20

can be conveniently used to store 150 integer numbers in a contiguous structure that can be viewed as consisting of 10 rows and 15 columns. Similarly the array declared in BASIC by

```
DIM X$(120)
```

can be used to alphabetize a small list containing no more than 120 names. Once stored in an array, data can be accessed directly. For example, if we ask to examine the 40th name in our list of 120 names, we do not need to examine the first 39 names.

For general implementation, an n-dimensional array is represented in PSEUDO as

```
VAR    NAME (d1, d2,. . . , dn) : other attributes
```

where d1, d2,. . . , dn are integers.

For example:

```
VAR    SIMPLE(4, 5, 7)  :  REAL
```

defines SIMPLE to be a three-dimensional array of size $4 \times 5 \times 7 = 140$ in which each location stores only numeric data of type real. Most high-level languages have facilities for array structures.

2-3   Linked Lists

A structure involved in many data processing activities is the **ordered list** of data items. Typical examples are alphabetical lists of names, a master payroll file containing information about employees in ascending order of social security number, or lists sorted by days of the year or chronologically sequenced events. Such a data set can be represented by a one-dimensional array in which the jth subscript corresponds to the jth item in the ordered list.

When such ordered lists contain a large number of entries, developing efficient means of updating them is a matter of great concern. In general, data processing activity pertaining to an ordered list involves:

1. **Accessing** the jth element of the list where, if n is the length of the list, then $1 \leqslant j \leqslant n$

2. **Inserting** a new element between positions j and $(j + 1)$ in the list, while maintaining the correct order

3. **Deleting** the jth element from the list, while preserving the order of the list

   If, for example, we have a list of student ID numbers in ascending order

   ```
   (1121, 1125, 1172, 1180, 1195)
   ```

to which another ID 1175 is to be added, then we want this list to remain in proper order:

```
(1121, 1125, 1172, 1175, 1180, 1195)
```

Similarly if an existing ID, such as 1125, is to be deleted from this new list, then the list should properly appear as

```
(1121, 1172, 1175, 1180, 1195)
```

upon completion.

Although small ordered lists can be implemented with ease using arrays, maintenance of longer ordered lists in this type of contiguous storage structure becomes very expensive because of the number of data that must be moved for each operation. A quick look at the previous example should convince you that the tasks of inserting in and deleting from an ordered list containing thousands of data items require considerable data movement up and down the list. If, in a large company, the master list of employees arranged in ascending order of their social security number is updated frequently by insertions and deletions, then the array is a highly inefficient way of accomplishing such an update. What we need is a structure that *minimizes* such wholesale data movement.

In Chapter 1, we introduced a sorting method (called the POINTER SORT) that, *without physically moving the data to be sorted,* achieved sorting by merely rearranging the pointers to data items in a parallel array. By eliminating the necessity of interchanging character strings, the use of these pointers makes the sorting algorithm more efficient from the perspective of data movement and, consequently, run time. Note that, at the same time, the algorithm becomes less efficient from the perspective of memory utilization because of the "data about data" maintained by the pointers. This tradeoff between efficiency in run time and memory utilization must be weighed continually when you select a data structure. Although a great deal more will be said about sorting techniques in a later chapter, the example of the POINTER SORT illustrates that, if you can afford the memory overhead of storing data about data, then run time efficiency often can be enhanced.

Like the array of pointers used in the POINTER SORT example, a linked list is a structure that leads to algorithms that minimize data movement as insertions and deletions occur in an ordered list. Each element—called a **node**—in a linked list contains not only a data field but also one **pointer** (in the sense of an *address*) to other nodes in the list. The pointer system in the linked list structure eliminates the need for wholesale movement of data in memory, because all that is needed to keep track of the position of a node in the list is to update its pointer. Thus, insertions, deletions, and extensions of the list become significantly more economical in processing time than they are in an array in which proper positioning of the data items up and down the list is mandatory. A linked list thus maintains data items in a **logical order** rather than in a **physical order.**

Singly Linked Lists

A **singly linked list** is a linked list in which each node contains only one link field pointing to the next node in the list. The first node in the list is pointed to by a HEAD pointer. The last node in the list has a link field containing a NULL flag indicating "end of list." Figures 2-1 and 2-2 on pages 24 and 25 show the physical and logical representations of a linked list containing 5 data nodes arranged in alphabetical order. The physical representation in Figure 2-1 could be 2 parallel arrays. Alternatively, some languages (for example, Pascal) offer their users the capability to declare **records,** contiguous allocations of memory that are subdivided into **fields** of potentially different data types such as DATA and LINK in Figure 2-1. In such a language, the physical representation in Figure 2-1 could be one array of records. Again, depending upon the language used, memory for such records could be allocated at compilation time (**static allocation**) or execution time (**dynamic allocation**). Such a dynamic record-oriented approach is highlighted in the Pascal supplement at the end of this chapter. Within the chapter, we represent linked lists as parallel arrays, thereby retaining language independence.

In the world of applications . . .

Operating systems typically grant their users disk storage in units called **blocks.** On the magnetic disk itself, a block is a contiguous area capable of storing a fixed number of data; for example, a block in DEC's well-known RSTS timesharing system is 512 bytes. As a user enters data into a disk file, the system must grant additional blocks of storage as they are needed. In such a timesharing environment, although each block represents a physically contiguous storage area on the disk, it may not be possible for the operating system to give a user blocks that are physically next to each other. Instead, when a user needs an additional storage block, the operating system may put information into the current block about where the next block is located. In effect, a **link** is established from the current block to the next block. By the time a naive user has completed entering a 4-block file, it may well be scattered over the entire disk surface, as indicated in the diagram.

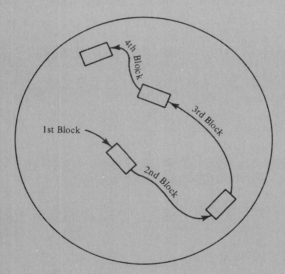

Although this may seem like an ingenious way of extending files indefinitely, one pays a price for such scattered blocks. Namely, the read/write head that seeks and puts data on the disk surface is forced to move greater distances, thereby slowing system performance. To combat such inefficiencies, shrewd users can often take advantage of options that allow them to pre-allocate the disk storage that will be required for a file. Moreover, system managers may occasionally bring down the entire system to rebuild disks, a process that entails copying all files that are presently scattered over the old disk onto a new disk in physically contiguous form.

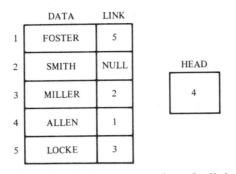

Figure 2-1   Physical representation of a linked list.

We shall demonstrate the processing of a singly linked list structure by examining a procedure to find the average of numeric data items stored in a linked list. The procedure itself must also determine the number of nodes in the list (n) in order to calculate the sum.

```
PROCEDURE AVERAGE(HEAD,LINK,DATA,MAX,AVE)

(*Determine the average of real—valued nodes in a linked list.*)
(*LINK and DATA arrays are as in Figure 2—1, with MAX representing*)
(*the size of these arrays.*)

VAR   N,MAX,HEAD,POINTER,LINK(MAX): INTEGER
VAR   AVE,SUM,DATA(MAX) : REAL
      POINTER:=HEAD
      N:=0
      SUM:=0
          WHILE    POINTER <> NULL DO
              ⌈SUM:=SUM + DATA(POINTER)⌉
              │N:=N + 1                 │
              ⌊POINTER:= LINK(POINTER) ⌋
          ENDWHILE
          AVE:= SUM/N
          WRITE 'AVERAGE OF', N, --->
              ---> 'DATA ITEMS IN THE LIST = ' , AVE
END   AVERAGE
```

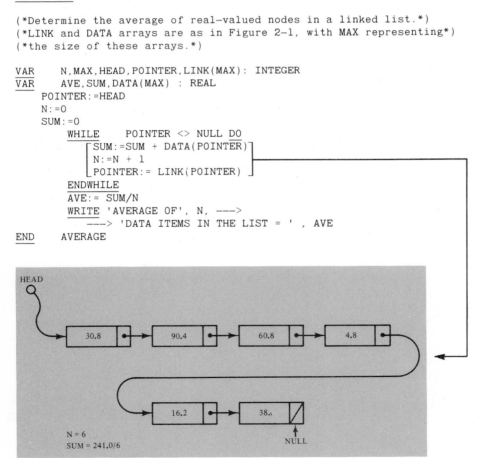

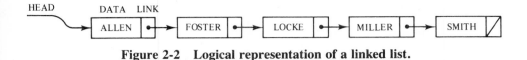

HEAD   DATA LINK

Figure 2-2   Logical representation of a linked list.

Insertions and Deletions

The algorithm described in the AVERAGE procedure illustrates how to traverse all the nodes in a linked list. The primary usefulness of this structure, however, is in minimizing the processing time for data insertion into and deletion from the list. These operations are carried out without disturbing the position of the data because they require rearranging only pointers. Suppose, for example, we have an alphabetically arranged linked list that appears as shown in Figure 2-3 on page 26.

If we now wish to add a node containing PRIM to the list, then all we need to do is to store PRIM in an available memory location outside of the list, such as that one pointed to by P in Figure 2-4 on page 27. We then rearrange the pointer link of the node containing OLP to point to the node containing PRIM, and the pointer link of the node containing PRIM to point to the node containing SINGH. This logically maintains the alphabetical order of the data in the nodes without physically moving any of the existing nodes.

In order to implement the procedure for inserting a node in an already existing singly linked list, it is necessary to have a procedure that supplies an unused node from the pool of available unused memory. We call this procedure GETNODE. Similarly, when a node in the linked list is no longer needed, we should be able to return it to the pool of available nodes. RETURNNODE is a procedure that does this. In some languages, such as Pascal, procedures equivalent to GETNODE and RETURNNODE are provided. We shall first show how GETNODE and RETURNNODE can be implemented in languages where such provisions are not made. Essentially, you need only store the available pool of nodes as a separate linked list with its own head pointer AVAIL. Because the order of nodes is not important in this available space list, all insertions and deletions can occur at its head. One possible method of initializing such an available space follows, along with GETNODE and RETURNNODE procedures.

```
PROCEDURE INITIALIZE(AVAIL,LINK,N)

(*Initialize an available space list to be used by procedures *)
(*GETNODE and RETURNNODE. The head of the list is location 1.*)
(*This value is returned in the head pointer AVAIL.*)
(*Thereafter, location I is linked to location I+1.*)

VAR        AVAIL,N,I,LINK(N):INTEGER

FOR I:= 1 TO (N-1)
    [LINK(I):=I+1]
ENDFOR
LINK(N):=NULL
AVAIL:=1
END INITIALIZE
```

	LINK
AVAIL = 1	2
2	3
3	4
⋮	⋮
N − 2	N − 1
N − 1	N
N	NULL

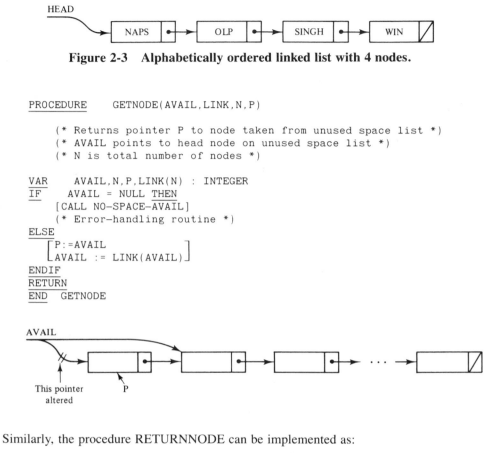

Figure 2-3 Alphabetically ordered linked list with 4 nodes.

```
PROCEDURE    GETNODE(AVAIL,LINK,N,P)

    (* Returns pointer P to node taken from unused space list *)
    (* AVAIL points to head node on unused space list *)
    (* N is total number of nodes *)

VAR    AVAIL,N,P,LINK(N) : INTEGER
IF    AVAIL = NULL THEN
    [CALL NO-SPACE-AVAIL]
    (* Error-handling routine *)
ELSE
    ┌P:=AVAIL           ┐
    └AVAIL := LINK(AVAIL)┘
ENDIF
RETURN
END  GETNODE
```

Similarly, the procedure RETURNNODE can be implemented as:

```
PROCEDURE    RETURNNODE(AVAIL,LINK,N,P)

    (* Same parameters as GETNODE except *)
    (* now P is to be returned to available space list *)

VAR    AVAIL,N,P,LINK(N) : INTEGER
    ┌LINK(P) := AVAIL┐
    └AVAIL := P      ┘
RETURN
END RETURNNODE
```

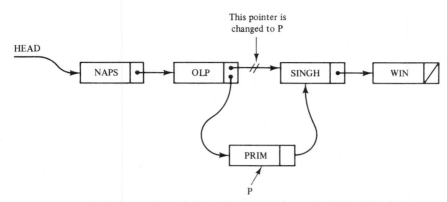

Figure 2-4 Insertion of the node PRIM into the linked list in Figure 2-3.

Finally, the procedure INSERTNODE inserts a node, pointed to by P, into a linked list pointed to by HEAD, immediately after the node pointed to by PREV:

```
PROCEDURE    INSERTNODE (N,LINK,HEAD,P,PREV)
VAR      N,LINK(N),HEAD,P,PREV : INTEGER

     (* Insert node pointed to by P *)
     (* after node pointed to by PREV. *)
     (* Assumes P already obtained via *)
     (* other means (e.g., GETNODE) and *)
     (* filled with appropriate data. *)
     (* The condition PREV = NULL is *)
     (* used to indicate insertion *)
     (* at the head of the list.*)

IF PREV = NULL THEN (*Insert at front*)
  ⌈LINK(P) := LINK(PREV)⌉
  ⌊HEAD := P          ⌋
ELSE
  ⌈LINK(P) := LINK(PREV)⌉
  ⌊LINK(PREV) := P     ⌋
ENDIF
RETURN
END  INSERTNODE
```

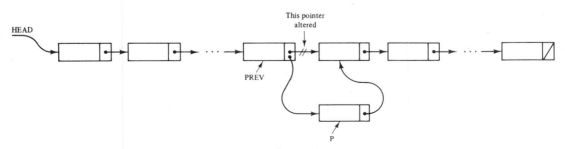

You should also note that the conditional test in INSERTNODE to determine whether the insertion is occurring at the front of the list can be eliminated if a special PREFIRST, or **dummy header,** node is maintained. This technique will be discussed in more detail later in this chapter; it then will be followed as a convention throughout the remainder of the text.

When you desire to delete an existing node from the list, you can merely alter the pointers to reflect this change. Again, *no movement of data occurs*. For example, given the list in Figure 2-4, the diagram of Figure 2-5 outlines what must be done if we wish to delete the node containing OLP.

The procedure to delete can be implemented in a fashion similar to INSERTNODE. When a data node is deleted from the list, this node is returned to the pool of unused available nodes. In the following procedure, DELETENODE, a node pointed to by P and preceded by a node pointed to by PREV is deleted and returned to the list of available nodes.

```
PROCEDURE    DELETENODE (N,LINK,HEAD,P,PREV,AVAIL)
VAR       N,LINK(N),HEAD,P,PREV,AVAIL:INTEGER

    (* Delete node pointed to by P *)
    (* and preceded by the node pointed *)
    (* to by PREV. *)
    (* The condition PREV = NULL signals *)
    (* deletion of first node *)

    IF  PREV = NULL THEN (*Delete first node*)
        [HEAD:=LINK(HEAD)]
    ELSE
        [LINK(PREV):=LINK(P)]
CALL   RETURNNODE(AVAIL,LINK,N,P)
RETURN
END   DELETENODE
```

As in INSERTNODE, the special test for deletions of the first node can be eliminated by the technique of maintaining a dummy header node at the beginning of the list.

2-4   Variations on Linked List Structures

Dummy Headers

A PREFIRST, or dummy header, node in the list before the first actual data node can often contain useful information about the structure (for example, the number of nodes). A query algorithm can then determine the status of the list by examining the contents of the PREFIRST node. This amounts to adding one more node to the list. Figure 2-6 illustrates this concept. Additions to and deletions from the list require changing this information-keeping field in the dummy header node of the list.

There is another distinct advantage of the dummy header node. If the list becomes empty and a dummy header node is not used, then the HEAD pointer for the list must be made NULL. But if the dummy header node is present, then the HEAD pointer never needs to be changed to NULL, because it always points to this dummy header. This convention can serve to simplify the coding involved in procedures INSERTNODE and

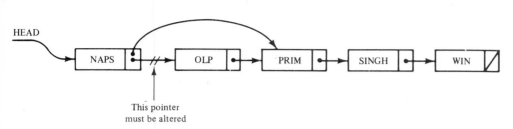

HEAD

NAPS — OLP — PRIM — SINGH — WIN

This pointer
must be altered

Figure 2-5   Deletion of a node from the linked list in Figure 2-4.

DELETENODE by removing the special handling previously required for inserts and deletes at the beginning of the list. You will write these simplified procedures as an exercise at the end of the chapter. Because of the convenience offered by a dummy header node, we will use it for all linked lists.

Circular Linked Lists

Although linked lists are satisfactory in many instances, the presence of a null pointer at the end of the list makes this structure most efficient only if the entire list is to be processed; the efficiency of such list processing algorithms decreases when the linked list is to be processed beginning at an arbitrary point in the list. In such situations, it would be desirable to be able to enter the list anywhere and process it with efficiency independently of the entry point. In other words, we need a linked list that has no beginning or end.

Circular linked lists are precisely such data structures. A **singly linked circular list** is a linked list in which the last node of the list points to the first node in the list. Notice that in circular list structures, there are no NULL links. Figure 2-7 depicts a singly linked circular list.

In the procedures INSERTNODE and DELETENODE we had prior knowledge about *where* in the list insertions and deletions were to be performed. In general, this information may have to be determined through a routine that searches the entire list. Because search algorithms require time proportional to half the length of the list, run time can be substantial if the list is very long. As an example, suppose we have a singly linked list in which we wish to insert a node A pointed to by POINT1 just before a node B pointed to

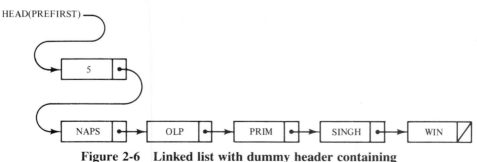

HEAD(PREFIRST)

5

NAPS — OLP — PRIM — SINGH — WIN

**Figure 2-6   Linked list with dummy header containing
information about the length of the list.**

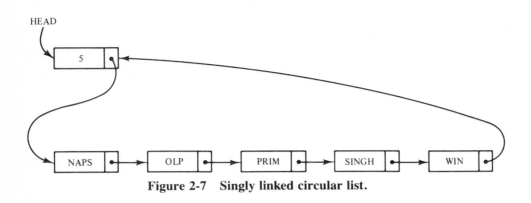

Figure 2-7   Singly linked circular list.

by POINT2. We can change the link field of A to point to B, but we do not know the address of (that is, a pointer to) the node preceding B. If we are to depend upon the current structure of the list then we must search the list for B—an inefficient procedure we wish to avoid. Figure 2-8 highlights this dilemma.

Doubly Linked Circular List

A satisfactory way of getting around the difficulty presented in Figure 2-8 is a **doubly linked circular list** in which each node has two pointers, a *forward link* and a *backward link*. The forward link is a pointer to the next node in the list, whereas the backward link points to the preceding node. Figure 2-9 illustrates a doubly linked circular list. This list

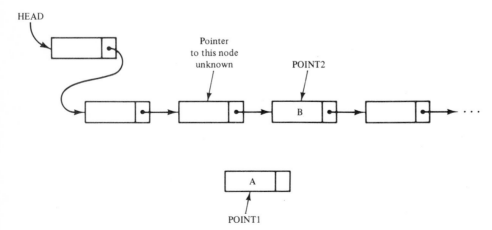

Figure 2-8   To insert node A before node B, we need to know the address of the node preceding B. In a singly linked structure this requires time-consuming sequential searching.

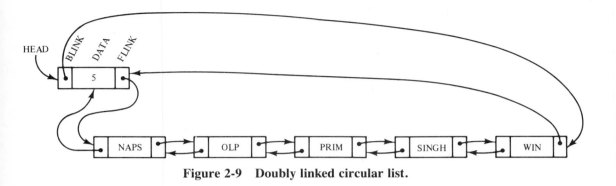

Figure 2-9   Doubly linked circular list.

has 5 nodes (plus a dummy header), each having a forward link (FLINK) and a backward link (BLINK); FLINK points to the successor node, whereas BLINK is a pointer to the predecessor node. Because the list is circular, BLINK of the first node must point to the last node, and FLINK of the last node must point to the first node. Inserting a node into a doubly linked list, or deleting one from it, is a much easier task because we do not have to search the list sequentially to locate a preceding node. The following PSEUDO INSERT-NODE-DOUBLE procedure inserts a node pointed to by POINT1 (already obtained via GETNODE or other means) into a doubly linked list just *before* a node pointed to by POINT2. Figure 2-10 indicates the action taken by this procedure.

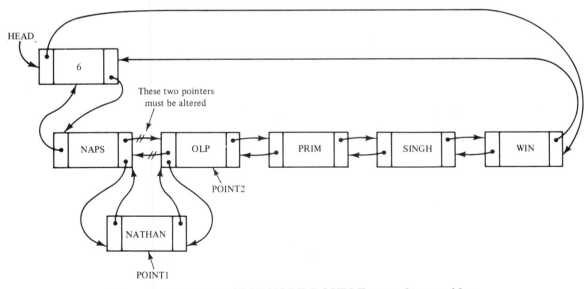

Figure 2-10   The INSERT-NODE-DOUBLE procedure avoids a time-consuming sequential search by using a doubly linked circular list.

```
PROCEDURE   INSERT—NODE—DOUBLE(FLINK,BLINK,N,HEAD,POINT1,POINT2)
VAR   BLINK(N),FLINK(N),N,POINT1,POINT2,HEAD,PREV: INTEGER

   (* Insert node pointed to by POINT1 into doubly *)
   (*    linked list before the node pointed to by *)
   (*      POINT2.                                  *)

   PREV:=BLINK(POINT2)
   FLINK(POINT1):=POINT2
   BLINK(POINT1):=PREV
   FLINK(PREV):=POINT1
   BLINK(POINT2):=POINT1


RETURN
END   INSERT—NODE—DOUBLE
```

Note that the procedure INSERT-NODE-DOUBLE illustrates how streamlined insert and delete procedures become when a dummy header is used. In particular, because the empty list appears as shown in Figure 2-11, the procedure works without any awkward checking of whether the list is empty or whether the insertion is being made at the front of the list.

The following procedure DELETE-NODE-DOUBLE deletes a node pointed to by POINT1 from a doubly linked list and returns the node to the storage pool of available nodes.

```
PROCEDURE   DELETE—NODE—DOUBLE(FLINK,BLINK,N,HEAD,POINT1)
VAR         BLINK(N),FLINK(N),N,POINT1,HEAD : INTEGER

   (* Delete node pointed to by POINT1 *)
   (*    from doubly linked list.      *)
   FLINK(BLINK(POINT1)) :=FLINK(POINT1)
   BLINK(FLINK(POINT1)) :=BLINK(POINT1)
   CALL  RETURNNODE(POINT1)

RETURN
END   DELETE—NODE—DOUBLE
```

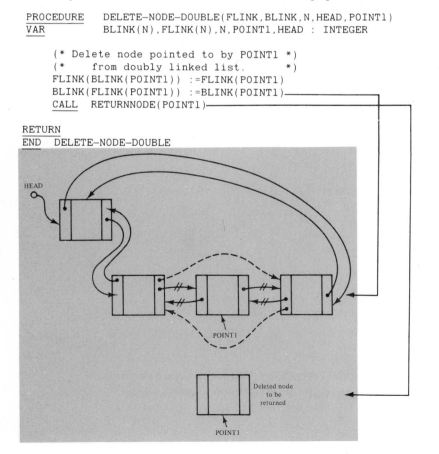

HEAD

POINT1

Deleted node to be returned

POINT1

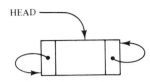

**Figure 2-11   Empty doubly linked list. Note how a dummy
header simplifies procedures in this situation.**

We shall end this chapter by noting that a doubly linked list is a special case of a structure known as a **multilinked list.** Because each link field determines an order in which the nodes of a list are to be processed, we can establish a different link field for every different order in which we wish to process the nodes in a list. Figure 2-12 illustrates such a multilinked list. By following the IDLINK fields, we traverse the list in ID-NUMBER order; by following the NAMELINK fields, we traverse the list in alphabetical order by NAME.

SUMMARY

It is evident that the linked list structures discussed in this chapter have endless possibilities for use in all kinds of data processing activities involving frequent insertions and deletions. The price one pays for this efficiency in the processing of insertions and deletions is the inability to access directly an element within the list. That is, finding an item in a singly linked list requires searching the list sequentially, starting at the head node. Variations on the linked list structure, such as using a dummy header node and double linking, can serve to streamline list processing algorithms at the expense of using slightly more memory. As we progress, we will see that linked lists often serve as the basis for a variety of more complex data structures.

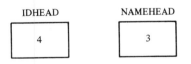

	IDHEAD	NAMEHEAD
	4	3

	NAME	ID-NUMBER	NAMELINK	IDLINK
1	SINGH	8316	4	NULL
2	OLP	4212	5	5
3	NAPS	6490	2	1
4	WIN	1330	NULL	2
5	PRIM	5560	1	3

**Figure 2-12   Multilink list. A different link field can be
established for any desired order of processing nodes.
NAMELINK processes the list in alphabetical order by name;
IDLINK traverses the list by ID-NUMBER.**

KEY TERMS

Linked list

One-dimensional array

Vector

Node

Pointer

Logical order

Physical order

Singly linked list

Records

Fields

Static allocation

Dynamic allocation

Dummy header

Circular linked list

Doubly linked list

Multilinked list

EXERCISES

1. In what way is the data structure involved with the POINTER SORT in Chapter 1 *not* a linked list?

2. Write a program equivalent to the PSEUDO procedure AVERAGE.* Test run your program with several data items.

3. Modify the PSEUDO POINTER SORT procedure of Chapter 1 using a linked list, and then run your program.

4. Translate the PSEUDO procedures INSERTNODE and DELETENODE into another programming language.*

5. Write a program that deletes the last node in a linked list.*

6. Initialize a one-dimensional array of size 50 with alphabetic data. Sort the array without physically disturbing the data in the array.

7. Rewrite the PSEUDO procedures INSERTNODE and DELETENODE using linked lists with dummy headers.

8. Write a program that employs the procedure INSERT-NODE-DOUBLE.*

9. Write a program that employs the procedure DELETE-NODE-DOUBLE.*

10. What are advantages of storing information about a list in a PREFIRST node?

11. Write a procedure for deleting a node from a doubly linked circular list.*

12. Write a procedure for inserting a node in a singly linked circular list.*

13. Write a procedure for deleting a node from a singly linked circular list.*

PROGRAMMING PROBLEMS

1. The Wing and A Prayer Airline Company maintains 4 scheduled flights per day, which they identify by the numbers 1, 2, 3, and 4. For each of these flights, they keep an alphabetized list of passengers. The database for the entire airline could hence be viewed as 4 linked lists. Your task is to write a program that sets up and maintains this database by handling commands of the following form:

*Use any appropriate programming language.

```
Command---->ADD
Flight number---->3
Passenger name---->BROWN

Command---->DELETE
From flight number---->1
Passenger name---->SMITH

Command---->LIST
Flight number---->2
(list alphabetically all passengers for the specified flight)
```

You may assume that this program is continually on-line, with the passenger lists maintained in main memory at all times.

2. Develop a line-oriented text editor that assigns a number to each line of text and then maintains the lines in a linked list by line number order (similar to the fashion in which BASIC programs are maintained on many systems). Your program should be able to process the commands:

```
I line number "text"
    (instruction to insert "text" at line number)

L line1 - line2
    (instruction to list line1 through line2)

D line1 - line2
    (instruction to delete line1 through line2)
```

3. Write a program that, given a file of text, will add those words in the text that are marked by special delimiting brackets [ ] to an index, which will be printed after the text itself has been formatted and printed. Words in this index should be listed in alphabetical order with a page number reference for each page of text on which they are delimited by the special brackets. Note that this program would be part of a word processing system an author could use in developing a book with an index of terms.

4. Write a program that allows input of an arbitrary number of polynomials as coefficient and exponent pairs. Store each polynomial as a linked list of coefficient/exponent pairs ordered in descending order by exponent. Note that the coefficient/exponent pairs need not be input in descending order; it is the responsibility of your program to put them in that order. Your program should then be able to evaluate each of the polynomials for an arbitrary argument X and be able to output each of the polynomials in the appropriate descending exponent order. Be sure that your program works for all "unusual" polynomials such as the zero polynomial, polynomials of degree 1, and constant polynomials.

If you work in Pascal . . .

The following Pascal program demonstrates the loading and then traversal of a singly linked list (with dummy header) containing employee records. As mentioned, Pascal offers its users several tools that greatly facilitate the development of data structures requiring pointers. In particular, this program makes use of Pascal's *dynamic memory allocation* achieved via pointer variables and the supplied new procedure. Essentially a pointer variable such as *p* in the program below will contain the absolute memory address of a Pascal record. Here a record type called *empinfo* has been established in the TYPE declarations for the program. Records of type *empinfo* will contain fields:

- idno—employee identification number

- initials—employee's first and middle initials

- lastname—employee's last name

- salary—employee's hourly salary

- next—a pointer variable leading to the next employee on the list

Notice that variables of the type *eptr* are special pointer variables to be used only as pointers in a Pascal program. The distinction between *p* and *p^* respectively is the distinction between the memory address itself and the contents of the record located at that memory address. The dynamic memory management system defined as a part of the Pascal standard conveniently replaces the procedures INITIALIZE, GETNODE, and RETURN-NODE developed in this chapter. Instead, the Pascal command *new(p)* may be used to obtain *dynamically* (as the program executes) a pointer *p* to an available node. Similarly, there is a Pascal procedure *dispose(p)*, which can be invoked to return the node pointed to by *p* to the Pascal-maintained available space pool.

```
    program linklist(input,output);
TYPE
   eptr = ^empinfo;
   empinfo = RECORD
               idno : integer;
               initials : ARRAY [1..2] OF char;
               lastname : ARRAY[1..9] OF char;
               salary : real;
               next : eptr
            END;
VAR
   head,prev,p : eptr;  (* Pointer variables *)
   number,i,j : integer;
   BEGIN
     readln(number);
     (* Initialize the dummy header *)
     new(head);
     head^.next:=NIL;
     prev:=head;
     (* Loop to load the list *)
     FOR i:= 1 TO number DO
```

```
     BEGIN
        new(p);
        readln(p^.idno);
        readln(p^.initials);
        readln(p^.lastname);
        readln(p^.salary);
        prev^.next:=p;
        p^.next:=NIL;
        prev:=p
     END;
   (* Next loop to print the list *)
   writeln;writeln;
   writeln('**ECHO BACK DATA**');
   writeln;writeln;
   p:=head;
   WHILE p^.next <> NIL DO
     BEGIN
        p:=p^.next;
        writeln(p^.idno);
        writeln(p^.initials);
        writeln(p^.lastname);
        writeln(p^.salary);
        writeln;
     END
END.
```

Sample Run of Program:

```
4
 118
RD
KRAMER
 8.74
 448
AL
SPAN
 9.83
 737
GG
BRELL
 6.27
 806
HB
MEYER
 5.19


**ECHO BACK DATA**


     118
RD
KRAMER
 8.740000E+00
```

```
        448
AL
SPAN
 9.830000E+00

        737
GG
BRELL
 6.270000E+00

        806
HB
MEYER
 5.190000E+00
```

3

String and Character Manipulation

Man does not live by words alone, despite the fact that he sometimes has to eat them.

ADLAI STEVENSON (1900–1965)

3-1 Introductory Considerations

The manipulation of character strings plays an important role in a wide variety of computer applications. Text editing, computer-assisted instruction, and attempts to have computers interact with users in natural languages are just a few examples of such applications. Some languages, like SNOBOL, COBOL, PL/1, and certain dialects of BASIC, provide a great number of tools to allow their users to manipulate character strings easily. Others, like FORTRAN and Pascal, often require their users to write these string manipulation tools themselves in the form of procedures and functions. In this chapter, we shall explore how the data structures used to store strings influence the ways in which the latter can be manipulated. You can then apply such considerations to enhance programs in those languages that have weak built-in string-handling capabilities. If you use a language that provides a library of string-handling tools, this chapter should provide you with a deeper understanding of what is happening "under the surface" when you use such tools; this will help you to write more efficient programs.

We will examine our string manipulation tools with respect to the following typical operations:

1. **Assignment:** The copying of one string variable into another. For example, if STR1 and STR2 are two string variables in PSEUDO, then the statement STR1 := STR2 should copy the contents of STR2 into STR1 without destroying the contents of STR2.

2. **Concatenation:** The joining together of two character strings. The concatenation of the strings "BIRD" and "DOG" is the string "BIRDDOG."

3. **Pattern matching:** The searching of one string for an occurrence of another string. For instance, the string "BASEBALL" occurs in the string "MODERN BASEBALL HISTORY" beginning at position 8.

4. **Substring operations:** It may be desirable to examine characters I through J of a given string. For example, the substring consisting of the 4th through 7th characters in the string "TALE OF TWO CITIES" is the substring "E OF."

5. **Insertion:** In text-editing applications, one frequently wishes to insert a given string in the middle of another string. The insertion of "AND " at position 6 of the string "SALT PEPPER" results in the string "SALT AND PEPPER."

6. **Deletion:** The opposite of insertion. To delete the substring occupying positions 5 through 13 of "SALT AND PEPPER" results in the string "SALTER."

We shall explore 3 types of structural techniques that can be used to store strings:

1. Fixed length string method

2. Workspace and index table method

3. Linked list method

In our discussion of each of these methods, we shall continually evaluate their performance with respect to the 6 string operations described above. It will soon become apparent that there is no one method that is best for all 6 types of operations. Instead, based on a thorough knowledge of their relative merits, you must choose the method that best suits a particular application.

3-2   Fixed Length String Method

The **fixed length string method** has the advantage of being the easiest to program. Unfortunately, as we shall see, it can also result in a tremendous waste of memory and severely restrict the length that a string can attain. Consequently, its use is limited to those situations in which you have the luxury of large amounts of excess memory (situations that occur far less often than we would like). The general idea behind this method is that string variables are allocated to handle the maximum possible string length that is envisioned for a particular application. As strings are entered into such locations, those strings that do not attain this maximum length are left-justified and padded with blanks (or null characters) on the right. The padding with blanks becomes memory for which you are charged but which you cannot effectively use.

As an example, suppose that we wanted to manipulate a piece of text consisting of up to 50 lines (strings) of a maximum length of 80 characters each. In PSEUDO, we could then declare the following array:

```
VAR STR(50) :  CHARACTER(80)
```

Then the text

```
IF PROGRAMMERS WROTE PROGRAMS
THE WAY THAT BUILDERS BUILT
BUILDINGS, THEN THE FIRST WOODPECKER
THAT CAME ALONG WOULD
DESTROY CIVILIZATION.
```

would be stored as the 5 strings appearing in Figure 3-1 on page 43.

Note that, for this choice of strings, well over half of the memory locations in STR(1) through STR(5) are being wasted. Also, although procedures for the 6 operations cited in section 3-1 can be written with relative ease using the fixed length method, other more subtle inefficiencies and limitations of this method will become apparent.

Before considering the problems of this method, you should know a generally useful function, LENGTH, which takes as arguments a fixed length string variable and the maximum number of characters (MAXLEN) that it may contain, and returns the actual length of the string in the function name: that is, the maximum possible length minus the number of padded blanks. Hence the LENGTH of STR(1) in Figure 3-1 is 29. The procedure assumes that the parameter MAXLEN is at least 1.

```
FUNCTION LENGTH(STR,MAXLEN)
      (*Returns the actual length of the string in STR.*)
      (*STR has a maximum possible length of MAXLEN *)
VAR STR : CHARACTER(MAXLEN)
VAR MAXLEN,I : INTEGER
FOR I := MAXLEN TO 1 STEP -1 DO
   [ IF STR(I) <> " " THEN
                [ LENGTH := I
                  RETURN      ]
     ENDIF                         ]
ENDFOR
LENGTH:=0
RETURN
END LENGTH
```

Now consider how the fixed length method lends itself to the operation of string concatenation. The procedure given below will (apparently) concatenate the strings STR1 followed by STR2, producing STR3, each of maximum length N.

```
PROCEDURE CONCAT-FL(STR1,STR2,STR3,N)
      (* Concatenate STR1, STR2 - producing STR3 *)
VAR STR1,STR2,STR3 : CHARACTER(N)
VAR I,N : INTEGER
FOR I := 1 TO LENGTH(STR(1)) DO
   [STR3(I) := STR1(I)]
ENDFOR
FOR I := LENGTH(STR1) + 1 TO LENGTH(STR2)+LENGTH(STR1) DO
   [STR3(I) := STR2(I-LENGTH(STR1))]
ENDFOR
RETURN
END CONCAT-FL
```

One limitation of the above procedure, however, is that success may not be guaranteed if the maximum length of the result string is the same as that of the 2 operand strings.

The only way to guarantee a successful operation is to specify that the result string must be declared longer than the 2 operand strings combined. Another alternative is to provide for appropriate error handling when the concatenation is impossible. This is illustrated in the following version of the procedure CONCAT-FL, in which it is assumed that the maximum length of each string is N.

```
PROCEDURE CONCAT-FL(STR1,STR2,STR3,N)
      (*Concatenate STR1, STR2 - producing STR3 of maximum length N*)
VAR STR1,STR2,STR3 : CHARACTER(N)
VAR I,N : INTEGER
IF LENGTH(STR1) + LENGTH(STR2) > N THEN
      [CALL ERROR-HANDLER]
      [RETURN           ]
ENDIF
FOR I := 1 TO LENGTH(STR(1)) DO
      [STR3(I) := STR1(I)]
ENDFOR
FOR I := LENGTH(STR1) + 1 TO LENGTH(STR2) + LENGTH(STR1) DO
      [STR3(I) := STR2(I-LENGTH(STR1))]
ENDFOR
RETURN
END CONCAT-FL
```

Notice, however, that neither of these alternatives is acceptable. Forcing the resultant string to be twice as long will result in an increasing waste of memory. On the other hand, specifying certain concatenations as impossible due to the combined length of the 2 strings can be easily avoided in both the workspace/index table and linked list methods.

As a second example of the problems inherent in the fixed length method, consider this short procedure to handle the operation of insertion.

```
PROCEDURE INSERT-FL(MASTERSTR, INSTR, POS,N)
      (*Procedure to insert INSTR in MASTERSTR, beginning at *)
      (* character position POS *)
      (* N is the maximum length of each string *)
VAR MASTERSTR, INSTR : CHARACTER(N)
VAR POS,I,N : INTEGER
      (* First "move over" the tail-end of MASTERSTR *)
FOR I := LENGTH(MASTERSTR) TO POS STEP -1 DO
      [MASTERSTR(I+LENGTH(INSTR)) := MASTERSTR(I)]
ENDFOR
      (* Next insert INSTR in vacated space *)
FOR I := 1 TO LENGTH(INSTR) DO
      [MASTERSTR(I+POS-1) := INSTR(I)]
ENDFOR
RETURN
END INSERT-FL
```

POS   LENGTH (MASTERSTRING)

Move this substring
over to make
room for INSTR

STR(1)	IF PROGRAMMERS WROTE PROGRAMS	51 blanks
STR(2)	THE WAY THAT BUILDERS BUILT	53 blanks
STR(3)	BUILDINGS, THEN THE FIRST WOODPECKER	44 blanks
STR(4)	THAT CAME ALONG WOULD	59 blanks
STR(5)	DESTROY CIVILIZATION.	59 blanks

Figure 3-1   Appearance of 5 stored strings.

One shortcoming of the procedure INSERT-FL as it stands is the potential problem of string "overflow" similar to that which appeared in concatenation. This may be easily remedied by inserting a quick check on the string lengths involved.

```
PROCEDURE INSERT-FL(MASTERSTR, INSTR, POS, N)
       (* Procedure to insert INSTR in MASTERSTR, beginning at *)
       (* character position POS *)
VAR MASTERSTR, INSTR : CHARACTER(N)
VAR POS,I,N : INTEGER
IF LENGTH(MASTERSTR) + LENGTH(INSTR) > N THEN
    [CALL ERROR-HANDLER]
    [RETURN           ]
ENDIF
       (* First "move over" the tail-end of MASTERSTR *)
FOR I := LENGTH(MASTERSTR) TO POS+1 STEP -1 DO
    [MASTERSTR(I+LENGTH(INSTR)) := MASTERSTR(I)]
ENDFOR
       (* Next insert INSTR in vacated space *)
FOR I := 1 TO LENGTH(INSTR) DO
    [MASTERSTR(I+POS-1) := INSTR(I)]
ENDFOR
RETURN
END INSERT-FL
```

Another more subtle problem in the insert procedure for fixed length strings is the efficiency of the algorithm. For instance, to insert the string "AND " at position 6 of the string "SALT PEPPER" we are required actually to move 10 bytes of memory. This problem tends to compound itself as longer strings become involved, with the result that frequent insertions (and deletions) may degrade the performance of a character manipulation program that employs the fixed length method. This problem of reducing the processing operations required for insertions and deletions is one that *only* the linked list method can gracefully handle.

3-3   Workspace/Index Table Method

We introduce the **workspace/index table method** by giving an example from a language that employs it in its string-handling package. In BASIC-PLUS, you need not declare a maximum length for a particular string variable. Instead, you are given "dynamic" storage allocation for string variables that may contain anywhere from 0 to 255 characters. Before we explain in detail the implementation method used in BASIC-PLUS, you should attempt to specify what the output would be from the following BASIC-PLUS program segment

(LSET is a special type of assignment operator that ensures left-justification and padding with blanks):

```
10 LET A$ = "COFFEE"
20 LET B$ = A$
30 LSET A$ = "TEA"
40 PRINT B$
```

If you answered that line 40 would result in the printing of the string "COFFEE," you gave the expected wrong answer. Actually, the output would be "TEA," and the reason is the manner in which BASIC-PLUS keeps track of strings. The idea behind this method is that one large memory workspace is allocated to storing all strings. Then 2 index tables are maintained—one that contains where in the workspace each particular string starts, and one that contains the length of each string. This principle is illustrated in Figure 3-2.

Suppose now that we were to add a 3rd string to the collection in Figure 3-2. All that we need to know is where the free portion of the workspace begins—in this case it begins at location 10. We place the string starting at that location, add appropriate entries to our index tables, and adjust the pointer to the beginning of the free memory. This threefold process is illustrated in Figure 3-3 for the addition of the string "CREAM."

We can now explain the surprising result that occurred in our earlier BASIC-PLUS example. Consider how the assignment of one string to another would be handled in a language that kept track of strings by this method. It would not be efficient to store a 2nd copy of the same string of characters. All that is needed is to add an entry to our index table that points to the same string of characters in the workspace. This principle as it relates to our BASIC-PLUS example is given in Figure 3-4.

Figure 3-5 illustrates what happens when we change the contents of the string variable *A$* via the LSET instruction in line 30. Had we used a normal LET assignment statement, a new workspace area would have been assigned to *A$*. However, LSET assigns data to a string variable without changing that variable's location in the workspace. From Figure 3-5, it should now be immediately clear why our initial example produced such unexpected output.

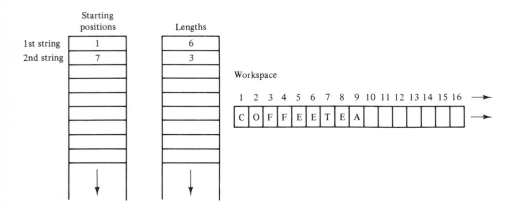

**Figure 3-2   The BASIC-PLUS method of handling strings. All
strings are stored in a large workspace, and 2 index tables keep
track of the beginning and length of each string.**

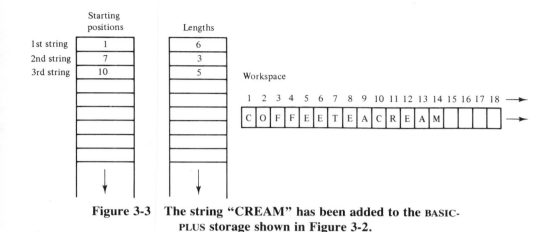

Figure 3-3 **The string "CREAM" has been added to the** BASIC-
PLUS storage shown in Figure 3-2.

Processing/Efficiency Considerations of the Workspace/Index Table Method

With regard to assignment, we have already seen that the workspace/index table method substitutes a relatively small amount of bookkeeping for the character-by-character copying used with the fixed length string method. It is also clear that strings do not waste memory as they did in the fixed length method. With the workspace/index method, memory allocation is **dynamic** in the sense that *a string gets only the amount of workspace it needs at the time it needs it.* The problem of what to do when a string no longer needs the memory it once occupied is one we shall take up later in the section on garbage collection.

Of the other string operations mentioned in 3-1, only concatenation and insertion present any real problem. In both cases, the difficulty is that the resultant string must grow

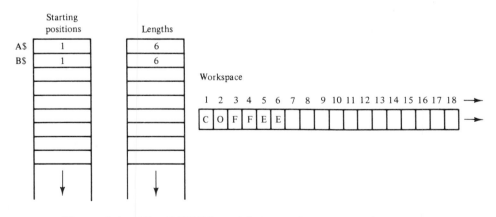

Figure 3-4 **After LET B$ = A$, but before LSET A$ = "TEA."**
Instead of storing a second copy of a string, BASIC-PLUS **simply**
adds a new entry to the indexes.

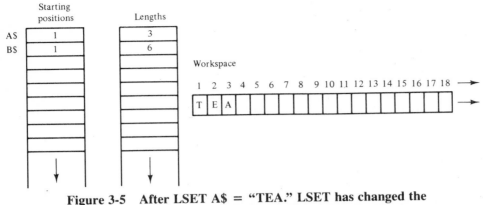

**Figure 3-5 After LSET A\$ = "TEA." LSET has changed the
string *A\$* to "TEA" without changing the location of *A\$*.**

in length, and the workspace/index table method does not allow for any growing room
without finding a completely new workspace area for the resulting string. That is, insertions and concatenations in which the resultant string is also an operand do not allow a
string to grow in place, but rather require that the entire string be recopied to some free
memory space.

To illustrate how the operation of insertion could be handled by a PSEUDO procedure,
suppose that we wanted to give ourselves the capability of handling 100 strings taking up
a total workspace area of no more than 10,000 characters. To do this we would need to
allocate:

1. An index table, START, of starting positions for strings 1, 2, 3, . . . , 100.

2. An index table, LEN, of lengths for strings 1, 2, 3, . . . , 100.

3. A workspace array, WORKSP, of size 10,000 characters.

4. A pointer, FREESP, to the beginning of the free space in the workspace.

Figure 3-6 illustrates our PSEUDO design.
Given this stage setting, let us now consider the procedure INSERT-WI, which will
insert string *J* in string *I* beginning at position POS.

```
PROCEDURE INSERT-WI(I,J,POS,START,LEN,WORKSP,FREESP)
      (* Insert Jth string in Ith string beginning at position POS *)
VAR I,J,POS,K,FREESP,OLDSTARTI,OLDLENI : INTEGER
VAR START(100), LEN(100) : INTEGER
VAR WORKSP : CHARACTER(10000)
      (* Store information on old string I *)
OLDSTARTI := START(I)
OLDLENI := LEN(I)
      (* Get new location for string I in WORKSP *)
START(I) := FREESP
LEN(I) := LEN(I) + LEN(J)
      (* Update FREESP pointer *)
FREESP := FREESP + LEN(I)
      (* Now build new string *)
```

```
FOR K := 1 TO POS-1 DO
    [WORKSP(START(I)+K-1) := WORKSP(OLDSTARTI + K -1)]
ENDFOR
FOR K := 1 TO LEN(J) DO
    [WORKSP(START(I)+POS+K-2) := WORKSP(START(J)+K-1)]
ENDFOR
FOR K := POS+LEN(J) TO LEN(I) DO
    [WORKSP(START(I)+K) := WORKSP(OLDSTARTI + K - POS)]
ENDFOR
RETURN
END INSERT-WI
```

For example, CALL INSERT-WI(1,3,4) with the data from Figure 3-6—that is, when the *I*th string is "COFFEE" and the *J*th string is "CREAM"—would alter our data structures in the fashion pictured in Figure 3-7 on page 48.

An analysis of the procedure INSERT-WI yields the following observations about the workspace/index table method:

1. Unlike the fixed length method, this method (generally) poses no problem with an insertion forcing a string to become too large.

2. Like that of the fixed length method, the workspace/index table insert routine requires the actual moving of a lot of bytes (characters) of memory. Hence the latter method offers no advantage in this regard.

3. Although generally a string will not be too large for the workspace/index table method, some provision should be made (and none is in the above procedure) as to what should be done when the addition of another string forces the FREESP pointer above 10,000.

4. When the FREESP pointer goes above 10,000, are we necessarily out of workspace? As we have manipulated our string workspace area by adding, deleting, concatenating,

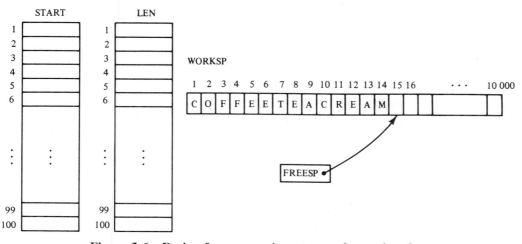

Figure 3-6   Design for PSEUDO insert procedure using the workspace/index table method.

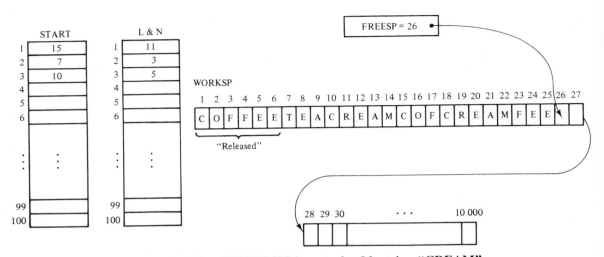

**Figure 3-7 How INSERT-WI inserts the *J*th string "CREAM"
into the *I*th string "COFFEE."**

and inserting strings, we have no doubt released some workspace area that was once occupied. The only problem is that our FREESP pointer is now beyond such areas. We must consider how such workspace can be reclaimed as usable workspace.

Garbage Collection

The problem of how to reclaim **usable workspace** generally can be classified as (believe it or not) a problem of **garbage collection.** A graphic illustration of the difficulty as it relates to the workspace/index table method of string handling is given in Figure 3-8.

We will discuss 2 strategies for handling this problem. Both require declaring and maintaining 2 additional indexes that store information on garbage areas. These correspond to START and LEN on the beginning positions and lengths of strings. That is, as a string area is released, we will record its starting position and length in index tables GAR-START and GAR-LEN, respectively (Figure 3-9). One alternative is now to consult these 2 free space indexes whenever we wish to add a string. If the indexes indicate that some garbage area is large enough to accommodate the string we wish to add, then we can reclaim that space. Otherwise, we use the FREESP pointer to take space from the end of the WORKSP area.

FREESP = 73

WORKSP

1	12 13	24 25	38 39	49 50	58 59	65 66	72 73	10 000
Actual data	Released	Actual data	Released	Actual data	Released	Actual data		

**Figure 3-8   Current status of WORKSP shows much released
space that is not usable because FREESP points to 73.**

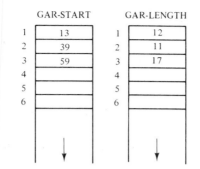

Figure 3-9   Garbage area index tables for Figure 3-8.

One of the main drawbacks of this alternative is that a fair amount of extra processing must be done each time we wish to add a string. Therefore, we recommend a 2nd alternative called **compaction,** which also makes use of the information in the GAR-START and GAR-LEN tables, although less frequently. The idea behind compaction is that only the FREESP pointer controls where a new string will be added; that is, new strings are added only at the end of the WORKSP area. However, when the addition of a new string would force the FREESP pointer beyond the limit of the WORKSP area, we then perform a compaction procedure that uses the information on the starting positions and lengths of garbage areas to roll down the good strings on top of them, hence freeing up area at the end of the workspace. Figure 3-10 graphically illustrates the compaction process on a small scale.

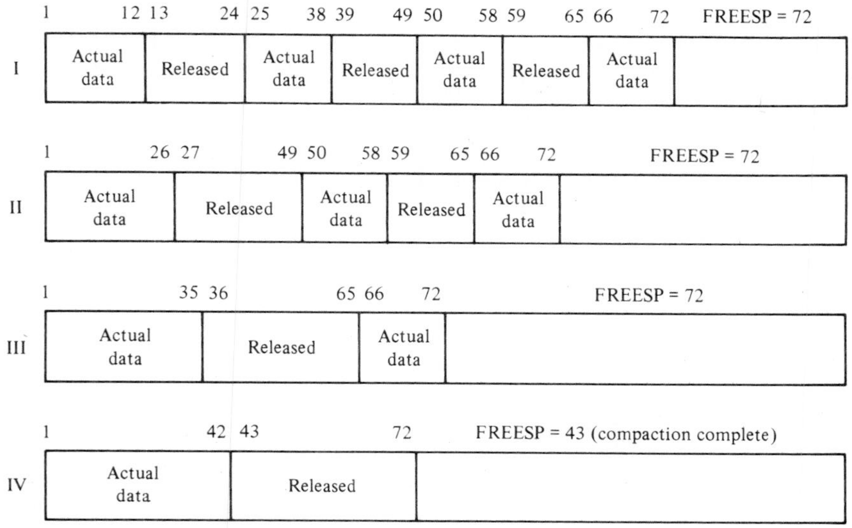

Figure 3-10   The compaction process. To release new space at the end of the workspace, good strings are rolled down into garbage areas indicated by GAR-START and GAR-LENGTH.

We will now examine a more complete version of the procedure INSERT-WI in which appropriate calls are made to procedures to perform compaction and error handling. You will write the compaction routine as an exercise at the end of the chapter.

```
PROCEDURE INSERT-WI(I,J,POS,START,LEN,WORKSP,FREESP)
     (* Insert Jth string in Ith string beginning at position POS. *)
VAR I,J,POS,K,FREESP,OLDSTARTI,OLDLENI : INTEGER
VAR START(100), LEN(100) : INTEGER
VAR WORKSP : CHARACTER(10000)
IF FREESP+LEN(I)+LEN(J) > 10001 THEN
     [CALL COMPACT]
ENDIF
     (* Still not enough free space? *)
IF FREESP+LEN(I)+LEN(J) > 10001 THEN
    ⌈CALL ERROR-HANDLER⌉
    ⌊RETURN             ⌋
ENDIF
     (* Store information on old string I *)
OLDSTARTI := START(I)
OLDLENI := LEN(I)
     (* Get new location for string I in WORKSP *)
START(I) := FREESP
LEN(I) := LEN(I) + LEN(J)
     (* Update FREESP pointer *)
FREESP := FREESP + LEN(I)
     (* Now build new string *)
FOR K := 1 TO POS-1 DO
     [WORKSP(START(I)+K-1) := WORKSP(OLDSTARTI + K -1)]
ENDFOR
FOR K := 1 TO LEN(J) DO
     [WORKSP(START(I)+POS+K-2) := WORKSP(START(J)+K-1)]
ENDFOR
FOR K := POS+LEN(J) TO LEN(I) DO
     [WORKSP(START(I)+K) := WORKSP(OLDSTARTI + K - POS)]
ENDFOR
     (* Now call to update tables for garbage areas *)
CALL ADD-TO-GARBAGE(OLDSTARTI, OLDLENI)
RETURN
END INSERT-WI
```

3-4 Linked List Method

Although the workspace/index table method gracefully solves the problems of having to declare a maximum possible string length and then wasting memory when strings are shorter than that length, it does not adequately solve the problem of having to move a tremendous number of data when insertions and deletions occur on a large scale. Only the **linked list method** handles both of these problems. However, we shall see that it is not without its own set of problems.

We shall view each string as a circular double linked list as described in Chapter 2. Each node in the list contains a back pointer, a forward pointer, and a data portion consisting of (for the moment) a single character. Clearly, for each such string, we need a pointer to the dummy header node for the list, and, for later use, we also want to keep track of the length of each string. The following conventions will be assumed throughout this section:

1. The array HEAD contains pointers to the dummy header of each string.

2. The array LEN contains the lengths of each string.

3. The back pointer for each node will be referred to as BLINK, the forward pointer as FLINK, and the data portion as DATA.

Figure 3-11, which pictures the three strings "COFFEE," "TEA," and "CREAM," should clarify these conventions.

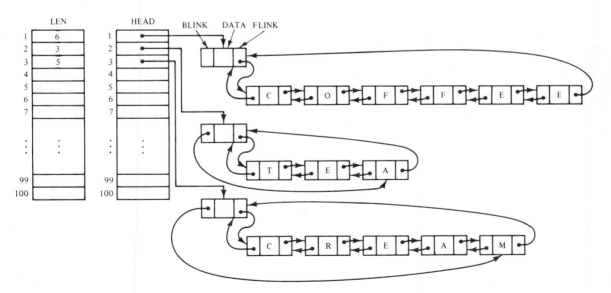

Figure 3-11   The three strings "COFFEE," "TEA," and "CREAM" in a circular doubly linked list with indexes for the length and dummy header location of each string.

In the world of applications . . .

All of us are familiar with coded messages in which the words and symbols are intricately combined to produce a logical text. Perhaps one of the more interesting episodes of this kind is the mystery novel *Postern of Fate* by Agatha Christie. The mystery is based on some underlined words in a book, which are accidentally found and **concatenated** to yield the clue to a murder:

Mary Jordan did not die naturally. It was one of us. I think I know which one.

At least one software company, Prosoft, Inc. of North Hollywood, California, seems to have removed the mystery surrounding the efficient garbage collection of string space for the workspace/index method of string handling used in many microcomputer versions of BASIC. To quote their catalog:

When a BASIC program changes a string, it moves it to a new place in memory, and leaves a hole in the old place. Eventually, all available memory gets used up and BASIC has to push the strings together to free up some space. This takes time. Lots of time. The computer stops running for seconds or minutes, and you may even think it's crashed.*

The brochure goes on to claim that, for a BASIC program using 1000 string variables, the garbage collection algorithm used by Prosoft's Trashman program outperforms the standard Radio Shack TRSDOS operating system method by a margin of 3.5 seconds to 179.6 seconds—an improvement of 98 percent; clear evidence that a better algorithm can make a real difference!

*Reprinted courtesy of The Tesler Software Corporation, Prosoft Catalog #3.

Assignment of one string to another could be handled in a fashion very similar to the workspace/index table method; that is, instead of physically creating 2 identical strings, having rather 2 entries in HEAD point to the same string. Pattern matching presents no real problem and is examined in an exercise at the end of the chapter. Substring operations do present a problem and will be discussed in greater detail later. Insertion, deletion, and concatenation (which may be viewed as a special case of insertion) can be handled elegantly and efficiently using the linked list method. The following is a procedure, INSERT-LL, to insert the string pointed to by HEAD(J) into the string pointed to by HEAD(I) beginning at position POS.

```
PROCEDURE INSERT-LL(I,J,POS,N)
     (* Insert Jth string in Ith string beginning at position POS *)
VAR I,J,POS,P,K,HEAD(N),LEN(N),N:INTEGER
VAR FIRSTINJ, LASTINJ,BLINK(N),FLINK(N):INTEGER
     (* Traverse Ith string to position POS *)
P := HEAD(I)
FOR K := 1 TO POS DO
     ⌈P := FLINK(P)          ⌉
     ⌊(* Now link it in *)⌋
ENDFOR
```

```
FIRSTINJ := FLINK(HEAD(J))
LASTINJ := BLINK(HEAD(J))
BLINK(FIRSTINJ) := BLINK(P)
FLINK(LASTINJ) := P
FLINK(BLINK(P)) := FIRSTINJ
BLINK(P) := LASTINJ
RETURN
END INSERT—LL
```

This procedure closely parallels the insertion procedure for linked lists described in Chapter 2. There is one difference, however. In Chapter 2, we were concerned with inserting only one node. Here we are inserting an entire collection of nodes; we are inserting one linked list within another (Figure 3-12). This is done with relative ease because our implementation of a doubly linked list gives us convenient pointers to both the 1st and last nodes in the list.

Problems with the Linked List Method

A recurrent theme in this text will be that the study of data structures is to a great extent acquiring knowledge about the relative advantages and disadvantages of different data storage techniques. In the string-handling application, we have seen that the linked list method allows both dynamic string allocation with no practical limit on string length and extremely efficient insertion and deletion operations. However, that does not mean that the linked list method is a universal cure-all that should be used in all applications.

Three general problem areas exist. First, the perceptive reader will have already noticed that, although the procedure INSERT-LL achieves a very efficient insertion, it renders the *J*th string thereafter inaccessible *as a separate entity.* This is because the pointers within the *J*th string had to be altered to chain it into the *I*th string.

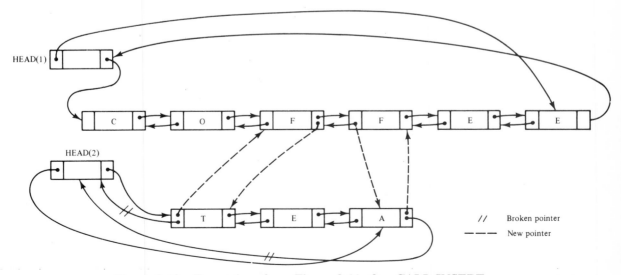

Figure 3-12   Two strings from Figure 3-11 after CALL INSERT-LL(1,2,4).

Second, consider an application in which operating with substrings is of more importance than insertion and deletion. With both the fixed length and the workspace/index table methods, the substring consisting of the *I*th through the *J*th characters could be directly accessed because the characters within any given string are physically next to each other. Accessing the same substring via the linked list implementation requires beginning at the initial character in the string and traversing the entire string until the *I*th character is reached. Our implementation of a string as a doubly linked list allows this process to be made somewhat more efficient. In particular, the length of the string from which we want to extract a substring could be checked to determine if the substring occurs in the front or back half. If it is in the back half, the pointer to the last character in the string could be used to begin a traversal from the rear of the list until we reach the desired substring. This still would require, however, a sequential processing of the list until the desired substring is found. Hence, for substring operations, the linked list method just does not stack up to either of the other two methods. (See Chapter 4 for a formal definition of the term *stack up*.)

A 3rd problem arises in the efficiency of memory utilization for the linked list method as we have described it here. If the data portion of a node in the linked list contains merely one character, then the 2 pointers associated with that node could require 4 to 8 times more memory than the data. That is, only 11 to 20 percent of memory is being utilized to store the data in which we are really interested; the rest of memory is storing data about data.

This memory utilization problem may be somewhat alleviated by making the data portion of a node a **cluster** of characters. Suppose, for instance, we choose a cluster size of 4 characters. Then the same strings given in Figure 3-11 would appear as shown in Figure 3-13. Here we have used the symbol ~ to represent a null character; that is, a character that is always ignored when the string is processed.

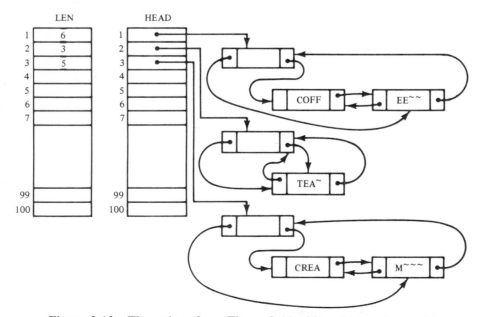

Figure 3-13   The strings from Figure 3-11 with a cluster size = 4.

Notice that, although this technique has enabled us to devote a greater percentage of memory to storage of data, a significant complication has been added in that our code must always account for null characters. For example, if we wish to insert the 2nd string from Figure 3-13 in the 1st string beginning at position 4, the scheme pictured in Figure 3-14 emerges.

Here the node containing "COFF" had to be split into the two nodes "COF~" and "F~~~" to achieve an effective insertion. As you might have expected, we have had to trade off one feature for another. To gain more effective memory utilization, we have had to make our program code more cumbersome and less efficient in its execution time.

SUMMARY

String operations are vital to all types of data processing needs. In this chapter, we have seen that a variety of data structure techniques can be used to implement strings. Each technique carries with it a set of advantages and disadvantages that must be carefully weighed when considering its use in a given application. The table on the following page highlights the strong and weak points of each method.

KEY TERMS

Assignment	Insertion	Garbage collection
Concatenation	Deletion	Compaction
Pattern matching	Fixed length method	Linked list method
Substring operations	Workspace/index table method	String length
		Cluster

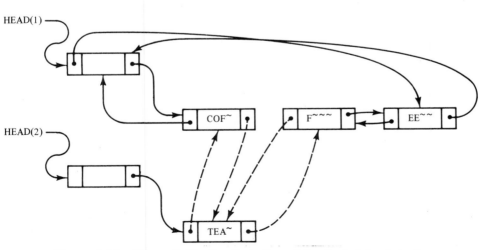

Figure 3-14   Figure 3-13 after insertion of the 2nd string into the 1st, beginning at position 4.

Advantages and disadvantages of the three string manipulation methods.

Method \ Characteristic	Concatenation	Pattern Matching	Substring Operations	Insertions and Deletions	Memory Utilization	Assignment
Fixed Length	Awkward because combined lengths may overflow fixed length limit	Requires sequential searching from beginning of string	Substrings are directly accessible	Large-scale movement of characters required	Very inefficient unless all strings of uniform length	Large-scale movement of characters required
Workspace Index	Requires large-scale movement of characters, but no length limitations	Requires sequential searching from beginning of string	Substrings are directly accessible	Large-scale movement of characters required	Very efficient	May be done via pointers to avoid data movement
Linked List	May be done via pointers to avoid data movement	Requires sequential searching from beginning of string	Substrings are not directly accessible	May be done via pointers to avoid data movement	Dependent upon cluster size	May be done via pointers to avoid data movement

EXERCISES

Using any appropriate programming language:

1. Write a string assignment procedure for the workspace/index table method.

2. Write a string assignment procedure for the linked list method.

3. Write a string concatenation procedure for the workspace/index table method.

4. Write a string concatenation procedure for the linked list method.

5. Write a pattern matching procedure for the fixed length method.

6. Write a pattern matching procedure for the workspace/index table method.

7. Write a pattern matching procedure for the linked list method.

8. Write a procedure to handle the substring operations described in 3-1 for the fixed length method.

9. Write a procedure to handle the substring operations described in 3-1 for the workspace/index table method.

10. Write a procedure to handle the substring operations described in 3-1 for the linked list method.

11. Write a procedure to handle substring deletion for the fixed length method.

12. Write a procedure to handle substring deletion for the workspace/index table method.

13. Write a procedure to handle substring deletion for the linked list method.

14. Write the procedure COMPACT as called for in the routine INSERT-WI.

PROGRAMMING PROBLEMS

1. Modify the airline reservation system or the line-oriented text editor (which you developed for Programming Problems (1) and (2) in Chapter 2) so that the strings involved are implemented via the workspace/index table method or the linked list method. (See Pascal supplement.)

2. In computer-assisted instruction it is often necessary to match a user's response against the correct answer to a question. When this response is in the form of a string, it may be desirable to allow spelling that is "almost correct." Think of a computer-assisted instruction application in which string responses would be appropriate, suitably define an "almost correct" spelling, and implement the corresponding pattern matching procedure in a complete program.

If you work in Pascal . . .

The Pascal program given below represents an initial solution to Programming Problem (2) in Chapter 2: implementation of a line-oriented text editor. In this program, the fixed length method is used to handle strings. Programming problem (1) of this chapter asks that you appropriately modify the program, using the workspace/index table or linked list method. Note that the CASE statement in the main loop of the program uses an ELSE CASE to trap erroneous input. This is a nonstandard, but very useful, feature made available in OMSI Pascal-1.

```pascal
program texted(input,output);

(* Line-oriented text editor *)

TYPE
  alfa = ARRAY[1..80] OF char;
  ptr = ^tentry;
  tentry = RECORD
             lineno : integer;
             linetext : alfa;
             next : ptr
           END;
VAR
  command : char;
  number,i,stop : integer;
  newline : alfa;
  head,link : ptr;

  PROCEDURE insert(VAR number : integer; VAR newline : alfa);

  (* Insert newline text at specified line number *)

  LABEL
    123;  (* Used to exit procedure *)
  VAR
    prev,p : ptr;
  BEGIN
    prev:=head;
    link:=head^.next;
    WHILE link <> NIL DO
      BEGIN
        IF link^.lineno = number
          THEN
            BEGIN
              link^.linetext:=newline;
              GOTO 123  (* Exit procedure *)
            END(*IF*);
        IF link^.lineno > number
          THEN
```

```
                BEGIN
                  new(p);
                  p^.lineno:=number;
                  p^.linetext:=newline;
                  p^.next:=link;
                  prev^.next:=p;
                  GOTO 123   (* Exit procedure *)
                END(*IF*);
              prev:=link;
              link:=link^.next
            END(*WHILE*);
            (*INSERT AT END*)
            new(p);
            p^.lineno:=number;
            p^.linetext:=newline;
            p^.next:=NIL;
            prev^.next:=p;
    123:(*EXIT PROCEDURE*)
       END(*INSERT*);

    PROCEDURE delete (VAR number : integer);

    (* Delete specified line number *)

    LABEL
       123;  (* Used only to exit procedure *)
    VAR
       prev : ptr;
     BEGIN
        prev:=head;
        link:=head^.next;
        WHILE link <> NIL DO
          BEGIN
            IF link^.lineno= number
              THEN
                BEGIN
                  prev^.next:=link^.next;
                  dispose(link);
                  GOTO 123   (* Exit procedure *)
                END(*IF*);
              prev:=link;
              link:=link^.next
           END(*WHILE*);
    123:(*EXIT PROCEDURE*)
        END(*DELETE*);

    PROCEDURE list(VAR start,stop : integer);

    (*List lines from start to stop *)
```

```
    LABEL
      123;  (* Used only to exit procedure *)
    VAR
      i : integer;
     BEGIN
       link:=head^.next;
       WHILE link <> NIL DO
        BEGIN
          IF link^.lineno > stop
            THEN GOTO 123;  (* Exit procedure *)
          IF link^.lineno >= start
            THEN
             BEGIN
               write(link^.lineno);
               writeln(link^.linetext)
             END(*IF*);
           link := link^.next
        END (*WHILE*);
123:(*EXIT PROCEDURE*)

    END(*LIST*);
  BEGIN

    (* Begin main program processing *)

    new(head);
    head^.next:=NIL;
     REPEAT
       writeln('NEXT COMMAND');
       read(command);
       CASE command OF
         'I':
          BEGIN
            read(number);
            read(newline);
            insert(number,newline)
          END(* CASE FOR 'I' *);
         'D':
          BEGIN
            read(number);
            delete(number)
          END(* CASE FOR 'D'*);
         'L':
          BEGIN
            read(number,stop);
            list(number,stop)
          END(* CASE FOR 'L' *);
         'Q': BEGIN END; (* Do nothing *)
         ELSE writeln('ERROR, TRY AGAIN')
        END(* CASE*);
       readln;
     UNTIL command = 'Q'
  END(*PROGRAM*).
```

Sample run:

```
NEXT COMMAND
I 10 INPUT A,B
NEXT COMMAND
I 20 PRINT A,B,C
NEXT COMMAND
I 15 C=A+B
NEXT COMMAND
L 10 30
     10 INPUT A,B
     15 C=A+B
     20 PRINT A,B,C
NEXT COMMAND
D 15
NEXT COMMAND
L 10 30
     10 INPUT A,B
     20 PRINT A,B,C
NEXT COMMAND
I 2 REM REMEMBER TO DOCUMENT ALL PROGRAMS
NEXT COMMAND
I 4 REM BUT THIS IS SUCH A DUMB PROGRAM
NEXT COMMAND
L 1 9999
      2 REM REMEMBER TO DOCUMENT ALL PROGRAMS
      4 REM BUT THIS IS SUCH A DUMB PROGRAM
     10 INPUT A,B
     20 PRINT A,B,C
NEXT COMMAND
I 6 REM LET'S MAKE THE PROGRAM DISAPPEAR
NEXT COMMAND
D 10
NEXT COMMAND
D 20
NEXT COMMAND
D 30
NEXT COMMAND
L 1 9999
      2 REM REMEMBER TO DOCUMENT ALL PROGRAMS
      4 REM BUT THIS IS SUCH A DUMB PROGRAM
      6 REM LET'S MAKE THE PROGRAM DISAPPEAR
NEXT COMMAND
Q
```

4

Queues and Stacks

The past is but the beginning of a beginning.

H. G. WELLS (1866–1946)

4-1 Introductory Considerations

In Chapter 2 we introduced the linked list as a data structure specifically designed to handle conveniently the insertion and deletion of entries in an ordered list. In this chapter, we will discuss 2 special types of lists characterized by restrictions imposed on the way in which entries may be inserted and removed. One of these structures, a **queue,** is a **first-in-first-out** (sometimes referred to as **FIFO) list.** Insertions are limited to one end of the list, whereas deletions may occur only at the other end. Typically, these 2 ends of the list are called the **rear** and **front,** respectively, and must be continually maintained via FRONT and REAR pointers. The conceptual picture that emerges from the notion of a queue is that of a waiting line; for example, jobs waiting to be serviced by a computer or cars forming a long line at a busy toll booth.

The other structure that we will study is a **last-in-first-out** (sometimes referred to as **LIFO) list,** known as a **stack.** In a stack, both insertions and deletions occur at one end only. Hence, a stack may be maintained with a single pointer to the *top* of the list of elements. Stacks are frequently used as a storage structure in everyday life. For instance, to maintain an orderly suitcase, the smart traveler will pack a wardrobe such that the last item packed will be the 1st to be worn. Perhaps the best visual example of a stack is that of the pop-up mechanism to store trays for a cafeteria line. The terminology used to describe stack operations reinforces this analogy. Removing the top entry from the stack is **popping** the stack, whereas adding a new entry is **pushing** the stack (Figure 4-1).

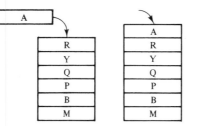

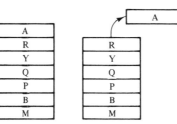

Figure 4-1   A stack can be thought of as the pop-up mechanism used to store cafeteria trays. Adding an item is called *pushing* onto the stack (top); removing one is called *popping* from the stack (bottom).

4-2   Queues

Let us consider computer jobs being scheduled in a batch processing environment, a nice example of a queue in use. We will further suppose that all job names are 6 characters or less and that jobs are scheduled strictly in the order in which they arrive. Then an array and 2 pointers can be used to implement the scheduling queue.

```
VAR   FRONT, REAR, ARRAYSIZE   :   INTEGER
VAR   QUEUE(ARRAYSIZE)   :   CHARACTER(6)
```

Here ARRAYSIZE represents the maximum number of entries the array QUEUE may contain. We shall see that this is different from the maximum number of entries that the queue may contain at a given time in processing.

If the FRONT and REAR pointers are initially set to 1 and 0, respectively, the state of the queue before any insertions or deletions appears as shown in Figure 4-2.

Recalling that insertions may be made only at the rear of the queue, suppose that job NEWTON now arrives to be processed. The queue changes to look like Figure 4-3. If job NEWTON is followed by PAYROL, the queue must change to look like Figure 4-4, which shows that the addition of any ITEM to the queue requires two steps:

```
REAR := REAR + 1
QUEUE(REAR) := ITEM
```

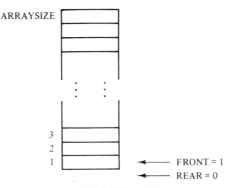

Figure 4-2 Stack with FRONT pointer set at 1 and REAR pointer set at 0.

If the system is now ready to process NEWTON, the front entry must be removed from the queue to an appropriate location designated by ITEM (Figure 4-5, page 66). Here the instructions:

```
ITEM := QUEUE(FRONT)
FRONT := FRONT + 1
```

achieve the desired effect.

It should be clear from the preceding discussion that the conditions in Figure 4-6 on page 67 signal the associated special situations. The conditions allow us to develop our brief two-line sequences for adding to and removing from a queue into full-fledged procedures capable of sending back an appropriate flag should the requested operation not be successful.

```
PROCEDURE  REMOVE(QUEUE, ARRAYSIZE, FRONT, REAR, ITEM, EMPTY)

     (* General procedure to remove FRONT entry from QUEUE*)
     (* and return it in ITEM.  EMPTY flag returned as FALSE *)
     (* if operation successful, and TRUE if QUEUE is empty. *)
```

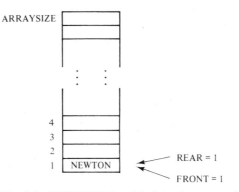

Figure 4-3 The job NEWTON is added to the rear of the stack.

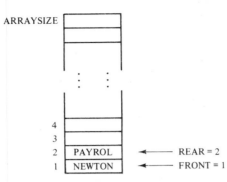

Figure 4-4 PAYROL is added after NEWTON.

```
VAR  QUEUE(ARRAYSIZE), ITEM : CHARACTER(6)
VAR  FRONT, REAR, ARRAYSIZE : INTEGER
VAR  EMPTY : BOOLEAN

IF  REAR < FRONT THEN
    [EMPTY := TRUE]
ELSE
   ┌EMPTY := FALSE
   │ITEM := QUEUE(FRONT)
   └FRONT := FRONT + 1
ENDIF
RETURN
END  REMOVE
```

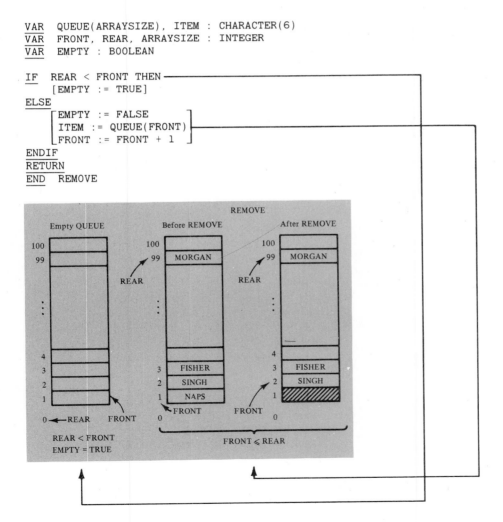

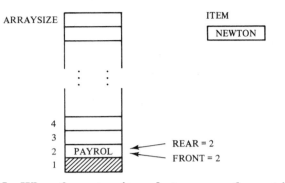

Figure 4-5 **When the system is ready to process the next job, it removes NEWTON to the location designated by ITEM.**

```
PROCEDURE  ADD(QUEUE, ARRAYSIZE, FRONT, REAR, ITEM, FULL)

    (* General procedure to add ITEM to REAR of QUEUE. *)
    (* FULL flag returned as FALSE if operation is successful *)
    (* and as TRUE if the QUEUE is full. *)

VAR  QUEUE(ARRAYSIZE), ITEM : CHARACTER(6)
VAR  FRONT, REAR, ARRAYSIZE : INTEGER
VAR  FULL : BOOLEAN

IF  REAR = ARRAYSIZE THEN
      [FULL := TRUE]
ELSE
      ┌FULL := FALSE
      │REAR := REAR + 1
      └QUEUE(REAR) := ITEM
ENDIF
RETURN
END  ADD
```

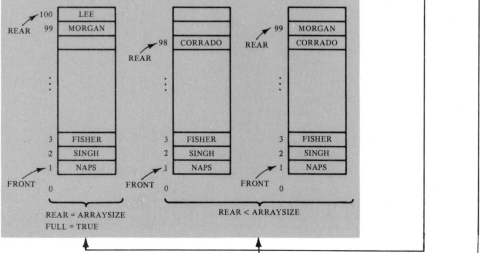

Condition	Special situation
REAR < FRONT	Empty queue
FRONT = REAR	One-entry queue
REAR = ARRAYSIZE	No more entries may be added to queue

Figure 4-6   Special situations that can occur in the stack, and the conditions that signal them.

As it now stands, our implementation of a queue as a scheduling structure for jobs in a batch environment functions effectively until REAR = ARRAYSIZE. Then a call to ADD returns FULL as TRUE even though only a small percentage of slots in the array may actually contain data items *currently* in the queue structure. In fact, we should be able to use slots 1 through 997 again (Figure 4-7). This is not necessarily undesirable. For example, it may be that the mode of operation in a given batch environment is to process 1000 jobs, then print a statistical report on these 1000 jobs, and finally clear the queue to start another group of 1000 jobs. In this case, the queue pictured in Figure 4-7 is the ideal structure, because data about jobs are not lost even after they have left the queue.

However, if the goal of a computer installation were to provide continuous scheduling of batch jobs, without interruption after 1000 jobs, then the queue of Figure 4-7 would not be effective. One strategy that could be employed to correct this situation is to move the active queue down the array upon reaching the condition REAR = ARRAYSIZE, as illustrated in Figure 4-8. Should the queue contain a large number of items, however, this strategy would not be satisfactory because it would require moving all of the individual data items. We will discuss 2 other strategies that allow the queue to operate in a continuous *and* efficient fashion—a **circular implementation** and a **linked list implementation.**

Circular Implementation of a Queue

This technique essentially allows the queue to **wrap around** upon reaching the end of the array. This transformation is illustrated by the addition of the item UPDATE to the queue in Figure 4-9.

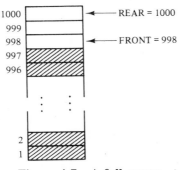

Figure 4-7   A full queue.

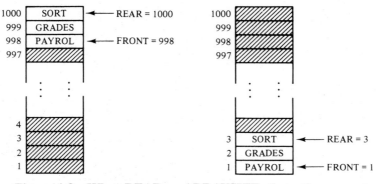

Figure 4-8   When REAR = ARRAYSIZE, the active queue is moved down.

To handle the pointer arithmetic necessary for this implementation of a queue, we must make the FRONT and REAR pointers behave in a fashion analogous to an odometer counter on a car that has exceeded its mileage capacity. A convenient way of doing this is to introduce the MOD operator where:

$$M \text{ MOD } N = \text{ remainder of dividing integer } M \text{ by integer } N$$

(For example, 5 MOD 3 = 2 and 10 MOD 7 = 3.) It is immediately clear from Figure 4-9 that REAR < FRONT will no longer suffice as a condition to signal an empty queue. To derive this condition, consider what remains after we remove an item from a queue that has only a single item in it. There are 2 possible situations, as illustrated in Figure 4-10.

An inspection of both cases reveals that, after the lone entry has been removed, the relationship

```
(REAR MOD ARRAYSIZE) + 1 = FRONT
```

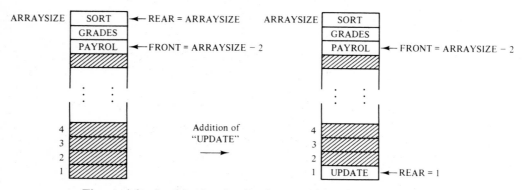

Figure 4-9   In this circular implementation, the queue wraps around when UPDATE is added.

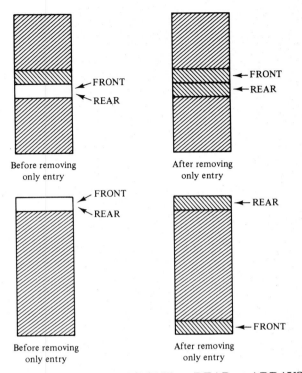

**Figure 4-10   Top: case 1   FRONT = REAR < ARRAYSIZE.
Bottom: case 2   FRONT = REAR = ARRAYSIZE.**

holds between the pointers. There is a problem, however, with immediately adopting this as a check for an empty queue. This same relationship between pointers also exists when the queue is full *if* we allow all slots in the array to be occupied at any one time!

This apparent contradiction can be avoided easily if one memory slot is sacrificed; that is, if we view a queue with ARRAYSIZE − 1 entries as a full queue. Then the test for fullness is met when the REAR pointer lags 2 behind FRONT (including consideration for wraparound). The results are summarized in Figure 4-11.

FRONT = REAR	One-entry queue
(REAR MOD ARRAYSIZE) + 1 = FRONT	Empty queue
(REAR MOD ARRAYSIZE) + 2 = FRONT	Full queue

**Figure 4-11   Implementing a circular queue, at most
ARRAYSIZE − 1 entries.**

Linked List Implementation of a Queue

The linked list method allows the queue to be completely dynamic with size restrictions imposed only by the pool of available nodes. Essentially, the queue is represented as a linked list with an additional REAR pointer to the last node in the list so that the list need not be traversed to find this node. To reduce the necessity of handling special cases, we follow the strategy established in Chapter 2 of having a dummy header, which carries no actual data, as the first node in the list. Hence the queue containing PAYROL, GRADES, and SORT would appear as in Figure 4-12. A special FRONT pointer need not be maintained, because LINK(HEAD) leads directly to the 1st item in the queue.

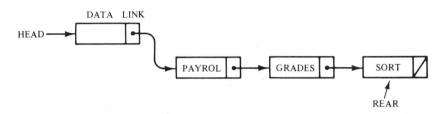

Figure 4-12   Linked list implementation of a queue with 3 data nodes and a dummy header.

Figure 4-13 summarizes the conditional checks that signal an empty, one-entry, or full queue.

Empty queue $\longrightarrow$ REAR = HEAD

One-entry queue $\longrightarrow$ REAR = LINK(HEAD)

Full queue $\longrightarrow$ Handled by GETNODE procedure of Chapter 2

Figure 4-13   Conditional checks for special situations in the linked list implementation.

Appropriate procedures for handling additions to and removals from the queue follow:

```
PROCEDURE  ADD(HEAD, REAR, ITEM, LINK, DATA, N, AVAIL)

    (* Add ITEM pointed to by P to QUEUE pointed to by REAR. *)
    (* QUEUE is maintained via linked list with LINK, *)
    (* DATA, N, and AVAIL as specified in Chapter 2. *)

VAR  HEAD, REAR, AVAIL, P, N, LINK(N) : INTEGER
VAR  DATA(N), ITEM : CHARACTER(6)

CALL  GETNODE(AVAIL, LINK, N, P)

    (* GETNODE handles no space available situation. *)

DATA(P) := ITEM
LINK(P) := NULL
LINK(REAR) := P
REAR := P
RETURN
END  ADD
```

QUEUE before ADD

P node obtained via GETNODE

Inserted

QUEUE after ADDing SORT

```
PROCEDURE  REMOVE (HEAD, REAR, ITEM, EMPTY, LINK, DATA, N, AVAIL)

    (* Remove ITEM pointed to by P from QUEUE pointed to by REAR. *)
    (* QUEUE is maintained via linked list with LINK, *)
    (* DATA, N, and AVAIL as specified in Chapter 2. *)
    (* EMPTY returned as TRUE when list is empty. *)
```

```
VAR  HEAD, REAR, AVAIL, P, N, LINK(N) : INTEGER
VAR  DATA(N), ITEM : CHARACTER(6)
VAR  EMPTY : BOOLEAN

IF  HEAD = REAR THEN ─────────────────────────────────────────┐
     [EMPTY := TRUE]
ELSE
     ┌ EMPTY := FALSE
     │ P := LINK(HEAD)
     │ ITEM := DATA(P)
     │ LINK(HEAD) := LINK(P)
     │ IF  REAR = P THEN    (* Removed from one-entry queue *)
     │      [REAR := HEAD]
     │ ENDIF
     └ CALL  RETURNNODE(AVAIL, LINK, N, P)    (* As per Chapter 2 *)
ENDIF
RETURN
END  REMOVE
```

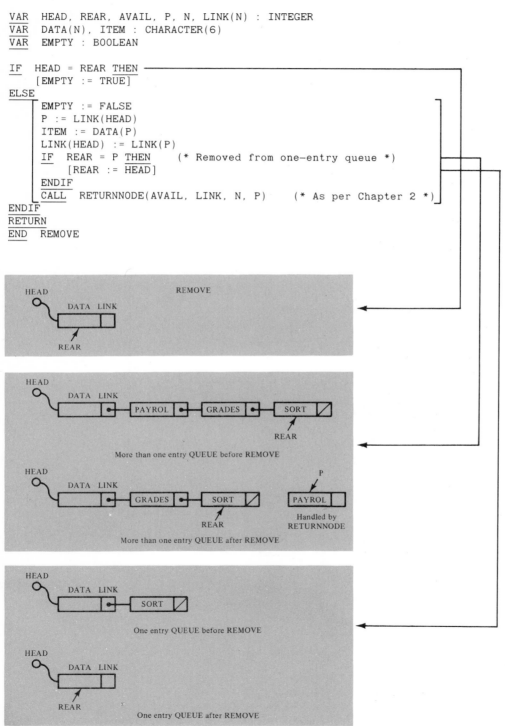

REMOVE

More than one entry QUEUE before REMOVE

More than one entry QUEUE after REMOVE

Handled by RETURNNODE

One entry QUEUE before REMOVE

One entry QUEUE after REMOVE

Priority Queues

So far we have used a batch scheduling application as an example of how a queue might be used in an operating system. Typically, such batch scheduling might also give higher priorities to certain types of jobs. For instance, at a university computer center, students in introductory computer science courses may receive the highest priority for their jobs to encourage a quick turnaround. Students in upper-division courses may have the next highest priority, whereas jobs related to faculty research, which require a great deal of computation, get the lowest possible priority. These types of jobs could be called A, B, and C, respectively. Any A job is serviced before any B or C job, regardless of the time it enters the service queue. Similarly, any B job is serviced before any C job. A data structure capable of representing such a queue would require just one FRONT pointer but 3 rear pointers—one each for A, B, and C.

A queue with 8 jobs waiting to be serviced might appear as shown in Figure 4-14, which tells us that STATS, PRINT, and BANK are the A jobs awaiting service; COPY and CHECK the B jobs, and UPDATE, AVERAG, and TEST the C jobs. If a new A job PROB1 were to arrive for service, it would be inserted at the end of the A queue, between BANK and COPY. Because jobs can be serviced only by leaving the front of the queue, PROB1 would be processed before any of the B or C jobs.

Because insertions in such a **priority queue** need not occur at the absolute rear of the queue, it is clear that an array implementation may require moving a substantial number of data when an item is inserted at the rear of one of the higher priorities. To avoid this, you can use a linked list to great advantage when implementing a priority queue. If a dummy header is included at the beginning of the list, the empty conditions for any given priority are:

Figure 4-14
**A priority queue
with 8 jobs at
3 priority levels.**

```
HEAD  = REAR1 ---> For priority 1, the
                     highest priority

REAR1 = REAR2 ---> For priority 2
     .             .
     .             .
REAR(n-1) = REARn ---> For priority n
```

The specifics of writing procedures to add to a given priority or remove from a priority queue are included as exercises at the end of the chapter.

4-3   Stacks

An Application in Compiler Design

Compilers for all languages allow for some sort of **subroutine call.** Of key importance to any subroutine structure is that the return from a subroutine must be to the instruction immediately following the call that originally transferred control to the subroutine. For example, in the partial coding:

```
PROGRAM  MAIN
      .
      .
      .
CALL  SUB1
PRINT Q
      .
      .
END   MAIN
```

In the world of applications . . .

In order to process jobs efficiently, an operating system in a computer installation makes use of a queue structure. The queue consists of an input device, a channel, an input buffer, the central processing unit (CPU), another channel, an output buffer, and an output device.

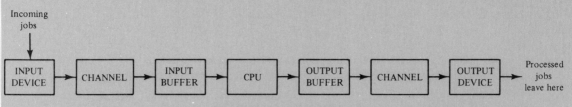

Queue structure in job processing

A channel may be a special-purpose small computer, or even a part of the main computer. Once the channel has received instructions from the operating system, it can operate independently of the CPU. The data for the input job are sent to the input buffer under channel control. The input buffer can accept data at slow speeds, and release them to the CPU at high speeds. Once the data have been processed by the CPU, they are released to the output buffer at a high speed. At this point, the data from another job are entering at the rear of the queue under the instructions of the operating system, into the input device. The processed data under channel control are now being released from the output buffer to the output device.

Because the CPU operates at nanosecond speeds, sometimes the operating system makes use of several such queues to keep the CPU occupied and achieve high efficiency in processing.

```
 PROCEDURE   SUB1

        .
        .
        .
 CALL  SUB2
 A := A + B

        .
        .
        .
 RETURN
 END  SUB1
 PROCEDURE   SUB2

        .
        .
        .
 CALL   SUB 3
 P := P -Q

        .
        .
        .
 RETURN
 END  SUB2
 PROCEDURE   SUB3
        .
        .
 RETURN
 END  SUB3
```

the order of operation would be:

1. Leave MAIN and transfer to SUB1

2. Leave SUB1 and transfer to SUB2

3. Leave SUB2 and transfer to SUB3

4. Return from SUB3 to the instruction P : = P − Q in SUB2

5. Return from SUB2 to the instruction A : = A + B in SUB1

6. Return from SUB1 to the instruction PRINT Q in MAIN

7. End of MAIN

Each time a CALL is made, the machine must remember where to return when that subroutine is completed. (For those of you who have programmed in micro assembler, the numerous PUSH operations given in this type of language are precisely implementations of a stack structure.)

A structure capable of storing the data necessary to handle calls and returns in this sequence would be a **memory stack.** In such a stack, items can enter and leave *only* at one end of the stack—the *top*. Hence, the preceding partial coding would generate a stack that develops as illustrated in Figure 4-15. Each time a CALL is made, a return address is placed, or *pushed,* onto the top of the stack. Each time a RETURN is executed, the top

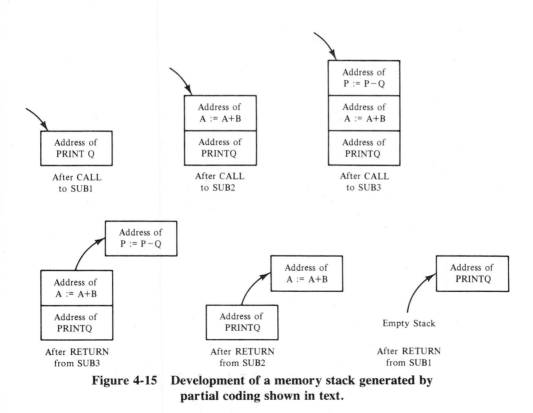

Figure 4-15 **Development of a memory stack generated by partial coding shown in text.**

item on the stack is *popped* to determine the memory address to which the RETURN should be made. The nature of the LEAVE-RETURN sequence for subroutines makes it crucial that the 1st return address accessed be the last one that was remembered by the computer. Because there is only one point, the *top*, at which data may enter or exit a stack, it is the ideal data structure to be used for this *last-in-first-out* (LIFO) type of operation.

This description of the method by which a compiler actually implements subroutine calls is just one illustration of the utility of stacks. We shall return in Chapter 5 to a more difficult type of subroutine usage called **recursion,** and we will examine in detail the role of the stack in handling such a **recursive call.** Now, however, we will consider 2 ways of implementing a stack.

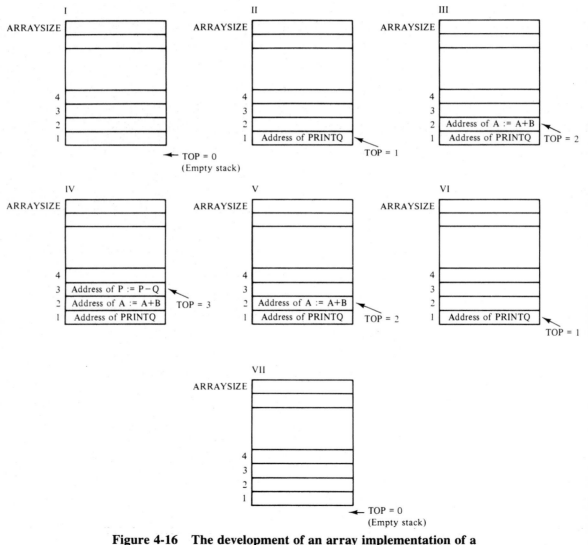

Figure 4-16   The development of an array implementation of a stack generated by the partial coding in the text.

Array Implementations of a Stack

A strategy similar to that used for an array implementation of a queue can be followed. However, because insertions and deletions occur at the same end of a stack, only one pointer will be needed, instead of the 2 required for a queue. We will call that pointer TOP and use Figure 4-16 to trace it through our previous subroutine example.

Thus, to push an entry in ITEM onto the stack, the 2 operations

```
TOP := TOP + 1
STACK(TOP) := ITEM
```

must occur. Popping an entry from the stack into ITEM requires:

```
ITEM := STACK(TOP)
TOP := TOP - 1
```

Complete procedures that take into account the boundary conditions of a full and empty stack follow:

```
PROCEDURE  PUSH(ITEM, STACK, ARRAYSIZE, TOP, FULL)

    (*Push ITEM onto STACK.  FULL is a flag indicating whether or *)
    (*not there is room on STACK to perform this operation.        *)

VAR   ARRAYSIZE, STACK(ARRAYSIZE)  : INTEGER

    (*For this procedure, we are assuming the STACK contains *)
    (*integer data with room for ARRAYSIZE entries *)

VAR   ITEM, TOP : INTEGER
VAR   FULL : BOOLEAN
IF    TOP = ARRAYSIZE   THEN
      [FULL := TRUE]
ELSE
      ⌈FULL := FALSE      ⌉
      │TOP := TOP + 1     │
      ⌊STACK(TOP) := ITEM⌋
ENDIF
RETURN
END    PUSH


PROCEDURE   POP(ITEM, STACK, ARRAYSIZE, TOP, EMPTY)

    (*Pop top element in STACK into ITEM. EMPTY is a flag to *)
    (*indicate whether or not operation successful.*)

VAR    ARRAYSIZE, STACK(ARRAYSIZE) : INTEGER
VAR    ITEM, TOP : INTEGER
VAR    EMPTY : BOOLEAN
IF    TOP = 0   THEN
      [EMPTY := TRUE]
ELSE
      ⌈EMPTY := FALSE      ⌉
      │ITEM := STACK(TOP)  │
      ⌊TOP := TOP - 1      ⌋
ENDIF
RETURN
END    POP
```

Linked List Implementation of a Stack

When we choose a linked list implementation, we are trading a relatively small amount of memory space needed to maintain pointers for the dynamic allocation of stack space. Following our usual convention of maintaining a dummy header node at the beginning of a linked list, a stack with the 3 entries 18, 40, 31 would appear as shown in Figure 4-17.

The condition to test for an empty stack would then be TOP = HEAD. A full stack occurs only when the GETNODE procedure for the linked list reports that there is no available space. Full procedures to push and pop the stack now become nothing more than inserts and deletes from the beginning of a linked list. As such, they are special cases of the procedures already developed in Chapter 2; you will write them as exercises at the end of the chapter.

SUMMARY

A queue is a first-in-first-out (FIFO) data structure used in processing of data such as job scheduling in a large university computer environment. There are 2 basic pointers, FRONT and REAR, associated with this structure. New data items to be processed are added to the rear of the queue, and the data item that is about to be processed is removed from the front of the queue. The process of cars entering and leaving a car wash is a familiar analogy.

A stack is a last-in-first-out (LIFO) data structure. There is only one pointer, TOP, associated with a stack. Implementation of subroutines and functions in many high-level languages are accomplished via stack structures. In a football game, when many players pile up on top of the ball carrier, the order in which they untangle themselves from the pile is typical of the way data items are processed in a stack.

KEY TERMS

Queue	Pop	MOD
FIFO	Push	Priority queue
LIFO	REAR	TOP
Stack	FRONT	

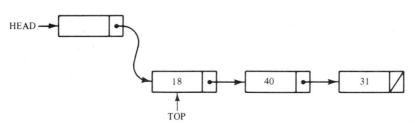

Figure 4-17   A linked list implementation of a stack with 3 data nodes and a dummy header.

EXERCISES

Using any appropriate programming language:

1. Given the discussion of circular queues presented in this chapter, determine a valid initial setting for the FRONT and REAR pointers in a circular queue.

2. Develop a calling convention and associated procedure to remove an item from a queue with *n* priorities.

3. Develop a calling convention and associated procedure to add an item to a queue with *n* priorities.

4. Develop a calling convention and associated procedure to push an item onto a stack implemented with a linked list.

5. Develop a calling convention and associated procedure to pop an item from a stack implemented with a linked list.

6. Develop a calling convention and associated procedure to add an item to a circular queue.

7. Develop a calling convention and associated procedure to remove an item from a circular queue.

PROGRAMMING PROBLEMS

1. The Wing and a Prayer Airline Company is becoming increasingly concerned about the amount of fuel being wasted as its planes wait to land at and take off from world famous O'Hair Airport. Write a program to simulate the operation of one day's activity at O'Hair and report on the times spent waiting to land and take off by each Wing and a Prayer flight. Input data to your program should include:

   - Average number of Wing and a Prayer arrivals each hour

   - Average number of other airline arrivals each hour

   - Average number of Wing and a Prayer departures each hour

   - Average number of other airline departures each hour

   - Number of available runways

   - Average time runway in use for an arrival

   - Average time runway in use for a departure

   Your program should maintain two queues: one for arrivals waiting for a runway, and one for departures waiting for a runway.

2. In a suitable high-level language of your choice, develop a program to simulate the processing of batch jobs by a computer system. The scheduling of these jobs should be handled via a queue (or priority queue for more of a challenge). Examples of commands that your program should be able to process are:

```
ADD (to add an entry to queue)
DELETE (to take an item out of the queue)
STATUS (to report on items currently in queue)
```

3. In a suitable high-level language, develop a program to simulate the arrival of customers in a waiting line at a bank. Factors to consider in such a program would be the average time it takes to service one customer, the average number of customers that arrive in a given time period, and the number of service windows maintained by the bank. Statistics such as the length of time the average customer has to spend in the waiting line could be very helpful in the bank's future planning.

4. If you are working in Pascal, consider the Pascal supplement that follows these problems. In it, procedures are given for pushing and popping a stack of characters implemented by the linked list method. However, checks for an empty stack condition are not given in either of the procedures. Modify these procedures so that they appropriately signal the empty stack condition. Then design a complete program to process the stack by handling PUSH, POP, and STATUS instructions in the manner of Problem 2 above.

5. Here is a problem typically encountered in text processing/formatting applications. Given a file of text, that text delimited by special bracketing symbols [ ] is to be considered a footnote. Footnotes, when encountered, are not to be printed as normal text but are instead stored in a footnote queue. Then, when the special symbol # is encountered, all footnotes currently in the queue are printed and the queue should be returned to an empty state. This problem also will allow you to make good use of string storage techniques!

If you work in Pascal . . .

Below we give Pascal procedures to push and pop a stack represented with a linked list implementation. In each case, the data on the stack consist of single character items. The pointer topc is used to point to the top of the stack. The procedure STACKC is used for pushing, and the procedure UNSTACKC is used for popping.

```
TYPE
    .
    .
    .
    ptrc = ^chstack;
    chstack = RECORD
                  ch : char;
                  next : ptrc
                END;


VAR
    .
    .
    .
    topc : ptrc;
    .
    .
    PROCEDURE stackc(VAR x:char);
    VAR
      p : ptrc;
     BEGIN
       new(p);
       p^.ch:=x;
       p^.next:=topc;
       topc:=p
     END(*STACKC*);


    PROCEDURE unstackc(VAR x:char);
    VAR
      p:ptrc;
     BEGIN
       p:=topc;
       x:=topc^.ch;
       topc:=topc^.next;
       dispose(p)
     END(*UNSTACKC*);
```

5

Applications of Stacks

It is hard to think at the top.

STRINGFELLOW BARR

5-1 Introductory Considerations

Often the logic of problems for which stacks are a suitable data structure involves the necessity to **backtrack,** to return to a previous state. For instance, consider the problem of finding your way out of a maze. One approach to take would be to probe a given path in the maze as deeply as possible. Upon finding a dead end, you would need to backtrack to previously visited maze locations in order to try probing other paths. Such backtracking would require recalling these previous locations in the reverse order from which you visited them. Not many of us need to find our way out of a maze. However, the designers of compilers are faced with an analogous backtracking situation in the evaluation of arithmetic expressions. As you scan the expression A * B/C + D in left-to-right order, it is impossible to tell upon initially encountering the asterisk whether or not you should apply the indicated multiplication operation to A and the immediately following operand. Instead, you must probe further into the expression to determine whether an operation with a higher priority occurs. While you undertake this probing of the expression, you must stack previously encountered operation symbols until you are certain when they can be applied.

5-2 Parsing and Evaluation of Arithmetic Expressions Using Stacks

Compounding the backtracking problem just described, there are often many different ways of representing the same algebraic expression. For example, the assignment statements

```
Z := A * B/C + D
Z := (A * B)/C + D
Z := ((A * B )/C) + D
```

should all result in the same order of arithmetic operations even though the expressions involved are written in distinctly different form. The process of collapsing such different expressions into one unique form is called **parsing** the expression, and one frequently used method of parsing relies heavily upon stacks.

Postfix, Prefix, and Infix Notation

Usual algebraic notation is often termed **infix** notation: the arithmetic operator appears *between* the two operands to which it is being applied. Infix notation may require parentheses to specify a desired order of operations. For example, in the expression A/B + C, the division will occur first. If we want the addition to occur first, the expression must be parenthesized as A/(B + C).

Using **postfix*** notation, the need for parentheses is eliminated because the operator is placed directly *after* the two operands to which it applies. Hence, A/B + C would be written as AB/C + in postfix form. This says:

1. Apply the division operator to A and B

2. To that result, add C

The infix expression A/(B + C) would be written as ABC + / in postfix notation. Reading this postfix expression from left to right, we are told to:

1. Apply the addition operator to B and C

2. Divide that result into A

Although relatively short expressions such as the ones in the preceding paragraphs can be converted from infix to postfix via an intuitive process, a more systematic method is required for complicated expressions. We propose the following algorithm for humans (and will soon consider a different one for computers):

1. *Completely* parenthesize the infix expression to specify the order of all operations

2. Move each operator to the space held by its corresponding right parenthesis

3. Remove all parentheses

Consider this three-step method as it applies to the expression

    A/B^C + D*E - A*C

1. Completely parenthesizing this expression yields:

    (((A/(B^C)) + (D*E)) - (A*C))

2. Moving each operator to its corresponding right parenthesis, we obtain:

    (((A/ (B^C)) + (D*E)) - (A*C))

3. Removing all parentheses, we are left with:

    ABC^/DE*+AC*−

---

*Also called **reverse Polish** notation after the nationality of its originator, the Polish logician Jan Lukasiewicz.

Had we started out with:

A / B^C - (D*E - A*C)

our three-step procedure would have resulted in:

((A / (B^C)) - ((D*E) - (A*C)))

Removing the parentheses would then yield:

ABC^/DE*AC*--

In a similar way, an expression can be converted into **prefix** form, in which an operator immediately *precedes* its two operands. The conversion algorithm for infix to prefix specifies that, after completely parenthesizing the infix expression with order of priority in mind, we move each operator to its corresponding left parenthesis. Applying the method to:

A/B^C + D*E - A*C

gives us

((A/(B^C)) + ((D*E) - (A*C)))

and finally the prefix form:

+/A^BC-*DE*AC

The importance of postfix and prefix notations in parsing arithmetic expressions is that these notations are completely free of parentheses. Consequently, an expression in postfix (or prefix) form is in **unique form.** In the design of compilers, this parsing of an expression into postfix form is crucial because having a unique form for an expression greatly simplifies its eventual evaluation. Thus, in handling an assignment statement, a compiler must:

1. Parse it into postfix form

2. Apply an evaluation algorithm to the postfix form

We shall limit our discussion here to postfix notation. The techniques we will cover are easily adaptable to the functionally equivalent prefix form.

Converting Infix Expressions to Postfix

First consider the problem of parsing an expression from infix to postfix form. Our three-step procedure is not easily adaptable to machine coding. Instead, we will use an algorithm that has as its essential data structures:

1. A string INFIX containing the infix expression

2. A stack OPSTACK, which may contain:

- Arithmetic operators: " +," " −," "*," and "/"

- Parentheses: "(" and ")"

- A special delimeter: "#"

3. A string POSTFIX containing the final postfix expression

To eliminate details that would only clutter the main logic of the algorithm, we will assume that the string representing the infix expression contains only arithmetic operators, parentheses, the delimiting character "#," and operands that consist of a single character each. We will also omit consideration of the exponentiation operator ^, which will be covered in a later exercise. Thus, our algorithm will convert infix expressions of the form

$$A * B + (C - D/E)\#$$

into postfix notation.

The description of the algorithm is as follows:

1. Define a function INFIX-PRIORITY, which takes an operator, parenthesis, or # as its argument and returns an integer as described in the table below:

Character	*	/	+	−	(	)	#
Returned value	2	2	1	1	3	0	0

2. Define another function STACK-PRIORITY, which takes the same possibilities for an argument and returns an integer as:

Character	*	/	+	−	(	)	#
Returned value	2	2	1	1	0	unde-fined	0

3. Push # onto OPSTACK as its first entry

4. Read the next character CH from the INFIX string

5. Test CH and:

- If CH is an operand, append it to the POSTFIX string.

- If CH is a right parenthesis, then pop entries from stack and append them to POSTFIX until a left parenthesis is popped. Discard both left and right parentheses.

- If CH is #, pop all entries that remain on the stack and append them to the POSTFIX string.

- Otherwise, pop from the stack and append to the POSTFIX string operators whose STACK-PRIORITY is greater than or equal to the INFIX-PRIORITY of CH. Then stack CH.

6. Repeat steps (4) and (5) until CH is the delimiter #.

The key to the algorithm is the use of the stack to hold operators from the infix expression that appear to the left of another given operator even though that latter operator must be applied first. The defined functions INFIX-PRIORITY and STACK-PRIORITY are used to specify this priority of operators and the associated pushing and popping operations. The entire process is best understood by carefully tracing through an example, as shown in Figure 5-1.

The PSEUDO procedure for implementing the algorithm follows. You will develop subordinate subroutines and functions as an exercise at the end of the chapter.

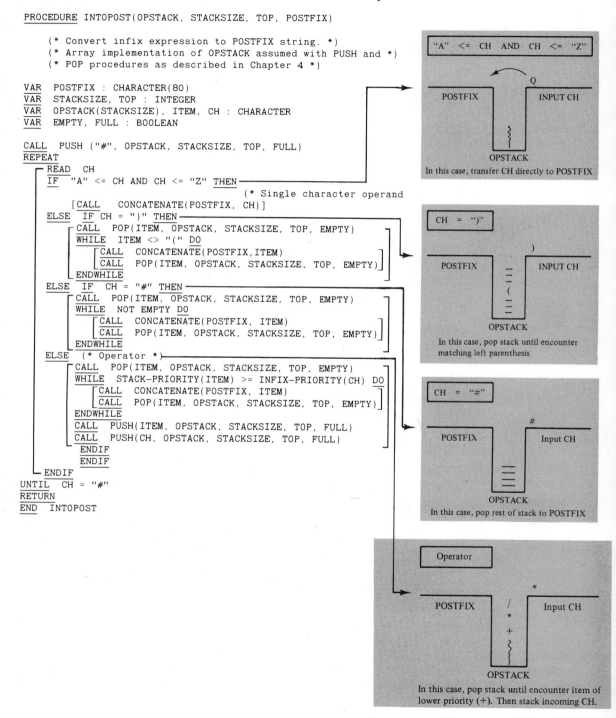

```
PROCEDURE INTOPOST(OPSTACK, STACKSIZE, TOP, POSTFIX)

    (* Convert infix expression to POSTFIX string. *)
    (* Array implementation of OPSTACK assumed with PUSH and *)
    (* POP procedures as described in Chapter 4 *)

VAR   POSTFIX : CHARACTER(80)
VAR   STACKSIZE, TOP : INTEGER
VAR   OPSTACK(STACKSIZE), ITEM, CH : CHARACTER
VAR   EMPTY, FULL : BOOLEAN

CALL  PUSH ("#", OPSTACK, STACKSIZE, TOP, FULL)
REPEAT
    READ  CH
    IF  "A" <= CH AND CH <= "Z" THEN
                        (* Single character operand
        [CALL   CONCATENATE(POSTFIX, CH)]
    ELSE  IF CH = ")" THEN
        CALL  POP(ITEM, OPSTACK, STACKSIZE, TOP, EMPTY)
        WHILE  ITEM <> "(" DO
            [CALL   CONCATENATE(POSTFIX,ITEM)
             CALL   POP(ITEM, OPSTACK, STACKSIZE, TOP, EMPTY)]
        ENDWHILE
    ELSE  IF  CH = "#" THEN
        CALL  POP(ITEM, OPSTACK, STACKSIZE, TOP, EMPTY)
        WHILE  NOT EMPTY DO
            [CALL   CONCATENATE(POSTFIX, ITEM)
             CALL   POP(ITEM, OPSTACK, STACKSIZE, TOP, EMPTY)]
        ENDWHILE
    ELSE  (* Operator *)
        CALL  POP(ITEM, OPSTACK, STACKSIZE, TOP, EMPTY)
        WHILE  STACK-PRIORITY(ITEM) >= INFIX-PRIORITY(CH) DO
            [CALL   CONCATENATE(POSTFIX, ITEM)
             CALL   POP(ITEM, OPSTACK, STACKSIZE, TOP, EMPTY)]
        ENDWHILE
        CALL  PUSH(ITEM, OPSTACK, STACKSIZE, TOP, FULL)
        CALL  PUSH(CH, OPSTACK, STACKSIZE, TOP, FULL)
        ENDIF
        ENDIF
    ENDIF
UNTIL  CH = "#"
RETURN
END  INTOPOST
```

"A" <= CH AND CH <= "Z"

Q

POSTFIX   INPUT CH

OPSTACK

In this case, transfer CH directly to POSTFIX

CH = ")"

)

POSTFIX   INPUT CH

(

OPSTACK

In this case, pop stack until encounter matching left parenthesis

CH = "#"

#

POSTFIX   Input CH

OPSTACK

In this case, pop rest of stack to POSTFIX

Operator

*

POSTFIX /   Input CH
         *
         +

OPSTACK

In this case, pop stack until encounter item of lower priority (+). Then stack incoming CH.

CH	OPSTACK	POSTFIX	Commentary
			Push #
A			Read CH
		A	Append CH to POSTFIX
*			Read CH
	* #		Stack CH
B			Read CH
		AB	Append CH to POSTFIX
+			Read CH
	+ #	AB*	Pop *, append * to POSTFIX, push CH
(			Read CH
	(+ #		Push CH
C			Read CH
		AB*C	Append CH to POSTFIX
−			Read CH
	− (+ #		Push CH
D			Read CH
		AB*CD	Append CH to POSTFIX
/			Read CH
	/ − (+ #		Push CH
E			Read CH
		AB*CDE	Append CH to POSTFIX
)			Read CH
	+	AB*CDE/−	Pop and append to POSTFIX until (reached
#			Read CH
		AB*CDE/−+#	Pop and append rest of stack to CH

**Figure 5-1   Translation of the infix expression A * B + (C − D/E)#
using the algorithm in the text.**

Evaluating Postfix Expressions

Once an expression has been parsed into postfix form, another stack plays an essential role in its final evaluation. As an example, consider the postfix expression from Figure 5-1:

AB*CDE/-+#

Let us suppose that the symbols A, B, C, D, and E had associated with them the values:

Symbol	Value
A	5
B	3
C	6
D	8
E	2

To evaluate such an expression, we repeatedly read characters from the postfix expression. If the character read is an operand, push the value associated with it onto the stack. If it is an operator, pop two values from the stack, apply the operator to them, and push the result back on the stack. The technique is illustrated for our current example in Figure 5-2.

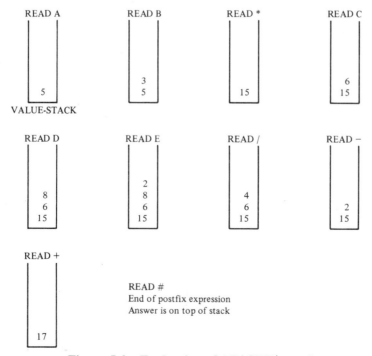

Figure 5-2 Evaluation of AB*CDE/ − + #.

Assuming functions VALUE, which will return the value associated with a particular symbol, and EVAL, which will return the result of applying an operator to 2 values, the PSEUDO procedure to evaluate a postfix expression is given by:

```
PROCEDURE  EVALUATE-POSTFIX (ANSWER, VALUESTACK, STACKSIZE, TOP)
        (* Procedure to evaluate a postfix expression and return result *)
        (* in ANSWER. *)
        (* Array implementation of the VALUESTACK is assumed. *)

VAR  VALUESTACK(STACKSIZE) : REAL (80)
VAR  CH : CHARACTER
VAR  V, V1, V2 : REAL
VAR  TOP : INTEGER
VAR  STACKSIZE : INTEGER
VAR  EMPTY, FULL : BOOLEAN

READ CH
WHILE CH <> "#" DO
    IF  "A" <= CH AND CH <= "Z"  THEN    (*Operand*)
          V = VALUE(CH)
          CALL PUSH(V, VALUESTACK, STACKSIZE, TOP, FULL)
    ELSE
          CALL  POP(V2, VALUESTACK, STACKSIZE, TOP, EMPTY)
          CALL  POP(V1, VALUESTACK, STACKSIZE, TOP, EMPTY)
          V = EVAL(V1, V2, CH)
          CALL  PUSH(V, VALUESTACK, STACKSIZE, TOP, FULL)
    ENDIF
    READ CH
ENDWHILE
CALL POP(ANSWER, VALUESTACK, STACKSIZE, TOP, EMPTY)
RETURN
END EVALUATE-POSTFIX
```

5-3 Recursion

In section 4-3, we indicated that stacks are an essential data structure in a compiler's implementation of subroutine calls. Many compilers, however, will not allow a subroutine to call on itself, a **recursive** call. In this section, we will discuss the role of the stack in compilers that do allow recursive calls, for example, Pascal and PL/1. We will also show how a stack can be used to implement recursive algorithms in languages like COBOL, FORTRAN, and BASIC, which do not allow recursive calls. This will be important in coming chapters, because we will use recursion to elegantly describe many algorithms.

Towers of Hanoi Problem

We introduce recursion with a problem that, although impractical, is excellent for illustrating the technique involved. According to legend, there existed in ancient Hanoi a monastery where the monks had the painstaking task of moving a collection of N stone disks from one pillar, designated as pillar A, to another, designated as pillar C. Moreover, the relative ordering of the disks on pillar A had to be maintained as they were moved to pillar C. That is, as illustrated in Figure 5-3, the disks were to be stacked in largest to smallest fashion beginning from the bottom. Additionally, the monks were to observe the following rules in moving disks:

- Only one disk could be moved at a time

- No larger disk could ever reside on a pillar on top of a smaller disk

- A 3rd pillar B could be used as an intermediate to store one or more disks while they were being moved from their original source A to their destination C

Consider the following recursive solution to this problem.

1. If $N = 1$, merely move the disk from A to C.

2. If $N = 2$, move 1st disk from A to B. Then move 2nd disk from A to C. Then move 1st disk from B to C.

3. If $N = 3$, call upon the technique already established in (2) to move the first 2 disks from A to B using C as an intermediate. Then move the 3rd disk from A to C. Then use the technique in (2) to move 2 disks from B to C using A as an intermediate.

4. For general N, use the technique already established to move $N - 1$ disks from A to B using C as an intermediate. Then move one disk from A to C. Then again use the technique already established to move $N - 1$ disks from B to C using A as an intermediate.

Notice that the technique described here calls upon itself, but switches the order of parameters in so doing. This can be formalized in the following PSEUDO procedure:

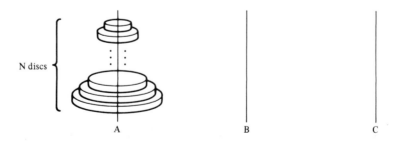

Figure 5-3 Towers of Hanoi problem. The monks must move N disks in order from pillar A to pillar C.

```
PROCEDURE HANOI (N, SOURCE, DESTINATION, INTERMEDIATE)
VAR  L1, L2  :  LABEL
VAR  N :  INTEGER
VAR  SOURCE, DESTINATION, INTERMEDIATE: CHARACTER
IF   N = 1 THEN
     ⎡WRITE "MOVE DISK FROM", SOURCE, "TO" --->⎤
     ⎢--->       DESTINATION                  ⎥
     ⎣RETURN                                  ⎦
ENDIF
CALL  HANOI (N-1, SOURCE, INTERMEDIATE, DESTINATION)
(* In every recursive call HANOI works with value of N less one *)
L1: WRITE  "MOVE DISK FROM", SOURCE, "TO", DESTINATION
    CALL  HANOI(N-1, INTERMEDIATE, DESTINATION, SOURCE)
L2: RETURN
    END  HANOI
```

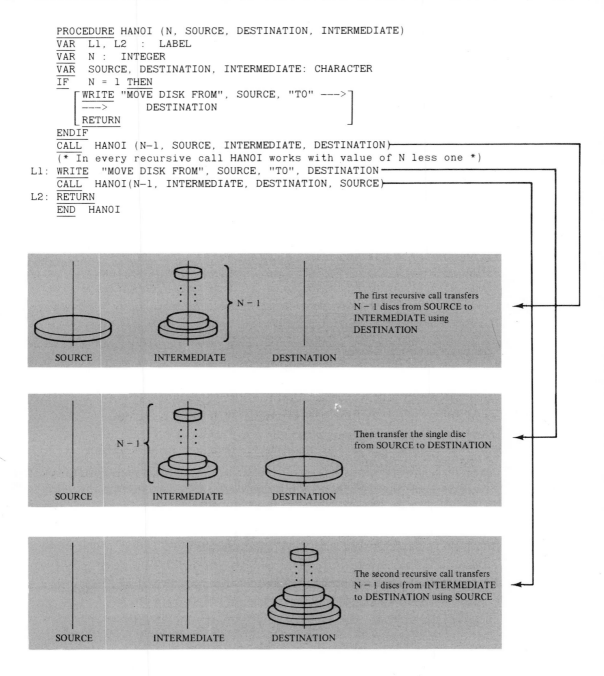

The first recursive call transfers N − 1 discs from SOURCE to INTERMEDIATE using DESTINATION

SOURCE   INTERMEDIATE   DESTINATION

Then transfer the single disc from SOURCE to DESTINATION

SOURCE   INTERMEDIATE   DESTINATION

The second recursive call transfers N − 1 discs from INTERMEDIATE to DESTINATION using SOURCE

SOURCE   INTERMEDIATE   DESTINATION

Because we have a CALL to HANOI within the procedure HANOI, this represents a recursive CALL. Although such a procedure is easy to write in PSEUDO, it is somewhat more difficult to *understand thoroughly!*

The key to understanding the procedure is to be aware of what a compiler must do when the recursive call is made. The difficulty with handling recursion is that, because we call a procedure from within that procedure, eventually a return will be made to that same procedure. However, because the call also involves changing the values of the procedure's parameters, the old values of the parameters will have been destroyed upon return *unless they were preserved before the recursive call*. The best way of preserving them is to stack them with the return address. Thus, a recursive call involves stacking not only a return address but also the values of all parameters essential to the current state of the procedure. In this sense, it is crucial that procedures which are recursively called receive actual working copies of their parameters rather than merely the memory addresses of the calling program's variables. That is, recursively called procedures should receive parameters *by value*, not *by reference*. To illustrate, we will trace through the actions taken when a call of the form

```
CALL HANOI (3, "A", "C", "B")
```

is initiated.

1. N is not 1, so the condition in the IF statement is false.

2. CALL HANOI ($N-1$, SOURCE, INTERMEDIATE, DESTINATION) is encountered with A, B, and C as 1st, 2nd, and 3rd arguments. Because this represents a recursive call, some stacking must be done:

```
                            B (intermediate)
                            C (destination)
                            A (source)
           L1               3 (N)
   _____     _____
   Return address stack     Parameter stack
```

3. Reenter HANOI. Notice that as we enter this time, the procedure's view of the parameters is $N = 2$, SOURCE = A, DESTINATION = B, and INTERMEDIATE = C. Because N is not 1, the condition in the IF statement is false.

4. CALL HANOI ($N - 1$, SOURCE, INTERMEDIATE, DESTINATION) is encountered. Because this is a recursive call, stacking occurs:

```
                            C (intermediate)
                            B (destination)
                            A (source)
                            2 (N)
                            B (intermediate)
                            C (destination)
           L1               A (source)
           L1               3 (N)
   _____     _____
   Return address stack     Parameter stack
```

5. We reenter HANOI with N = 1, SOURCE = A, DESTINATION = C, and INTERMEDIATE = B. Because $N = 1$, the condition in the IF statement is true.

6. Hence:

```
MOVE DISK FROM A TO C
```

is output and a RETURN triggers a popping of a return address (L1) and four parameters ($N = 2$, SOURCE = A, DESTINATION = B, and INTERMEDIATE = C).

```
                            B (intermediate)
                            C (destination)
                            A (source)
            L1              3 (N)
    ----------------------  ------------------
    Return address stack    Parameter stack
```

7. Because the return address popped was L1:

```
MOVE DISK FROM A TO B
```

is output and:

```
CALL HANOI (N-1, INTERMEDIATE, DESTINATION, SOURCE)
```

is encountered with $N = 2$, SOURCE = A, DESTINATION = B and INTERMEDIATE = C.

8. The call pushes a return address and 4 parameters onto the stacks.

```
                            C (intermediate)
                            B (destination)
                            A (source)
                            2 (N)
                            B (intermediate)
                            C (destination)
            L2              A (source)
            L1              3 (N)
    ----------------------  ------------------
    Return address stack    Parameter stack
```

9. We reenter HANOI, this time with $N = 1$, SOURCE = C, DESTINATION = B, INTERMEDIATE = A.

10. Because $N = 1$, the IF statement generates the output:

```
MOVE DISK FROM C TO B
```

and a RETURN.

11. The RETURN pops values from both stacks and we return to L2 with $N = 2$, SOURCE = A, DESTINATION = B, INTERMEDIATE = C.

12. But L2 is a RETURN statement itself, so both stacks are popped again and we return to L1 with $N = 3$, SOURCE = A, DESTINATION = C, INTERMEDIATE = B, and both stacks temporarily empty.

13. Line L1 triggers the output:

```
MOVE DISK FROM A TO C
```

and we are immediately at another call:

```
CALL HANOI (N-1, INTERMEDIATE, DESTINATION, SOURCE)
```

Hence the temporary empty status of the stacks is changed to

```
                              B (intermediate)
                              C (destination)
                              A (source)
            L2                3 (N)
     _____      _____
     Return address stack     Parameter stack
```

14. Reenter HANOI with $N = 2$, SOURCE = B, DESTINATION = C, INTER-MEDIATE = A. Because N is not 1, another CALL:

```
CALL HANOI (N-1, SOURCE, INTERMEDIATE, DESTINATION)
```

is executed and more values are stacked:

```
                              A (intermediate)
                              C (destination)
                              B (source)
                              2 (N)
                              B (intermediate)
                              C (destination)
            L1                A (source)
            L2                3 (N)
     _____      _____
     Return address stack     Parameter stack
```

15. Reenter HANOI with $N = 1$, SOURCE = B, DESTINATION = A, INTER-MEDIATE = C. Because $N = 1$, output:

```
MOVE DISK FROM B TO A
```

and RETURN.

16. The return prompts the popping of both stacks. The return address popped is L1 with parameters $N = 2$, SOURCE = B, DESTINATION = C, INTERMEDIATE = A. Statement L1 causes output:

```
MOVE DISK FROM B TO C
```

with the stacks left at:

```
                              B (intermediate)
                              C (destination)
                              A (source)
            L2                3 (N)
     _____      _____
     Return address stack     Parameter stack
```

17. The output from L1 is followed by:

```
CALL HANOI (N-1, INTERMEDIATE, DESTINATION, SOURCE)
```

so pushed onto the stacks are:

```
                                A (intermediate)
                                C (destination)
                                B (source)
                                2 (N)
                                B (intermediate)
                                C (destination)
              L2                A (source)
              L2                3 (N)
        --------------------    ------------------
        Return address stack     Parameter stack
```

18. Reenter (for the last time) HANOI with $N = 1$, SOURCE = A, DESTINATION = C, INTERMEDIATE = B. Because $N = 1$, output:

MOVE DISK FROM A TO C

and RETURN.

19. But now the RETURN pops RETURN address L2 from the stack, so return to L2 with $N = 2$, SOURCE = B, DESTINATION = C, INTERMEDIATE = A:

```
                                B (intermediate)
                                C (destination)
                                A (source)
              L2                3 (N)
        --------------------    ------------------
        Return address stack     Parameter stack
```

20. L2 is another RETURN, so pop the stacks again. Return address popped is L2, the same RETURN statement. But this time the RETURN will transfer control back to the original calling procedure and

WE ARE DONE!

Long-winded as this narrative is, it is *essential* that you understand it. Recursive procedures are crucial to many of the algorithms used in data structures, and you can acquire the necessary familiarity with recursion only by convincing yourself that it really works. If you have some doubts or are not sure you understand, we recommend you trace through the HANOI procedure with $N = 4$ (be prepared to go through lots of paper!).

The key to writing recursive procedures is *always to leave a way out*. Suppose, for instance, that the IF statement were to be left out of our previous HANOI procedure. This would trigger an endless sequence of CALLs never interrupted by a RETURN. The outcome is predictable—the program soon runs out of stack space. Such erroneous recursive calls are typically met with a "stack overflow" error message in languages that allow recursion.

Recursive Algorithms Implemented Nonrecursively

We are still faced with a dilemma if we have an elegant recursive algorithm but a language that does not support recursion. There is a systematic technique for implementing recursive algorithms in such languages. Essentially, the technique involves:

- Substituting appropriate GOTOs for CALLs and RETURNs

- Using stack(s) to store return addresses and preserve necessary parameters prior to a recursive call

- Using assignment statements to simulate the passage of arguments that a CALL statement would allow

To illustrate the method, we will use a nonrecursive version of the HANOI algorithm in PSEUDO. We will assume the existence of 3 stacks—ISTACK, CSTACK, LSTACK—composed of INTEGER, CHARACTER, and LABEL data, respectively. Each stack is further assumed to have its own top pointer—ITOP, CTOP, and LTOP, respectively.

```
            PROCEDURE  NONRECURSIVE-HANOI (N,SOURCE,DESTINATION,INTERMEDIATE)
            VAR   N,ARRAYSIZE,ISTACK(ARRAYSIZE),ITOP,CTOP,LTOP : INTEGER
            VAR   SOURCE,DESTINATION,INTERMEDIATE,TEMP,CSTACK(ARRAYSIZE) : CHARACTER
            VAR   ENTRY,L1,L2,L,LSTACK(ARRAYSIZE) : LABEL
            VAR   EMPTY,FULL : BOOLEAN
            (* L is a label variable that can take on a fixed label as a value *)
   ENTRY:   IF  N = 1 THEN
                WRITE "MOVE DISC FROM", SOURCE, "TO", DESTINATION

                (*Now simulate RETURN*)

                CALL  POP (N,ISTACK,ARRAYSIZE,ITOP,EMPTY)
                CALL  POP (INTERMEDIATE,CSTACK,ARRAYSIZE,CTOP,EMPTY)
                CALL  POP (DESTINATION,CSTACK,ARRAYSIZE,CTOP,EMPTY)
                CALL  POP (SOURCE,CSTACK,ARRAYSIZE,CTOP,EMPTY)
                CALL  POP (L,LSTACK,ARRAYSIZE,LTOP,EMPTY)
                IF  EMPTY  THEN
                    [RETURN]
                ELSE
                    [GOTO L ]
                ENDIF
            ENDIF
```

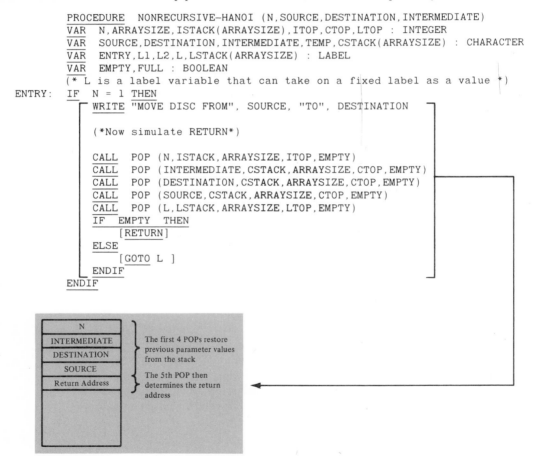

N
INTERMEDIATE
DESTINATION
SOURCE
Return Address

The first 4 POPs restore previous parameter values from the stack

The 5th POP then determines the return address

```
            (* Simulate 1st recursive call from previous version *)
            (* Stack parameters *)

            CALL   PUSH (N,ISTACK,ARRAYSIZE,ITOP,FULL)
            CALL   PUSH (SOURCE,CSTACK,ARRAYSIZE,CTOP,FULL)
            CALL   PUSH (DESTINATION,CSTACK,ARRAYSIZE,CTOP,FULL)
            CALL   PUSH (INTERMEDIATE,CSTACK,ARRAYSIZE,CTOP,FULL)
```

```
         (* Arrange parameter passing *)

         N := N-1
         TEMP := INTERMEDIATE
         INTERMEDIATE  := DESTINATION
         DESTINATION  := TEMP

         (* Stack return address *)

         CALL    PUSH (L1,LSTACK,ARRAYSIZE,LTOP,FULL)

         (* Actual CALL replaced by GOTO *)

         GOTO  ENTRY
L1:      WRITE   "MOVE DISC FROM", SOURCE, "TO", DESTINATION

         (* Next simulate 2nd recursive call in HANOI *)
         (* Stack parameters *)

         CALL   PUSH (N,ISTACK,ARRAYSIZE,ITOP,FULL)
         CALL   PUSH (SOURCE,CSTACK,ARRAYSIZE,CTOP,FULL)
         CALL   PUSH (DESTINATION,CSTACK,ARRAYSIZE,CTOP,FULL)
         CALL   PUSH (INTERMEDIATE,CSTACK,ARRAYSIZE,CTOP,FULL)

         (* Simulate parameter passing for 2nd call *)

         N := N-1
         TEMP := INTERMEDIATE
         INTERMEDIATE := SOURCE
         SOURCE  := TEMP

         (* Stack return address *)

         CALL    PUSH (L2,LSTACK,ARRAYSIZE,LTOP,FULL)

         (* Actual CALL replaced by GOTO *)

         GOTO  ENTRY

         (* The remaining lines simulate the RETURN appearing *)
         (* in line L2 of previous recursive HANOI. *)
         (* First pop parameters from stack *)

L2:      CALL    POP (N,ISTACK,ARRAYSIZE,IPOP,EMPTY)
         CALL    POP (INTERMEDIATE,CSTACK,ARRAYSIZE,CTOP,EMPTY)
         CALL    POP (DESTINATION,CSTACK,ARRAYSIZE,CTOP,EMPTY)
         CALL    POP (SOURCE,CSTACK,ARRAYSIZE,CTOP,EMPTY)
         CALL    POP (L,LSTACK,ARRAYSIZE,LTOP,EMPTY)
         IF    EMPTY THEN
             [RETURN]
         ELSE
             [GOTO L ]
         ENDIF
         END  NONRECURSIVE-HANOI
```

When you compare this to the previous recursive HANOI procedure, you should note that each recursive CALL and RETURN is replaced by a considerable number of statements. CALLS are replaced by a series of push operations, assignment statements, and finally a GOTO. RETURNS are replaced by a reverse series of pop operations and then, conditionally, either a GOTO or a true RETURN to the original calling procedure. This increase in the number of statements should not be interpreted as meaning that the non-recursive version of the program is less efficient; we are merely doing what the system would otherwise do for us. Frequently, judicious choosing of the data items to be stacked can make the nonrecursive version of the algorithm more efficient in both stack space and run time. Hence, there is an argument for removing recursion even in those languages that allow it.

Unfortunately, such nonrecursive versions of recursive algorithms cannot conveniently be coded in a *structured* style. This is because a RETURN following a recursive CALL may lead to any one of several possible locations in the procedure, depending upon the return address popped from the stack. In our nonrecursive PSEUDO procedure, we have used a GOTO statement in which the destination is a LABEL type variable L to implement this type of branching. We have the freedom to do this in a noncompiled language such as PSEUDO. Although languages such as FORTRAN and BASIC do not allow LABEL type variables, the same effect can be achieved using a COMPUTED GOTO (in FORTRAN) and an ON-GOTO (in BASIC).

Recursion, Stacks, and Backtracking

One classic type of problem ideally suited to recursion is that of **backtracking.** At the beginning of this chapter, we gave an illustration of backtracking logic as it is used when you try to find a path out of a maze. You must explore numerous paths before you find the appropriate one. Upon exploring a given path and determining that it can lead only to a dead end, you must retrace the points on the path in reverse order—backtrack—until you reach a point at which you can try an appropriate new path. This concept of trial-and-

In the world of applications . . .

In the *Pascal User Manual and Report,* Niklaus Wirth and Kathleen Jensen made famous a diagrammatic representation of Pascal syntax. A syntax diagram that defines a Pascal *statement* is presented below. One interesting feature of this diagram is that the term *statement* is used 8 times in the definition of *statement*. The diagrams of Wirth and Jensen are recursive in nature, and they point out the fact that the syntax of most computer languages can be recursively defined. This is of tremendous importance in the writing of compilers, many of which rely heavily upon recursion to analyze source programs. In fact, one well-known technique of compiler writing is called *recursive descent* compiling. If you intend to study compilers, you had better understand the intricacies of recursion!

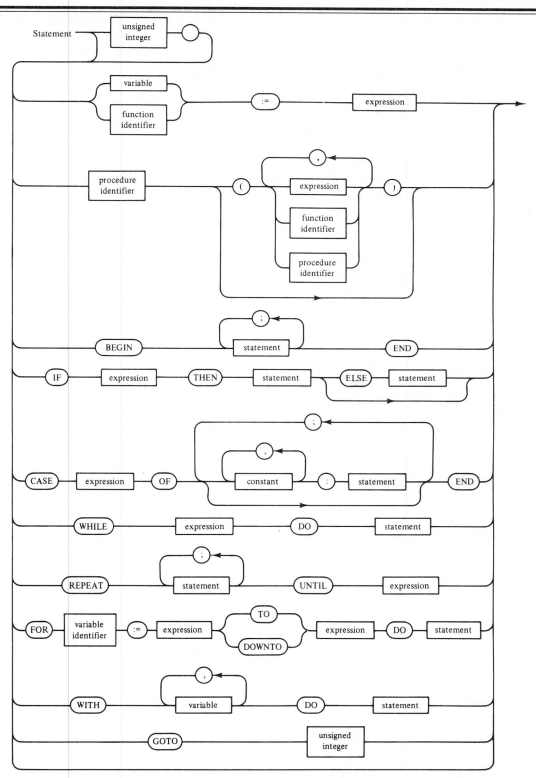

error backtracking is illustrated in Figure 5-4. The retracing in reverse order of points that have been visited previously is where a stack comes into play. The stack can be explicitly maintained by the programmer or implicitly maintained by recursion.

The 8 Queens Problem

A backtracking problem that has long intrigued chess fanatics is the *8 Queens* problem, which requires determining the various ways in which 8 queens could be configured on a chess board so that none of them could access any other queen. (The rules of chess allow a queen to move an arbitrary number of squares in a horizontal, vertical, or diagonal fashion.) Figure 5-5 illustrates one such configuration.

Applying backtracking logic to this problem, we could attempt to find a "path" to a configuration by successively trying to place a queen in each column of a chessboard until we reach a *dead end:* a column in which the placement of queens in prior columns makes it impossible to place the queen being moved. This situation is pictured in Figure 5-6. When we reach this dead end, we must backtrack one column (to column 5 in the case of Figure 5-6) and attempt to find a new placement for the queen in the previous column. If placement in the previous column is impossible, we must backtrack yet another column to attempt the new placement. This backtracking through previous columns continues until we finally are able to reposition a queen. At that point, we can begin a new *path* by again attempting to position queens on a column-by-column basis until another dead end is reached or until a fully successful configuration is developed.

The key to a program that finds all possible 8 queens configurations is a procedure that attempts to place a queen in a given square and, if successful, recursively calls itself to attempt the placement of another queen in the next column. Such a procedure in skeleton form follows:

```
PROCEDURE PLACEQUEEN(I,J)

    (* If possible, place queen in row I and column J of chessboard *)
    (* and then "recurse" to place queen in next column *)

    IF no immediate danger at position I,J THEN
      ┌─IF J = 8 THEN
      │   └─[CALL TALLY-CONFIGURATION]
      │ ELSE
      │     ┌─Mark position I,J as occupied┐
      │     │ FOR K := 1 TO 8
      │     │   └─[CALL PLACEQUEEN(K,J+1)]
      │     │ ENDFOR
      │     └─Remove mark from position I,J┘
      └─ENDIF
        ENDIF
    RETURN
    END PLACEQUEEN
```

Note that this procedure has been intentionally left unfinished. Still to be resolved are such issues as:

- The initial call(s) to PLACEQUEEN.

- How to represent the chessboard.

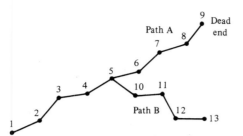

Figure 5-4   The backtracking problem as illustrated by maze solution. Upon reaching a dead end for path A, you must retrace steps 9 → 8 → 7 → 6 → 5 before you can try new path B.

- How to check whether placing a queen at position I,J puts it in immediate danger. That is, how to determine whether there is currently another queen sharing the same row, column, or diagonal.

The resolution of these issues is left for your enjoyment in the Programming Problems at the end of the chapter.

In the next chapter, we will begin a careful study of data structures known as trees. We will see to an even greater degree the power and elegance of recursive algorithms; without recursion, an analysis of trees would be virtually impossible.

SUMMARY

Parsing of expressions, and hence the use of a stack structure, is an essential part of compiler design. When an expression is parsed into a postfix or prefix form, it is rendered into an essentially unique form free of parentheses.

Additionally, as the Tower of Hanoi algorithm shows, recursive procedures use stacks extensively and can be cumbersome to code. Modern programming languages have imple-

							Q
		Q					
Q							
			Q				
					Q		
	Q						
						Q	
				Q			

Figure 5-5   One successful 8 queens configuration; no queen has access to any other.

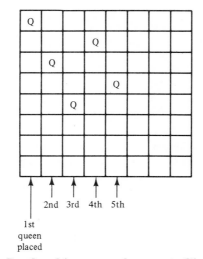

Figure 5-6   Dead end in queen placement. Given previous 5 placements, queen cannot be placed in 6th column. Must backtrack and attempt to reposition in column 5. If that fails, backtrack to column 4, and so on.

mented recursion to save the user the trouble of this stack-oriented coding. Older languages such as BASIC and FORTRAN do not allow recursive subroutine calls. Regardless of whether you work in a language that allows recursion, you should thoroughly understand the details of how a stack is used in recursive calls.

Recursion is a powerful technique and will be used heavily in the coming chapter about tree structures.

KEY TERMS

Backtracking	Prefix	Recursion
Parsing	Infix priority	Stack
Infix	Stack priority	Towers of Hanoi
Postfix		

EXERCISES

1. What is a stack structure?

2. What are the infix, postfix, and prefix forms of the expression:
   A + B *(C − D)/(P − R) ?

3. What are stack priorities of (,), *, /, +, −, and #?

4. What are infix priorities of (,), *, /, +, −, and #?

5. Stand between 2 parallel mirrors and see how recursion works for you.

PROGRAMMING PROBLEMS

1. In the problems for Chapters 2 and 3, you developed a passenger list processing system for the various flights of the Wing and a Prayer Airline Company. Wing and a Prayer management would now like you to extend this system so that it processes logical combinations of flight numbers. For example, the command

       LIST 1 OR 2

   should list all passengers whose name appears on the flight 1 list or the flight 2 list. Your program should also accept the logical operators *and* and *not* and allow parenthesized logical expressions obeying the standard logical hierarchy

   not

   and

   or

2. Implement in a high-level language the algorithm to parse an infix expression into postfix form.

3. Implement in a high-level language the algorithm to evaluate an expression given in postfix form.

4. Using your results from Programming Problems (2) and (3), write a program that will call for input of an infix expression and output the proper evaluation of that expression.

5. Add to your program from Programming Problem (4) the ability to parse expressions that contain the exponentiation operator ^.

6. Write a program that will parse infix expressions into prefix form.

7. Using stacks, write a program that will call for input of an integer N and will output all permutations of N.

8. Write a program to call for input of a decimal number and convert it to its binary equivalent using the method described in the following flowchart:

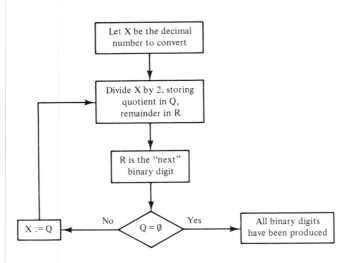

Note that this method produces the binary digits for the given number in reverse order. One strategy for printing out the digits in the correct order would be to store them in an array as they are produced and then print out the array. However, this strategy would have the drawbacks of allocating unnecessary storage for an array and then limiting the size of the binary number to the size of the array. Your program is *not* to employ this strategy. Rather, call for input of the decimal number in your main program and then immediately transfer control to a procedure that in turn is called recursively, stacking the binary digits as they are produced. Once division by 2 yields 0, the succession of "returns" can be used to print out the digits one-by-one as they are popped from this stack.

9. Write a recursive program that will call for input of an integer N and output the value N factorial.

10. The Nth Fibonacci number is defined by

> 1 if N is 1
> 1 if N is 2
> The sum of the previous two Fibonacci numbers otherwise

Write a recursive procedure to compute the Nth Fibonacci number.

11. Euclid devised a clever algorithm for computing the greatest common divisor of two integers. According to Euclid's algorithm:

$$GCD(M,N) = \begin{cases} GCD(N,M) \text{ if } N > M \\ M \text{ if } N = 0 \\ GCD(N, M \text{ MOD } N) \text{ if } N > 0 \end{cases}$$

Write a recursive procedure to compute greatest common divisors via Euclid's method.

12. Write a program that will accept commands of the following form:

1. INPUT♭var, name

2. var. name = Infix expression involving var. names and $+, -, *, /$

3. PRINT♭var. name

4. GO

Essentially these commands are to be stored in an array of strings until the GO command is entered. Once GO is entered, your program should execute the previously stored commands. "Execute" here means:

1. For an INPUT command: Send a question mark to the terminal and allow the user to enter a real number, which is then stored in "var. name."

2. For an assignment statement: Parse the expression into postfix form and then evaluate it, storing the result in the "var. name" on the left of the equality sign.

3. For a PRINT instruction: Write to the terminal the numerical contents of the specified "var. name."

To make things (relatively) easy, you may assume a syntax that:

1. Allows only one "var. name" following INPUT or PRINT

2. Allows one blank space after the keywords INPUT and PRINT and no blank spaces anywhere else

3. Allows "var. names" consisting of one uppercase alphabetical character

For an additional challenge, enable your program to handle successfully the exponentiation operator "^" within assignment statement expressions. The following example should illustrate the need for care in handling this exponentiation operator:

$$3^{2^2} = 3^4, \quad not \quad 9^2$$

13. Write a program to analyze football team scores by computing the point spread for any team A playing any team B. Your program should compute the point spreads for:

- Level I analysis: Team A played team B in past

- Level II analysis: Average point spreads for situations such as:
                    A played C—point spread 3
                    C played B—point spread 7

                                        Total point spread 10

- Level III analysis: Average point spreads for situations such as:
                    A played C—point spread 3
                    C played D—point spread −14 (C lost)
                    D played B—point spread 7

                                        Total point spread −4

- Level IV analysis: Average point spreads for situations such as:
                    A played C—point spread 3
                    C played D—point spread −14 (C lost)
                    D played E—point spread 21
                    E played B—point spread 4

                                        Total point spread 14

All level II point spreads are then averaged for a final level II point spread figure. Point spreads are similarly averaged for levels III and IV. Items that potentially need to be stacked in this program include:

- Accumulated point spread at current position

- Number of scores reflected in the accumulated point spread at current position

- Current position: that is, team A playing team B

- Path to the current position: that is, teams played to get to the current position

14. Write a program to complete the Eight Queens problem.

If you work in Pascal . . .

The program given below represents a recursive Pascal implementation of the Towers of Hanoi problem discussed in this chapter.

Program listing:

```
     program recursivehanoi(input,output);
VAR
  numberdiscs : integer;
  source,intermediate,destination : char;
  PROCEDURE hanoi(numberdiscs:integer;source,intermediate,destination:char);
   BEGIN
     IF numberdiscs = 1
       THEN
       writeln('MOVE DISC FROM ',source,' TO ',destination)
       ELSE
         BEGIN
           hanoi(numberdiscs-1,source,destination,intermediate);
           writeln('MOVE DISC FROM ',source,' TO ',destination);
           hanoi(numberdiscs-1,intermediate,source,destination)
         END
   END;
BEGIN
   write('NUMBER OF DISCS?');readln(numberdiscs);
   write('FROM?');readln(source);
   write('TO?');readln(destination);
   write('USING?');readln(intermediate);
   writeln;
   hanoi(numberdiscs,source,intermediate,destination)
 END.
```

Sample run:

```
NUMBER OF DISCS?4
FROM?A
TO?B
USING?C

MOVE DISC FROM A TO C
MOVE DISC FROM A TO B
MOVE DISC FROM C TO B
MOVE DISC FROM A TO C
MOVE DISC FROM B TO A
MOVE DISC FROM B TO C
MOVE DISC FROM A TO C
MOVE DISC FROM A TO B
MOVE DISC FROM C TO B
MOVE DISC FROM C TO A
MOVE DISC FROM B TO A
MOVE DISC FROM C TO B
MOVE DISC FROM A TO C
MOVE DISC FROM A TO B
MOVE DISC FROM C TO B

Ready
```

Tree Structures

I don't have to look up my family tree because I know
that I'm the sap.

FRED ALLEN (1894–1956)

6-1 Introductory Considerations

Most people are aware of the genealogical trees that allow a family of individuals to trace
their ancestry. In this sense, a genealogical tree is simply a way of expressing a hierarchical
relationship between parents, children, brothers, sisters, cousins, aunts, uncles, and so
on. The crucial relationship in such a genealogical tree is that between parent and child.
Such a parent–child relationship is an excellent example of a **hierarchical** relationship in
which there exists a well-defined order of precedence between the 2 items being related.
In computer science, a **tree** is *a data structure that represents hierarchical relationships
between individual data items*.

To introduce some of the terminology of tree structures, we will consider the record
of a student at a typical university. In addition to the usual statistical background information such as social security number, name, and address, a typical student record might
contain listings for a number of courses, exams and final grades in each course, overall
grade point average, and other data relating to the student's performance at the college.

Figure 6-1 is an example of a tree structure representing such a student record. As
in genealogical trees, at the highest level (0) of a tree is its **root** (also called the **root
node**). Here STUDENT is the root node. The nodes NAME, ADDRESS, SSN, COURSE,
and GPA, which are directly connected to the root node, are the **child nodes** of the **parent
node** STUDENT. The child nodes of a given parent constitute a set of **siblings.** Thus,
NAME, ADDRESS, SSN, COURSE, and GPA are siblings. In the hierarchy represented
by a tree, the child nodes of a parent are one level lower than the parent node. Thus
NAME, ADDRESS, SSN, COURSE, and GPA are at level 1 in Figure 6-1.

107

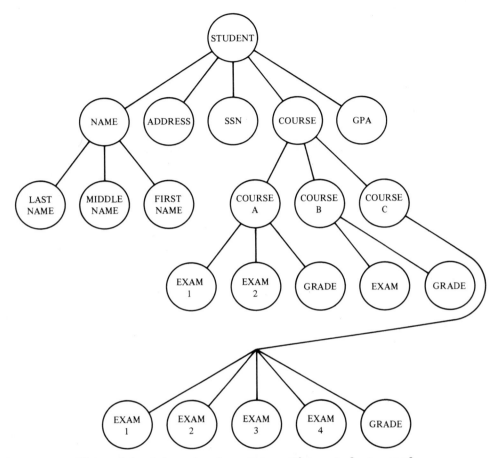

Figure 6-1 A tree structure representing a student record.

A link between a parent and its child is called a **branch** in a tree structure. Each node in a tree except the root must descend from a parent node via a branch. Thus LAST NAME, MIDDLE NAME, and FIRST NAME in Figure 6-1 descend from the parent node NAME. The root of the tree is the **ancestor** of all the nodes in the tree. Each node may be the parent of any number of nodes in the tree. A node with no children is called a **leaf node.** In Figure 6-1, GPA is a leaf node. LAST NAME, MIDDLE NAME, FIRST NAME, EXAM1, and EXAM2 also are leaf nodes.

A **subtree** is a subset of a tree that is itself a tree; the tree in Figure 6-2 is a subtree of the tree in Figure 6-1. This subtree has the root node NAME. Similarly, the tree in Figure 6-3 is another subtree of the tree in Figure 6-1. Notice that the tree in Figure 6-3 is a subtree of both the tree in Figure 6-1 and the tree in Figure 6-4 on page 110.

Given this intuitive background, we can now precisely define a tree in recursive fashion as a set of nodes that:

- Is either empty, or

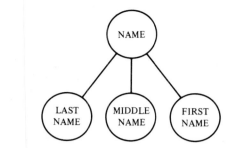

Figure 6-2   A subtree of the tree shown in Figure 6-1.

- Has a designated node called the *root* from which descend zero or more subtrees. Each subtree itself satisfies the definition of a tree.

It is important to emphasize the recursive fashion in which a tree is defined. (It should serve as a strong hint that most tree-processing algorithms also will be recursive.)

6-2   Binary Trees

One of the most important of all tree structures is the **binary tree.** In a binary tree, each node has *no more than two child nodes,* each of which may be a leaf node. In other words, in a binary tree each node has two subtrees (null or non-null) known as the **left subtree** and the **right subtree.** Figure 6-5 is an example of a binary tree. Notice that both children of " − " are leaf nodes, whereas only the left child of "*" is a leaf node. The left subtree of the root " + " appears in Figure 6-6 on page 111. As another example, the right subtree of the right subtree of " + " is given by Figure 6-7.

From this example it should be apparent that if we sever the branch linking a child node to a parent node, the child node becomes the root of a subtree. This is consistent with the recursive definition of a tree given in 6-1. For example, breaking the branch between the child node "*" and the parent node " + " in Figure 6-5 gives us the subtree of Figure 6-8, which is a tree structure whose root is "*." We also emphasize that binary trees are not symmetric structures; interchanging the right and left subtrees in any of the preceding figures yields a new and different tree.

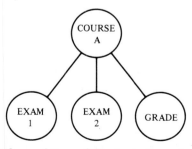

Figure 6-3   Another subtree of the tree shown in Figure 6-1; also a subtree of the tree shown in Figure 6-4.

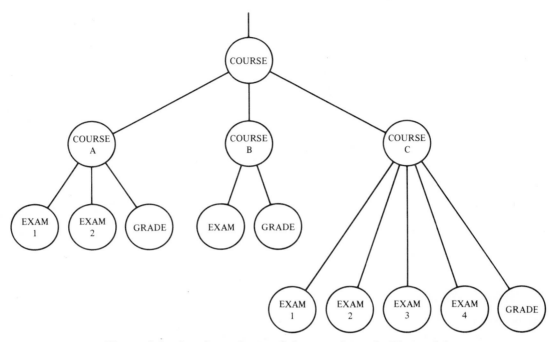

Figure 6-4 Another subtree of the tree shown in Figure 6-1.

Tree structures arise quite naturally in both computer science and data processing applications. In data processing, file index schemes and hierarchical data base management systems, such as the Information Management System (IMS) available from IBM, typically make use of tree structures. We will say more about such file-oriented applications of trees in the final two chapters. Here we will consider the computer science application of using binary trees to represent algebraic expressions. The hierarchy of algebraic operators involved in mathematical expressions can be graphically represented by the hierarchical nature of a tree structure.

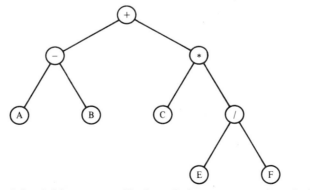

Figure 6-5 A binary tree. Each node has no more than 2 child nodes.

Figure 6-6 Left subtree of the root " + " in Figure 6-5.

The tree in Figure 6-5 is evidence of this because, when viewed in the proper way, it represents the arithmetic expression shown in Figure 6-9. This expression was obtained by traversing the tree in Figure 6-5 in a certain manner.

Contemporary compilers make use of tree structures in obtaining forms of an arithmetic expression for efficient evaluation. As discussed in Chapter 5, there are basically 3 forms of an arithmetic expression—infix, prefix, and postfix. You should recall that the forms of the expression in Figure 6-9 are:

$$(A - B) + C * (E/F) \quad \text{infix}$$

$$+ - AB*C/EF \quad \text{prefix}$$

$$AB - CEF/* + \quad \text{postfix}$$

All three of these forms are immediately available to us if we know exactly how the corresponding tree should be traversed. **Traversing** a tree means processing it such that each node is visited only once. The **inorder traversal** of the binary tree for an arithmetic expression gives us the expression in the *infix* form—the readily recognizable form of Figure 6-9. The **preorder traversal** of the corresponding tree leads us to the *prefix* form of the expression, whereas the **postorder traversal** of the same tree yields the *postfix* form of the expression.

6-3 Implementation of Binary Trees

There are two methods of implementing a binary tree structure. One, which does not require the overhead of maintaining pointers, is called a **linear representation;** the other, known as the **linked representation,** uses pointers.

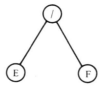

**Figure 6-7 The right subtree of the right subtree of " + " in
Figure 6-5.**

In the world of applications . . .

The front page headline in the January 23, 1984 issue of *Computerworld* proclaimed the UNIX operating system from AT&T Technologies "the operating system of the 80s." The article went on to point out that one of the reasons for the popularity of UNIX was its "hierarchical file system." In effect, the UNIX file directory system can be viewed as a large tree structure similar to that pictured below.

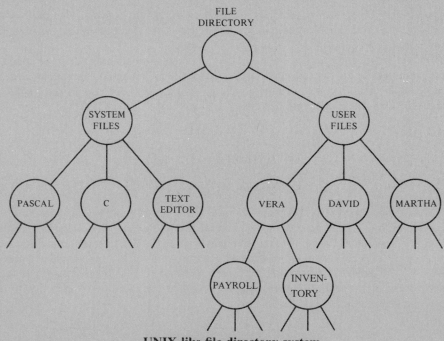

UNIX-like file directory system

Each interior node of the tree can be viewed as a directory containing various system information about those files or subdirectories that are its descendants. Hence, in the diagram, files can be broken down into system files and user files. System files consist of the Pascal library, the C library, and the text-editing system. User directories are called VERA, DAVID, and MARTHA. One of the very convenient features of UNIX is that it allows the user to extend this tree structure as deep as desired. For instance, in the tree directory structure above, we see that user VERA has created subdirectories for files related to PAYROLL and INVENTORY. DAVID and MARTHA have similarly partitioned subdirectories. A UNIX command language then allows users to traverse these various subdirectories in a fashion consistent with file security. The extreme popularity of this tree-structured approach is rapidly making UNIX one of the rare operating systems that is able to migrate from one computer system to another.

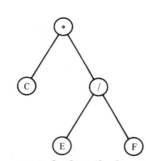

Figure 6-8 **Subtree created when the branch between the child node "*" and the parent node " + " in Figure 6-5 is severed.**

Linear Representation of a Binary Tree

The **linear representation** method of implementing a binary tree uses a one-dimensional array of size $(2^{d+1} - 1)$ where d is the **depth** of the tree—the maximum level of any node in the tree. In the tree of Figure 6-5, the root " + " is at the level 0, the nodes " − " and "*" are at level 1, and so on. The deepest level in this tree is the level of "E" and "F," level 3. Therefore, $d = 3$ and this tree will require an array of size $2^{3+1} - 1 = 15$.

Once the size of the array has been determined, the following method is used to represent the tree:

1. Store the root in the 1st location of the array.

2. If a node is in location n of the array, store its left child at location $2n$, and its right child at location $(2n + 1)$.

With the aid of this scheme, the tree of Figure 6-5 is stored in the array IMPBIN of size 15 shown in Figure 6-10. Locations IMPBIN(8) through IMPBIN(13) are not used.

The main advantages of this method lie in its simplicity and the fact that, given a child node, its parent node can be determined immediately. If a child node is at location N in the array, then its parent node is at location $N/2$ (integer division). Another merit of this method is that it can be implemented easily in older languages such as BASIC and FORTRAN in which only static memory allocation is directly available.

In spite of its simplicity and ease of implementation, the linear representation method has all the trappings that come with physically ordering items. Insertion or deletion of a node causes considerable data movement up and down the array, using an excessive amount of processing time; because insertions and deletions are major data processing activities, algorithms must be developed to maximize their processing efficiency. Also, there usually are wasted memory locations (such as locations 8 through 13 in our example) due to partially filled trees.

Figure 6-9 **Expression represented by the tree in Figure 6-5.**

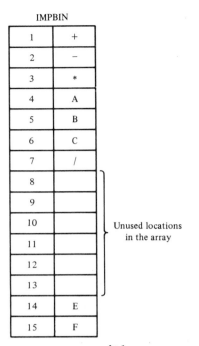

IMPBIN

Figure 6-10 Using the array size $(2^{d+1} - 1)$ and the storage method described in the text, the tree in Figure 6-5 is stored in this linear representation.

Linked Representation of a Binary Tree

Because each node in a binary tree may have 2 child nodes, a node in a linked representation has 2 pointer fields, one for each child, and one or more data fields containing specific information about the node itself. When a node has no children, the corresponding pointer fields are NULL.

Figure 6-11 is a linked representation of the binary tree of Figure 6-5. The LLINK and RLINK fields are pointers to (memory addresses of) the left child and the right child of a node. Notice that *an operand in the tree of an arithmetic expression is always a leaf node*.

Although for most purposes the linked representation of a binary tree is most efficient, it does have certain disadvantages. Namely:

1. Wasted memory space in null pointers. The representation in Figure 6-11 has 10 null pointers.

2. Given a node, it is difficult to determine its parent.

3. Its implementation algorithm is more difficult in languages that do not offer dynamic storage techniques; for example, FORTRAN, BASIC, and COBOL.

The disadvantage (1) can be offset by **threading** the tree, a technique discussed in Chapter 7. Drawback (2) can be overcome by adding a parent pointer field to a node if you can

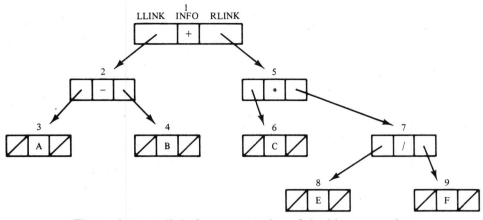

Figure 6-11   A linked representation of the binary tree in Figure 6-5.

afford the luxury of using more memory. Drawback (3) is not serious, because a programmer can develop in *any* language procedures analogous to the PSEUDO GETNODE and RETURNNODE of Chapter 2.

In older languages such as BASIC and FORTRAN, you can implement the linked representation of a binary tree by the use of arrays for both pointers and data fields. For example, by using 3 arrays we can implement the tree of Figure 6-11 as shown in Figure 6-12, using the strategy of building the left subtree for each node before considering the right subtree. The numbers on top of the cells in Figure 6-11 represent the addresses given by the LLINK and RLINK pointer arrays.

In the linked representation, insertions and deletions involve no data movement except the rearrangement of pointers. Suppose we wish to modify the tree in Figure 6-5 to that which appears in Figure 6-13. (This change might be needed due to some recent modification in the expression represented by Figure 6-5.) The insertion of the nodes containing " − " and "P" into the tree structure can be achieved easily by simply adding the nodes " − " and "P" in the next available spaces in the array and correspondingly adjusting the pointers. For the implementation of the tree shown in Figure 6-11, the effect of this insertion is given by Figure 6-14; the adjusted pointers and data fields have been under-

	INFO	LLINK	RLINK
1	+	2	5
2	−	3	4
3	A	NULL	NULL
4	B	NULL	NULL
5	*	6	7
6	C	NULL	NULL
7	/	8	9
8	E	NULL	NULL
9	F	NULL	NULL

Figure 6-12   Implementation of the binary tree in Figure 6-11 using 3 arrays.

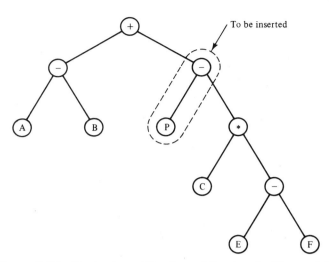

Figure 6-13 Desired modification of the tree in Figure 6-5.

scored. Notice that the change in row 1 of RLINK and the additional rows 10 and 11 are all that is necessary. No data items were moved.

Similarly, if we wish to shorten the tree in Figure 6-5 by deleting the nodes "*" and "C," then all we must do is rearrange the pointers to obtain the altered tree, as shown in Figure 6-15.

The preceding examples indicate that, as far as processing efficiency is concerned, the linked representation seems to be more efficient, particularly where frequent insertions and deletions are required. A more formal statement of the algorithm underlying such insertions and deletions will be given later in this chapter, when list maintenance using a binary tree is discussed.

	INFO	LLINK	RLINK
1	+	2	10
2	–	3	4
3	A	NULL	NULL
4	B	NULL	NULL
5	*	6	7
6	C	NULL	NULL
7	/	8	9
8	E	NULL	NULL
9	F	NULL	NULL
10	–	11	5
11	P	NULL	NULL

Figure 6-14   Modification of Figure 6-11 by insertions of the nodes " – " and "P" into the tree shown in Figure 6-5. (Underscoring indicates new or adjusted fields.)

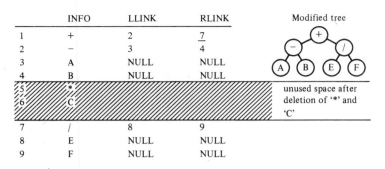

	INFO	LLINK	RLINK
1	+	2	<u>7</u>
2	–	3	4
3	A	NULL	NULL
4	B	NULL	NULL
5	*		
6	C		
7	/	8	9
8	E	NULL	NULL
9	F	NULL	NULL

unused space after deletion of '*' and 'C'

Figure 6-15   Modification of tree by deletion of nodes "*" and "C." (Underscoring indicates a new or adjusted field.)

6-4   Binary Tree Traversals

As noted earlier, traversing a tree means processing the tree such that each node is visited only once.

Preorder Traversal

Preorder traversal (which leads to prefix expressions) of a binary tree entails the following three steps:

1. Process the root node

2. Process the left subtree

3. Process the right subtree

These 3 **ordered steps** are recursive. Once the root of the tree is processed, we go to the root of the left subtree, and then to the root of the left subtree of the left subtree, and so on until we can go no further. Following these 3 steps, the preorder traversal of the tree of Figure 6-5 yields the expression

```
+-AB*C/EF
```

which is the prefix form of the expression in Figure 6-9.

The preorder traversal of an existing linked binary tree with a root node at location ROOT can be accomplished recursively using the following PSEUDO procedure:

```
PROCEDURE    PREORDERTRAV(ROOT)
GLOBAL VAR   N,LLINK(N),RLINK(N) : INTEGER
GLOBAL VAR   INFO(N) : CHARACTER
VAR   ROOT : INTEGER

     (* LLINK and RLINK are pointer arrays to left and right children *)
     (* respectively. INFO is a one-character data field. *)
```

```
IF  ROOT = NULL THEN
              [RETURN]
ENDIF
CALL  PROCESS(INFO(ROOT))
         (* PROCESS represents an *)
         (* arbitrary procedure *)
         (* designed to process *)
         (* a given node. *)
CALL  PREORDERTRAV(LLINK(ROOT))
CALL  PREORDERTRAV(RLINK(ROOT))
RETURN
END  PREORDERTRAV.
```

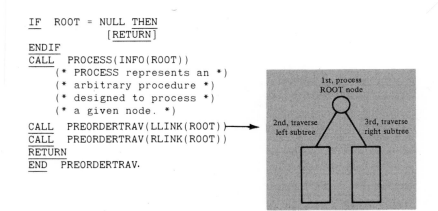

Applying PREORDERTRAV to the tree of Figure 6-5, we obtain the prefix expression:

```
+-AB*C/EF
```

For languages not allowing recursion, a nonrecursive procedure using a stack as described in Chapter 5 can be written to accomplish a preorder traversal. The PSEUDO version of a nonrecursive preorder procedure is given below, with the procedures and parameters PUSH, POP, and STACK as defined in Chapter 4.

```
PROCEDURE   PREORDER-STACK-TRAV (ROOT)
GLOBAL VAR   N,LLINK(N),RLINK(N) : INTEGER
GLOBAL VAR   INFO(N) :CHARACTER
VAR   ROOT,VAL,TOP,M,STACK(M) : INTEGER
VAR   EMPTY,FULL : BOOLEAN

     (* LLINK and RLINK are pointer arrays of arbitrary size. *)
     (* LLINK(VAL) points to the left child of the node pointed to by *)
     (* VAL. RLINK(VAL) points to the right child of the same node. *)

EMPTY := FALSE
VAL := ROOT
CALL INITIALIZE-STACK (TOP, STACK, M)   (* Call to initialize stack *)
IF   VAL = NULL THEN
    [PRINT "NULL TREE"]
    [EMPTY := TRUE    ]
ENDIF
WHILE     NOT EMPTY DO
    IF VAL <> NULL THEN
       [CALL PROCESS (INFO(VAL))
        (* Push pointer to right subtree onto stack. *)
        IF RLINK(VAL) <> NULL THEN
           [CALL PUSH(RLINK(VAL), TOP, STACK, M, FULL)]
        ENDIF
        (* Now process the left subtree. *)
        VAL := LLINK(VAL)
    ELSE
       [(* No more movement to left. Start popping stack. *)
        (* If it is empty, we are done. *)
        CALL POP(VAL, TOP, STACK, M, EMPTY)
    ENDIF
ENDWHILE
RETURN
END   PREORDER-STACK-TRAV
```

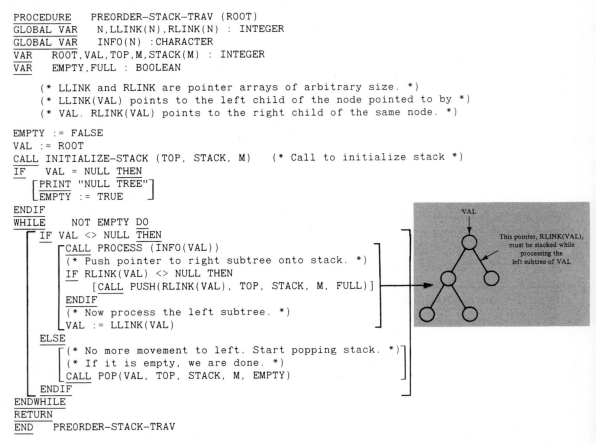

Using the PREORDER-STACK-TRAV procedure, the preorder traversal of the tree in Figure 6-5 (with its corresponding implementation from Figure 6-12) can be traced through as shown in Figure 6-16.

Inorder Traversal

The inorder traversal of a binary tree (which results in an infix expression) proceeds as outlined in the following three ordered steps:

1. Process the left subtree

2. Process the root node

3. Process the right subtree

It should be noted that steps (1) and (3) are recursive. By carefully following these steps for the tree of Figure 6-5, we obtain the readily recognizable infix expression

```
A-B+C*E/F
```

Without parentheses, this infix expression is not algebraically equivalent to the order of operations reflected in the tree of Figure 6-5. The fact that prefix and postfix notations do not require parentheses to avoid such ambiguities makes them distinctly superior to infix notation for evaluation purposes.

A more formal statement of the recursive algorithm for an inorder traversal is given in the following PSEUDO procedure:

```
PROCEDURE   INORDERTRAV(ROOT)
GLOBAL VAR  N,LLINK(N),RLINK(N) : INTEGER
GLOBAL VAR  INFO(N) : CHARACTER
VAR   ROOT : INTEGER
```

ITERATION	STACK (of VAL pointers)	OUTPUT
1	5	+
2	4 / 5	+-
3	4 / 5	+-A
4	5	+-AB
5	7	+-AB*
6	7	+-AB*C
7	9	+-AB*C/
8	9	+-AB*C/E
9		+-AB*C/EF

Figure 6-16   Preorder traversal of the tree in Figure 6-5 as performed by PREORDER-STACK-TRAV.

```
      (* LLINK and RLINK are pointer arrays to left *)
      (* and right children respectively. *)

IF    ROOT = NULL THEN
      [RETURN]
ENDIF
CALL    INORDERTRAV(LLINK(ROOT))
CALL    PROCESS(INFO(ROOT))
CALL    INORDERTRAV(RLINK(ROOT))
RETURN
END    INORDERTRAV
```

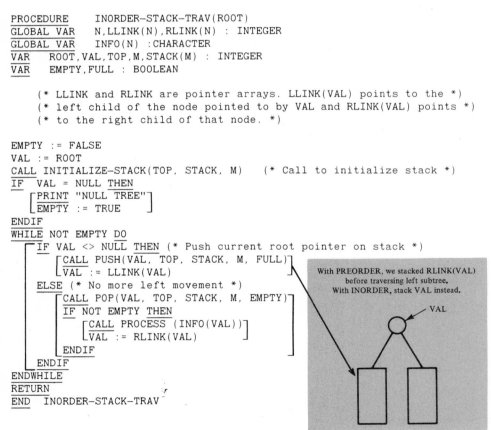

This can be easily implemented in those languages which allow recursive calls. For computer languages without this capability, we suggest the following nonrecursive procedure, which utilizes a stack.

```
PROCEDURE     INORDER-STACK-TRAV(ROOT)
GLOBAL VAR    N,LLINK(N),RLINK(N) : INTEGER
GLOBAL VAR    INFO(N) :CHARACTER
VAR    ROOT,VAL,TOP,M,STACK(M) : INTEGER
VAR    EMPTY,FULL : BOOLEAN

      (* LLINK and RLINK are pointer arrays. LLINK(VAL) points to the *)
      (* left child of the node pointed to by VAL and RLINK(VAL) points *)
      (* to the right child of that node. *)

EMPTY := FALSE
VAL := ROOT
CALL INITIALIZE-STACK(TOP, STACK, M)    (* Call to initialize stack *)
IF  VAL = NULL THEN
    [PRINT "NULL TREE"
     EMPTY := TRUE    ]
ENDIF
WHILE NOT EMPTY DO
      IF VAL <> NULL THEN (* Push current root pointer on stack *)
         [CALL PUSH(VAL, TOP, STACK, M, FULL)
          VAL := LLINK(VAL)                    ]
      ELSE (* No more left movement *)
         [CALL POP(VAL, TOP, STACK, M, EMPTY)
          IF NOT EMPTY THEN
             [CALL PROCESS (INFO(VAL))
              VAL := RLINK(VAL)        ]
          ENDIF                              ]
      ENDIF
ENDWHILE
RETURN
END  INORDER-STACK-TRAV
```

Applying this procedure to the tree of Figure 6-5, implemented with the linked representation given in Figure 6-12, results in the successive iterations shown in Figure 6-17.

ITERATION	STACK (of VAL pointers)	OUTPUT
1	1	
2	2, 1	
3	3, 2, 1	
4	2, 1	A
5	1	A−
6	4, 1	A−
7	1	A−B
8	5	A−B+
9	6, 5	A−B+
10	5	A−B+C
11	7	A−B+C*
12	8, 7	A−B+C*
13	7	A−B+C*E
14	9	A−B+C*E/
15		A−B*C*E/F

Figure 6-17   Inorder traversal of the tree in Figure 6-5 as performed by INORDERTRAV.

Postorder Traversal of a Binary Tree

Postorder traversal of a binary tree (which results in a postfix expression) entails these three ordered steps:

1. Process the left subtree

2. Process the right subtree

3. Process the root node

The postorder traversal can be implemented recursively in PSEUDO by the procedure POSTORDERTRAV:

```
PROCEDURE    POSTORDERTRAV(ROOT)
GLOBAL VAR   N,LLINK(N),RLINK(N) : INTEGER
GLOBAL VAR   INFO(N) : CHARACTER
VAR   ROOT : INTEGER

     (* LLINK and RLINK are pointer arrays to left *)
     (* and right children respectively. *)

IF   ROOT = NULL THEN
        [RETURN]
ENDIF
CALL    POSTORDERTRAV(LLINK(ROOT))
CALL    POSTORDERTRAV(RLINK(ROOT))
CALL    PROCESS(INFO(ROOT))
RETURN
END    POSTORDERTRAV
```

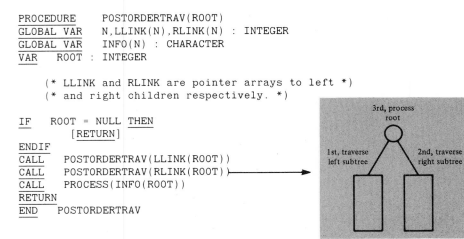

Applying this procedure to the tree of Figure 6-5, we obtain the postfix expression

```
AB-CEF/*+
```

You can replace the POSTORDERTRAV procedure with a nonrecursive algorithm using a stack in a fashion similar to what we have already done for preorder and inorder traversals; this has been left as an exercise at the end of the chapter.

6-5   An Application of Binary Trees in Maintaining Ordered Lists

Besides being used to represent arithmetic expressions in such areas as compiler design, trees arise naturally wherever a hierarchical relationship between data items exists. In particular, consider the following example of such a relationship existing between data items in a tree:

> For any given data item X in the tree, every node in the left subtree of X contains only items that are less than or equal to X with respect to a particular type of ordering. Every node in the right subtree of X contains only items that are greater than or equal to X with respect to the same ordering.

We will hereafter frequently refer to this property as the **ordering property for binary trees**. For instance, the tree in Figure 6-18 illustrates this property with respect to alphabetical ordering. You can quickly verify that an inorder traversal of this tree (in which the processing of each node consists merely of printing its contents) leads to the alphabetized list:

```
     ALLEN
     DAVIS
    EVENSON
  FAIRCHILD
   GARLOCK
    GREEN
    KELLER
    MILLER
    NATHAN
   PERKINS
    SMITH
    TALBOT
  UNDERWOOD
   VERKINS
    ZELLER
```

Moreover, insertion of a new string into such an ordered tree is a fairly easy process that may well require significantly fewer comparisons than insertion into a linked list. Consider, for example, the steps necessary to insert the string SALINAS into the tree in such a fashion as to maintain the ordering property. We must:

1. Compare SALINAS to MILLER. Because SALINAS is greater than MILLER, follow the right child pointer to TALBOT.

2. Compare SALINAS to TALBOT. Because SALINAS is less than TALBOT, follow the left child pointer to PERKINS.

3. SALINAS is greater than PERKINS. Hence follow the right child pointer to SMITH.

4. SMITH is a leaf node, so SALINAS may be added as one of its children. The left child is chosen because SALINAS is less than SMITH.

The resulting tree for this sample insertion is given in Figure 6-19.

The preceding algorithm implies that insertion of new nodes will always occur at the leaf nodes of a tree. As with insertion into a linked list, no data are moved; only pointers are manipulated. However, unlike the steps required by a linked list representation, we do not have to traverse the list *sequentially* to determine where the new node belongs. Instead, using the **insertion rule:**

- If less than, go left

- Otherwise, go right

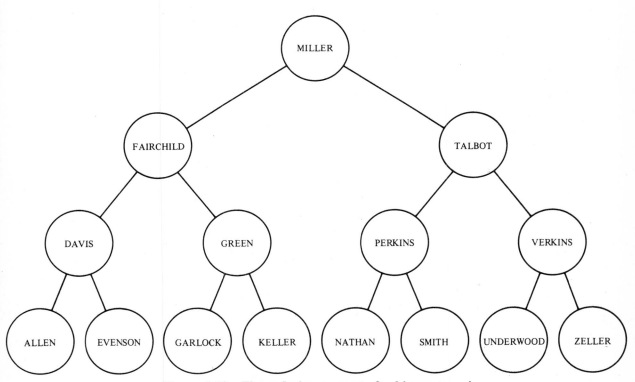

Figure 6-18   The ordering property for binary trees is represented with respect to alphabetical ordering.

we need merely traverse one branch of the tree to determine the position for a new node. Provided that the tree maintains a full shape, the number of nodes on a given branch will be at most

$$\log_2 N + 1$$

where N is the total number of nodes in the tree. By **full,** we mean that all nodes with only one child must have a leaf node as that only child. Hence, adding ROBERTS to the tree of Figure 6-19 by the insertion rule would destroy the fullness of the tree: the only child of SMITH no longer would be a leaf node.

Given this definition of full, the $\log_2 N + 1$ figure for the maximum number of nodes on a branch emerges immediately upon inspection or, more formally, using a proof by mathematical induction. Our purpose here, however, is not to detail such a proof but rather to emphasize that a binary tree presents an alternative to a linked list structure for the type of processing involved in maintaining ordered lists. Moreover, it is a particularly attractive

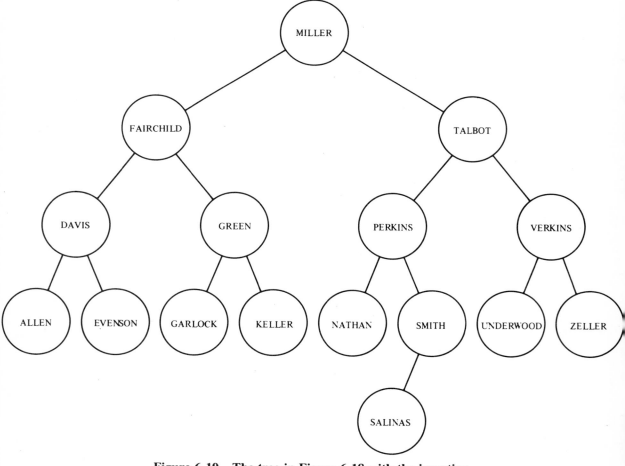

**Figure 6-19   The tree in Figure 6-18 with the insertion
SALINAS.**

alternative when the tree is full, because substantially fewer comparisons are needed to locate where in the structure an insertion is to be made. For instance, if N is 1024, the linked list may require as many as 1024 comparisons to make an insertion. Because $\log_2 1024$ is 10, the full binary tree method will require at most 11. This difference becomes even more dramatic as N gets larger. For an ordered list with 1,000,000 entries, a linked list may require that many comparisons; the full binary tree requires a mere 21 comparisons.

Such attractiveness rarely comes without corresponding disadvantages, and this case is no exception. For instance, deleting from an ordered list maintained with a binary tree is more complex than deleting from one maintained with a linked list. Suppose we wish to remove TALBOT from the list represented by the tree in Figure 6-18. Two questions arise:

1. Can such a deletion be achieved merely by manipulating pointers?

2. If so, what does the resulting tree look like?

The answers to both of these questions are given in the algorithm in the next section.

Deletion Algorithm for Lists Maintained with Binary Trees

All that is necessary to represent an ordered list with a binary tree is that, for each node in the tree:

1. The left subtree contain only items less than or equal to it

2. The right subtree contain only items greater than or equal to it

With the preservation of this ordering property as the primary goal in processing a deletion, one acceptable way of restructuring the tree of Figure 6-18 after deleting TALBOT appears in Figure 6-20; essentially, SMITH moves up to replace TALBOT in the tree. The choice of SMITH to replace TALBOT is made because SMITH represents the greatest data item in the left subtree of the node containing TALBOT. As long as we choose this greatest item in the left subtree to replace the item being deleted, we guarantee preservation of the crucial ordering property that enables the tree to represent the list accurately.

Given this general motivation for choosing a node to replace the one being deleted, let us now outline a case-by-case analysis of the deletion algorithm. Throughout this analysis, we assume that we have a pointer P to the item that we wish to delete. The pointer P may be:

1. The root pointer for the entire tree, or

2. The left child pointer of the parent of the node to be deleted, or

3. The right child pointer of the parent of the node to be deleted.

Figure 6-21 highlights these 3 possibilities; the algorithm applies whether (1), (2), or (3) holds.

We will examine 3 cases of node deletion on a binary tree:

1. The node to be deleted has a left child

2. The node to be deleted has a right child but no left child

3. The node to be deleted has no children

Case 1. The node pointed to by P—that is, the node to be deleted—has a left child. In this case, because we have a non-null left subtree of the node to be deleted, our previous discussion indicates that we must find the greatest node in that left subtree. If the node pointed to by LLINK(P) has no right child, then the greatest node in the left subtree of P is LLINK(P) itself. Figure 6-22 pictorially describes this situation; the dotted lines indicate new pointer values.

The PSEUDO coding to achieve this pointer manipulation is given by:

```
X := P
P := LLINK(X)
RLINK(P) := RLINK(X)
CALL RETURNNODE(X)
```

where LLINK and RLINK refer to the left and right child pointer arrays described earlier in this chapter.

If the node pointed to by LLINK(P) does have a right child, then to find the greatest node in the left subtree of P we must follow the right branch leading from LLINK(P) as

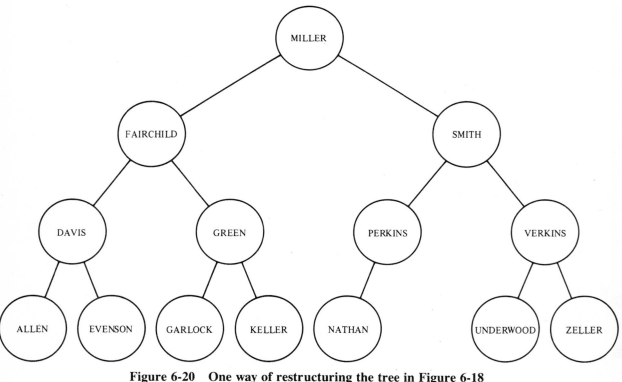

Figure 6-20   One way of restructuring the tree in Figure 6-18 after deleting TALBOT.

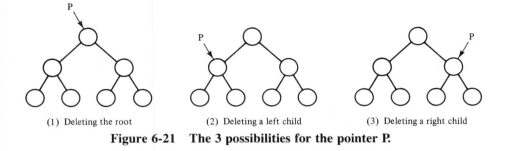

(1) Deleting the root   (2) Deleting a left child   (3) Deleting a right child

Figure 6-21   The 3 possibilities for the pointer P.

deeply as possible into the tree. Figure 6-23 gives the schematic representation, with the pointer changes necessary to complete the deletion. The coding necessary for this slightly more complicated version of Case 1 is:

```
X := P
Q := RLINK (LLINK(X))
QPARENT := LLINK(X)

(* Q will eventually point to node to replace P. *)
(* QPARENT will point to Q's parent. *)
(* The following loop forces Q as deep as possible *)
(* along the right branch leaving LLINK(P). *)

WHILE RLINK(Q) <> NULL DO
    ┌Q := RLINK(Q)          ┐
    └QPARENT := RLINK(QPARENT)┘
ENDWHILE

(* Having found node Q to replace P, adjust pointers *)
(* to appropriately link it into the tree. *)

RLINK(Q) := RLINK(X)
P := Q
RLINK(QPARENT) := LLINK(Q)
LLINK(Q) := LLINK(X)
CALL RETURNNODE(X)
```

Figure 6-22   Case 1 with LLINK(P) having no right children.

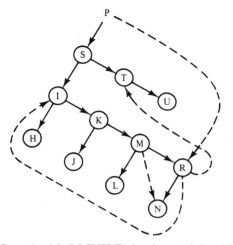

Figure 6-23 Case 1 with LLINK(P) having a right child. Node containing R is the one chosen to replace the deleted node.

Case 2. The node pointed to by P—that is, the node to be deleted—has a right child but no left child. This case is substantially easier than Case 1, and is described in Figure 6-24. The necessary PSEUDO coding is:

```
X := P
P := RLINK(X)
CALL RETURNNODE(X)
```

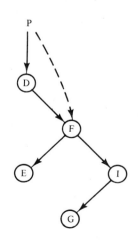

Figure 6-24 Case 2: The node pointed to by P has a right but no left child.

Case 3. The node pointed to by P—that is, the node to be deleted—has no children. As indicated in Figure 6-25, this is the easiest of all the cases. It can be compactly handled by the same PSEUDO coding used for Case 2 or, more directly, by:

```
X := P
P := NULL
CALL RETURNNODE(X)
```

It is important to note that, in all 3 cases, the deletion of a node from the tree involved only pointer manipulation and no actual data movement. Hence, in a list maintained with a binary tree, we are able to process both insertions and deletions by the same pure pointer manipulation that makes linked lists so desirable. Moreover, the binary tree approach apparently allows us to locate insertion or deletion points much faster than a linked list representation would. However, there are aspects of the binary tree method that tarnish its performance in comparison to a linked list. In particular:

1. The binary tree method requires more memory in two respects. First, each node has two pointers instead of the one required in a singly linked list. This proliferation of pointers is particularly wasteful because many of the pointers may be null. Second, we presently can traverse the tree in order only by using recursive techniques. Even in a language that allows recursion, a substantial amount of overhead is needed to maintain the stack used by recursive calls.

2. The ($\log_2 N + 1$) efficiency of the binary tree method is only an optimal, not a guaranteed, efficiency. It is contingent upon the tree's remaining full. In the worst possible case, data entering the tree structure in the wrong order can cause the tree to degenerate into a glorified linked list. (Try to identify what this worst case is.)

Hence, a theme that has already emerged in previous chapters must be reiterated. There are no absolute answers to data structure questions; rather, the best you can hope for is to know the relative advantages of various structures and to apply this knowledge to particular situations. In the next chapter, we will introduce variations on tree structures that allow you to *partially* overcome the two problems cited above.

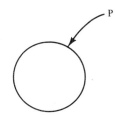

Figure 6-25   Case 3: The node pointed to by P has no children. P must be set to null and the node returned.

SUMMARY

Tree structures are heavily used in representing hierarchical data relationships. A binary tree has only a left subtree and a right subtree. Postorder, inorder, and preorder traversals of a binary tree can be used in parsing expressions, statistical analyses, or sort and search routines.

There are always advantages and disadvantages for any given data structure, and a tree is by no means an exception. Despite the storage occupied by the pointers necessary to maintain a tree, search and sort algorithms using a binary tree are highly efficient in processing time. We will examine more diverse uses of trees in later chapters.

KEY TERMS

Tree	Left subtree	Preorder traversal
Root	Right subtree	Postorder traversal
Node	Left child	Depth of a tree
Child	Right child	
Binary tree	Inorder traversal	

EXERCISES

1. Draw a binary tree for the expression:

```
A * B - (C + D) * (P/Q)
```

2. Using a preorder traversal of the tree from Exercise (1), obtain the prefix form of the expression.

3. If you are familiar with COBOL or Pascal, represent the following record as a binary tree:

COBOL Version:

```
01 STUDENT-REC.
    02 NAME.
        03 FIRST-NAME   PIC X(10).
        03 LAST-NAME    PIC X(10).
    02 YEAR-OF-STUDY.
        03 FIRST-SEM    PIC XX.
        03 SECOND-SEM   PIC XX.
```

Pascal Version:

```
NAME = RECORD
        FIRSTNAME : ARRAY [1..10] OF CHAR;
        LASTNAME : ARRAY [1..10] OF CHAR
        END;

YEAR = RECORD
        FIRSTSEM : ARRAY [1..2] OF CHAR;
        SECONDSEM : ARRAY [1..2] OF CHAR
        END;

STUDENTREC = RECORD
        STUDENTNAME : NAME;
        YEAROFSTUDY : YEAR
        END;
```

4. Discuss the relative merits of maintaining an ordered list by a binary tree, a singly linked list, and a doubly linked list.

5. Discuss how the order in which data are entered into a binary tree representation of a list affects the *fullness* of the tree. Identify the best and worst possible cases.

6. Develop a complete PSEUDO procedure to process the insertion of a node into the binary tree representation of an ordered list.

7. Develop a complete PSEUDO procedure to process the deletion of a node from a binary tree representation of an ordered list. This will essentially require that you combine into one module the 3 cases discussed in the chapter.

PROGRAMMING PROBLEMS

1. Modify the airline reservation system you developed for the Wing and a Prayer Airline Company in Programming Problem (1) of Chapter 3 so that the alphabetized lists are maintained with binary trees instead of linked lists.

2. Write a program that reads an expression in its prefix form and builds the binary tree corresponding to that expression. Then write procedures to print the infix and postfix forms of the expression using inorder and postorder traversals of this tree. Then see if you can write a program to evaluate the expression represented by the tree. If you are working in Pascal, the supplement at the end of this chapter may help get you started.

3. Write a program in a suitable high-level language to implement a recursive postorder traversal for a binary tree.

4. In a suitable high-level language, write a program that uses a stack to achieve a nonrecursive postorder traversal of a binary tree.

5. Using a linear representation of a binary tree, write a program to achieve inorder, preorder, and postorder traversals of the tree.

6. Re-do Programming Problem (1) or (2) from Chapter 2, maintaining the lists involved by using binary trees instead of linked lists.

7. Here is a problem encountered in the writing of statistical analysis software. Given an arbitrarily long list of unordered numbers with an arbitrary number of values appearing in it, determine and print out the marginal distribution for this list of numbers. That is, count how many times each different value appears in the list and then print out each value along with its count. This final output should be arranged from smallest to largest value. This problem can be solved in elegant fashion using trees. An example of such output as produced by the COSAP (Conversationally Oriented Statistical Analysis Package) of Lawrence University appears below.

```
Command? MARGINALS JUDGE
Do you want the statistics (Yes or No) *? No
```

```
              Outagamie County Criminal Cases, 1973-74

                   M A R G I N A L F R E Q U E N C I E S

   Variable  JUDGE     JUDGE BEFORE WHOM CASE BROUGHT (2)
   Value label      Value       Absolute          Relative
                                Frequency          Frequency


      SHAFER         1           677              80.8%
      CANE           2            88              10.5%
      VANSUS         3            26               3.1%
      MYSE           5            47               5.6%



   838  Valid      0  Missing       838  Total Observations.
```

8. Here is a problem from the area of text analysis but with logic similar to that of Programming Problem (7). Given a file containing some arbitrary text, determine how many times each word appears in the file. Your program should output in alphabetical order the words that appear in the file, with their frequency counts. For an added challenge, do not assume any maximum word length; this will enable you to combine trees with the string-handling methods you learned in Chapter 3.

9. Many compilers offer the services of a cross-referencing program to aid in debugging. Such cross-referencers will list in alphabetical order all the identifiers that appear in a program and the various lines of the program that reference them. A sample of what a cross-referencer for a BASIC program might produce as output follows. (*'s in this output indicate references where the identifier may potentially be changed.) Write such a cross-referencer for your favorite language.

```
OLD SORTCL

Ready

LIST
SORTCL  11:13 AM         04-Jul-83
10 DIM A$(150)
15 INPUT 'CLASS NAME';C$
17 OPEN C$+'.LST' FOR OUTPUT AS FILE #1%
20 INPUT 'HOW MANY';N
30 FOR I=1 TO N
40 INPUT 'STUDENT NAME';A$(I)
50 NEXT I
60 FOR I=1 TO N-1
70 FOR J=1 TO N-1
80 X$=A$(J)
90 Y$=A$(J+1)
100 IF X$<=Y$ THEN 130
110 A$(J)=Y$
120 A$(J+1)=X$
130 NEXT J
140 NEXT I
150 PRINT\PRINT\PRINT\PRINT\PRINT
160 FOR I=1 TO N
170 PRINT #1,A$(I);TAB(20);'__/__/__/__/__/__/__/
```

```
180 NEXT I
190 END

Ready

RUN %CREF

Lawrence CREF V1.2
Input? SORTCL
Output <KB:>?
Options?


        Cross Reference Listing of SORTCL.BAS on 04-Jul-83 at 11:14 AM



    Variables


    A$( )       10      *40      80      90     *110     *120      170

    C$         *15      17

    I          *30      40      50     *60      70      140     *160
               170     180

    J          *70      80      90      110     120     130

    N          *20      30      60      70      160

    X$         *80      100     120

    Y$         *90      100     110



    Line Numbers



    #   130     100



    KB:SORTCL.CRF created, run time was 1.9 seconds.
    There were 8 identifiers and line numbers,
    and 36 references to them.
```

10. A relatively easy game to implement with a binary tree is to have the computer try to guess an animal about which the user is thinking by asking the user a series of YES/NO questions. A node in the binary tree to play this game could be viewed as

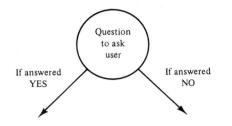

YES/NO pointers can lead to:

1. Another question

2. The name of the animal

3. NULL

If NULL, have your program ask the user for a new question that uniquely defines the animal being thought of, and then add this new question to the growing binary tree database.

If you work in Pascal . . .

The following Pascal program will allow input of a prefix expression, such as $-+AB+CD\$$ (with '$\$$' as delimiting character), and then build the binary tree corresponding to that expression. However, the program is incomplete in that calls are made to nonexistent procedures to achieve preorder, inorder, and postorder traversals of the tree. You should have written these procedures as Programming Problem (2).

```
    program traversal(input,output);
CONST
    delim = '$';
TYPE
    ptr = ^treenode;
    treenode = RECORD
                    lchild:ptr;
                    data:char;
                    rchild:ptr
                END;
    charset = SET OF char;
VAR
    root : ptr;
    token : char;
    operators : charset;

    PROCEDURE bildtree(root : ptr);
    BEGIN
        read(token);
        IF token IN operators
            THEN
            BEGIN
            root^.data:=token;
            new(root^.lchild);
            bildtree(root^.lchild);
            new(root^.rchild);
            bildtree(root^.rchild)
            END
            ELSE IF token <> delim THEN
            BEGIN
            root^.data:=token;
            root^.lchild:=NIL;
            root^.rchild:=NIL
            END
    END;

    (* The procedure BILDTREE will correctly build a binary tree *)
    (* corresponding to any prefix expression that is entered. The *)
    (* three traversals called in the main program are left as *)
    (* exercises for the student. *)
```

```
BEGIN

   operators:=['+','-','/','*'];

   (* Initialize tree *)

   new(root);
   root^.lchild:=NIL;
   root^.rchild:=NIL;

   (* Allow entry of prefix expression and build corresponding tree *)

   bildtree(root);

   (* Now call on the three traversals *)

   writeln;
   preorder(root);
   writeln;
   inorder(root);
   writeln;
   postorder(root);
END.
```

Variations on
Tree Structures

As the twig is bent, the tree inclines.

VIRGIL (70–19 B.C.)

7-1   Introductory Considerations

In Chapter 6, we discussed using a binary tree as an efficient alternative to a linked list. *Efficiency* in this context referred to speed of processing the list as opposed to storage utilization. In sections 7-2 and 7-3 we will discuss two techniques, **threading** and **height-balancing,** used to improve significantly the processing speed of a list implemented with a binary tree. Be forewarned that both of these techniques require additional data storage for each tree node; the conflict of speed versus storage again emerges. This tradeoff, along with the complexities involved in implementation, means that you should carefully weigh a decision to use either technique in a given application.

The primary motivation for threading a tree is *to eliminate the need for recursion* (or simulating recursion) *in traversing a tree*. The elegance of recursion in expressing an algorithm can sometimes hide the fact that it may be a very costly technique. Preserving all necessary local parameters before a recursive call requires both time and stack space. Hence, it may well be better to use an algorithm that is free from the overhead associated with recursion even if it is not as compactly stated. In threading a tree, we will use the numerous pointer locations that are normally null in a linked representation of a binary tree to store information that will lead us through a specified tree traversal in a completely nonrecursive fashion.

Whereas threading is used to enhance efficiency in traversing a tree, height-balancing is aimed at maximizing the speed with which insertions and searches in a tree are handled.

In particular, if we restrict our attention to a tree satisfying the

- Left subtree less than

- Right subtree greater than

property described in the last chapter, it is clear that nodes distributed in a tree with many short branches represent a far more efficient structure than the same collection of nodes distributed in a tree with relatively few long branches. For example, although trees A and B in Figure 7-1 contain the same data nodes, tree B requires significantly fewer comparisons for insertions and searches than tree A. This is because tree B is *full* in the sense defined in Chapter 6. However, we have no guarantee that a full tree will develop if we merely insert nodes in any arbitrary order. Indeed, many orders of insertion result in trees that are decidedly not full. To maintain a perfectly full tree requires considerable data shifting each time a node is inserted. Height-balancing, on the other hand, allows the tree to be maintained in a form that is relatively full and yet requires only a few pointer manipulations each time a node is inserted.

7-2   Threaded Binary Trees

Consider the linked representation of a binary tree in figure 6-11 on page 108. There are 10 wasted fields taken up by null pointers. These could be effectively used to point to significant nodes chosen according to a traversal scheme to be used for the tree. For the inorder traversal of the binary tree in Figure 6-11, note that the node "A" comes before "−" and that "B" is preceded by "−" but followed by the root node "+." With an inorder traversal, we could therefore adjust the null RLINK of the node containing "B" to point to the node containing "+" and the LLINK of the node containing "B" to point to its predecessor node "−." The inorder traversal of this tree yields the expression:

A−B+C*E/F

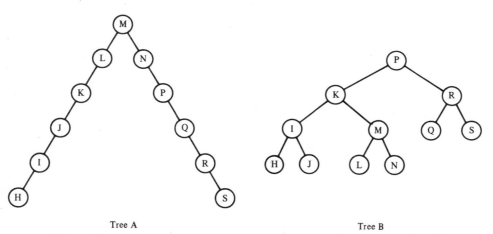

Tree A   Tree B

Figure 7-1   Both trees contain the same data nodes, but the many short branches of tree B require fewer comparisons for insertions and searches.

Notice that "B" comes after " − " but before " + ." Similarly, because "E" is preceded by "*" but followed by "/," the left null link of the node containing "E" should, in our scheme, point to "*"; the right null link of "E" should point to "/."

Because we are arranging pointers to the **inorder predecessor** and **successor** of a leaf node, we will call these pointers **inorder threads.** Following a thread pointer allows us to ascend strategically one or more appropriate levels in the tree without relying on recursion. Figure 7-2 is the transformed version of Figure 6-11, with threads indicated by dotted lines. Threads that take the place of a left child pointer indicate the inorder predecessor, whereas those taking the place of a right child pointer lead to the inorder successor.

The 2 threads on the left and right of Figure 7-2 are the only loose threads at this stage. To correct this, we shall assume that *a threaded binary tree is the left subtree of a root node whose right child pointer points to itself.* According to this convention, an empty threaded binary tree will appear as shown in Figure 7-3. This choice of a **dummy root node** for a threaded binary tree is similar to the convention of using a dummy header for a linked list that we adopted in Chapter 2. By initially setting the pointers as indicated in Figure 7-3, we avoid having to treat the empty tree as a special case in our algorithms that process threaded trees.

In order to keep track of which pointers are threads, we shall include 2 additional Boolean fields in each node. One of these fields, TLPOINT, will be used to indicate whether the left link of the node is a normal pointer or a thread. TRPOINT will be used analogously for the right link. Let N be a pointer to a node. We will follow the convention that

```
TLPOINT(N) = FALSE
```

means that LLINK(N) is a normal pointer. Similarly

```
TLPOINT(N) = TRUE
```

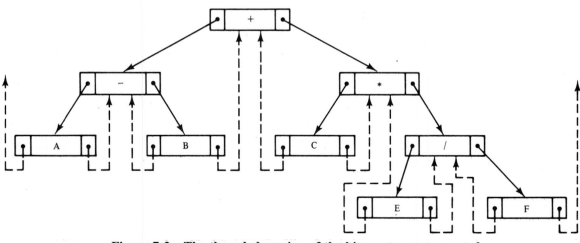

Figure 7-2   The threaded version of the binary tree represented in Figure 6-11.

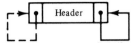

Figure 7-3   An empty threaded binary tree containing only the dummy root node.

means that the left link of N is a thread pointer. Similar interpretations hold for TRPOINT(N) = TRUE and TRPOINT(N) = FALSE. This Boolean information identifying various pointers only helps to facilitate PSEUDO algorithms for different *modes of traversing the tree*. When we incorporate the header and Boolean information into the tree of Figure 7-2, it takes the form of Figure 7-4.

To achieve an inorder traversal of the tree in Figure 7-4, we must proceed from each given node to its inorder successor. This inorder successor is determined by one of 2 methods depending upon whether the right child pointer to the node in question is a thread or a normal pointer. If it is a thread, then it leads us directly to the inorder successor. If it is not a thread, then we must follow the right child pointer to the node it references and, from there, follow left child pointers until we encounter a left thread. To convince yourself of this, consider the threaded tree that is given in Figure 7-5 on page 142. In this tree, to get the inorder successor of the node containing "M," we must first follow the right child

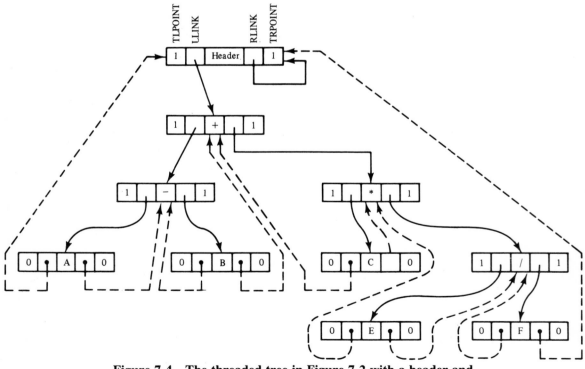

Figure 7-4   The threaded tree in Figure 7-2 with a header and Boolean information added.

pointer from "M" to "V" and then go left as deep as possible in the tree, finally arriving at the node containing "Q." Note also that this general strategy of *proceeding one to the right, then left as deep as possible* in combination with the *initial setting of the right child pointer to the header node* ensures that the inorder traversal begins with the proper node.

The following PSEUDO procedure more formally expresses the algorithm for the threaded inorder traversal discussed. Note that it is achieved without any need for recursion or the use of a stack to simulate recursion.

```
PROCEDURE  THREADED-INORDER(ROOT)

(* Performs a threaded inorder traversal of the tree with *)
(* dummy root node pointed to by ROOT *)

(* Global variables are used to maintain the links, threads, *)
(* and data portions of the tree structure *)

GLOBAL VAR   N,LLINK(N),RLINK(N) : INTEGER
GLOBAL VAR   DATA(N) : CHARACTER (* or other appropriate type *)
GLOBAL VAR   TLPOINT(N),TRPOINT(N) : BOOLEAN
VAR  ROOT,P : INTEGER
P := ROOT
REPEAT

    (* The following IF statement alters P to point *)
    (* to its inorder successor *)

    IF  TRPOINT(P) THEN
        [ P := RLINK(P)]
    ELSE
        [ P := RLINK(P)
          WHILE  NOT TLPOINT(P) DO
              P := LLINK(P)
          ENDWHILE                ]
    ENDIF

    (* P now has been changed to point to its inorder successor *)

    (* Next check to see whether or not we have returned to the *)
    (* ROOT, i.e., completed the traversal *)

    IF  P <> ROOT THEN
        [ WRITE  (DATA(P))]
    ENDIF
UNTIL  P = ROOT
RETURN
END   THREADED-INORDER
```

You should carefully trace through this procedure on the tree in Figure 7-5. Verify that the procedure gracefully prints nothing when the ROOT pointer refers to an empty tree. A few minor modifications to the procedure will yield a new procedure, REVERSE-THREADED-INORDER(ROOT), that will employ the predecessor threads to do a reverse inorder traversal. Note that, if a given application requires only forward traversing of the

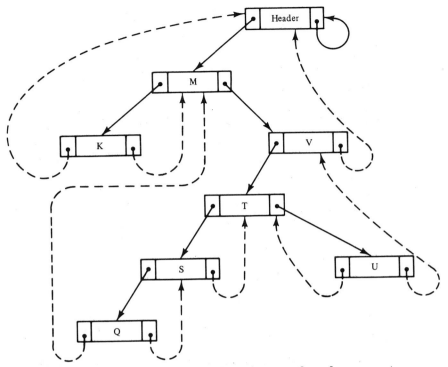

Figure 7-5 **If the right child pointer is not a thread, you must go to the node referenced by it and then follow left child pointers until you encounter a left thread. Trace the process here to find "Q" as the inorder successor of "M."**

tree, there is no necessity to maintain these predecessor threads. In that case, the left child pointers of the leaf nodes could remain NULL or perhaps even thread the tree for a preorder or postorder traversal. (See the Exercises at the end of the chapter.)

Insertions into a Threaded Tree

A valid question at this stage is, "Where do the threads come from?" In our examples so far, they have merely been drawn as dotted line pointers in the context of an already existing tree. We stress, however, that in practice threads cannot exist unless they are continually maintained as nodes are added to the tree. In this discussion, we will develop a procedure to insert a node into a binary tree. Our criterion for insertion will be the preservation of the ordering property cited in Chapter 6: for any given node, its left subtree can contain only data less than or equal to it, whereas its right subtree can contain only data greater than or equal to it. In order to ensure that this property holds for the dummy root node, we stipulate that:

> The data portion of the dummy root node should be initialized to a value greater than any other data item that might appear in the tree.

Given this criterion, insertions require that the node to be inserted travel down a branch of the tree following the *less than, go left; greater than, go right* **insertion rule.** Upon reaching a thread (a null pointer in an unthreaded tree), the new node is inserted appropriately as the left or right child. Figures 7-6 and 7-7 on pages 144 and 145 highlight the pointer manipulations that must occur in each of these cases.

These pointer manipulations are achieved by the following PSEUDO procedure INSERT-THREADED. Notice that, as is essential to any efficient insertion algorithm, no data are moved within the tree.

```
PROCEDURE  INSERT-THREADED(ROOT,ITEM)

(* Procedure to insert ITEM into threaded tree *)
(* pointed to by ROOT *)

(* Global variables are used to maintain the links, threads, and *)
(* data portions of the tree structure *)

GLOBAL VAR  N,LLINK(N),RLINK(N) : INTEGER
GLOBAL VAR  DATA(N) : CHARACTER (* or other appropriate type *)
GLOBAL VAR  TLPOINT(N),TRPOINT(N) : BOOLEAN
VAR   ITEM : CHARACTER (* or other appropriate type *)
VAR   ROOT,Q,PARENTQ : INTEGER
VAR   LEFT : BOOLEAN

(* Begin by calling on GETNODE of Chapter 2 *)

CALL  GETNODE(P)
DATA(P) := ITEM

(* Next allow this new node to travel down appropriate branch of *)
(* tree until insertion spot found *)

Q := ROOT
PARENTQ := NULL
REPEAT
      IF  ITEM < DATA(Q) THEN
          PARENTQ := Q
          Q := LLINK(Q)
          LEFT := TRUE
      ELSE
          PARENTQ := Q
          Q := RLINK(Q)
          LEFT := FALSE
      ENDIF
UNTIL  (LEFT AND TLPOINT(PARENTQ)) OR
          (NOT LEFT AND TRPOINT(PARENTQ))

(* Now insert P as left or right child of PARENTQ *)

TLPOINT(P) := TRUE
TRPOINT(P) := TRUE
IF  LEFT THEN
      LLINK(P) := LLINK(PARENTQ)
      RLINK(P) := PARENTQ
      LLINK(PARENTQ) := P
      TLPOINT(PARENTQ) := FALSE
```

UNTIL conditional controlling REPEAT

QPARENT

Leaf node may be reached with
LEFT AND TLPOINT(PARENTQ)
OR
Leaf node may be reached with
NOT LEFT AND TRPOINT(PARENTQ)

QPARENT

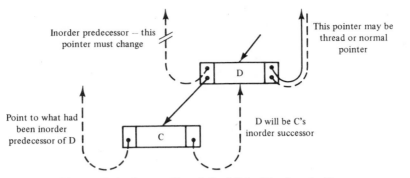

Inorder predecessor — this pointer must change

This pointer may be thread or normal pointer

D

Point to what had been inorder predecessor of D

D will be C's inorder successor

C

Figure 7-6 Insert C as left child of leaf node D.

```
ELSE
    ┌RLINK(P) := RLINK(PARENTQ)┐
    │LLINK(P) := PARENTQ       │
    │RLINK(PARENTQ) := P       │
    └TRPOINT(PARENTQ) := FALSE ┘
ENDIF
RETURN
END  INSERT-THREADED
```

Deletion of a node from a threaded tree can be handled by considering the cases we discussed in Section 6-5. The only additional consideration is maintenance of the Boolean threads. Hence, a threaded tree emerges as a structure with very little overhead. The only new fields required are the threads, and, in practice, they typically can be incorporated into the signs of the left and right child pointers. They thus represent a true bargain. By spending very little, you gain both the time and stack space required for recursion.

7-3 Height-Balanced Trees

Height-balanced binary trees, on the other hand, represent an alternative that often may not be worth the additional storage space and developmental complexities introduced for the sake of increasing speed. After describing the method, we shall discuss some considerations that may help you decide whether to height-balance a tree in a particular application.

The technique was developed in 1962 by researchers Adelson-Velskii and Landis.* (Hence, height-balanced trees are also referred to as **AVL trees.**) Height-balancing attempts to maintain trees that possess the ordering property of Section 6-5 in a form close to fullness, thereby ensuring rapid insertions and searches. One of the costs is that each node of the tree must store an additional item called its **balance factor.** The balance factor of a node is defined to be *the difference between the height of the node's left subtree and the height of the node's right subtree.* In this context, the **height** of a tree is *the number of nodes visited in traversing a branch that leads to a leaf node at the deepest level of the tree.* An example of a tree with computed balance factors for each node is given in Figure 7-8.

*Adelson-Velskii, G. M., and Landis, Y. M., 1962. An algorithm for the organization of information. *Dokl. Acad. Nauk. SSSR*, 146:263–266.

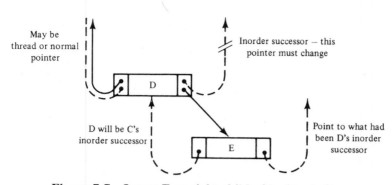

Figure 7-7   Insert E as right child of leaf node D.

A tree is said to be height-balanced if all of its nodes have a balance factor of 1, 0, or − 1. Hence, the tree in Figure 7-8 is not height-balanced. Note that every tree that is full is also height-balanced; however, the converse is not true. (Convince yourself of this by constructing an example.) The AVL technique used to keep a tree in height-balance requires that each time an insertion is made according to the insertion rule specified in Section 6-5, you must:

1. Let the node to be inserted travel down the appropriate branch, keeping track along the way of the deepest level node on that branch that has a balance factor of + 1 or − 1. This particular node is called the **pivot node,** for reasons that will soon be apparent.

2. Inclusive of and below the pivot node, recompute all balance factors along the insertion path traced in (1). It will be shown that no nodes other than these can possibly change their balance factors using the AVL method.

3. Determine whether the absolute value of the pivot node's balance factor switched from 1 to 2.

4. If there was such a switch as indicated in (3), perform a manipulation of tree pointers centered at the pivot node to bring the tree back into height balance. Because the visual

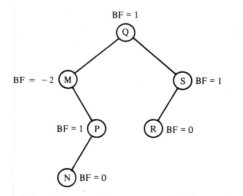

Figure 7-8   A tree with computed balance factors.

effect of this pointer manipulation is to "rotate" the subtree whose root is the pivot node, the operation is frequently referred to as an **AVL-rotation.**

We shall cover these steps in reverse order because, until you fully understand the nature of the AVL-rotation, it will not be apparent why the pivot node is chosen as specified in (1).

AVL-Rotations

In this discussion we assume that steps (1), (2), and (3) in the last section have all been completed and that we have a pointer, PIVOT, to the deepest level node whose balance factor has switched from an absolute value of 1 to 2. In practice, PIVOT may be the root pointer for the entire tree or the child pointer of a parent node inside the tree. The pointer manipulations required to rebalance the tree necessitate division into 4 cases identified by the direction of the "guilty" insertion relative to the pivot node. They are:

1. The insertion occurred in the left subtree of the left child of the pivot node

2. The insertion occurred in the right subtree of the right child of the pivot node

3. The insertion occurred in the right subtree of the left child of the pivot node

4. The insertion occurred in the left subtree of the right child of the pivot node

Case 1.   The insertion that unbalanced the tree occurred in the left subtree of the left child of the pivot node. In this case, the situation pictured in Figure 7-9 must have occurred. Our only criterion for rebalancing the tree is preservation of the ordering property for binary trees. Hence, if we could force a rotation (merely through changes in pointers) that made the tree pointed to by PIVOT appear as in Figure 7-10, the rebalancing would be complete. The procedure to achieve this rotation is:

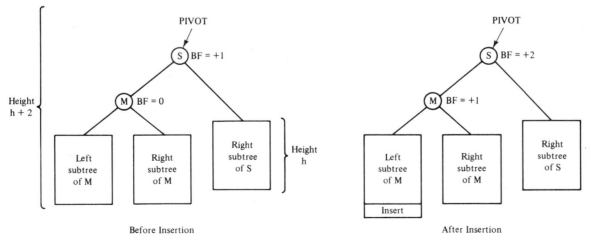

Before Insertion   After Insertion

**Figure 7-9   Case 1: The insertion occurred in the left subtree of
the left child of the pivot node.**

```
PROCEDURE  LEFT-OF-LEFT(PIVOT)

(* Perform AVL rotation for Case 1 on subtree pointed to by PIVOT *)
(* GLOBAL LLINK,RLINK,DATA arrays defined as in Chapter 6 *)
(* GLOBAL BF array is additional field in node used to store the *)
(* balance factor *)

GLOBAL VAR  N,LLINK(N),RLINK(N),BF(N) : INTEGER
GLOBAL VAR  DATA(N) : CHARACTER
VAR  P,Q,PIVOT : INTEGER

(* Begin by altering the necessary pointers *)

P := LLINK(PIVOT)
Q := RLINK(P)
RLINK(P) := PIVOT
LLINK(PIVOT) := Q
PIVOT := P

(* Then readjust the balance factors that had been

BF(PIVOT) := 0
BF(RLINK(PIVOT)) := 0
RETURN
END  LEFT-OF-LEFT
```

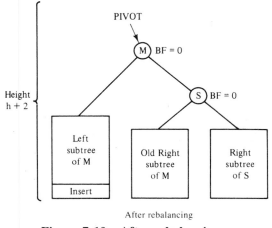

Case 2. The insertion that unbalanced the tree occurred in the right subtree of the right child of the pivot node. This case is pictured in Figure 7-11. Figure 7-12 indicates the rebalancing that should occur. Again, the idea is to rotate the tree around the pivot node, except that this time the rotation must occur in the opposite direction.

The PSEUDO RIGHT-OF-RIGHT(PIVOT) procedure necessary to achieve this rotation is left as an exercise at the end of the chapter. It is essentially a mirror image of the LEFT-OF-LEFT procedure.

After rebalancing

Figure 7-10   After rebalancing.

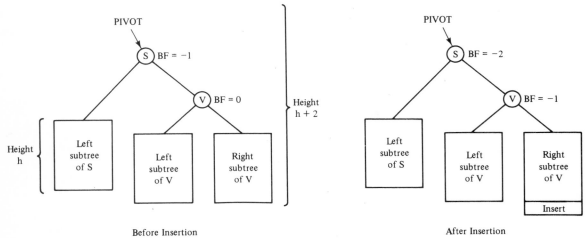
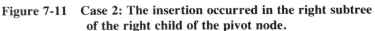

Before Insertion   After Insertion

**Figure 7-11   Case 2: The insertion occurred in the right subtree
of the right child of the pivot node.**

Case 3.   The insertion causing the imbalance occurred in the right subtree of the left child of the pivot node. In this case, the PSEUDO procedure to perform the pointer manipulations necessary to rebalance the tree will require subdivision into 3 subcases. They are best described in the diagrammatic form of Figures 7-13, 7-14, and 7-15 on pages 150–152.

Upon first glance, the need for splitting Case 3 into 3 subcases may not be apparent. Indeed, all 3 subcases require nearly identical pointer changes. However, the subtle point of differentiation among the 3 lies in how the balance factors are reset after the rotation has occurred. This subtlety is taken into account in the following PSEUDO procedure to handle Case 3:

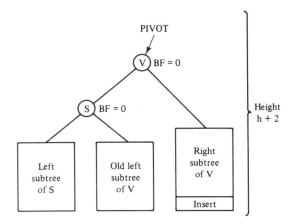

Figure 7-12   After rebalancing.

```
PROCEDURE  RIGHT-OF-LEFT(PIVOT)

    (* Perform AVL rotation for Case 3 on subtree *)
    (* pointed to by PIVOT *)

    (* GLOBAL LLINK, RLINK, DATA, and BF arrays *)
    (* as in LEFT-OF-LEFT procedure *)

GLOBAL VAR  N,LLINK(N),RLINK(N),BF(N) : INTEGER
GLOBAL VAR  DATA(N) : INTEGER
VAR PIVOT,X,Y : INTEGER

(* First adjust pointers in fashion to perform AVL rotation *)

X := LLINK(PIVOT)
Y := RLINK(X)
LLINK(PIVOT) := RLINK(Y)
RLINK(X) := LLINK(Y)
LLINK(Y) := X
RLINK(Y) := PIVOT
PIVOT := Y

(* Then reset balance factors according to subcase *)

IF  BF(PIVOT) = 0 THEN  (* Subcase #1 *)
   ⌈BF(LCHILD(PIVOT)) := 0⌉
   ⌊BF(RCHILD(PIVOT)) := 0⌋
ELSE IF  BF(PIVOT)= 1 THEN  (* Subcase #2 *)
   ⌈BF(PIVOT) := 0

    BF(LCHILD(PIVOT)) := 0
   ⌊BF(RCHILD(PIVOT)) := -1
ELSE                        (* Subcase #3 *)
   ⌈BF(PIVOT) := 0
    BF(LCHILD(PIVOT)) := 1
   ⌊BF(RCHILD(PIVOT)) := 0
   ENDIF
ENDIF
RETURN
END  RIGHT-OF-LEFT
```

Case 4.   The insertion causing the imbalance in the tree occurred in the left subtree of the right child of the pivot node. Case 4 is to Case 3 as Case 2 is to Case 1; you will write the procedure LEFT-OF-RIGHT(PIVOT) as an exercise at the end of the chapter.

Why Does the AVL Height-Balancing Technique Work?

When people first study the AVL algorithm, it is often not apparent to them why the pivot node must be the *deepest* node along the path of insertion that has a balance factor of $+1$ or -1. After all, it would seem that the diagrams in Figures 7-11 through 7-15 work equally well as long as PIVOT points to any node along the insertion path that has a change in the magnitude of its balance factor from 1 to 2. However, three rather subtle factors are involved in the selection of the pivot node to be not just *any* node with balance factor $+1$ or -1 along the insertion path but *the deepest* such node.

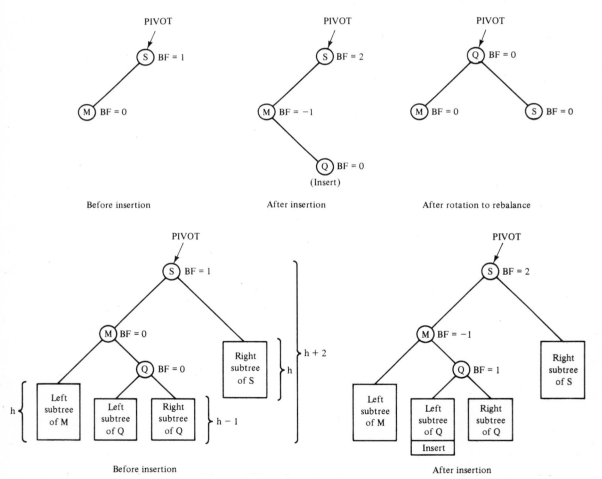

Figure 7-13   Case 3, subcase #1.

First, it is quite evident that we must choose a node whose original balance factor is $+1$ or -1 as the pivot node. Such nodes are the only candidates for points at which the tree can go out of height-balance. Any node with balance factor 0 can at worst change to $+1$ or -1 after insertion, therefore not requiring any rotation at all.

Second, whether or not a rotation takes place, *the only balance factors in the entire tree that will be affected are those of nodes inclusive of and below the pivot node along the insertion path*. In situations where a rotation does occur, this is evident from Figures 7-11 through 7-15. In all 4 cases of AVL-rotation, the overall height of the subtree pointed to by PIVOT is the same after the rotation as before it. In situations where no rotation occurs, the balance factor of the pivot node must change from either 1 to 0 or from -1 to 0; it cannot remain what it was originally. This is because every node below it on the insertion path must have an original balance factor of 0. Consequently, there is no way that an insertion can "hide" in a fashion not affecting the balance factor of the pivot node. However, the fact that the pivot node changes to a 0 balance factor in such situations again means that the rest of the tree above the pivot node is unaffected by the insertion.

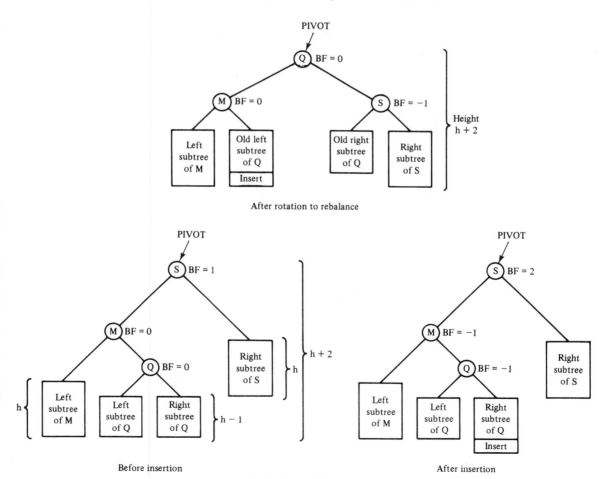

Figure 7-14   Case 3, subcase #2.

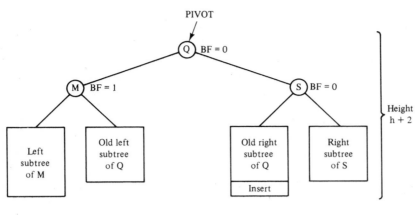

After rotation to rebalance

Figure 7-15   Case 3, subcase #3.

Third, if we do not choose the deepest level node with a balance factor equal to $+1$ or -1, we run the risk of having an AVL-rotation only partially rebalance the tree. Figure 7-16 indicates how this could occur.

With this rationale in mind, we are now able to present convincingly a complete PSEUDO procedure to process an insertion into a height-balanced tree, recompute all affected balance factors, and perform an AVL-rotation if necessary:

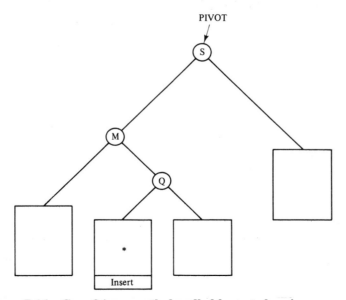

Figure 7-16   Case 3 incorrectly handled by not choosing proper pivot. AVL-rotation only partially rebalances the tree.

```
PROCEDURE  AVL-INSERT(ROOT,ITEM)

(* Procedure to insert ITEM into the height-balanced tree *)
(* pointed to by ROOT *)

(* Global arrays LLINK,RLINK,DATA,BF used to maintain the tree *)

GLOBAL VAR  N,LLINK(N),RLINK(N),BF(N) : INTEGER
GLOBAL VAR  DATA(N) : CHARACTER
VAR  ROOT,P,PIV,PIVPARENT,IN,INPARENT,Q : INTEGER

(* First obtain tree node for ITEM via *)
(* GETNODE procedure of Chapter 2 *)


CALL  GETNODE(P)
DATA(P) := ITEM
LLINK(P) := NULL
RLINK(P) := NULL
BF(P) := 0


(* Then check for empty tree *)

IF ROOT = NULL THEN
    ⌈ROOT := P⌉
    ⌊RETURN  ⌋
ENDIF

(* Pointer IN keeps track of insertion point, with its parent *)
(* INPARENT.  Pointer PIV keeps track of pivot node, with its parent *)
(* PIVPARENT *)

IN := ROOT
PIV := ROOT
INPARENT := NULL
PIVPARENT := NULL

(* Search for insertion point and pivot node *)

REPEAT
    ⌈IF  BF(IN) <> 0 THEN                    ⌉
    │   ⌈PIV := IN              ⌉           │
    │   ⌊PIVPARENT := INPARENT⌋           │
    │ ENDIF                                │
    │ INPARENT := IN                       │
    │ IF  ITEM < DATA(IN) THEN             │
    │    [IN := LLINK(IN)]                 │
    │ ELSE                                 │
    │    [IN := RLINK(IN)]                 │
    ⌊ ENDIF                                ⌋
UNTIL  IN = NULL
```

```
(* Insert node as left or right child of INPARENT *)

IF ITEM < DATA(INPARENT) THEN
    [LLINK(INPARENT) := P]
ELSE
    [RLINK(INPARENT) := P]
ENDIF

(* Now recompute balance factors between PIV and INPARENT. *)
(* By definition of pivot node, all these balance factors must *)
(* change by 1 in direction of insertion *)

Q := PIV
REPEAT
    IF  ITEM < DATA(Q) THEN
        BF(Q) := BF(Q) + 1
        Q := LLINK(Q)
    ELSE
        BF(Q) := BF(Q) -1
        Q := RLINK(Q)
    ENDIF
UNTIL  Q := NULL

(* Need to rotate?  If not, can now return *)

IF -1 <= BF(PIV) AND BF(PIV) <=1 THEN
    [RETURN]
ENDIF

(* AVL-rotation is necessary.  Call on appropriate procedure *)
(* passing one of ROOT,LLINK(PIVPARENT), or RLINK(PIVPARENT) as *)
(* the pointer to the pivot node *)

IF  ITEM < DATA(PIV) THEN
    IF  ITEM < DATA(LLINK(PIV)) THEN
        IF  PIV = ROOT THEN
            [CALL  LEFT-OF-LEFT (ROOT)]
        ELSE  IF  PIV = LLINK(PIVPARENT) THEN
            [CALL  LEFT-OF-LEFT (LLINK(PIVPARENT))]
        ELSE
            CALL  LEFT-OF-LEFT (RLINK(PIVPARENT))
            ENDIF
        ENDIF
    ELSE
        IF  PIV = ROOT THEN
            [CALL  RIGHT-OF-LEFT (ROOT)]
        ELSE  IF  PIV = LLINK(PIVPARENT) THEN
            [CALL  RIGHT-OF-LEFT (LLINK(PIVPARENT))]
        ELSE
            CALL  RIGHT-OF-LEFT (RLINK(PIVPARENT))
            ENDIF
        ENDIF
    ENDIF
```

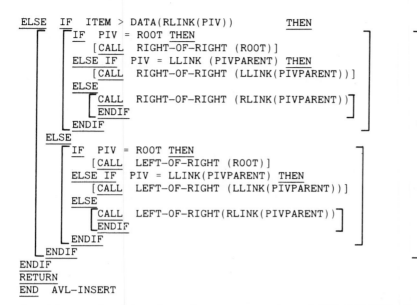

```
ELSE  IF  ITEM > DATA(RLINK(PIV))          THEN
           IF  PIV = ROOT THEN
               [CALL  RIGHT-OF-RIGHT (ROOT)]
           ELSE IF  PIV = LLINK (PIVPARENT) THEN
               [CALL  RIGHT-OF-RIGHT (LLINK(PIVPARENT))]
           ELSE
               [CALL  RIGHT-OF-RIGHT (RLINK(PIVPARENT))
                ENDIF
           ENDIF
      ELSE
           IF  PIV = ROOT THEN
               [CALL  LEFT-OF-RIGHT (ROOT)]
           ELSE IF  PIV = LLINK(PIVPARENT) THEN
               [CALL  LEFT-OF-RIGHT (LLINK(PIVPARENT))]
           ELSE
               [CALL  LEFT-OF-RIGHT(RLINK(PIVPARENT))
                ENDIF
           ENDIF
      ENDIF
ENDIF
RETURN
END  AVL-INSERT
```

A subtle question arises from the PSEUDO version of AVL-INSERT. Consider the segment:

```
IF  PIV = ROOT THEN
    [CALL  LEFT-OF-LEFT (ROOT)]
ELSE IF  PIV = LLINK(PIVPARENT) THEN
    [CALL  LEFT-OF-LEFT (LLINK(PIVPARENT))]
ELSE
    [CALL  LEFT-OF-LEFT(RLINK(PIVPARENT))
     ENDIF
ENDIF
```

Why could this lengthy segment from AVL-INSERT not be replaced by the single PSEUDO instruction CALL LEFT-OF-LEFT(PIV)? The answer lies in the fact that the procedure LEFT-OF-LEFT alters the argument that is sent to it. What we wish to alter in the segment above is *not* the variable PIV but rather one of the variables ROOT, LINK(PIVPARENT), or RLINK(PIVPARENT). The simple CALL LEFT-OF-LEFT(PIV) would leave the variables we wish to change unaffected.

Height-Balancing—Is It Worth It?

The height-balancing procedure is clearly a nontrivial algorithm. Moreover, the algorithm to delete a node from a height-balanced tree is no easier; you will write it as an exercise at the end of the chapter. Adelson-Velskii and Landis were able to demonstrate that their method would guarantee a maximum branch length proportional to $\log_2 N$, where N is the number of nodes in the tree. This means that the insertion efficiency for a height-balanced tree will be, in terms of orders of magnitude, roughly equivalent to that for a full tree. Compared to the worst case efficiency of N for a nonbalanced tree, it is clear that the AVL method can make a difference. Whether the difference is worth the added developmental costs is, as always, a consideration tied to a particular application.

The real problem in this regard, however, is that it is often impossible to have a realistic appraisal in the design stage of just how much height-balancing will mean to overall run time efficiency. There is a real dilemma here. You may not be able to estimate accurately beforehand the precise advantages or costs of height-balancing. Consequently, if you do employ height-balancing and it then turns out that system performance would have been adequate without it, you have wasted a considerable amount of development time. We recommend a rather empirical approach to this problem. Unless for some reasons the need for height-balancing is obvious, design and write the application without it. However, leave enough storage space in the tree nodes to accommodate balance factors. (Note that you can get by with a mere two bits in this regard if storage is at a real premium.) After empirically testing the performance of your application without height-balancing, make the decision whether or not to rewrite insertion and deletion routines to incorporate height-balancing.

7-4 General Trees

Our introduction to the topic of trees cited the example of genealogical trees similar to that appearing in Figure 7-17. However, thus far we have been strictly enforcing a birth control rule of no more than 2 children per node. Seemingly, we must now relax this rule if we are to represent **general trees** such as our genealogical example.

In a general tree, a node can have any number of children, so the implementation of a general tree is more complex than that of a binary tree. One alternative is to use a maximum but fixed number of children for each node. This strategy, however, has the disadvantage of being very wasteful of memory space taken up by null nodes. Another equally wasteful technique is to allow variable size nodes. This plan requires providing extra memory space to store the size of the node. Additionally, algorithms needed to handle a variable size node structure are much less elegant than those for tree structures with fixed size nodes. Figure 7-18 shows a tree structure with variable size nodes.

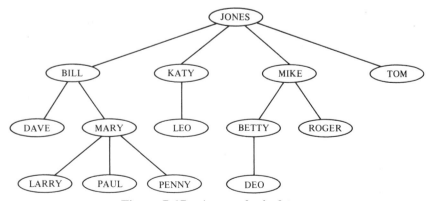

Figure 7-17   A genealogical tree.

In the world of applications . . .

General trees are used in almost all aspects of scientific study. One intriguing application is in what is known as the *8 Coins Puzzle*. There are 8 coins, one of which is heavier than the others. The purpose is to design a strategy to isolate this coin. A general tree such as shown here can be effectively used to identify this biased coin. Suppose we label coins

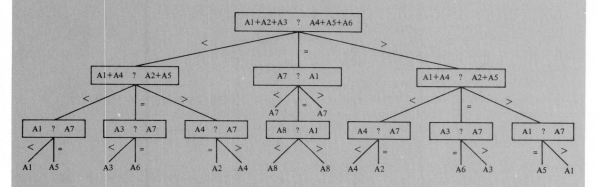

as A1, A2, . . . , A8. We start at the root and compare the total weight of A1 + A2 + A3 with that of A4 + A5 + A6. If the former weight is lesser or greater than the latter, we follow an appropriate branch on the tree marked by "<" or ">." The diagram is self-explanatory and we eventually identify this coin at the leaf node level.

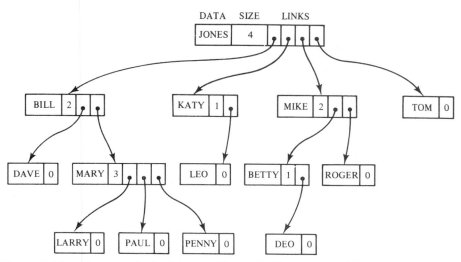

Figure 7-18 The genealogical tree in Figure 7-17, represented with variable size nodes.

Binary Tree Representation of General Trees

A more practical way of implementing a general tree is to use its binary representation. This requires that each node have only 2 pointer fields. The first pointer points to the leftmost child of the node, and the second pointer identifies the next sibling to the right of the leftmost child. Because the children of a node taken in this context form an ordered set of nodes, we can regard the leftmost child of a node as FIRSTCHILD and the sibling to the right of this node as NEXTSIBLING. We will henceforth adopt this terminology for the two link fields involved with the binary tree representation of a general tree. Figure 7-19 gives the binary representation of the general genealogical tree shown in Figure 7-17.

Implementation algorithms for binary tree representations of general trees can be elegantly written in languages equipped with dynamic storage allocation. However, in languages such as BASIC and FORTRAN, which lack this facility, arrays can be used for pointers and data. For example, the tree of Figure 7-17 can be stored as shown in Figure 7-20. Once again, remember that arrays used in this manner will almost always leave unused memory locations. The scheme used to fill the arrays in Figure 7-20 was to store a node before any of its children, and then to store recursively the leftmost child.

Traversals of a General Tree Implemented with a Binary Tree

Because the binary implementation scheme for a general tree is nothing more than a special interpretation of a binary tree, all of the traversals defined for a binary tree clearly can be performed for a general tree. A more relevant question than that of whether a traversal

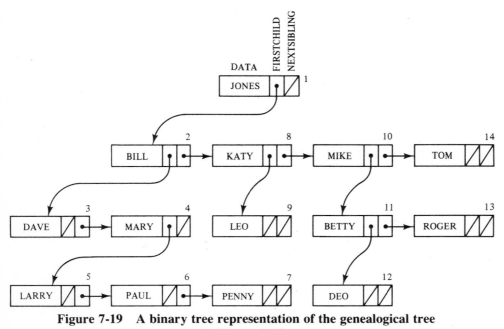

Figure 7-19   A binary tree representation of the genealogical tree in Figure 7-17.

can be accomplished, however, is: What is the significance of the order in which the nodes of a general tree are visited when its corresponding binary tree is traversed? Of particular interest in this regard are preorder and postorder traversals.

You should verify at this point that the preorder traversal algorithm for a binary tree applied to Figure 7-19 yields the listing:

```
JONES
     BILL
          DAVE
          MARY
               LARRY
               PAUL
               PENNY
     KATY
          LEO
     MIKE
          BETTY
               DEO
          ROGER
     TOM
```

The indentation here has been added to highlight the fact that the preorder traversal will recursively:

1. Process a parent node, and then

2. Process the child nodes from left to right

Relative to the general tree pictured in Figure 7-17, we see that the effect of the preorder traversal is to fix on a node at one level of the tree and then run through all of that node's children before progressing to the next node at the same level. There is a hint here of a generalized nested loop situation, which we will soon see has some interesting applications.

LOCATION	DATA	FIRSTCHILD	NEXTCHILD
1	JONES	2	0
2	BILL	3	8
3	DAVE	0	4
4	MARY	5	0
5	LARRY	0	6
6	PAUL	0	7
7	PENNY	0	0
8	KATY	9	10
9	LEO	0	0
10	MIKE	11	14
11	BETTY	12	13
12	DEO	0	0
13	ROGER	0	0
14	TOM	0	0

Figure 7-20   The tree in Figure 7-17 stored in arrays for data and pointers. "0" represents a null pointer.

Postorder traversal also is of interest in a binary tree representation of a general tree. Verify that postorder traversal of Figure 7-19 yields the listing:

```
PENNY
PAUL
LARRY
MARY
DAVE
LEO
DEO
ROGER
BETTY
TOM
MIKE
KATY
BILL
JONES
```

In general, the postorder traversal works its way up from the leaf nodes of a tree, ensuring that no given node is processed until all nodes in the subtree below it have been processed.

Ternary Tree Representation of a General Tree

An alternate to a binary tree representation of a general tree that uses a node containing three pointers is called a **ternary tree** representation. In it, the left-to-right order of siblings along any given level of the tree is more efficiently maintained. A given node within the tree appears as in Figure 7-21. In this scheme:

1. LSIBLING is a pointer to the left sibling of the given node relative to a binary tree representation of the ordered list of siblings at this level

2. RSIBLING is a pointer to the right sibling of the given node relative to a binary tree representation of the ordered list of siblings at this level

3. CHILDREN is a pointer to a binary tree representation of the ordered list of children of a given node.

Thus, a ternary tree representation of the general tree of Figure 7-17 that maintains the left-to-right order of siblings is given by Figure 7-22.

Interestingly enough, a close perusal of the ternary tree representation of Figure 7-22 will show that it is composed of strategically located binary trees (highlighted by dotted lines for those who lack time for a close perusal). For example, an inorder traversal of the binary tree encircled by the dotted line numbered 2 yields the listing

```
BILL
KATY
MIKE
TOM
```

This is precisely the left-to-right order of the siblings that are the children of JONES in Figure 7-17! Similarly, an inorder traversal of the binary tree encircled by the dotted line numbered 6 yields the left-to-right order of the children of MARY in Figure 7-17. Thus,

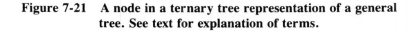

Figure 7-21 **A node in a ternary tree representation of a general tree. See text for explanation of terms.**

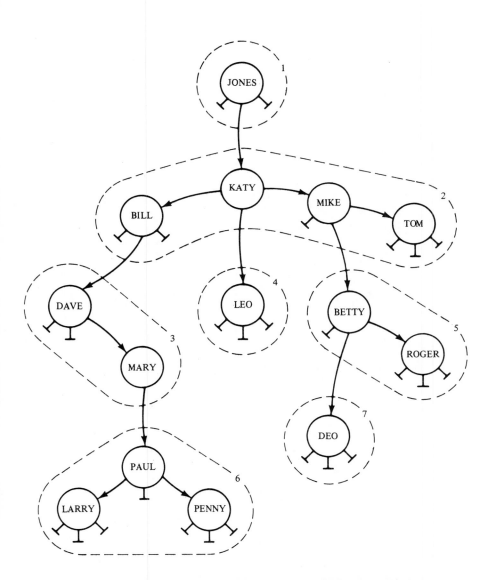

Figure 7-22 **Ternary tree representation of Figure 7-17 (the symbol ⊥ is used to emphasize NULL pointers).**

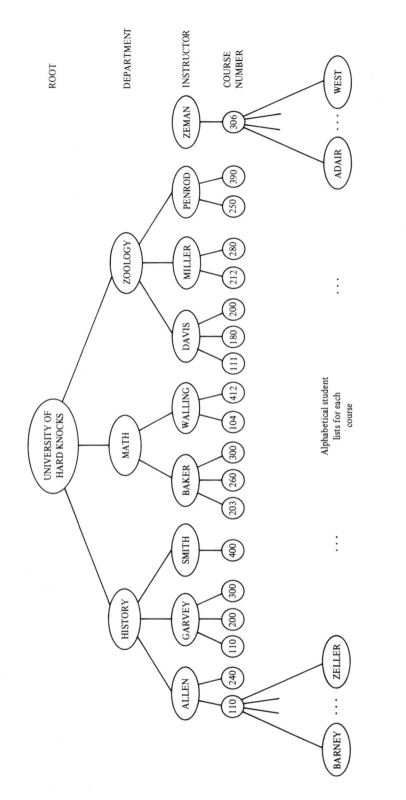

ROOT

DEPARTMENT

INSTRUCTOR

COURSE
NUMBER

Alphabetical student
lists for each
course

Figure 7-23 Database for the University of Hard Knocks.

the LSIBLING and RSIBLING pointers are tied to the ordering of children relative to an inorder traversal of an appropriate binary subtree of the entire structure. The CHILDREN pointer, on the other hand, is actually the root pointer to a binary tree that, in turn, represents an ordered list of children at the next deeper level.

The implications of the ternary tree representation in the area of database management are relatively profound. At first glance, it would seem that the only difference is that we are charged for one extra pointer per node. However, consider for a moment the following application, which is a typical problem encountered in database management. A university has a list of departments, which it wishes to maintain in alphabetical order. Each department has a list of professors, which also is to be kept in alphabetical order relative to that department. Each professor teaches a list of courses; this course list is to be kept in order by course number. Finally each course has a list of students enrolled, also to be kept in alphabetical order. Figure 7-23 illustrates such a database for a university (with enrollments kept small enough to fit conveniently on one page).

Now consider the maintenance that is likely to be necessary for this tree-structured database. Insertions and deletions will frequently occur at the class section and student enrollment level. The tenure density at this institution will control the next level, but this type of processing will not occur as often at the higher levels of the tree. Insertions and deletions in a large database necessarily force considerations of efficiency. If this tree is implemented with the binary tree representation of a general tree, each class list, each list of courses taught, and each list of departmental faculty becomes essentially a linked list. As such, each list's insertion and search efficiency is proportional to the number of members in the list. However, with the ternary tree representation of this general tree, each sublist within the data is implemented with the binary tree method of Section 6-5. Hence, insertion and deletion efficiency could well be proportional to the $\log_2 N$ figure we have cited previously. To ensure maximum efficiency, each binary tree sublist could be threaded and/or height-balanced. Clearly, for such a list-oriented database, the third pointer of the ternary tree representation is a relatively small price to pay for the added efficiency achieved.

In regard to traversing a general tree represented by the ternary tree method, we can duplicate the order of nodes visited by the preorder and postorder traversals of a binary tree representation. However, although the order can be duplicated, the method is slightly different. Suppose, for example, that we wish to achieve the equivalent of a preorder traversal with a ternary representation. We must ensure that, immediately after processing a given node, we process *in order* all the children of that node. But to process *in order* all the children of a node, we need merely call on an inorder traversal of the tree whose root node is referenced by the CHILDREN pointer of the node in question. That is, we essentially duplicate the effect of a preorder traversal for a binary representation by recursively calling on an inorder traversal for the tree of children! The procedure can be written quite elegantly in PSEUDO:

```
PROCEDURE   TERNARY-PREORDER(ROOT)

(* Achieve preorder traversal of general tree represented *)
(* by ternary tree implementation. *)

(* Tree structure is represented by global arrays *)
(* LSIBLING,CHILDREN,DATA, and RSIBLING *)
```

```
GLOBAL VAR  N,LSIBLING(N),CHILDREN(N),RSIBLING(N) : INTEGER
GLOBAL VAR  DATA(N) : CHARACTER (* or other appropriate type *)
VAR  ROOT : INTEGER
IF  ROOT <> NULL THEN
    CALL  TERNARY-PREORDER(LSIBLING(ROOT))

    (* Then apply appropriate process to root node *)

    CALL  PROCESS (ROOT)

    (* Then visit the children *)

    CALL  TERNARY-PREORDER(CHILDREN(ROOT))

    (* Finally continue on at sibling level *)

    CALL  TERNARY-PREORDER(RSIBLING(ROOT))
ENDIF
RETURN
END  TERNARY-PREORDER
```

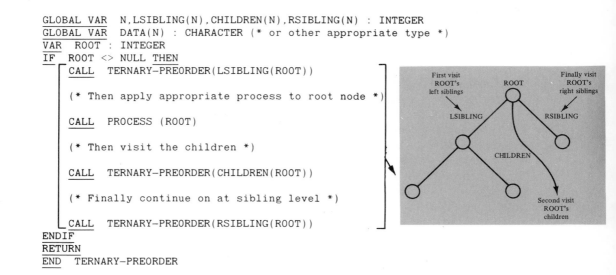

SUMMARY

In Chapters 6 and 7, trees have emerged as one of the most potent of all data structures. They combine the insertion/deletion capabilities of a linked list with a $\log_2 N$ efficiency (as opposed to N for a linked list). Moreover, threading and height-balancing offer enhancements that you can choose to tailor the efficiency of tree processing to a particular application. We have seen examples of how trees can be used in the parsing of algebraic expressions and in database management. The Programming Problems will further serve to highlight the use of trees in databases, statistical analysis packages, and artificial intelligence (game playing). Moreover, we have just begun to see the power of trees. Further applications of trees will be explored in Chapter 12 when we talk about the use of indexes in file searching.

KEY TERMS

Threaded tree
Inorder predecessor
Inorder successor

Height-balanced tree
AVL-rotation
General tree

Binary tree representation of
  general tree
Ternary tree representation of
  general tree
Tree-structured database

EXERCISES

1. Redraw the threads in Figure 7-4 to indicate preorder and postorder traversals of the tree.

2. Adapt the PSEUDO procedure for a threaded inorder traversal to a high-level language.

3. Write a PSEUDO procedure for the preorder traversal diagram suggested in Exercise (1).

4. Write a PSEUDO procedure for the postorder threaded traversal of the binary tree in Exercise (1).

5. Why is the inorder traversal of a general tree not appropriate?

6. Modify the PSEUDO procedure TERNARY-PREORDER to obtain the postorder traversal of a general tree.

7. Write a PSEUDO procedure that uses the predecessor pointers in a threaded binary tree to generate a reverse inorder traversal.

8. Write a PSEUDO procedure to delete a node from a threaded binary tree.

9. Write a PSEUDO procedure to delete a node from a height-balanced tree.

10. Convince yourself that a height-balanced tree is not necessarily full by drawing an example that is height-balanced but not full.

11. Complete the PSEUDO procedures RIGHT-OF-RIGHT and LEFT-OF-RIGHT for insertion of a node into a height-balanced tree.

12. Consider the following drawing of a binary tree. Draw the tree after the data item "A" has been inserted and the tree has been height-balanced.

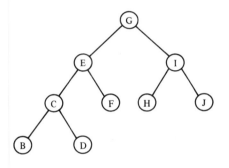

13. Repeat Exercise (12) for the insertion of "D" and the corresponding height-balancing of the following tree.

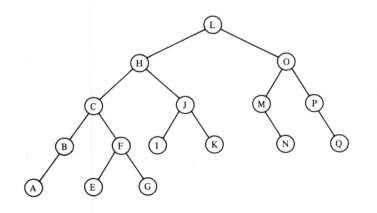

PROGRAMMING PROBLEMS

1. The Wing and a Prayer Airline Company of Programming Problem (1) in Chapter 2 is expanding their record-keeping database. This database may now be pictured hierarchically as:

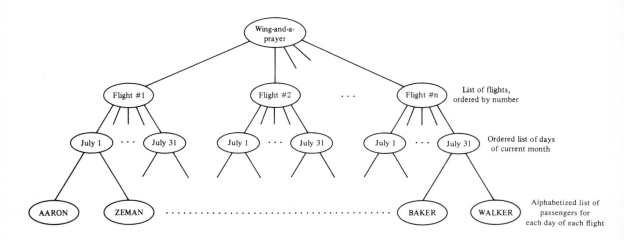

Write a program to maintain this database. Your program should process requests to add, delete, or list:

- Specified flight number

- Specified day of the month (relative to a flight number)

- Specified passenger or all passengers (relative to given flight number and day of the month)

2. The Pascal supplement at the end of this chapter loads and then prints the ternary preorder traversal of the family tree that appears in Figure 7-17. Modify this procedure to print out the postorder traversal for the ternary tree representation of the general family tree. Additionally, use this supplement as a starting point to experiment with:

- Different orders of loading the tree

- Different orders of traversing the tree

- Different methods of graphically representing the tree on a character printer

3. Many statistical analysis packages support a "cross-tabulation" command designed to explore the relationship between statistical variables. A cross-tabulation between two variables merely produces a two-dimensional table containing a frequency count for each possible ordered pair of values of the two variables. However, these statistical packages typically allow this type of analysis to proceed even further than merely exploring two variables. For instance, in a legal system database, we might be interested in cross-tabulating a defendant's age with the judge before whom he/she stood trial. We may then wish to cross-tabulate this result with the sex of the defendant. The output produced by the COSAP statistical package of Lawrence University for this type of request is given following this problem. Of interest in this output is the fact that the value of the control variable (SEX in this case) is held fixed at 1 while the cross-tabulation table for the two primary variables (AGEBRACK and JUDGE) is printed. Then the next largest value for SEX is fixed and another AGEBRACK by JUDGE table is produced. This could continue for larger values of SEX (provided we were capable of using more than two sexes). Note that this type of output is not limited to just one control variable. There may be an arbitrary number of control variables and tables to cycle through. Moreover, the variables have an arbitrary number of observations and are all in arbitrary order. Yet for each variable the list of possible values is always printed out in smallest to largest order! The general tree structure that emerges for handling cross-tabulations is:

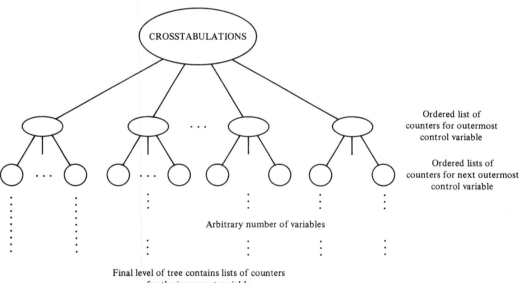

Write a program to handle the task of producing statistical cross-tabulations. Pattern its output after the sample that follows.

```
Command? CROSSTABS
Enter variables for CROSSTABULATION? AGEBRACK/JUDGE/SEX
Enter Options?
            4 categories for JUDGE        ⎫  Arbitrary number of
            8 categories for AGEBRACK      ⎬  variables should be
            2 categories for SEX           ⎭  allowed here
CROSSTABS will print   2   8 by  4 tables.
Proceed (Yes or No) *? YES
```

                    CRIMINAL HISTORY DATABANK

                  C R O S S T A B U L A T I O N

AGEBRACK by JUDGE by SEX

AGEBRACK   REGROUPED AGE (4R) OF PERSON CHGD
JUDGE   JUDGE BEFORE WHOM CASE BROUGHT (2)

Controlling for...
SEX   SEX OF PERSON CHARGED (3)   Value =   1   MALE


```
                    JUDGE
                    :SHAFER:CANE  :VANSUS:MYSE  :  Row
           Count :     1:    2:     3:     5:  Total
AGEBRACK           ──────:──────:──────:──────:
_<18         1 :      1     0      0      0       1

18-20        2 :    157    11      1     19     188

21-24        3 :    103     8      4     16     131

25-29        4 :     58    14      3      6      81

30-39        5 :     58     4      2      1      65

40-49        6 :     40     5      1      1      47

50-71        7 :     27     1      0      1      29

DKNA         9 :    117    37      7      2     163

          Column     561    80     18     46     705
          Total
```

Cross-tabulation table for smallest value of SEX

```
AGEBRACK   REGROUPED AGE (4R) OF PERSON CHGD
JUDGE      JUDGE BEFORE WHOM CASE BROUGHT (2)

Controlling for...
SEX        SEX OF PERSON CHARGED (3)            Value =    2  FEMALE
```

	Count	JUDGE SHAFER 1	CANE 2	VANSUS 3	MYSE 5	Row Total
AGEBRACK						
_<18	1 :	0	0	1	0	1
18–20	2 :	29	0	6	0	35
21–24	3 :	18	1	0	1	20
25–29	4 :	14	0	1	0	15
30–39	5 :	21	1	0	0	22
40–49	6 :	7	0	0	0	7
50–71	7 :	5	1	0	0	6
DKNA	9 :	22	5	0	0	27
Column Total		116	8	8	1	133

Cross-tabulation table for next value of SEX

4. Trees find significant application in the area of artificial intelligence and game playing. Consider, for instance, the game of FIFTEEN. In this game, 2 players take turns selecting digits between 1 and 9 with the goal of selecting a combination of digits that adds up to 15. Once a digit is chosen, it may not be chosen again by either player. Rather than immediately considering a tree for the game of FIFTEEN, let us first consider a tree for the trivial game of SEVEN with digits chosen in the range 1 to 6. A tree that partially represents the states that may be reached in this game is:

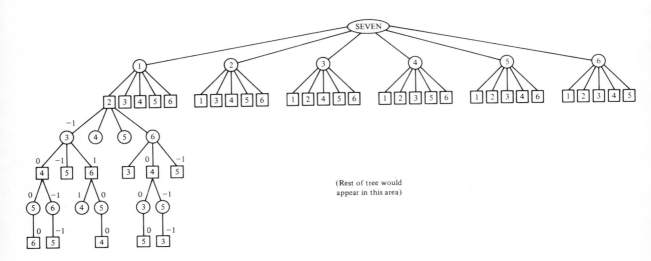

(Rest of tree would appear in this area)

In this tree, circular nodes represent the states that may be reached by the player who moves first (the computer), and square nodes represent the states that may be reached by the player who moves second (a human opponent). The $+1$, 0, or -1 attached to each node represent weighting factors designed to help the computer choose the most advantageous move at any given stage of the game. The rule used to compute these weighting factors is:

- If the node is a leaf node, its weight is determined by some static weighting function. In this case, the static weighting function used was to assign $+1$ to a leaf node representing a computer win, 0 to a leaf node representing a draw, and -1 to a leaf node representing a human win.

- If the node is a node from which the computer will move (that is, a state occupied by the human opponent), then the weighting factor of the node is the maximum of the weighting factors of its children.

- If the node is a node from which the human opponent will move, then the weighting factor of the node is the minimum of the weighting factors of its children.

In its turn, the computer should always choose to move to the node having the maximum possible weighting factor. The rationale behind this technique, called the *minimax* technique, is that the computer will move in such a way as always to maximize its chances of winning. The human opponent, if she or he is playing intelligently, will always move to that node having a minimum weighting factor. Thus, in the partial game tree shown, the computer would choose to select 4 if the human had been naive enough to select the 6 node with weighting factor $+1$.

Write a program to build a weighted game tree for the game of FIFTEEN and then have the computer play against a human opponent. Note that this game is really the game of tic-tac-toe if you consider the matrix given below.

4	9	2
3	5	7
8	1	6

All winning tic-tac-toe paths add up to 15.

Give some consideration to time and memory utilization efficiency of your algorithm. Many games simply cannot be completely represented by a tree. Consequently, a partial game tree is built in which the leaf nodes may not actually be the final move made in the game. In such situations, the static weighting function applied to the leaf nodes in the game tree requires a bit more insight to develop.

5. Write a program to print out the nodes of a tree level by level; that is, all level 0 nodes, followed by all level 1 nodes, followed by all level 2 nodes, and so on. As a hint in getting started, note that this program will afford an excellent opportunity to practice using a queue in addition to a tree.

If you work in Pascal . . .

The following Pascal program uses dynamic memory allocation to load a ternary tree representation of the family tree that appears in Figure 7-17. As indicated in the attached run, children are entered for each node until a delimiting asterisk is typed. The procedure TERNARYPREORDER then traverses the tree, using the variable LEVEL to control a simple graphic representation of the tree. Slight modifications in this program can dramatically alter the order in which nodes on the tree are processed. See Programming Problem (1) for some ideas in this regard.

Program listing:

```
        program testtree(input,output);

    TYPE
      string = ARRAY [1..6] OF char;
      treeptr = ^treenode;
      treenode = RECORD
                     lsibling : treeptr;
                     data : string;
                     children : treeptr;
                     rsibling : treeptr
                  END;


    VAR
      name : string;
      root : treeptr;
      level : integer;

      PROCEDURE insert(VAR name : string; VAR root : treeptr);

        {INSERTS NAME INTO TREE POINTED TO BY ROOT VIA
         INSERTION RULE OF CHAPTER 6}

      VAR
        p,q : treeptr;

    BEGIN
      p:=root;
      new(q);
      q^.lsibling:=NIL;
      q^.rsibling:=NIL;
      q^.data:=name;
      q^.children:=NIL;
      IF p=NIL
        THEN
         root:=q
      ELSE
```

```
        BEGIN
          WHILE p<>NIL DO
            BEGIN
              IF (name < p^.data) AND (p^.lsibling = NIL)
                THEN
                  BEGIN
                    p^.lsibling := q;
                    p:=NIL
                  END
                ELSE
                IF (name > p^.data) AND (p^.rsibling = NIL)
                  THEN
                    BEGIN
                      p^.rsibling := q;
                      p:=NIL
                    END
                  ELSE
                  IF name < p^.data
                    THEN
                    p:=p^.lsibling
                    ELSE
                    p:=p^.rsibling
            END
      END
  END;
{END INSERT}


PROCEDURE loadtree(VAR root : treeptr);

  {GETS FAMILY MEMBER NAMES FROM USERS AND CALLS ON INSERT TO
   BUILD TREE}

VAR
  name : string;

  BEGIN
    IF root <> NIL
      THEN
       BEGIN
         loadtree(root^.lsibling);
         write('ENTER CHILDREN FOR ',root^.data,' ---->');
          REPEAT
            readln(name);
            IF name[1] <> '*'
              THEN
              insert(name,root^.children)
          UNTIL name[1] ='*';
         loadtree(root^.children);
         loadtree(root^.rsibling)
      END
  END;
{END LOADTREE}
```

```
        PROCEDURE ternarypreorder(VAR root : treeptr);

         {TERNARY PREORDER WITH LEVEL USED FOR INDENTATION EFFECT}

        VAR
          i :integer;

         BEGIN
           IF root <> NIL
             THEN
               BEGIN
                 ternarypreorder(root^.lsibling);
                 FOR i:= 1 TO (level+1) DO write('        ');
                 writeln(root^.data);
                 level:=level+1;
                 ternarypreorder(root^.children);
                 level:=level-1;
                 ternarypreorder(root^.rsibling)
               END
         END;
         {END TERNARYPREORDER}

        BEGIN

         {INITIALIZE TREE}

         root:=NIL;
         write('FAMILY NAME-->');
         readln (name);
         insert(name,root);

         {THEN LOAD CHILDREN INTO TREE}

         loadtree(root);
         writeln('***********************************');
         level:=0;
         ternarypreorder(root)
        END.
```

Sample run:

```
FAMILY NAME-->JONES
ENTER CHILDREN FOR JONES  --->BILL
KATY
MIKE
TOM
*
ENTER CHILDREN FOR BILL   --->DAVE
MARY
*
```

```
ENTER CHILDREN FOR DAVE    ---->*
ENTER CHILDREN FOR MARY    ---->LARRY
PAUL
PENNY
*
ENTER CHILDREN FOR LARRY   ---->*
ENTER CHILDREN FOR PAUL    ---->*
ENTER CHILDREN FOR PENNY   ---->*
ENTER CHILDREN FOR KATY    ---->LEO
*
ENTER CHILDREN FOR LEO     ---->*
ENTER CHILDREN FOR MIKE    ---->BETTY
ROGER
*
ENTER CHILDREN FOR BETTY   ---->DEO
*
ENTER CHILDREN FOR DEO     ---->*
ENTER CHILDREN FOR ROGER   ---->*
ENTER CHILDREN FOR TOM     ---->*
*************************************
        JONES
              BILL
                    DAVE
                    MARY
                          LARRY
                          PAUL
                          PENNY
              KATY
                    LEO
              MIKE
                    BETTY
                          DEO
                    ROGER
              TOM
```

Multidimensional Arrays and Sparse Matrices

But as soon as we wish to grasp this being, it slips
between our fingers, and we find ourselves faced with a
pattern of duality, with a game of reflections.

JEAN-PAUL SARTRE (1905–1980)

8-1 Introductory Considerations

In preceding chapters, we have frequently used singly dimensioned arrays. In fact, they have been used as the data structure from which other more sophisticated data structures such as linked lists, stacks, queues, and trees have been built. However, in Chapter 9, which is about graphs and networks, it will become necessary to consider arrays of dimension higher than one. Of particular importance will be the **two-dimensional array,** or **matrix,** in which the position of a data element must be specified by giving 2 coordinates, typically called **row** and **column coordinates.** For example in PSEUDO, the declaration

```
VAR GRID(6,5) : INTEGER
```

specifies the data structure with a sample assignment of values pictured in Figure 8-1.
When, in procedural statements, we specify the entry

```
GRID(5,4)
```

we are in fact referring to the entry in the 5th row and 4th column of GRID (as marked by an asterisk in Figure 8-1).

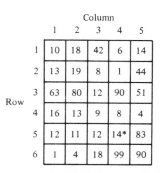

Figure 8-1   Structure established by <u>VAR</u> GRID(6,5) : INTEGER.

8-2 Implementing a Multidimensional Array

Within main memory, storage locations are not arranged in the gridlike pattern of Figure 8-1. Instead, they are arranged in **linear sequence** beginning with location 1,2,3, . . . , and so on. Because of this, there must be manipulations "behind the scenes" when a program requests the entry in the 5th row and 4th column of a two-dimensional array. Essentially, the coordinates of 5th row and 4th column must be transformed into an address in this linear sequence of memory locations. The nature of the transformation is dependent upon how the designers of the compiler have chosen to arrange the programmer's mental image of rows and columns within the linear sequence of memory locations. Suppose that we have chosen to store the 30 entries in the two-dimensional array GRID as indicated in Figure 8-2. According to this arrangement, the 1st row would take up the first 5 locations in the list allocated for the array, the 2nd row the 2nd 5 locations, and so on. The entry in the 5th row and 4th column would in fact be located in the 24th position within the list. In general, the *I*th row and *J*th column must be transformed into the

        (5 * (I - 1) + J)th

position in the list. In even more general terms, if *NCOL* is the number of columns in the array, then the entry in the *I*th row and *J*th column is given as the

        (NCOL * (I - 1) + J)th

entry in the linear list corresponding to the two-dimensional array. Most high-level computer languages implement two- (and higher-) dimensional arrays in such a **row major** fashion, and do so in a way that is largely transparent to the applications programmer.

10	18	42	6	14	13	19	8	1	44	63	80	12	90	51	16	13	9	8	4	12	11	12	14*	83	1	4	18	99	90
1	2	3	4	5	6	7	8	9	10	11	12	13	14	15	16	17	18	19	20	21	22	23	24	25	26	27	28	29	30

Figure 8-2   Linear storage of data from Figure 8-1.

However, all programmers should be aware that multidimensional arrays are inherently less efficient than one-dimensional arrays because of the computations required by the transformation from row-and-column to linear address each time an entry of the array is accessed. Such a transformation is often called a **mapping function.**

Those readers who have programmed in FORTRAN will recall that, when you initialize a two-dimensional array with a DATA statement, you must list the entries for the array by column—that is, first column followed by second, then third, and so on. This is because FORTRAN is one of the few high-level languages that chooses to store a multidimensional array in **column major** order, as indicated in Figure 8-3.

To access the entry in the *I*th row and *J*th column of a two-dimensional array stored in column major order, the transformation

```
NROW * (J-1) + I
```

is required, where *N*ROW represents the number of rows in the array. The fact that this transformation requires the number of rows but not the number of columns also explains why many FORTRAN compilers insist that a subroutine be informed of the number of rows, but not the number of columns, in an array passed down from a calling program.

Our discussion of sparse matrices in the next section will necessitate our understanding how compilers implement multidimensional arrays in general and two-dimensional arrays in particular. *We will assume for the remainder of this chapter that all two-dimensional arrays are implemented in row major order.*

When a source program makes reference to a simple variable—for example, COUNT— that variable name must be looked up (by methods to be described in Chapter 11) in a **symbol table** created by the compiler (Figure 8-4). Once the variable name COUNT is found in the symbol table, its memory address is known. This strategy works fine if COUNT is merely an ordinary variable; that is, it has one memory location. However, suppose the reference being made is to the two-dimensional array entry GRID(3,2). Looking up GRID in the symbol table of Figure 8-4 yields a memory address for it.

But the memory address from the symbol table in Figure 8-4 does not *directly* lead us to where the data in GRID are stored. Rather it leads us to what is commonly called a **dope vector** for the array. This dope vector contains information that will help us to interpret the array's actual data item once it is located. In particular, this dope vector information must include:

1. The **rank** of the array; that is, the number of dimensions of the array.

2. The number of entries in the 1st dimension, 2nd dimension, 3rd dimension, and so on. For a two-dimensional array, this amounts to the number of rows and columns.

3. The total number of entries in the array.

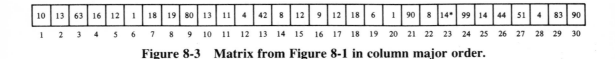

10	13	63	16	12	1	18	19	80	13	11	4	42	8	12	9	12	18	6	1	90	8	14*	99	14	44	51	4	83	90
1	2	3	4	5	6	7	8	9	10	11	12	13	14	15	16	17	18	19	20	21	22	23	24	25	26	27	28	29	30

Figure 8-3   Matrix from Figure 8-1 in column major order.

Identifier	Associated Memory Address
⋮	
COUNT	017646
⋮	
GRID	017422
⋮	

Figure 8-4 Symbol table for identifiers in a program.

4. The beginning address of the linear sequence of memory locations actually containing the array's data. A given data item's offset from this beginning address essentially determines its coordinate position in the multidimensional structure. (This last informational item is unnecessary if the array's data are always stored immediately after the dope vector.)

For example, if the data in the two-dimensional array GRID described earlier in this section actually begins at octal location 17442, then the dope vector corresponding to GRID would appear as shown in Figure 8-5. Note in particular that the dope vector contains information crucial to performing the row-and-column to linear address transformation that enables the applications programmer to think in terms of row and column although the computer is working in a linear sequence.

We remark here that everything we have said about two-dimensional arrays in particular can quite easily be generalized to arrays of dimension greater than 2. For instance, the declaration

```
VAR MGRIDS(2,3,4) :  INTEGER
```

generates an image of two 3 row by 4 column tables as illustrated for the sample assignment of values pictured in Figure 8-6.

RANK	2
NROW	6
NCOL	5
TOTENTRIES	30
BEG-ADD	Address of initial data location

Figure 8-5 Dope vector for the two-dimensional array GRID.

MGRIDS(2,2,3) would refer to the value 18 stored in the 2nd row and 3rd column of the 2nd occurrence in Figure 8-6. To store this data item in a linear sequence of memory locations would necessitate adopting one of 2 reasonable conventions:

1. Grouping together all the data associated with a given value of the leftmost subscript, the *left subscript major form,* or

2. Grouping together all the data associated with a given value of the rightmost subscript, the *right subscript major form.*

For example, the left subscript major form of the data in Figure 8-6 would appear in a linear list as pictured in Figure 8-7. As exercises at the end of the chapter, you will encounter the problems of translating a given three-dimensional coordinate to the appropriate position in the linear list and representing this same data in right subscript major form.

It should be clear that the total number of entries in a multidimensional array could quite easily exceed main memory limitations. For example, an array to store the coefficients for a 50 × 50 system of equations requires 2500 memory locations. In the next chapter we shall see that a two-dimensional array necessary to contain data about a transportation network involving 200 cities would require 40,000 memory locations. Yet, in actual applications, it quite often turns out that a very high percentage of these memory locations are filled with zeros. Such an array with a low percentage of non-zero entries is said to be *sparse,* and the data structure problem of a sparse array is to develop techniques that accurately represent the data it contains without wasting the memory required to store an exceedingly large number of zeros. In the remaining 2 sections of this chapter, we shall discuss 2 techniques for handling the sparse matrix problem—the generalized dope vector method and the linked list method.

8-3 Sparse Matrices and Generalized Dope Vector Implementation

Our previous discussion about dope vectors has focused upon what the compiler does beneath the surface for the applications programmer. Now, however, the sparse matrix problem will force us to look at a variation on dope vectors in which the data structure

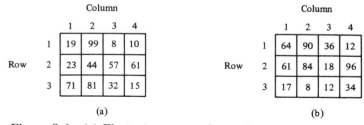

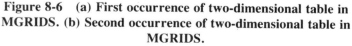

Figure 8-6   (a) First occurrence of two-dimensional table in MGRIDS. (b) Second occurrence of two-dimensional table in MGRIDS.

In the world of applications . . .

Sparse matrices have diversified uses in almost all areas of the natural sciences. One such application is in the equilibrium conditions across an electrical network. Kirchhoff's Laws of Electrical Equilibrium state:

1. The sum of incoming currents at each node is equal to the sum of the outgoing currents.

2. Around every closed loop, the sum of voltage is 0.

Now consider the electrical network shown below.

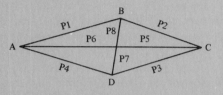

	P1	P2	P3	P4	P5	P6	P7	P8
A	-1	0	0	-1	0	1	0	0
B	1	-1	0	0	0	0	0	-1
C	0	1	-1	0	-1	0	0	0
D	0	0	1	1	0	0	1	0

The rows in the matrix represent nodes. The columns indicate directed electrical paths. − 1 is used to indicate a node where a path ends, 1 to indicate a node where a path begins, and 0 to indicate that the particular path does not meet the corresponding node. If we look at Node A, we notice that P1 and P4 end at A, whereas P6 starts at A. According to Kirchhoff's first law, the sum of incoming currents along P1 and P2 must equal the outgoing current along P6. Similarly, the second law is also completely manifested by the sparse matrix.

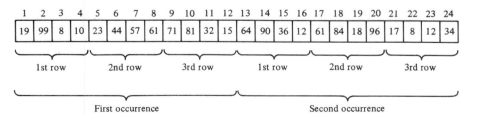

Figure 8-7 Left subscript major form for the data of Figure 8-6.

we are using is not built into the language. Hence, it must be maintained explicitly by the programmer using the tools available in the chosen language.

The **generalized dope vector method** for implementing sparse matrices is particularly effective for **band** matrices; that is, matrices in which the non-zero entries tend to cluster around the middle of each row. For square matrices, this is equivalent to saying that the non-zero values tend to cluster around the diagonal. Fortunately, in many applications, this is precisely what happens, thereby making the generalized dope vector method highly usable in the "real world." For such matrices, we are able to specify for each row the column numbers of the first and last non-zero entries. We will add this information to a dope vector for such a band matrix, enabling us actually to store in memory only those entries between the first non-zero entry and the last non-zero entry in each row. For example, suppose that we have a 5 × 14 band matrix called SPARSE as pictured in Figure 8-8. Then the linear sequence of data corresponding to the nonzero bands in this matrix could be stored as indicated in Figure 8-9. Notice that those zero values embedded within the band must be stored. Consequently, as the band of the matrix becomes wider, this method tends to lose its effectiveness.

To compensate for the leading and trailing zeros that are not stored, we must add some information to the dope vector for the array SPARSE. Such a generalized dope vector for the array pictured in Figure 8-8 is given in Figure 8-10. In this figure, although FIRSTNONZERO(I) and LASTNONZERO(I) are pictured as neighboring locations, they would in practice be the Ith locations in two parallel arrays, FIRSTNONZERO and LASTNONZERO.

Now the value for the Jth entry in the Ith row of SPARSE is obtained merely by:

1. Checking to see if J is less than FIRSTNONZERO(I) or greater than LASTNONZERO(I). If it is, then the value of SPARSE(I,J) is zero.

2. Otherwise SPARSE(I,J) is the Nth entry in the sequential list of data stored for the array, where N is calculated:

```
N := (LASTNONZERO(K) - LASTNONZERO(K) + 1) + (J - FIRSTNONZERO(I) + 1)
```

To avoid frequently recomputing the summation term in the expression above each time an array entry is accessed, we recommend storing the sum corresponding to the Ith row as part of the dope vector for the array. Following this convention, the dope vector for the sample matrix SPARSE with which we have been working would appear as shown in Figure 8-11 on page 186. Hence the computation of N in the situation described earlier becomes:

```
N := SUM(I) + (J - FIRSTNONZERO(I) + 1)
```

	1	2	3	4	5	6	7	8	9	10	11	12	13	14
1	0	83	19	40	0	0	0	0	0	0	0	0	0	0
2	0	0	0	91	0	42	12	0	0	0	0	0	0	0
3	0	0	0	0	0	18	4	0	0	0	0	0	0	0
4	0	0	0	0	0	0	0	0	71	64	0	13	0	0
5	0	0	0	0	0	0	0	0	0	0	0	0	21	40

Figure 8-8 Example of band matrix.

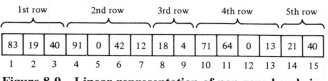

Figure 8-9 Linear representation of non-zero bands in Figure 8-8.

The NROW additional storage locations required to store these sums represent a small price to pay in order to avoid continually recomputing a sum of potentially many terms each time an array entry is accessed. We leave for the Exercises at the end of the chapter the question of whether the data stored in LASTNONZERO are now even necessary at all.

The development of procedures to assign data to and retrieve data from a specified location in a sparse matrix presents an excellent illustration of the advantages of modular programming. Such procedures can be written in a fashion that makes them virtually transparent to their calling program; the calling program sees little difference between working with an actual two-dimensional array and a generalized dope vector representation of such an array. In particular, the retrieval of values from the Ith row and Jth column of SPARSE would require no adjustment in the calling program other than the realization that the PSEUDO statement:

```
V := SPARSE(I,J)
```

RANK	2
NROW	5
NCOL	14
TOTENTRIES	70
BEG–ADD	
FIRSTNONZERO(1)	2
LASTNONZERO(1)	4
FIRSTNONZERO(2)	4
LASTNONZERO(2)	7
FIRSTNONZERO(3)	6
LASTNONZERO(3)	7
FIRSTNONZERO(4)	9
LASTNONZERO(4)	12
FIRSTNONZERO(5)	13
LASTNONZERO(5)	14

This entry dependent upon the memory allocation for the linear list of Figure 8-9

Figure 8-10 Generalized dope vector for matrix of Figure 8-8.

is now a call to a function procedure instead of a direct access to an entry in an actual two-dimensional array. The function procedure SPARSE follows:

```
PROCEDURE: FUNCTION SPARSE(I,J)
GLOBAL VAR  RANK, NROW, NCOL, TOTENTRIES : INTEGER
GLOBAL VAR LIST(-), FIRSTNONZERO(-), LASTNONZERO(-), SUM(-) -->
                                                : INTEGER

VAR  I,J,N : INTEGER

    (* LIST represents the global linear sequence of storage *)
    (* locations where the sparse array's non-zero bands *)
    (* are stored. *)

    (* Dope vector entries are assumed global and named *)
    (* as indicated in Figure 8-11. *)

    (* Hyphens used to indicate "appropriate" array *)
    (* dimensioning *)

IF J < FIRSTNONZERO(I) OR J > LASTNONZERO(I) THEN
    [ SPARSE := 0 ]
ELSE
    [ N := SUM(I) + (J - FIRSTNONZERO(I) + 1) ]
    [ SPARSE := LIST(N)                       ]
ENDIF
RETURN
END SPARSE
```

The assignment of values to the *I*th row and *J*th column of SPARSE is a situation for which the generalized dope vector procedure cannot be written in a completely transparent manner. This is because a function cannot appear on the left of the := operator in an assignment statement. Hence the assignment statement:

```
SPARSE(I,J) := V
```

in a calling program must be changed to:

```
CALL PUT(V,I,J)
```

where the procedure PUT is as follows:

```
PROCEDURE: PUT (I,J,V)

    (* Procedure to assign value V at the Ith row & Jth *)
    (* column of the matrix SPARSE, as implemented by the *)
    (* generalized dope vector technique. *)

GLOBAL VAR  RANK, NROW, NCOL, TOTENTRIES : INTEGER
GLOBAL VAR LIST(-), FIRSTNONZERO(-), LASTNONZERO(-), SUM(-) -->
                                                : INTEGER

VAR  I,J,V,N : INTEGER

    (* LIST represents the linear sequence of storage *)
    (* locations where the sparse array's non-zero bands *)
    (* are stored. *)
```

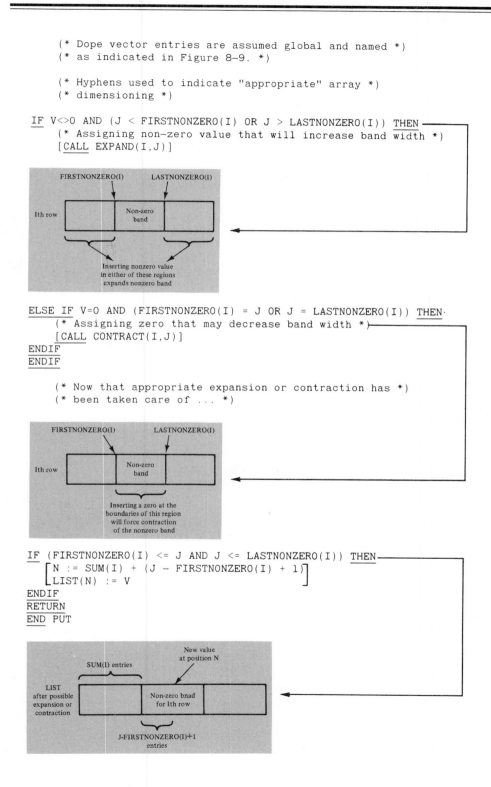

```
(* Dope vector entries are assumed global and named *)
(* as indicated in Figure 8-9. *)

(* Hyphens used to indicate "appropriate" array *)
(* dimensioning *)

IF V<>0 AND (J < FIRSTNONZERO(I) OR J > LASTNONZERO(I)) THEN
    (* Assigning non-zero value that will increase band width *)
    [CALL EXPAND(I,J)]
```

FIRSTNONZERO(I) LASTNONZERO(I)

Ith row   Non-zero band

Inserting nonzero value
in either of these regions
expands nonzero band

```
ELSE IF V=0 AND (FIRSTNONZERO(I) = J OR J = LASTNONZERO(I)) THEN
    (* Assigning zero that may decrease band width *)
    [CALL CONTRACT(I,J)]
ENDIF
ENDIF

    (* Now that appropriate expansion or contraction has *)
    (* been taken care of ... *)
```

FIRSTNONZERO(I) LASTNONZERO(I)

Ith row   Non-zero band

Inserting a zero at the
boundaries of this region
will force contraction
of the nonzero band

```
IF (FIRSTNONZERO(I) <= J AND J <= LASTNONZERO(I)) THEN
    [N := SUM(I) + (J - FIRSTNONZERO(I) + 1)]
    [LIST(N) := V]
ENDIF
RETURN
END PUT
```

New value
at position N

SUM(I) entries

LIST
after possible
expansion or
contraction

Non-zero bnad
for Ith row

J-FIRSTNONZERO(I)+1
entries

RANK	2
NROW	5
NCOL	14
TOTENTRIES	70
BEG–ADD	
SUM(1)	0
FIRSTNONZERO(1)	2
LASTNONZERO(1)	4
SUM(2)	3
FIRSTNONZERO(2)	4
LASTNONZERO(2)	7
SUM(3)	7
FIRSTNONZERO(3)	6
LASTNONZERO(3)	7
SUM(4)	9
FIRSTNONZERO(4)	9
LASTNONZERO(4)	12
SUM(5)	13
FIRSTNONZERO(5)	13
LASTNONZERO(5)	14

This entry is dependent upon the memory allocation for the linear list of Figure 8-9

Figure 8-11 Dope vector augmented with sums to avoid recalculation.

The call to EXPAND is intended to update the values stored in SUM, FIRSTNON-ZERO, and LASTNONZERO when the insertion of a non-zero entry will increase the size of the band in the *I*th row. The procedure EXPAND will also have to insert an appropriate sequence of zeros in LIST, shifting a designated portion of LIST to the right to do so.

The call to CONTRACT in PUT will appropriately check whether the insertion of a zero within the present non-zero band necessitates a contraction of that band. If this is the case, SUM, FIRSTNONZERO, and LASTNONZERO will be appropriately updated and a corresponding sequence of entries removed from LIST. Notice that we hope expansions or contractions of LIST within the procedures EXPAND and CONTRACT do not occur too often because the processing involved will significantly decrease the run time efficiency of the algorithm. You will write these two procedures as exercises at the end of the chapter.

Before beginning our discussion of the linked list method of implementing a sparse matrix, we should mention the notion of the **efficiency ratio** of the generalized dope vector method. This ratio is defined by the fraction:

$$\frac{\text{Number of storage locations used by generalized dope vector method}}{\text{Number of storage locations used by standard row major form}}$$

Because the generalized dope vector method requires 3 additional dope vector entries— SUM(*I*), FIRSTNONZERO(*I*), and LASTNONZERO(*I*)—for each row, it is clear that we achieve a desirable efficiency ratio of less than 1 only when the average band width for all rows in the array is 4 or more less than the number of columns in the matrix. For instance, in the sparse band matrix of Figure 8-8, the efficiency ratio would be:

$$\frac{\begin{array}{c}\text{15 memory locations to store the 5 non-zero bands}\\+\\\text{15 ''overhead'' locations for SUM, FIRSTNONZERO, LASTNONZERO}\end{array}}{\text{70 locations necessary for standard row major form}}$$

Here, because the average band width of 3 is 11 less than the number of columns in the matrix, a desirable efficiency ratio of 3/7 is achieved.

8-4 Linked List Implementation of a Sparse Matrix

The linked list implementation of a sparse matrix is completely dynamic and, instead of a dope vector, requires an array of pointers, each leading to a linked list storing the non-zero data in a given row of the sparse matrix. Each node in one of these linked lists needs to contain not only an entry from the matrix but also an indication of which column within that particular row is occupied by the data in the node. We further stipulate that, for efficiency in processing, each linked list be arranged in ascending order of column numbers within that row. Given these conventions, the 5 × 14 matrix SPARSE of Figure 8-8 would be represented as shown in Figure 8-12 on page 190.

Using the procedures GETNODE, INSERTNODE, and DELETENODE already developed in Chapter 2, a function SPARSE and a procedure PUT analogous to those for the generalized dope vector method in Section 8-2 are as follows:

```
PROCEDURE: FUNCTION SPARSE(I,J)
GLOBAL VAR HEAD(-), DATA(-), COL(-), NEXTCOL(-) : INTEGER
VAR I,J,P  :  INTEGER

     (* The arrays HEAD, DATA, COL, NEXTCOL of Figure 8-12 *)
     (* are assumed to be global parameters. *)

P := HEAD(I)

     (* We will assume, in PSEUDO, that the conditional test *)
     (*          P <> NULL AND COL(P) < J                    *)
     (* will unambiguously return FALSE when P = NULL. This *)
     (* may not be the case in an actual language implementation. *)
     (* See Exercise 12. *)

WHILE P <> NULL AND COL(P) < J
     [P := NEXTCOL(P)]
ENDWHILE
```

```
IF P=NULL THEN
     [ SPARSE := 0 ]
ELSE IF COL(P) > J THEN
     [ SPARSE := 0 ]
ELSE
     [ SPARSE := DATA(P) ]
ENDIF
ENDIF

RETURN
END SPARSE
```

Example of P = NULL case, suppose J = 8

Example of COL(P) > J case, suppose J = 6

WHILE loop left P pointing at this node

Example of ELSE case, J = 5

WHILE loop left P pointing at this node, 12 to be returned

```
PROCEDURE:  PUT(I,J,V)
GLOBAL VAR HEAD(-), DATA(-), COL(-), NEXTCOL(-) : INTEGER
VAR  I,J,V,P,PREV,Q  :  INTEGER

    (* The arrays HEAD, DATA, COL, NEXTCOL of Figure 8-12 *)
    (* are assumed to be global parameters, appropriately *)
    (* dimensioned. *)

P := HEAD(I)

    (* We will assume, in PSEUDO, that the conditional test *)
    (*        P <> NULL AND COL(P) < J                      *)
    (* will unambiguously return FALSE when P = NULL. This *)
    (* may not be the case in an actual language implementation. *)
    (* See Exercise 12. *)

WHILE P <> NULL AND COL(P) <J
    [PREV := P
     P := NEXTCOL(P)]
ENDWHILE
```

```
IF COL(P) = J AND V=0 THEN
    (* Assigning zero where non-zero entry had been. *)
    (* Call procedure to delete appropriate node from *)
    (* the Ith linked list. *)
    [ CALL DELETENODE(I,PREV,Q) ]
```

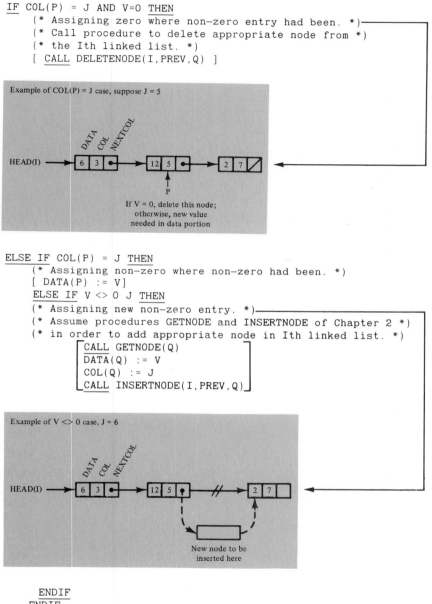

Example of COL(P) = J case, suppose J = 5

HEAD(I)

DATA COL NEXTCOL

6 | 3 | •   →   12 | 5 | •   →   2 | 7 | /

P

If V = 0, delete this node;
otherwise, new value
needed in data portion

```
ELSE IF COL(P) = J THEN
    (* Assigning non-zero where non-zero had been. *)
    [ DATA(P) := V]
    ELSE IF V <> 0 J THEN
    (* Assigning new non-zero entry. *)
    (* Assume procedures GETNODE and INSERTNODE of Chapter 2 *)
    (* in order to add appropriate node in Ith linked list. *)
        ⎡ CALL GETNODE(Q)
        ⎢ DATA(Q) := V
        ⎢ COL(Q) := J
        ⎣ CALL INSERTNODE(I,PREV,Q)⎦
```

Example of V <> 0 case, J = 6

HEAD(I)

DATA COL NEXTCOL

6 | 3 | •   →   12 | 5 | •   //   →   2 | 7 |

New node to be
inserted here

```
        ENDIF
      ENDIF
ENDIF

(* Assigning zero where zero had been requires no action *)

RETURN
END PUT
```

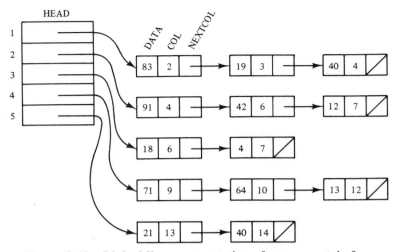

Figure 8-12   Linked list representation of sparse matrix from Figure 8-8.

Assuming that the data in a sparse matrix is of INTEGER type, the efficiency ratio for this linked list implementation of a sparse matrix drops below 1 only when the number of non-zero locations in the matrix is less than:

$$NROW * (NCOL - 1) / 3$$

To see this, note that each non-zero matrix entry requires 3 integers to represent it in the linked list implementation. Moreover, each row requires an integer head pointer. Thus, the total number of integers required to store N non-zero entries via the linked list method is:

$$NROW + N*3$$

Because we want to force the efficiency ratio:

$$\frac{NROW + N*3}{NROW * NCOL}$$

to be less than 1, we conclude that:

$$NROW + N*3 < NROW * NCOL$$
$$N*3 < NROW*NCOL - NROW$$
$$N < NROW*(NCOL - 1)/3$$

We close this chapter with a discussion of the relative merits of the linked list method compared to the generalized dope vector method.

1. It has been our experience that the linked list method is conceptually easier. Given already existing routines to insert in and delete from a linked list, it requires less detailed code.

2. Given suitable GETNODE and RETURNNODE procedures, the linked list method is completely dynamic. All insertions and deletions are processed by altering pointers instead of moving data. The generalized dope vector method, on the other hand, requires an initial static storage allocation for the maximum band width that is anticipated. Also, the dope vector method may require considerable data movement when the band width of a given row is altered.

3. The generalized dope vector method tends to save more storage when band matrices are involved. In particular, it requires a less sparse matrix to drop its efficiency ratio below 1.

4. The generalized dope vector method directly accesses a matrix entry via a computation instead of requiring the sequential search performed by the linked list method. This means that the dope vector method will access entries faster than the linked list method.

As with all data structure techniques, it is clear that the choice of which method to use is not black and white, but instead depends upon the particular application.

SUMMARY

A matrix is an important mathematical tool that will be used extensively in Chapter 9, which is about graphs and networks. As a data structure, a matrix must be implemented with space economy in mind. Because many matrices used in practice are large sparse matrices, they cannot be implemented simply as two-dimensional arrays. The 2 techniques given in this chapter are space-saving means of implementing such sparse matrices. A 3rd technique, called hashing subscripts, is explained in the programming exercises of Chapter 11.

KEY TERMS

Multidimensional array	Column major	Sparse matrix
Matrix	Dope vector	Generalized dope vector
Row major	Rank	method
Mapping function	Left subscript major	Band matrices
	Right subscript major	Linked list method

EXERCISES

1. What do the terms row major and column major mean? Left subscript major? Right subscript major?

2. What is a dope vector? A generalized dope vector?

3. What is sparse about a sparse matrix?

4. Is a two-dimensional $M \times M$ array more or less efficient than a one-dimensional array of extent $M \times M$?

5. Write the data elements of the three-dimensional array pictured in Figure 8-6 in a linear list arranged in right subscript major form.

6. Write the procedures EXPAND and CONTRACT as called in the procedure PUT for the generalized dope vector implementation of a sparse matrix.

7. Develop data structures and appropriate procedures to adapt the generalized dope vector method to a sparse three-dimensional array.

8. The linked list implementation of a sparse matrix as presented in 8-4 will allow access of an array entry only by first accessing the linked list corresponding to the row of the entry and then proceeding along that row until the appropriate column is found. For applications that frequently access the data in a sparse matrix *by columns,* this would be highly inefficient. Devise data structures and develop appropriate procedures that would allow either row or column access to entries of the matrix.

9. Specifically describe how your solution to Exercise (8) would affect the efficiency ratio of the sparse matrix representation.

10. Generalize the linked list method for sparse matrices so that it could be used for a sparse three-dimensional array.

11. Many languages (for example, Pascal) allow subscripts for an arbitrary range of ordinal values, not necessarily always starting at 1. Specify how this would affect the techniques developed in this chapter to translate multidimensional array coordinates into linear list positions.

12. A comment in PROCEDURE PUT for the linked list implementation of a sparse matrix hints that, when coded in a high-level programming language, the conditional test

$$P <> \text{NULL AND COL(P)} < J$$

may result in a run time error instead of unambiguously returning FALSE when P is NULL. What assumption is made about the way ANDs are evaluated in PSEUDO? If the language you use does not follow this same convention in evaluating ANDs, explain how the above test can be coded so that it will not result in a run time error.

13. Is the LASTNONZERO data stored in the generalized dope vector still necessary once the data in SUM have been added to the vector? Justify your answer.

14. What would the mapping function be for a three-dimensional array stored in left subscript major form? Right subscript major form?

PROGRAMMING PROBLEMS

1. Due to factors such as type of airplane, amount of pilot experience, and pilot geographic location, each of the pilots employed by the Wing and a Prayer Airline Company qualifies to fly on only a relatively small percentage of flights offered by this growing company. The information concerning for which flights a given pilot qualifies could be stored as a large Boolean array

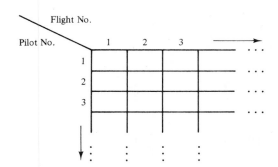

Help Wing and a Prayer by developing a program that will accept as input a flight or pilot number and then print all pilots or flights, respectively, that correspond to the input. Because a given pilot qualifies for only a small percentage of flights, a sparse matrix technique should be used to store the data.

2. *The Game of Life:* Invented by mathematician John H. Conway (*Scientific American,* October 1970, p. 120), this game models the growth and changes in a complex collection of living organisms. The model can be interpreted as applying to a collection of microorganisms, an ecologically closed system of animals or plants, or an urban development.

Start with a $N \times N$ checkerboard on which "counters" are to be placed. Each location has 8 neighbors. The counters are born, survive, or die during a "generation" according to the following rules:

- *Survival:* Counters with 2 or 3 neighboring counters survive to the next generation.

- *Death:* Counters with 4 or more neighbors die from overcrowding and are removed for the next generation. Counters with 0 or 1 neighbors die from isolation and are removed for the next generation.

- *Birth:* Each empty location that has exactly 3 counters in the 8 neighboring locations is a birth location. A counter is placed in the location for the next generation.

For example, on a 6 × 6 space the pattern on the left would look like the one on the right in the next generation:

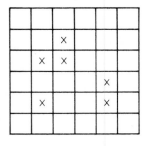

Certain patterns are stable:

Other patterns repeat a sequence:

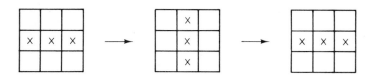

Because two $N \times N$ matrices are required to implement *The Game of Life*, it is clear that memory limitations could easily become a problem for a large N.

Choosing one of the sparse matrix methods described in this chapter, design a program in a high-level language to implement *The Game of Life*.

After initializing the first generation, print it out. Then calculate the next generation in another array and print this too. Repeat for a specified number of generations. Your output should be an "X" for live cells and a blank otherwise.

3. Develop a procedure that will translate (X, Y) Cartesian coordinates into the row and column subscripts of a two-dimensional array. Using this and one of the two sparse matrix strategies discussed in this chapter, implement in a high-level language a graphics program that will plot the graph of a specified equation by plotting points on the graph of the equation in a suitably dimensioned sparse matrix.

4. If you are familiar with linear algebra, implement the Gaussian elimination procedure to solve an $N \times N$ system of equations using one of the sparse matrix techniques discussed in this chapter.

5. For each of the two sparse matrix representations developed in this chapter, devise a system to perform typical matrix operations such as matrix addition, matrix multiplication, matrix inversion, and evaluation of determinants.

If you work in Pascal . . .

The following function is the Pascal equivalent of the PSEUDO function SPARSE developed in Section 8-3. The function assumes the following global declarations:

```
CONST   NUMBERROWS = 100;

TYPE    SPARSEPOINTER = ^SPARSENODE;
        SPARSENODE = RECORD
                          DATA : INTEGER;
                          COL : INTEGER;
                          NEXTCOL : SPARSEPOINTER
                     END;

VAR     HEAD : ARRAY [1..NUMBERROWS] OF SPARSEPOINTER;
```

If you use Pascal, we encourage you to code the Pascal version of the corresponding procedure PUT as an exercise.

```
FUNCTION SPARSE(I,J:INTEGER) : INTEGER;

  (* RETURN VALUE OF (I,J)TH POSITION IN SPARSE MATRIX *)

VAR     P : SPARSEPOINTER;
        NOEXIT : BOOLEAN;

BEGIN
 P:=HEAD[I];
 NOEXIT:=TRUE;
 WHILE  (P <> NIL) AND NOEXIT DO
  IF P^.COL < J THEN
    P^ := P^.NEXTCOL
  ELSE
    NOEXIT := FALSE;
 IF (P = NIL) OR (P^.COL > J) THEN
  SPARSE := 0
 ELSE
  SPARSE := P^.DATA
END;
```

9

Graphs and Networks

*I'd rather wake up in the middle of nowhere than in any
city on earth.*

STEVE McQUEEN

9-1 Introductory Considerations

In Chapters 6 and 7, trees were introduced as structures that could be used to describe a
certain type of relationship between data items. The tree structure is a special kind of
graph in which the relationship between parent and child is hierarchical. A general graph,
on the other hand, is a structure that represents a less restrictive relationship between data
items. A common example of a graph is a collection of cities and the roads between them;
2 cities are related if there is a route between them. Their relationship is not hierarchical
because traffic on the routes between cities can flow in either direction. Graphs are frequently applied in diverse areas such as artificial intelligence, cybernetics, chemical structures of crystals, transportation networks, electrical circuitry, and the analysis of programming languages. In this chapter, we shall examine graphs in general and then look
at some specific applications.

A **graph** is formally defined as a set of objects called nodes and edges. In this context,
a **node** is a data element of the graph; an **edge** is a path between 2 nodes. In an **undirected
graph** (Figure 9-1), an edge between 2 nodes is not directionally oriented. Thus, in an
undirected graph, if AG (A to G) is an edge, so is GA.

In a **directed graph** or **digraph,** the edges between nodes are directionally oriented.
In the directed graph of Figure 9-2, AB is an edge but BA is not an edge. Thus, there are
directed edges from A to B, B to C, C to D, and D to E. A directed edge is also called
an **arc.** The digraph of Figure 9-2 can be looked upon as expressing the alphabetical order
relationship between the letters in the nodes. We shall denote an arc from node x to node
y by $x \rightarrow y$.

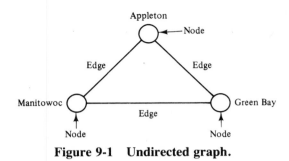

Figure 9-1 Undirected graph.

In order to use graphs effectively, we need to know which nodes are directly connected by an edge, and also which nodes are indirectly connected by a set of edges. For example, in Figure 9-2, A is directly connected to B, and B is indirectly connected to E via the arcs B → C, C → D, and D → E. In a digraph, therefore, we say that there is a **directed path connection** from node I to node J if and only if there is a sequence of nodes $I = I_1$, $I_2, \ldots, I_n = J$ such that I_{i-1} is connected to I_i via an arc. In Figure 9-2, there is no path from node E to node A, although there is a path from node A to E. Any graph is **connected** provided that there exists a path (of any kind) between any 2 nodes. A digraph is said to be **strongly connected** if, for any two nodes I and J, there is a directed path from I to J. A digraph is said to be **weakly connected** if, for any two nodes I and J, there is a directed path from I to J or J to I. The digraph in Figure 9-2 is weakly connected; however, it is not strongly connected because, for the nodes C and E, there is a directed path from C to E but none from E to C. The digraph shown in Figure 9-3 is strongly connected. Clearly, any digraph that is strongly connected is also weakly connected.

The **outdegree** of a node in a digraph is the number of arcs *exiting* from the node; the **indegree** of a node is the number of arcs *entering* the node. In Figure 9-3, the indegree of NEW YORK is 2 and its outdegree is 1. The indegree and outdegree of CHICAGO are 1 and 2, respectively. The indegree and outdegree of a node in a digraph indicate its relative importance in data processing of that graph. A node whose outdegree is 0 acts primarily as a depository of information and hence is called a **sink node.** A node whose indegree is 0 is called a **source node.** The fundamental input to output operation, which is common to all data processing activity and is shown in Figure 9-4, highlights this concept.

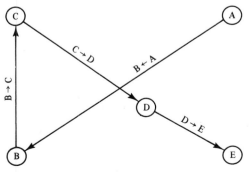

Figure 9-2 Directed graph.

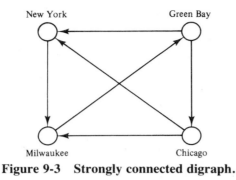

Figure 9-3 Strongly connected digraph.

A **cycle** in a directed graph is a directed path of length at least 1 that originates and terminates at the same node. In Figure 9-3:

New York → Milwaukee → Green Bay → New York is a cycle of length 3.

These concepts also hold for an undirected graph wherever they apply. Thus, a path between 2 nodes is a sequence of edges, directly or indirectly connecting the 2 nodes. There is a path between any 2 nodes in Figure 9-1. Because indegree and outdegree cannot apply to a node in an undirected graph, the **degree** of a node is defined as the number of edges connected directly to the node. In Figure 9-1, the degree of each node is 2.

9-2 Implementation of Graphs—The Adjacency Matrix

The physical structure of a graph (undirected or directed) can be conveniently represented by an **adjacency matrix** or **incidence matrix.** A graph containing *n* nodes can be represented by a matrix containing *n* rows and *n* columns. The matrix is formed by placing a 1 in the *i*th row and *j*th column (the (i,j)th entry) of the matrix if there is an edge between node *i* and node *j* of the graph. Consider the graph in Figure 9-5. Its adjacency matrix, as given in Figure 9-6, clearly shows whether or not there is an edge between any 2 nodes. For example, the presence of 1 in the 4th row of the 3rd column denotes an edge between nodes L and C; the 0 in the 1st row of the 5th column, by the same token, signifies the absence of an edge between the nodes A and R.

We stress that matrices are only a convenient way of thinking about the memory representation of a graph. You will *not* necessarily use a two-dimensional array to store a graph in memory. Clearly a graph with a substantial number of nodes could consume an

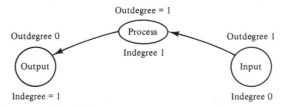

Figure 9-4 Indegrees and outdegrees of nodes.

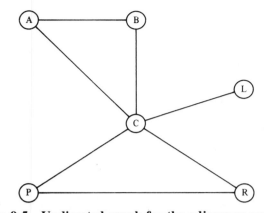

Figure 9-5   Undirected graph for the adjacency matrix in Figure 9-6.

inordinately large amount of memory if you used a two-dimensional array to implement it. Fortunately, most graphs are sparse matrices. Consequently, any of the space-saving techniques discussed in Chapter 8 can be used to implement the adjacency matrix for a graph. For the rest of this chapter, we will refer to the adjacency matrix M for a graph and use the notation:

$$M(I,J) <> 0 \quad \text{or} \quad M(I,J) = 0$$

to refer to the presence or absence, respectively, of an edge between nodes I and J in the graph. $M(I,J)$ could refer to a two-dimensional array or to a function call that retrieves a value from some sparse matrix representation. In this chapter, we will not be concerned with the details of the actual representation; instead, we will concentrate on the algorithms that manipulate a graph, regardless of its representation.

For an undirected graph such as that appearing in Figure 9-5, the ith row and ith column of the adjacency matrix must be identical. That is, it must be a **symmetric matrix.** The adjacency matrix of a digraph in most cases is not symmetric due to the directional nature of the arc from one node to another. Figure 9-7 shows the adjacency matrix of the digraph in Figure 9-2.

	A	B	L	C	R	P
A	0	1	0	1	0	0
B	1	0	0	1	0	0
L	0	0	0	1	0	0
C	1	1	1	0	1	1
R	0	0	0	1	0	1
P	0	0	0	1	1	0

Figure 9-6   Adjacency matrix for graph in Figure 9-5.

	A	B	C	D	E
A	0	1	0	0	0
B	0	0	1	0	0
C	0	0	0	1	0
D	0	0	0	0	1
E	0	0	0	0	0

Figure 9-7   Adjacency matrix for digraph in Figure 9-2.

The **length** of a path between nodes I and K is the number of nodes $I = J_1, J_2, \ldots,$ $J_n = K$ on the path from I to K minus 1 (that is, the number of edges). For example, in the graph of Figure 9-5, there are more than 2 paths between A and R: if we choose the path ABCR, then the length of this path is 3; if we choose the path ACR, then its length is 2. In many practical applications of graphs, it is important to know whether there is a path between nodes I and K and, if so, what the length of this path is.

To determine the answers, we need to use the algebraic notion of matrix multiplication. Briefly, the product of 2 square matrices A × B of the same order is another square matrix C such that the (i,j)th entry in C is the sum of the products of the corresponding entries from row i in A and column j in B.

Suppose we wish to multiply:

$$A = \begin{bmatrix} 2 & 3 & 4 \\ 1 & 6 & 7 \\ 2 & 1 & 3 \end{bmatrix} = \begin{bmatrix} a_{11} & a_{12} & a_{13} \\ a_{21} & a_{22} & a_{23} \\ a_{31} & a_{32} & a_{33} \end{bmatrix}$$

and:

$$B = \begin{bmatrix} 1 & 2 & 3 \\ 3 & 2 & 4 \\ 5 & 6 & 7 \end{bmatrix} = \begin{bmatrix} b_{11} & b_{12} & b_{13} \\ b_{21} & b_{22} & b_{23} \\ b_{31} & b_{32} & b_{33} \end{bmatrix}$$

then:

A × B = C

where the matrix C also has 3 rows and 3 columns:

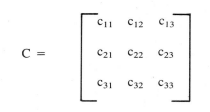

$$
C = \begin{bmatrix} c_{11} & c_{12} & c_{13} \\ c_{21} & c_{22} & c_{23} \\ c_{31} & c_{32} & c_{33} \end{bmatrix}
$$

$$c_{11} = a_{11} \times b_{11} + a_{12} \times b_{21} + a_{13} \times b_{31}$$

Similarly:

$$c_{ij} = a_{i1} \times b_{1j} + a_{i2} \times b_{2j} + a_{i3} \times b_{3j}$$

for $i = 1, 2, 3$ and $j = 1, 2, 3$.

Following this strategy we obtain:

$$
C = \begin{bmatrix} 31 & 34 & 46 \\ 54 & 56 & 76 \\ 20 & 24 & 31 \end{bmatrix}
$$

Note that in matrix multiplication A × B is not always the same as B × A. (Convince yourself by doing Exercise (6) at the end of the chapter. You will also write a PSEUDO procedure to perform such multiplication as an exercise; we shall assume this procedure is already written in our algorithm discussions.)

If M is the adjacency matrix of a graph, then non-zero entries in it represent those nodes joined together by a path of length 1. The matrix M^2 (M × M) identifies those nodes joined by paths of length 2. The presence of a non-zero number in the (i,j)th entry of M^2 indicates that the ith node and jth node have a path between them of length 2. In general, an integer r present in the (i,j)th entry of the matrix M^n is an indication that the ith and jth nodes in the original graph have r paths between them of length n. Consider the digraph of Figure 9-8 and the corresponding adjacency matrix in Figure 9-9.

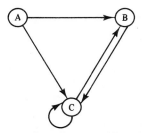

Figure 9-8   Digraph with number of paths computed using matrix multiplication in Figure 9-9.

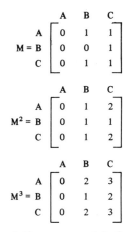

$$\begin{array}{c@{\quad}ccc}
 & A & B & C \\
M = \begin{array}{c} A \\ B \\ C \end{array} & \left[\begin{array}{ccc} 0 & 1 & 1 \\ 0 & 0 & 1 \\ 0 & 1 & 1 \end{array}\right]
\end{array}$$

$$M^2 = \begin{array}{c} A \\ B \\ C \end{array} \left[\begin{array}{ccc} 0 & 1 & 2 \\ 0 & 1 & 1 \\ 0 & 1 & 2 \end{array}\right]$$

$$M^3 = \begin{array}{c} A \\ B \\ C \end{array} \left[\begin{array}{ccc} 0 & 2 & 3 \\ 0 & 1 & 2 \\ 0 & 2 & 3 \end{array}\right]$$

Figure 9-9   Adjacency matrix for Figure 9-8.

The 2 in the 1st row of the 3rd column and in the 3rd row of the 3rd column of M^2 indicates that A and C are connected by 2 paths of length 2. Similarly, the 3 in the 1st row of the 3rd column in M^3 signifies 3 directed paths of length 3 from A to C; the 2 in the 3rd row of the 2nd column in M^3 denotes that C and B are connected by 2 paths of length 3.

At first glance, the claim that the (i,j)th entry of M^n tells us precisely the number of paths of length n between the 2 corresponding nodes may seem to be an extremely fortunate coincidence. The justification, however, lies in the principle of mathematical induction. An informal inductive argument will illustrate that there is an intuitive basis for the claim.

Suppose we know that the claim is valid for $n - 1$; that is, the (i,j)th entry of M^{n-1} is the number of paths of length $n - 1$ between nodes i and j. The validity of the claim for $n - 1$ indicates that the entries $a_{i1}, a_{i2}, \ldots, a_{in}$ along the ith row of M^{n-1} in Figure 9-10 are precisely the number of paths of length $n - 1$ from node i to node 1, node i to node 2, ..., node i to node n. The jth column of M contains 1's and 0's. A 1 in the kth row of column j indicates an edge connecting node k to node j.

If there are a_{ik} paths of length $n - 1$ from node i to node k, then each of these will generate a path of length n from node i to node j provided there is an edge connecting node k to node j. If there is no such edge, then no paths are generated. In terms of the coefficients used in Figure 9-10, this means that there are:

$$\sum_{K=1}^{n} a_{ik} m_{kj}$$

paths of length n from node i to node j. But:

$$\sum_{K=1}^{n} a_{ik} m_{kj}$$

is precisely the (i,j)th coefficient in the matrix M^n.

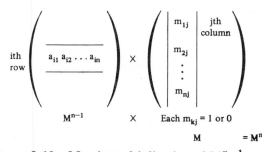

Figure 9-10 Matrix multiplication of M^{n-1} by M.

In addition to this matrix multiplication property, you can easily verify that, for an undirected graph, the row sum of the ith row in its adjacency matrix gives the degree of the ith node. The row sum of ith row and column sum of jth column in the adjacency matrix of a directed graph give the outdegree of the ith node and the indegree of the jth node, respectively.

In many applications, it is of interest to determine whether there is a path (or a directed path in a digraph) between any 2 nodes in a graph. The adjacency matrix also can be used to answer this question. You may have already surmised part of the answer. If the (i,j)th entry in M^n is non-zero, then this is a necessary and sufficient condition that there is a path of length n between the ith and jth nodes of the graph. Put differently, the (i,j)th entry of the matrix M^n is non-zero if and only if there is a path of length n between the corresponding nodes. Now the question arises: how many times do we multiply the adjacency matrix M by itself (what should n be?) to determine whether there exists a path between 2 arbitrary nodes?

Consider the simple digraph of Figure 9-11, the adjacency matrix M of which is given in Figure 9-12 on page 205. Because M^3, M^4, M^5, . . . are simply repetitions of M and M^2, all paths of length more than 2 are mere duplications of paths of length 1 or 2. This shows that there is a path from A to B (or B to A) if and only if there is a path of length 2 or less between them. Looking at M, we notice that there is indeed a path of length 1 from A to B and from B to A, although M^2 shows no path of length 2 from A to B.

When the graph contains more than 2 nodes, the situation is completely analogous. Suppose a graph contains r nodes. Then there is a path between ith and jth nodes if and only if the (i,j)th entry in at least one of the M, M^2, . . ., M^r matrices is not 0. The following PSEUDO procedure determines the existence of a path between any 2 nodes of a graph containing N nodes using this property of its adjacency matrix M. If a path between the designated nodes exists, the procedure returns FLAG with the value TRUE, otherwise FALSE is returned in FLAG.

Figure 9-11 Simple digraph corresponding to the adjacency matrix in Figure 9-12.

```
PROCEDURE FIND-PATH(M, N, I, J, FLAG)
VAR M(N, N), KPOWER (N, N), I, J, K, N: INTEGER
VAR FLAG:BOOLEAN
 (*Determine whether there is a path between I and J nodes*)
 (*in the graph represented by the N by N adjacency matrix*)
 (*M*)
FLAG:=FALSE
(*Check first for the easiest possible case*)
IF M(I, J) < > 0 THEN
   ┌ FLAG:=TRUE┐
   └ RETURN     ┘
ENDIF
 K:=2
WHILE K < N + 1 DO
  ┌CALL POWER (M, N, KPOWER, K)
  │   (*This call is to return in KPOWER the matrix M raised
  │    to the power K*)
  │ IF KPOWER (I, J) < > 0 THEN
  │    ┌ FLAG:=TRUE┐
  │    └RETURN      ┘
  │ ELSE
  │    [ K:=K + 1 ]
  └ ENDIF
```

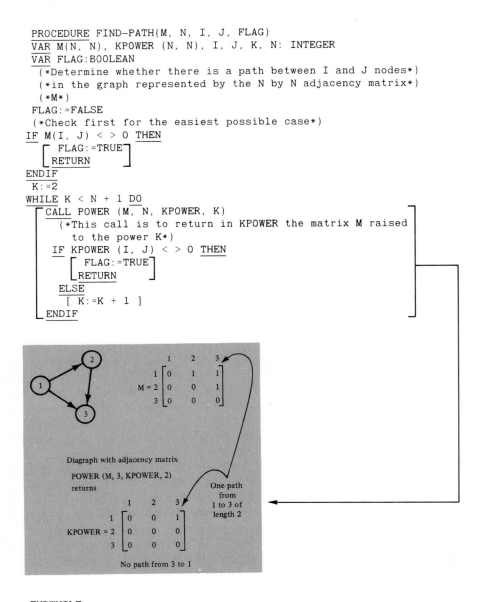

Diagraph with adjacency matrix

POWER (M, 3, KPOWER, 2)
returns

One path
from
1 to 3 of
length 2

No path from 3 to 1

```
ENDWHILE
RETURN
END FIND-PATH
```

Our procedure FIND-PATH uses another procedure POWER, which simply finds successive powers M, M × M, M × M × M, and so on of a square matrix M. You will write the procedure POWER as an exercise at the end of the chapter. When you implement FIND-PATH and POWER in a high level language, you can design the program to take advantage of the previously computed powers of the matrix.

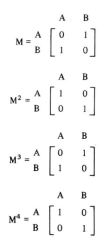

Figure 9-12   Adjacency matrix for digraph in Figure 9-11.

9-3   Graph Traversal

In many practical applications of graphs, there is a need to visit systematically all the nodes on a graph. One such application occurs when the organizers of a political campaign want their candidate to visit all important political centers. The presence or absence of direct transportation routes (edges) between such centers will determine the possible ways in which all the centers could be visited. At the moment, our only concern is to develop an algorithm that ensures that all nodes are visited. Later in the chapter we shall investigate how to determine the most economical way of visiting nodes.

Depth-First Search

The main logic of the **depth-first search** algorithm is analogous to the preorder traversal of a tree. It is accomplished recursively as follows:

1. Choose any node in the graph. Designate it as the *search node* and mark it as *visited*.

2. Using the adjacency matrix of the graph, find a node adjacent to the search node (that is, connected by an arc from the search node) that has not been visited yet. Designate this as the new search node (but remember the previous one) and mark it as visited.

3. Repeat (2) using the new search node. If no nodes satisfying (2) can be found, return to the previous search node and continue from there.

4. When a return to the previous search node in (3) is impossible, the search from the originally chosen search node is complete.

5. If the graph still contains unvisited nodes, choose any node that has not been visited and repeat steps (1) through (4).

The algorithm is called a depth-first search because the search continues progressively deeper in a recursive manner. To illustrate this procedure more clearly, we consider the directed graph in Figure 9-13. (Although our examples will illustrate the depth-first search for a directed graph, note that the algorithm also applies to undirected graphs.) Its adjacency matrix is shown in Figure 9-14. Suppose we have a procedure, SEARCH, that is invoked to begin a depth-first search from a given node on the graph. The steps followed by the algorithm for Figure 9-14 are:

1. Begin by marking C visited and invoking SEARCH (C).

2. Because both N and L are adjacent to C on the adjacency matrix of the graph, L is encountered first on a left to right scan of the C row, so go to L. Invoke SEARCH (L) and mark L as visited.

3. Because N is the only node adjacent to L, go to N, invoke SEARCH (N), and mark N as visited.

4. Because there is no node adjacent to N—that is, N has exhausted the search—go back to N's predecessor, L.

5. All nodes adjacent to L also have been visited, so return to C.

6. N is the next node adjacent to C. However, N already has been visited, so the search from C is now completed.

7. All nodes except P and B have been visited. Choose B next and mark it as visited. Because P is the only unvisited node adjacent to B, proceed to P and invoke SEARCH (P). N being the only node adjacent to P, go to N—which has already been visited. Then backtrack to B; the total search is complete.

Figure 9-15 highlights the steps of this algorithm. Before giving a formal statement of the algorithm in PSEUDO, we will first consider some definitions and applications that arise when it is applied to directed graphs. In Figure 9-15 there are 3 types of arcs. Double arrow arcs, known as **tree arcs,** indicate natural descent from one adjacent node to its next adjacent node in the depth-first search. Single arrow arcs represent **backward arcs.** Backward arcs indicate that there are cycles in the digraph. There are no backward arcs in Figure 9-15, consistent with there being no cycles in the graph in Figure 9-13. A graph with no cycles in it is also called an **acyclic graph.** (Note that an undirected graph cannot be acyclic. Why?) The dotted arcs are simply **cross arcs.** Notice that the depth-first search decomposes the graph into a set of trees with cross arcs connecting various nodes on different trees within this set. The set of these trees is called the **depth-first spanning forest** for the graph.

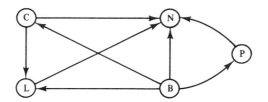

Figure 9-13 Directed graph illustrating a depth-first search.

	C	L	N	B	P
C	0	1	1	0	0
L	0	0	1	0	0
N	0	0	0	0	0
B	1	1	1	0	1
P	0	0	1	0	0

Figure 9-14   Adjacency matrix of graph in Figure 9-13.

As another example, consider the digraph in Figure 9-16. Beginning the depth-first search with A and choosing C as adjacent to A before B, we arrive at the spanning forest as shown in Figure 9-17. Notice that a different spanning forest is obtained each time the search is initiated at a different node.

A 2nd spanning forest is shown in Figure 9-18 on page 209, in which we applied the depth-first search algorithm beginning at node B. The node D was chosen adjacent to B before E.

In both spanning forests, there are back arcs; thus, the graph in Figure 9-15 contains cycles. We now have a simple test to determine whether a particular graph contains cycles. If a spanning forest of the graph has no back arcs, the graph contains no cycles.

Acyclic graphs are particularly useful in arranging various modules in order of priority in a large project. Suppose that a large job consists of modules A, B, C, and D. Suppose you must finish A first and C last, and you must do B before you start C and D. An acyclic graph such as that shown in Figure 9-19 establishes an ordering of the various modules. This linear ordering is expressed: *between any 2 modules X and Y, choose X to precede Y if there is an arc from X to Y.*

According to the digraph in Figure 9-19, the project should be performed in the order A, B, D, and C. The depth-first search can be used effectively to arrive at this ordering provided that the adjacency matrix representation of the graph forces the choice of B adjacent to A before C, and D adjacent to B before C. That is, we must use the adjacency

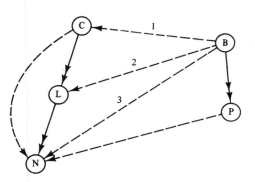

Figure 9-15   Depth-first search applied to Figure 9-14.

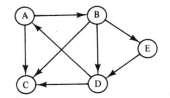

Figure 9-16   Directed graph with cycle.

matrix as it appears in Figure 9-20 on page 210 if the order of nodes visited by the depth-first search is to indicate the order in which modules are to be scheduled for completion of the project. Later in this chapter, we will consider this question: given an *arbitrary* adjacency matrix for a diagraph corresponding to the ordering of nodes in a project, is there an algorithm that can be invoked to reconstruct the adjacency matrix in such a way that the depth-first search corresponds to scheduling of the project modules in the fashion described for Figure 9-19? Such an algorithm is said to result in a **topological ordering** of the digraph nodes.

The PSEUDO procedure DF-SEARCH performs a depth-first search. The recursive PSEUDO procedure SEARCH-FROM that follows is used to visit each node and then progress deeper (if possible) along a given tree in the spanning forest of the graph.

```
PROCEDURE DF-SEARCH
  (*Depth-first search of graph with N nodes,*)
  (*represented by adjacency matrix M*)
GLOBAL VAR N: INTEGER
GLOBAL VAR M(N,N): INTEGER
GLOBAL VAR VISITED(N): BOOLEAN
VAR I: INTEGER
    (*Initialize visited array to FALSE*)
FOR I:=1 TO N DO
    [VISITED(I):= FALSE]
```

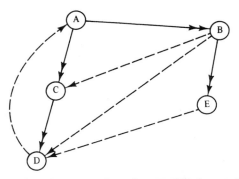

**Figure 9-17   Depth-first search and spanning forest derived from
graph in Figure 9-16.**

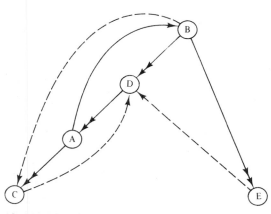

Figure 9-18   Spanning forest arising from different depth-first search of graph in Figure 9-16.

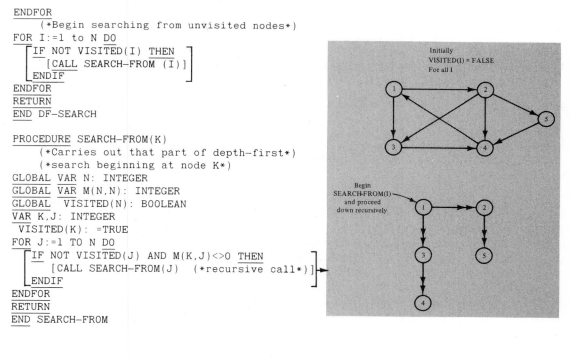

```
ENDFOR
      (*Begin searching from unvisited nodes*)
FOR I:=1 to N DO
      IF NOT VISITED(I) THEN
         [CALL SEARCH-FROM (I)]
      ENDIF
ENDFOR
RETURN
END DF-SEARCH

PROCEDURE SEARCH-FROM(K)
      (*Carries out that part of depth-first*)
      (*search beginning at node K*)
GLOBAL VAR N: INTEGER
GLOBAL VAR M(N,N): INTEGER
GLOBAL  VISITED(N): BOOLEAN
VAR K,J: INTEGER
   VISITED(K): =TRUE
FOR J:=1 TO N DO
      IF NOT VISITED(J) AND M(K,J)<>0 THEN
         [CALL SEARCH-FROM(J)  (*recursive call*)]
      ENDIF
ENDFOR
RETURN
END SEARCH-FROM
```

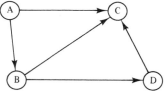

Figure 9-19   Digraph ordering nodes in sample project.

	A	B	D	C
A	0	1	0	1
B.	0	0	1	1
D	0	0	0	1
C	0	0	0	0

Figure 9-20   Adjacency matrix for digraph in Figure 9-19.

Breadth-First Search

Another widely used scheme for graph traversal is the **breadth-first search.** Although it can be used both for directed and undirected graphs, we shall describe it in relation to undirected graphs. Essentially the breadth-first search begins at a given node and then proceeds to all the nodes directly connected to that node. The following steps are involved in the algorithm:

1. Begin with any node, mark it as *visited*.

2. Proceed to the next node having an edge connection to the node in step (1). Mark it as visited.

3. Come back to the node in step (1), descend along an edge toward an unvisited node, and mark the new node as visited.

4. Repeat step (3) until all nodes adjacent to the node in step (1) have been marked as visited.

5. Repeat step 1 through 4 starting from the node visited in (2), then starting from the nodes visited in step (3) in the order visited. Keep this up as long as possible before starting a new scan.

Notice that the algorithm amounts to choosing a tree in the graph, visiting the root node, then visiting all nodes at level 1, level 2, and so on. A queue is a convenient structure to keep track of nodes that are visited during a breadth-first search. As a given node is visited, it is entered into the queue of nodes waiting to have their children visited. Once all the children of a given node have been visited, the node currently at the front of the queue is removed and all its children are visited.

As does a depth-first search, this algorithm results in a spanning forest for the graph. This spanning forest is called the **breadth-first spanning forest.** The undirected graph in Figure 9-21 yields the breadth-first spanning forest in Figure 9-22, assuming that we begin the traversal at P. You will write the implementation of a breadth-first search as an exercise at the end of the chapter.

In a breadth-first search, the graph is searched *broadly* by exploring all the nodes adjacent to a node; that is, by visiting all nodes on a given level of the chosen tree. In relational database applications, all graphs are first decomposed into spanning forests. Because a graph represents a *many-to-many* relationship between nodes (as opposed to the *one-to-many* hierarchical relationship in trees), graphs are first decomposed into a set of trees (a spanning forest) before they are stored. Database management systems use this concept extensively, as we will see in Chapter 12.

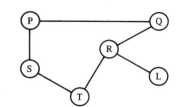

Figure 9-21   Undirected graph yielding Figure 9-22.

9-4   Networks

In many natural applications of graphs, not only the edges between nodes, but also the weights of these edges, play an important role. The **weight** of an edge is just its value. For example, an airline may be interested in not only the existence of an air route between 2 cities but also the shortest such air route. The distance between the 2 cities is the weight of the edge connecting the 2 cities. A graph with weighted edges such as the one in Figure 9-23 is called a **network.** An immediate question that arises in regard to this type of network is: What is the shortest path between any 2 given nodes of a network?

Before answering this question, consider a more general problem usually encountered in communication networks. Given a network, you must connect all the nodes in the network so that the total edge weight is minimized. In a telephone communication network, it is vital to link all cities in the network for the least possible cost. To solve this problem, we shall devise an algorithm that converts a network into a tree structure called the **minimum spanning tree** of the network.

Minimum Spanning Tree

This algorithm essentially results in a tree that contains branches chosen from the edges in the original network. Given an original network in which there is a path between any 2 nodes, the edges for the minimum spanning tree are chosen in such a way that:

1. Every node in the network must be included in the spanning tree

2. The overall edge weight of the spanning tree is the minimum possible that will allow the existence of a path between any 2 nodes in the tree

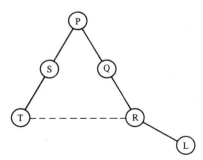

Figure 9-22   Breadth-first spanning forest from Figure 9-21.

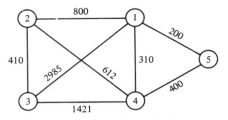

Figure 9-23   A network with weighted edges representing the distances between nodes.

In PSEUDO, the general algorithm to do this can be stated as

```
INCLUDE any node to begin with
REPEAT
   ┌─FOR all nodes not yet INCLUDED                              ─┐
   │   ┌─INCLUDE a node having an edge of minimal weight─┐        │
   │   │     connecting it to an already INCLUDED node   │        │
   │   └─ADD this node and edge to the tree             ─┘        │
   └─ENDFOR                                                      ─┘
UNTIL all nodes INCLUDED
```

Here the keywords INCLUDE and ADD imply in some sense the marking of nodes and edges as they are chosen for the minimal spanning tree.

Before getting into the details of a specific PSEUDO implementation of this algorithm, let us trace it for a small network to see why it works. Consider the network of Figure 9-23, the adjacency matrix of which is shown in Figure 9-24.

The algorithm allows us to begin with any node, so begin with INCLUDING node 1. We then enter the REPEAT loop of the algorithm, first searching for a node having an edge of minimum weight connecting it to node 1. Clearly, this is node 5, so node 5 is INCLUDED and the edge connecting node 1 to node 5 is ADDED to the tree. Next time through the REPEAT loop, we search for a node not yet INCLUDED (that is, node 2, 3, or 4) having an edge of minimal weight connecting it to an already INCLUDED node (that is, node 1 or 5). A visual scan of the network in Figure 9-23 will verify that the edge of weight 310 connecting node 4 to node 1 is the appropriate choice this time through the loop. Hence node 4 is INCLUDED and this edge is ADDED to the tree. Now verify that the edge connecting node 2 to node 4 and then the edge connecting node 3 to node 2 would be ADDED to complete construction of the minimal spanning tree. The result is shown in Figure 9-25.

	1	2	3	4	5
1	0	800	2985	310	200
2	800	0	410	612	0
3	2985	410	0	1421	0
4	310	612	1421	0	400
5	200	0	0	400	0

Figure 9-24   Adjacency matrix for network in Figure 9-23.

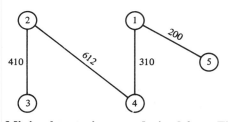

**Figure 9-25   Minimal spanning tree derived from Figures 9-23
and 9-24.**

It is obvious that, if the original network has a path between any 2 nodes, the minimum spanning tree constructed by this method also will have a path between any 2 nodes. It is perhaps not as obvious that the method will necessarily produce a tree of the minimal possible edgeweight allowing the existence of a path between any 2 nodes. An intuitive rationale as to why this indeed *must* be is given by the following argument. Consider any other method for choosing nodes and edges for the minimal spanning tree. Because our method allows us to start with any node, we could easily identify the choice at which our method and the proposed other method deviate. Let us group the nodes and edges for which the 2 methods dictate the same choice as indicated in Figure 9-26. The edge leaving the circled edges in Figure 9-26 identifies the choice at which the proposed method and our method deviate. That is, this edge cannot be an edge of minimal weight connecting a node outside the circle to one within the circle. There must be an edge of lesser weight connecting a node outside the circle to one within the circle. Such an edge is indicated by a dotted line in Figure 9-27.

It should now be obvious that Figure 9-27 has given us a spanning tree of smaller overall edgeweight than the one in Figure 9-26. Hence, we have informally shown that any other proposed method of selecting nodes and edges *cannot* result in a minimal overall edgeweight! Our prescribed method can always improve upon any method that dictates a different choice.

Having justified the minimum spanning tree algorithm on an intuitive basis, consider the formal statement of it in PSEUDO; the procedure MINSPAN assumes:

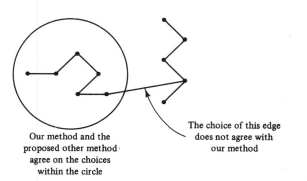

Our method and the
proposed other method
agree on the choices
within the circle

The choice of this edge
does not agree with
our method

**Figure 9-26   Comparison of 2 methods for constructing a
minimum spanning tree. See text.**

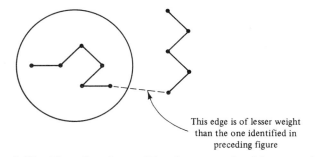

This edge is of lesser weight
than the one identified in
preceding figure

**Figure 9-27   The edge denoted by the arrow is of lesser weight
than the one identified in Figure 9-25.**

1. The existence of a global adjacency matrix M for the network in question. In practice, M may be an actual two-dimensional array or a function call that returns a value from some sparse matrix representation scheme.

2. A one-dimensional Boolean array INCLUDED that is indexed by the nodes in the network.

3. An external procedure FINDMIN(*I,J*) that returns in *I* and *J* the nodes determining an edge of minimal weight connecting a node *J* with INCLUDED(*J*) = FALSE to a node *I* with INCLUDED(*I*) = TRUE.

4. An external procedure ADDTOTREE(*I,J*) that can be called when we wish to add the edge connecting nodes *I* and *J* to the minimal spanning tree.

5. An external Boolean-valued function ALL(INCLUDED) that returns TRUE only when all locations in the Boolean array INCLUDED are true.

You will write the external procedures listed as exercises.

```
PROCEDURE MINSPAN
GLOBAL VAR  N,M(N,N): INTEGER
    (*In practice, M may be any appropriate sparse*)
    (*matrix representation of a network, not*)
    (*necessarily a two-dimensional array.*)
VAR  INCLUDED(N) : BOOLEAN
VAR  I,J,K : INTEGER
FOR K:= 1 TO N DO
    [ INCLUDED(K) : = FALSE ]
ENDFOR
 INCLUDED(1):=TRUE
REPEAT

    [ CALL FINDMIN(I,J)
      INCLUDED(I):=TRUE
      INCLUDED(J):=TRUE
      CALL ADDTOTREE(I,J) ]

UNTIL  ALL(INCLUDED)
RETURN
END MINSPAN
```

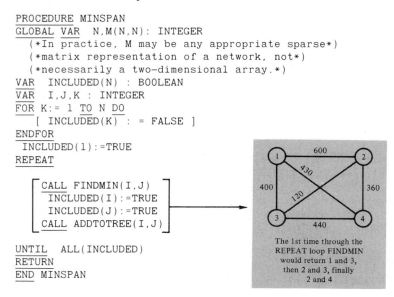

The 1st time through the
REPEAT loop FINDMIN
would return 1 and 3,
then 2 and 3, finally
2 and 4

9-5   The Shortest Path Algorithm

If we look at the minimal spanning tree of the graph in Figure 9-23, we find that this tree gives no indication of the shortest path between 2 nodes; only the *overall* edge weight is minimized. For instance, the minimum spanning tree pictured in Figure 9-25 does not include the shortest path between nodes 4 and 5, the direct edge of weight 400 that connects these nodes.

In this section we consider a network such as one shown in Figure 9-28, and give an algorithm that finds the shortest path between any 2 given nodes of the network. The network of Figure 9-28 could be thought of as representing airline routes between cities. An airline would be interested in finding the most economical route between any 2 given cities in the network. The numbers (weights) listed on the edges would, in this case, represent distances between cities. Thus, finding the shortest path from node 5 to node 2 would determine the minimal distance flown from node 5 to reach node 2.

To solve this problem, we first set up an adjacency matrix analogous to that in Figure 9-24. Suppose we want to find the shortest path from node 1 to node 3. From Figure 9-28, we note that this path should be $1 \rightarrow 2 \rightarrow 3$, yielding a total weight of $800 + 410 = 1210$. The algorithm to find such a path was first discovered by Dijkstra.*

Given a collection of nodes $1, 2, \ldots, N$, Dijkstra's algorithm revolves around 3 arrays in addition to the network's adjacency matrix M (or a suitable sparse matrix representation of M). These 3 arrays are identified as:

```
VAR   DISTANCE(N),PATH(N): INTEGER
VAR   INCLUDED(N): BOOLEAN
```

Identifying one node as the SOURCE, the algorithm proceeds to find the shortest distance from SOURCE to all other nodes in the network. At the conclusion of the algorithm, the shortest distance from SOURCE to node J is stored in DISTANCE(J), whereas PATH(J) contains the immediate predecessor of node J on the path determining this shortest distance. While the algorithm is in progress, DISTANCE(J) and PATH(J) are being updated continually until INCLUDED(J) is switched from FALSE to TRUE. Once this switch occurs, it is definitely known that DISTANCE(J) contains the *shortest* distance from SOURCE to J. The algorithm progresses until all nodes have been so included. Hence, Dijkstra's algorithm gives us the shortest distance from SOURCE to every other node in the network.

Given the SOURCE node, the algorithm can be divided into 2 phases—an *initialization* phase followed by an *iteration* phase in which nodes are included one by one in

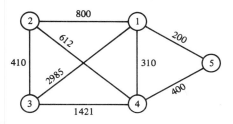

Figure 9-28   Network with edge weights representing distances.

*Dijkstra, E. W. 1954. A note on two problems in connection with graphs. *Numeriche Mathematik*, 1: 269–272.

the set of nodes for which the shortest distance from SOURCE is definitely known.

During the initialization phase, we must:

1. Initialize INCLUDED(SOURCE) to TRUE and INCLUDED(J) to FALSE for all other J.

2. Initialize the DISTANCE array via the rule

$$\text{DISTANCE}(J) = \begin{cases} 0 \text{ if } J = \text{SOURCE} \\ \text{M(SOURCE},J) \text{ IF M(SOURCE},J) <> 0 \\ \infty \text{ otherwise} \end{cases}$$

3. Initialize the PATH array via the rule:

$$\text{PATH}(J) = \begin{cases} \text{SOURCE if M(SOURCE},J) <> 0 \\ \text{undefined otherwise} \end{cases}$$

Given this initialization, the iteration phase can be expressed in a general form in PSEUDO as follows:

```
REPEAT
      FIND the node J which has the minimal DISTANCE
           among those nodes not yet INCLUDED.
      MARK J as now INCLUDED
      FOR each R not yet INCLUDED
          IF R is connected by an edge to J THEN
             [IF DISTANCE(J) + M(R,J)< DISTANCE(R) THEN
               [DISTANCE(R):=DISTANCE(J) + M(R,J)
                PATH(R):=J                         ]
             ENDIF                                  ]
          ENDIF
      ENDFOR
UNTIL ALL nodes are INCLUDED
```

The crucial part of the algorithm occurs within the innermost IF of the FOR loop. Figure 9-29 on page 219 provides a pictorial representation of the logic involved here. The circled nodes represent those nodes already INCLUDED prior to a given iteration of the REPEAT loop. Node J represents the node found in the first step of the REPEAT loop, whereas R represents another arbitrary node that has not yet been INCLUDED. The lines emanating from SOURCE represent the paths corresponding to the current entries in the DISTANCE array. For nodes within the circle—that is, those already INCLUDED—these paths are guaranteed to be the shortest distance paths. If J is the node having the minimal entry in DISTANCE among those not yet INCLUDED, we add J to the circle of INCLUDED nodes and then check to see if J's connections to other nodes not yet INCLUDED results in a newly found shorter path to such nodes. Referring to Figure 9-29 again, the sum of 2 sides of a triangle, DISTANCE(J) + M(J,R), may in fact be shorter than the 3rd side, DISTANCE(R). This geometric contradiction is possible because we are not dealing with true straight-sided triangles but rather with "triangles" whose sides may be very complicated paths through a network.

It is also apparent from Figure 9-29 why Dijkstra's algorithm works. As the node J in this figure is found to have the minimal DISTANCE entry from among all those nodes not yet INCLUDED, we may now INCLUDE it among the nodes whose minimal distance from the source is absolutely known. Why? Because the very fashion in which we update the DISTANCE and PATH arrays guarantees that nodes that will be INCLUDED in the future could never alter DISTANCE(J) and PATH(J). DISTANCE(J) is already minimal among DISTANCE(X) for any X that has not yet been INCLUDED.

To be sure you understand Dijkstra's complicated algorithm before you examine a formal PSEUDO version of it, trace it through on the network of Figure 9-28. Initially, we would have:

```
DISTANCE(2) = 800         PATH(2) = 1
DISTANCE(3) = 2985        PATH(3) = 1
DISTANCE(4) = 310         PATH(4) = 1
DISTANCE(5) = 200         PATH(5) = 1
```

in accordance with steps 2 and 3 of the initialization phase. According to the iteration phase of the algorithm, we would then, in order:

1. INCLUDE node 5; no changes in DISTANCE and PATH needed:

```
DISTANCE(2) = 800         PATH(2) = 1
DISTANCE(3) = 2985        PATH(3) = 1
DISTANCE(4) = 310         PATH(4) = 1
DISTANCE(5) = 200         PATH(5) = 1
```

2. INCLUDE node 4; update DISTANCE AND PATH to:

```
DISTANCE(2) = 800         PATH(2) = 1
DISTANCE(3) = 1731        PATH(3) = 4
DISTANCE(4) = 310         PATH(4) = 1
DISTANCE(5) = 200         PATH(5) = 1
```

[Note that it is shorter to go from node 1 to node 4 to node 3 than to follow the edge directly connecting node 1 to node 3.]

3. INCLUDE node 2; update DISTANCE and PATH to:

```
DISTANCE(2) = 800         PATH(2) = 1
DISTANCE(3) = 1210        PATH(3) = 2
DISTANCE(4) = 310         PATH(4) = 1
DISTANCE(5) = 200         PATH(5) = 1
```

[Now we find that traveling from node 1 to node 2 to node 3 is even better than the path determined in (3)!]

4. INCLUDE node 3 with (obviously) no changes made in DISTANCE or PATH.

The shortest path from node 1 to node 3 can be obtained in reverse order from the contents of the array PATH. It is $1 \rightarrow 2 \rightarrow 3$.

The PSEUDO version of Dijkstra's algorithm is the procedure SHORT-PATH, which in turn must call on procedures and functions INITIALIZE, FINDMIN, UPDATE, and ALL. The responsibilities of these procedures are documented; you will write them as exercises at the end of the chapter.

```
PROCEDURE SHORT-PATH(SOURCE)
     (*Determine shortest path from SOURCE to all other*)
     (*nodes in the network M. Shortest distances stored in*)
     (*global array DISTANCE. Nodes on shortest path stored*)
     (*in global array PATH.*)
  GLOBAL VAR  N,M(N,N),DISTANCE(N),PATH(N) : INTEGER
     (*The network M may be represented by two-dimensional*)
     (*array or suitable sparse matrix functions calls.*)
VAR   INCLUDED(N): BOOLEAN
VAR     J,R: INTEGER
CALL   INITIALIZE(SOURCE,INCLUDED)  (*Initialized global *)
(* arrays DISTANCE and PATH and local array INCLUDED *)
REPEAT
    ┌CALL FINDMIN(INCLUDED,J)
    │      (*This procedure call should return*)
    │      (*in J the node with minimal DISTANCE among those*)
    │      (*with INCLUDED entry still FALSE*)
    │ INCLUDED(J):=TRUE
    │ FOR R:=1 TO N DO
    │     ┌IF NOT INCLUDED(R) THEN
    │     │    ┌CALL UPDATE(R,J)
    │     │    │ (*Potentially alter DISTANCE(R) and PATH(R)*)
    │     │    └ (*based on inclusion of J*)
    │     └ENDIF
    └ ENDFOR
```

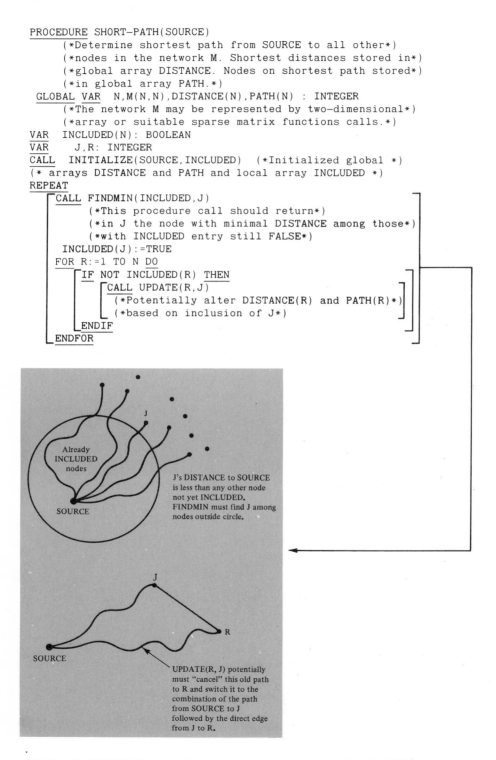

Already INCLUDED nodes

SOURCE

J

J's DISTANCE to SOURCE is less than any other node not yet INCLUDED. FINDMIN must find J among nodes outside circle.

J

R

SOURCE

UPDATE(R, J) potentially must "cancel" this old path to R and switch it to the combination of the path from SOURCE to J followed by the direct edge from J to R.

```
UNTIL ALL(INCLUDED)    (*Boolean function to signal all TRUE*)
RETURN
END SHORT-PATH
```

In the world of applications . . .

Swiss mathematician Leonhard Euler (pronounced "oiler") (1707–1783) was once given a problem by the townfolk of Königsberg, a city in the Soviet Union. The river flowing through the city wound around an island. There were several bridges over the river as shown in the drawing below.

   The people wanted to know if it was possible to walk through the city crossing each bridge only once. The solution to this puzzle was the birth of graph theory. For more on this path problem, read any good book on graph theory.

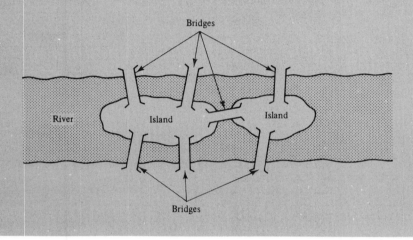

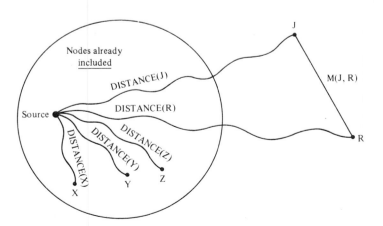

Figure 9-29   REPEAT loop logic in shortest path (Dijkstra's) algorithm.

A modification of Dijkstra's algorithm, developed by Floyd, uses slightly more computing time.* Floyd's algorithm computes the minimum value path matrix between any two nodes. Dijkstra's algorithm has a run time proportional to N^2 where N is the number of nodes in the network. Floyd's algorithm first initializes a matrix $P(I,J)$ to $M(I,J)$ if $M(I,J) <> 0$, to 0 if $I=J$ (diagonal entry), and to ∞ otherwise (no edge between I and J). If the network contains N nodes, then N passes are made in such a way that the Lth pass accomplishes:

$$P(I,J) = \text{Min} (P(I,J), P(I,L) + P(L,J))$$

This in turn achieves the shortest path value from node I to J not passing through a node whose subscript is greater than J.

The PSEUDO procedure MIN-PATH-FLOYD implements this algorithm. As an exercise, you will trace this procedure for the network of Figure 9-28 and compute the minimum path between node I and node J.

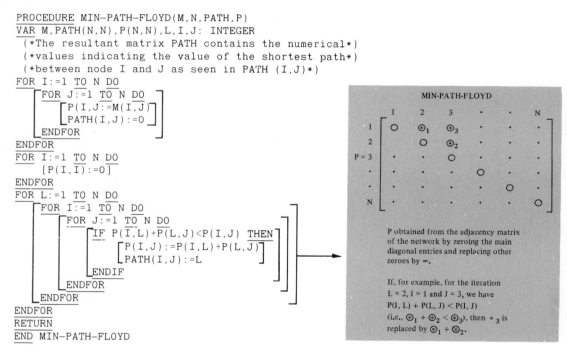

```
PROCEDURE MIN-PATH-FLOYD(M,N,PATH,P)
VAR M,PATH(N,N),P(N,N),L,I,J: INTEGER
  (*The resultant matrix PATH contains the numerical*)
  (*values indicating the value of the shortest path*)
  (*between node I and J as seen in PATH (I,J)*)
FOR I:=1 TO N DO
  [FOR J:=1 TO N DO
     [P(I,J:=M(I,J)]
      PATH(I,J):=0
   ENDFOR
ENDFOR
FOR I:=1 TO N DO
  [P(I,I):=0]
ENDFOR
FOR L:=1 TO N DO
  [FOR I:=1 TO N DO
     [FOR J:=1 TO N DO
        [IF P(I,L)+P(L,J)<P(I,J) THEN
           [P(I,J):=P(I,L)+P(L,J)]
            PATH(I,J):=L
         ENDIF
      ENDFOR
   ENDFOR
ENDFOR
RETURN
END MIN-PATH-FLOYD
```

MIN-PATH-FLOYD

P obtained from the adjacency matrix of the network by zeroing the main diagonal entries and replacing other zeroes by ∞.

If, for example, for the iteration $L = 2$, $I = 1$ and $J = 3$, we have $P(I, L) + P(L, J) < P(I, J)$ (i.e., $\otimes_1 + \otimes_2 < \otimes_3$), then $*_3$ is replaced by $\otimes_1 + \otimes_2$.

The matrix PATH can now be used to retrieve the shortest path as well, which you will do as an exercise. The run time efficiency of Floyd's algorithm has been estimated to be $O(N^3)$ where N is the number of nodes in the network.†

9-6 Topological Ordering

The graph of Figure 9-19 as represented by its adjacency matrix in Figure 9-20 essentially states that A precedes B, B precedes D, and D precedes C. Forcing a topological order on the adjacency matrix in Figure 9-20 means putting it into the form of Figure 9-30.

*Floyd, R. W. 1962. Algorithm 97: shortest path, *Communication of the Association for Computing Machinery* 5:345.

†Knuth, D.E. 1973. *The Art of Computer Programming*, Vol. 1. Fundamental Algorithms. Menlo Park, CA: Addison-Wesley.

	A	B	D	C
A	0	1	0	1
B	0	0	1	1
D	0	0	0	1
C	0	0	0	0

Figure 9-30   Topologically ordered adjacency matrix from Figure 9-20.

Once topologically ordered, the adjacency matrix is guaranteed to generate a depth-first search corresponding to the scheduling of modules in a project as described in Section 9-3.

An elegant human algorithm (its counterpart computer algorithm is not efficient because it takes a run time proportional to N^3 where N is the number of nodes) is as follows:

1. Initialize a variable L to 1.

2. Find the leftmost matrix column containing all zeros. This amounts to finding a node with no predecessors. If none exists you are done.

3. If found, assign it the numerical ordering L. This is the Lth node with precedence number L.

4. Increment L by 1.

5. Delete the found column and its corresponding row; that is, if the rth column contains all zeros, simply delete the rth row and rth column.

6. Repeat steps (2) through (5) until all the nodes have been assigned their precedence numbers.

This algorithm is carried out pictorially in Figures 9-31 through 9-33.

Rewriting the matrix again according to precedence numbers of rows, we get the matrix shown in Figure 9-30. Notice that all the entries below the main diagonal of this matrix are zeros. Such a matrix is also known as an **upper triangular** matrix.

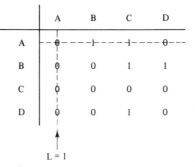

Figure 9-31   The precedence number of node A is 1. Thus, row A should be 1st row.

The PSEUDO procedure TOPOLOGICAL-ORDER makes use of 2 other procedures—
DELETE and BUILD—that you will write as exercises. The procedure DELETE simply
deletes the row and column corresponding to an assigned node and returns a reduced
matrix of an order less than the one passed to it. The procedure TOPOLOGICAL-ORDER
assumes that the graph has at least 2 nodes. The procedure BUILD then builds the new
matrix K which is in *upper triangular* form. The procedure TOPOLOGICAL-ORDER
assumes that the nodes in the corresponding digraph are designated numerically as 1,2,
. . ., N.

```
PROCEDURE TOPOLOGICAL-ORDER (M,K,TRACK,N)
VAR FLAG: BOOLEAN
VAR M(N,N),K(N,N),P,I,J,L,TRACK(N): INTEGER*)
  (*M is the adjacency matrix of an acyclic graph. K is an*)
  (*exact copy of M to begin with. The graph has N nodes*)
    FOR P:=1 to N DO
        [TRACK(P):= 0)]
    ENDFOR
    L:=0
    S:=N
    REPEAT (*keeps track of nodes*)
        L:=L+1
        (*S is the size of current matrix*)
        FOR J:=1 TO S DO (*J controls columns*)
            FLAG:=TRUE
            I:=1
            (*I controls rows*)
            WHILE (M(I,J)=0 AND FLAG) DO
                I:=I+1
                IF I > S THEN
                    FLAG:= FALSE
                    I:=N
                ENDIF
            ENDWHILE
        ENDFOR
            (*FALSE FLAG at the end of WHILE*)
            (*loop indicates a column with all zeros*)
            (*has been found*)
        IF NOT FLAG THEN
            CALL DELETE(M,J,S)
            TRACK(J):=L
        ENDIF
            (*After DELETE order of M has been reduced by 1*)
            (*The current size of M is S by S*)
            (*TRACK array keeps track of the precedence*)
            (*number of a node*)
    UNTIL L=N
    FOR I:=1 TO N DO
        IF TRACK(I)=0 THEN
        [ RETURN (*Graph is cyclic*)]
        ENDIF
    ENDFOR
    CALL BUILD(K,TRACK,N)
    RETURN
END TOPOLOGICAL-ORDER
```

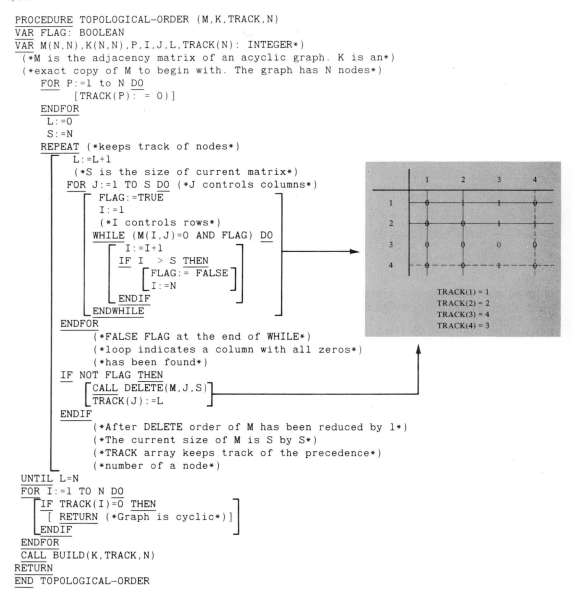

TRACK(1) = 1
TRACK(2) = 2
TRACK(3) = 4
TRACK(4) = 3

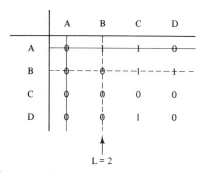

Figure 9-32 **The precedence number of node B is 2. Thus, row B should be 2nd row.**

As noted earlier, this procedure is not efficient and can be modified. One possible modification area is the WHILE loop, which simply looks for a column with all zeros. You will do this as an exercise.

SUMMARY

Graphs and networks represent general relationships between data objects called nodes. Traversal of graphs solves many important data processing problems. There are basically 2 types of traversals—depth-first search and breadth-first search. Modern database implementations decompose graphs into their spanning forests, for implementation.

Networks are essentially graphs with weighted edges. These are used in design analysis to minimize cost. Minimum spanning trees and shortest path algorithms are extensively used for applications such as electrical circuit analysis, communication networks, transportation systems, and the efficient scheduling of modules in a large project.

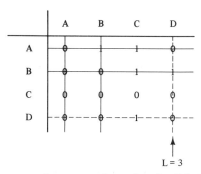

Figure 9-33 **The precedence number of node C is 3. Thus, row C should be 3rd row.**

KEY TERMS

Graph	Source node	Tree arc
Node	Cycle	Backward arc
Edge	Degree	Acyclic
Undirected	Adjacency matrix	Cross arcs
Directed graph	Incidence matrix	Spanning forest
Digraph	Symmetric matrix	Topological ordering
Arc	Length of a path	Breadth-first search
Directed path	Graph traversal	Network
Connected	Depth-first search	Weight of an edge
Strongly connected		Minimum spanning tree
Weakly connected		Shortest path
Outdegree		Upper triangular
Indegree		
Sink node		

EXERCISES

1. What kind of graph represents a hierarchical relationship?

2. What is the outdegree of a sink node?

3. What is the indegree of a source node?

4. Draw a graph that has cycles in it.

5. Define the term *spanning forest* as it is associated with a digraph.

6. When you multiply two square matrices A and B of the same order, is A × B = B × A?

7. What is a spanning tree?

8. Does the minimum spanning tree of a network give any indication of shortest path between nodes?

9. What is the indegree and outdegree of each node in the following graph?

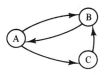

10. Write the adjacency matrix of the following graph:

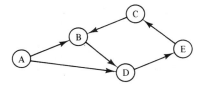

11. Write a program that stores the adjacency matrix of the digraph in Exercise (9) and calculates the sum of each row. What is the significance of such sums?

12. Consider the digraph:

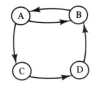

Use its adjacency matrix to find how many paths of length 3 exist from A to B.

13. Translate the PSEUDO procedure FIND-PATH into any high-level language. Test your program on an arbitrary graph containing 5 nodes.

14. Implement procedure POWER (M,N,KPOWER,K) which computes M × M, M × M × M, . . ., M × M × M . . . M for values of K from 1 to *N*.

15. Write the PSEUDO procedure FINDMIN that is called by procedure MINSPAN as discussed in this chapter.

16. Write the PSEUDO procedure ADDTOTREE that is called by procedure MINSPAN as discussed in this chapter.

17. Does the minimum spanning tree of a graph give the shortest distance between any 2 specified nodes?

18. Trace Floyd's algorithm as applied to the network of Figure 9-28 and obtain the matrix PATH.

19. Write a procedure in any high-level language that retrieves the shortest path between any 2 nodes of a network from the associated matrix PATH of procedure MIN-PATH-FLOYD.

20. Write in any high-level language the procedure DF-SEARCH used in the depth-first search.

21. Modify SEARCH-FROM so it can be used in a breadth-first search for the graph that follows:

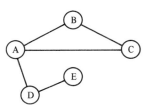

22. Compute A × B and B × A where B and A are square matrices used in Section 9-2.

23. If you have mathematical experience in proofs by induction, attempt to prove the validity of:

a. The minimal spanning tree algorithm
b. The shortest path algorithm

24. Remember that the adjacency matrix for a substantial graph or network usually will have to be implemented by the generalized dope vector or linked list representation of a sparse matrix. For each of the algorithms presented in this chapter, discuss how the choice of a sparse matrix representation would effect the run time efficiency of the algorithm.

25. Write the PSEUDO procedures and functions INITIALIZE, FINDMIN, UPDATE, and ALL that are called by SHORTEST PATH, which implements Dijkstra's algorithm.

PROGRAMMING PROBLEMS

1. The network below indicates air routes supported by Wing and a Prayer Airline Company. Design a program for Wing and a Prayer that will:
a. Compute the shortest path between any 2 nodes
b. Compute the shortest paths from one given node to all other nodes

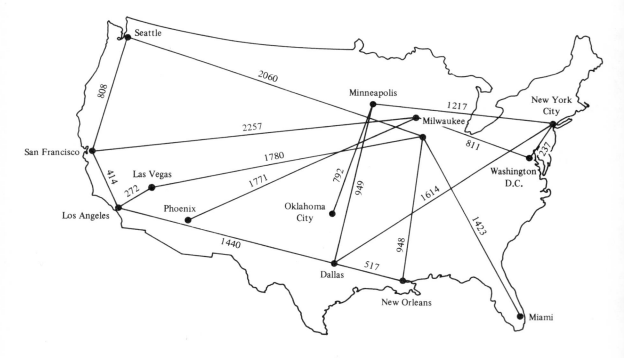

2. Consider the network

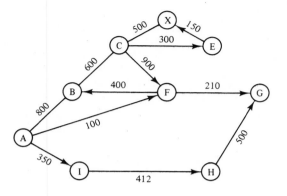

Write a complete program that gives the minimum spanning tree of this network.

3. Write a program that traverses the network from Programming Problem (1) using a breadth-first search. Then do the same for a depth-first search. Remember that a graph (or network) is said to be *connected* provided any 2 nodes are connected by some path. How might your depth-first or breadth-first procedure be used to test whether or not a network is connected?

4. In the Pascal supplement at the end of this chapter, a main program has been written (and verified with correct output) to reflect the logic of the PSEUDO version of the minimum spanning tree algorithm. The procedures that have been called are not given in the supplement; if you are familiar with Pascal, write these procedures.

If you work in Pascal . . .

The following program represents a Pascal implementation of the minimum spanning tree algorithm discussed in this chapter. The verifiably correct output follows the program. However, the procedures and functions FINDMIN, ADDTOTREE, and ALL have been declared *external* and do not appear in the listing. Programming Problem (4) asks that you write them and link them to our main program. Note in particular, because we are interested in only a printout of the edges in the minimal spanning tree, the ADDTOTREE procedure need not store the structure in memory, but need only appropriately send to the printer the data it receives. We have also added a call to a fourth external procedure, INPUTDATA, in the main program. This procedure is responsible for inputting the adjacency matrix of the network. For an additional challenge, try to represent the adjacency matrix by one of the sparse matrix methods discussed in Chapter 8.

```pascal
PROGRAM   MINSPANDEMO(INPUT,OUTPUT);
TYPE NETWORKARRAY = ARRAY[1..40, 1..40] OF INTEGER;
     (*Without sparse matrix representation, a maximum
       of 40 nodes may be accommodated.*)
     INCLUSIONARRAY = ARRAY [1..40] OF BOOLEAN;
VAR  N:INTEGER;
     M:NETWORKARRAY;
PROCEDURE FINDMIN(VAR I,J: INTEGER); EXTERNAL;
PROCEDURE ADDTOTREE(I,J: INTEGER); EXTERNAL;
FUNCTION ALL (INCLUDED: INCLUSIONARRAY): BOOLEAN; EXTERNAL;
PROCEDURE INPUTDATA : EXTERNAL;
PROCEDURE MINSPAN;
     VAR INCLUDED: INCLUSIONARRAY;
         I,J,K: INTEGER;
     BEGIN
         FOR K:=1 TO N DO INCLUDED[K]:=FALSE
       INCLUDED[1]:=TRUE;
       REPEAT
           FINDMIN(I,J);
           INCLUDED[I]:=TRUE;
           INCLUDED[J]:=TRUE;
           ADDTOTREE(I,J);
       UNTIL ALL (INCLUDED)
     END; (*OF MINSPAN*);

BEGIN (*MAIN*)
INPUTDATA;
MINSPAN
END.
```

Sample run:

```
INPUT THE NUMBER OF NODES→ 4
ENTER ROWS OF ADJACENCY MATRIX, ONE ROW PER LINE
0    500 800 600
500 0    100 110
800 100 0    510
600 110 510 0

ATTACH NODE 2 TO NODE 1
EDGEWEIGHT BETWEEN NODE( 2) AND NODE( 1) IS   500

ATTACH NODE 3 TO NODE 2
EDGEWEIGHT BETWEEN NODE( 3) AND NODE( 2) IS   100

ATTACH NODE 4 TO NODE 2
EDGEWEIGHT BETWEEN NODE( 4) AND NODE( 2) IS   110
```

10

Sorting

The people whose seats are farthest from the aisle
invariably arrive last.

AXIOM OF ORDERING

10-1   Introductory Considerations

There is practically no data processing activity that does not require the data to be in some order. **Ordering** or sorting data in an increasing or decreasing fashion according to some linear relationship among data items is of fundamental importance. Sort algorithms are designed with the following objectives:

1. Minimize exchanges or wholesale movement of data. When data items are large and the number of data items is excessive, swapping of data items takes an inordinate amount of processing time.

2. Move data from secondary storage to main memory in large blocks, because the larger the data block to be moved, the more efficient is the corresponding algorithm. This is a key part of **external sorting.**

3. If possible, retain all the data in main memory. In this case, random access into an array can be effectively used. This is a key part of **internal sorting.**

There are basically three main considerations that should affect a programmer's decision to choose from a variety of sorting methods:

1. Programming time

2. Execution time of the program

3. Memory or auxiliary space needed for the program environment

First, evaluate carefully the need for sorting data. It is pointless to write a complex program to sort a short file. If the number of records in the file is no more than 100, and each record no longer than 80 bytes, any sorting procedure probably would be adequate. However, when both the file size and the record size are large, minimize processing time by choosing an efficient sorting routine. Quite often, advance knowledge about the structure of the file and the data in it can help you to make a proper choice. However, if no such advance knowledge about the data is available, then you may need to assume the worst case scenario for the job. Unfortunately, there is no such thing as a "best" sorting method fitting all applications.

The efficiency of a sorting method is measured by the run time used for execution of the algorithm. When the file is large, choice of a proper sorting method resulting in the least possible run time is crucial. One sorting method may use different run times on different machines, and consequently you must consider machine environment in making this choice. The various sort algorithms considered in this chapter have been compared for their relative efficiencies as n, the number of items to be sorted, becomes larger; efficiency is usually proportional to some function of n. This function is denoted by $f(n)$; we use the notation $O(f(n))$ to mean *proportional to* $f(n)$. As we shall see later in this chapter, the efficiency of a sort routine falls between $O(n \log_2 n)$, and $O(n^2)$, the latter being the worst case.

Sometimes, in an effort to improve the efficiency of a sort, a more complex code introduces more variables, and hence the space needs of the program increase. The overhead placed on the software to fetch and execute instructions in a large program may create a Catch-22 situation. However, if the machine environment allows for ample memory capacity, and increasing program complexity increases program run time efficiency considerably, then it is worth the tradeoff.

Be careful to maintain a proper balance between program efficiency and readability. Making a subroutine call from inside of a FOR, WHILE, or REPEAT loop, although structured and readable, places an unusual demand on the software and slows the execution. If the subroutine involved is not very long, substitution of its code within these loops may be a better programming strategy—especially if the run time needs to be shortened. Often, the best opportunity to achieve this balance is when you translate from PSEUDO to actual program code.

10-2   Internal Sorts

The Bubble Sort

The **bubble sort** derives its name from the fact that the smallest data item bubbles up to the top of the sorted array.

The algorithm begins by comparing the top item of the array with the next, and swapping them if necessary. After $n - 1$ comparisons, the largest among a total of n items descends to the bottom of the array, to the nth location. The process is then reapplied to the remaining $n - 1$ items in the array. For n data items, the method requires $n(n - 1)/2$ comparisons and, on the average, almost one-half as many swaps. The bubble sort, therefore, is very inefficient in large sorting jobs. A modified version of the bubble sort has been given in Chapter 1 as the PSEUDO POINTER-SORT. Recall that this modified version used the bubble sort algorithm to rearrange an array of pointers without actually moving any data. The idea of the POINTER-SORT could be incorporated into any of the sorting algorithms we are about to describe.

In the world of applications . . .

Sorting lists of data can so consume resources that it can bring large computer systems to their knees. Consequently, there is big money in writing more versatile and faster generalized sorting software. Syncsort, Inc., is one of the world leaders in producing this type of software. In *Computerworld*, January 23, 1984, Syncsort took a full page advertisement to proclaim:

> We knew that the new hardware and software systems would create opportunities for the evolution of advanced sort programs. Speed would still be essential. But productivity would continue to skyrocket in importance. So that's why we bred Syncsort 2.5.
>
> You can expect savings in critical resources up to those shown (in the table below). And that can add up to a big increase in total systems throughput.

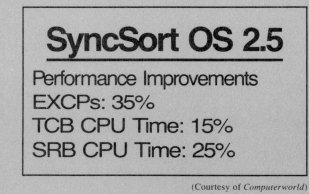

SyncSort OS 2.5
Performance Improvements
EXCPs: 35%
TCB CPU Time: 15%
SRB CPU Time: 25%

(Courtesy of *Computerworld*)

Want to put yourself in demand? Just learn how to write more efficient user-friendly sorting programs. It sure has worked for Syncsort!

The Insertion Sort

The main idea behind the **insertion sort** is to insert in the ith pass the ith element in A(1),A(2), . . . , A(i) in its rightful place. The following steps essentially define the insertion sort as applied to sorting into ascending order an array ALPHA containing N elements:

1. Set $J = 2$, where J is an integer

2. Check if ALPHA (J) < ALPHA ($J - 1$): if so interchange them; set $J = J - 1$ and repeat step (2) until $J = 1$

3. Set $J = 3, 4, 5, . . . , N$ and keep on executing step (2)

The following PSEUDO procedure describes the insertion sort for sorting the array ALPHA in ascending order:

```
PROCEDURE INSERTION (ALPHA, N)
(*This algorithm is insertion sort as applied to ALPHA containing*)
(*N alphanumeric elements*)
VAR S, ALPHA(N): CHARACTER
VAR N,I,J: INTEGER
(*Test for the trivial situation*)
IF N=0 OR N=1 THEN
    [RETURN]
ENDIF
FOR I:=2 TO N DO
    J:=I
    WHILE J>=2
        IF ALPHA(J)<ALPHA(J-1) THEN
            S:=ALPHA(J)
            ALPHA(J):=ALPHA(J-1)
            ALPHA(J-1):=S
        ENDIF
        J:=J-1
    ENDWHILE
ENDFOR
RETURN
END INSERTION
```

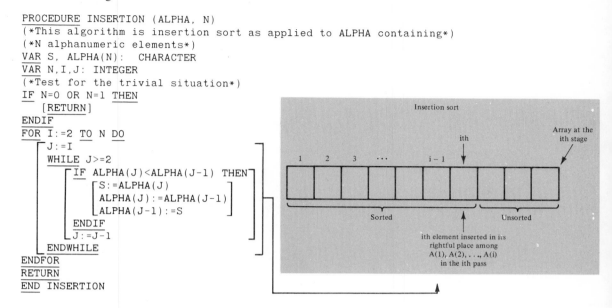

Figure 10-1 indicates the sorting achieved by the algorithm for each value of *I* for array ALPHA. In each row the data items are in sorted order relative to each other above the item with the asterisk; below this item the data are not affected.

Although the insertion sort is almost always better than the bubble sort, the time element in both methods is approximately the same—that is, it is proportional to n^2, where n is the number of the data items in the array. The number of interchanges needed in both the methods is on the average $(n^2)/4$, and in the worst cases is about $(n^2)/2$. Where the data are already partially ordered, the insertion sort will normally take less time than the bubble sort. The insertion sort is highly efficient if the array is already in almost sorted order.

ALPHA		I = 2		I = 3		I = 4		I = 5		I = 6
PAM	.	PAM	.	DAVE	.	ARON	.	ARON	.	ARON
SINGH	:	SINGH*:		PAM	:	DAVE	:	DAVE	:	BEV
DAVE	:	DAVE	:	SINGH*:		PAM	:	PAM	:	DAVE
ARON	:	ARON	:	ARON	:	SINGH*:		SINGH:		PAM
TOM	:	TOM	:	TOM	:	TOM	:	TOM* :		SINGH
BEV	:	BEV	:	BEV	:	BEV	:	BEV	:	TOM*

Figure 10-1 Insertion sort algorithm applied to ALPHA.

The Selection Sort

The main idea behind the **selection sort** is to find the smallest entry among in ALPHA(J), ALPHA($J + 1$), . . .,ALPHA(N), and then interchange it with ALPHA (J). This process is then repeated for each value of J. The PSEUDO procedure SELECTION gives this algorithm:

```
PROCEDURE SELECTION (ALPHA, N)
VAR S, ALPHA(N): CHARACTER
(*S carries the smallest element in the decreasing block *)
VAR I, J, K, N: INTEGER
(* The outer loop generates the block ALPHA(J),...,ALPHA(N) *)

(*The inner loop places the smallest in ALPHA (K) *)
FOR J:=1 TO N-1 DO
    K:=J
    S:=ALPHA(J)
    FOR I:=J+1 TO N DO
        IF ALPHA(I) < S THEN
            S:=ALPHA (I)
            K:=I
        ENDIF
    ENDFOR
        S:=ALPHA(J)
        ALPHA(J):=ALPHA(K)
        ALPHA(K):=S

ENDFOR
RETURN
END SELECTION
```

Selection sort

In the ith pass select lowest in A(i), A(i+1), ..., A(n) and swap it with A(i)

A(i) A(i+1) ··· ··· A(n)

A look at the last line of the outer loop of the procedure indicates that the selection sort always will be more efficient than the bubble sort or the insertion sort, because there are no more than $N - 1$ actual interchanges. Thus, if excessive swapping is involved, the selection sort should be chosen over the insertion sort and the bubble sort. Figure 10-2 outlines each iteration of the FOR loop of the procedure SELECTION as applied to the array ALPHA. Notice how the selection sort causes an item to leap over a whole section of the array to reach its proper place. Also notice that each column in Figure 10-2 is in the required sorted order beginning with and above the last item with an asterisk; that is, for each J the portion of the array ALPHA(1), ALPHA(2), . . ., ALPHA(J) is in the appropriate sorted order. In spite of the superiority of the selection sort over the bubble

ALPHA	J = 1	J = 2	J = 3	J = 4	J = 5
PAM	ARON*	ARON*	ARON*	ARON*	ARON*
SINGH	SINGH	BEV*	BEV*	BEV*	BEV*
DAVE	DAVE	DAVE*	DAVE*	DAVE	DAVE
ARON	PAM	PAM	PAM*	PAM*	PAM*
TOM	TOM	TOM	TOM	TOM	SINGH*
BEV	BEV	SINGH	SINGH	SINGH	TOM*

Figure 10-2   The FOR loop of SELECTION applied to ALPHA.

sort and the insertion sort, there is no significant gain in run time; its efficiency is also $O(n^2)$ for n data items.

Do not be misled by $O(n^2)$ efficiency of each of the preceding 3 sorts: the constants of proportionality in each of the 3 methods are different. Nonetheless, an $O(n^2)$ efficiency is severely limiting when n is reasonably large. It would be nice to reduce (n^2) and design algorithms whose run time is of the order $O(n^r)$ for $r < 2$.

The Shell Sort

We commented that the insertion sort was most efficient for data already almost sorted. This is the basis of the **shell sort.** Instead of sorting the entire array at once, it first divides the array into smaller segments, which are then separately sorted using the insertion sort. The array ALPHA originally appears as:

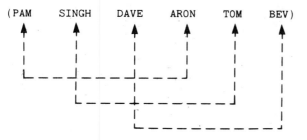

We first divide this into 3 segments of 2 elements each:

```
PAM     ARON ───► Segment 1
SINGH   TOM ────► Segment 2
DAVE    BEV ────► Segment 3
```

We then sort each of the segments:

```
ARON    PAM
SINGH   TOM
BEV     DAVE
```

The original array, partially sorted, now appears as:

```
(ARON   SINGH   BEV   PAM   TOM   DAVE)
```

We divide this partially sorted array as:

```
ARON    BEV   TOM  →Segment 1
SINGH   PAM   DAVE→Segment 2
```

The segments are sorted and the array ALPHA takes the form:

```
(ARON    DAVE    BEV    PAM    TOM    SINGH)
```

Finally, this array is sorted as one segment; DAVE and BEV, and TOM and SINGH get swapped to give us the sorted array:

```
( ARON    BEV    DAVE    PAM    SINGH    TOM)
```

The key to the shell sort algorithm is that the whole array is first fragmented into K segments for some number K, where K is preferably a prime number.* If the size of the array ALPHA is N, then the segments are:

```
ALPHA(1), ALPHA(K + 1), ALPHA(2K + 1), . . ., ALPHA(N/K + 1)
ALPHA(2), ALPHA(K + 2), ALPHA(2K + 2), . . ., ALPHA(N/K + 2)
                          .                         .
                          .                         .
                          .                         .
ALPHA(K), ALPHA(2K), ALPHA(3K), . . ., ALPHA(N/K + K)
```

Because each segment is sorted, the whole array is partially sorted after the first pass. For the next pass, the value of K is reduced, which increases the size of each segment— hence reducing the number of segments. The next value of K is also chosen so that it is relatively prime to its previous value. The process is repeated until $K = 1$, at which point the array is sorted. The insertion sort is applied to each segment, so each successive segment is partially sorted. Consequently, the later applications of the insertion sort became very efficient, dramatically increasing the overall efficiency of the shell sort.

The shell sort is also called the **diminishing increment sort** because the value of K (the number of segments) continually decreases. The method is most efficient if the successive values of K are kept relatively prime to each other. Knuth has mathematically estimated that, with relatively prime values of K, the shell sort will execute in an average time proportional to $O(n(\log_2 N)^2)$. However, the sort will work for any values of K, as long as the last value of K is 1. When the values of K are not relatively prime, then the efficiency of the shell sort is of the order $O(n^r)$ where $1 < r < 2$. This is less efficient than $O(n(\log_2 n)^2)$ for large values of n.

The shell sort thus is most efficient on arrays that are already nearly sorted. In fact, the first chosen value of K is large to ensure that the whole array is fragmented into small individual arrays, for which the insertion sort is highly effective. Each subsequent sort causes the entire array to be more nearly sorted, so that the efficiency of the insertion sort as applied to larger partially sorted arrays is increased. Trace through a few examples to convince yourself that the partially ordered status of the array for one value of K is not affected by subsequent partial sorts for a different value of K.

It is not clearly known with what value of K the shell sort should start, but Knuth suggests a sequence of values as 1, 3, 7, 15, . . . for reverse values of K; that is, the $(J + 1)$th value is 2 times Jth value plus 1. There are other possible values of K suggested by Knuth, but by and large the initial guess at the first value of K is all that you need. That initial guess will depend on the size of the array and, to some extent, on the type of data being sorted.

The PSEUDO procedure SHELLSORT sorts an array ALPHA of size N:

```
PROCEDURE SHELLSORT(ALPHA,N)
(*This procedure sorts an array alpha of size N*)
VAR S,I,J,K,ALPHA(N),N: INTEGER
I:=N/2
WHILE I>0 DO
```

*Knuth, D.E. 1973. *The Art of Computer Programming*, Vol. 3, Menlo Park, CA: Addison-Wesley.

```
┌J:=I
│REPEAT
│      ┌J:=J+1
│      │K:=J-I
│      │WHILE K>0 DO
│      │    .┌IF A(K)> A(K+I) THEN┐
│      │     │      S:=A(K)        │
│      │     │      A(K):=A(K+I)   │
│      │     │      A(K+I):=S      │
│      │     │      K:=K-I         │
│      │     ELSE                  │
│      │     │      K:=0           │
│      │     └ENDIF                │
│      └ENDWHILE
│UNTIL J=N
└I:=I/2
 ENDWHILE
 RETURN
 END SHELLSORT
```

The Quick Sort

Even though the shell sort provides a significant advantage in run time over its $O(n^2)$ predecessors, its average efficiency of $O(n(\log_2 n)^2)$ still may not be good enough for large arrays. The next group of methods, including quick sort, have the average execution time of $O(n(\log_2 n))$, which is seemingly the best that can be achieved. Compared to the shell sort's $O(n(\log_2 n)^2)$ or $O(n^r)$ for $1 < r < 2$, an $O(n(\log_2 n))$ efficient sort is often a good choice for large sorting jobs.

The purpose of the **quick sort** is to move a data item in the correct direction just enough for it to reach its final place in the array. The method, therefore, reduces unnecessary swaps, and moves an item a great distance in one move. A pivotal item near the middle of the array is chosen, and then items on either side are moved so that the data items on one side of the pivot are smaller than the pivot, whereas those on the other side are larger. The middle (pivot) item is now in its correct position. The procedure is then applied recursively to the 2 parts of the array, on either side of the pivot, until the whole array is sorted. We shall illustrate the mechanics of this method by applying it to an array of numbers. Suppose the array A initially appears as:

(15 20 5 8 95 12 80 17 9 55)

Figure 10-3 shows a quick sort applied to this array.

A(1)	A(2)	A(3)	A(4)	A(5)	A(6)	A(7)	A(8)	A(9)	A(10)
15*	20	5	8	95	12	80	17	9	55
9	20	5	8	95	12	80	17	( )	55
9	( )	5	8	95	12	80	17	20	55
9	12	5	8	95	( )	80	17	20	55
9	12	5	8	( )	95	80	17	20	55
9	12	5	8	15	95	80	17	20	55

Figure 10-3 Quick sort of an array.

The following steps are involved:

1. Remove the 1st data item, 15, mark its position and scan the array from right to left, comparing data item values with 15. When you find the 1st smaller value, remove it from its current position and put in position A(1). This is shown in line 2 of Figure 10-3.

2. Scan line 2 from left to right beginning with position A(2), comparing data item values with 15. When you find the 1st value greater than 15, extract it and store in the position marked by parentheses in line 2. This is shown in line 3 in Figure 10-3.

3. Begin the right to left scan of line 3 with position A(8) looking for a value smaller than 15. When you find it, extract it and store it in the position marked by the parentheses in line 3 of Figure 10-3.

4. Begin scanning line 4 from left to right at position A(3), find a value greater than 15, remove it, mark its position, and store it inside the parentheses in line 4. This is shown in line 5 of Figure 10-3.

5. Now, when you scan line 5 from right to left beginning at position A(7), you find no value smaller than 15. Moreover, you come to a parentheses position, position A(5). This is the location to put the 1st data item, 15, as shown in line 6 of Figure 10-3. At this stage 15 is in its correct place relative to the final sorted array.

Notice that all values to the left of 15 are less than 15, and all values to the right of 15 are greater than 15. The method will still work if 2 values are the same. The process can now be applied recursively to the 2 segments of the array on the left and right of 15.

The PSEUDO procedure QUICKSORT given here uses a stack to avoid recursion. You will write the recursive version of this procedure as an exercise at the end of the chapter.

```
PROCEDURE QUICKSORT (A, N)

(*This procedure sorts a numeric array A of size N in an*)
(*ascending order*)

VAR S, A(N), N, L, I, R, J, REF: INTEGER

        (*L is the left current position, R is the right current*)
        (*position, REF is the reference value *)
        L:=1
        R:=N

        (*We now begin to process the array A from A(R) to A(L) *)
        (*We call on the previously defined POP, PUSH in relation to*)
        (*stack STACK*)
```

```
REPEAT
   ┌ I:=L
   │ J:=R
   │ REF:=A(L)
   │ WHILE I<J DO
   │  ┌ (*Begin right to left scan*)
   │  │      WHILE REF <A(J) AND I<J DO ─────────────────────
   │  │           [J:=J-1]
   │  │      ENDWHILE
   │  │      IF J<>I THEN
   │  │           ┌A(I):=A(J)┐
   │  │           └I:=I+1   ┘
   │  │      ENDIF
   │  │      (*Begin left to right scan*)
   │  │      WHILE REF > A(I) AND I<J DO ─────────────────────
   │  │           [I:=I+1]
   │  │      ENDWHILE
   │  │      IF  J< >I THEN
   │  │           ┌A(J):=A(I)┐
   │  │           └J:=J-1   ┘
   │  │      ENDIF
   │  └ ENDWHILE
   │ (* I and J have met somewhere between L and R *)
   │ A(J):=REF
   │ (* Have I and J met at the right boundary?*)
   │ IF J=R THEN
   │      [R:=R-1]
   │ (* Have I and J met at the left boundary?*)
   │      ELSE IF I=L THEN
   │         ┌ [L:=L+1]
   │         │ (*I and J did not meet at boundaries*)
   │         │ (*Which segment,i.e.,below L*)
   │         │ (*or above R,is larger?*)
   │         │ ELSE IF (I-L) < (R-J) THEN
   │         │    ┌ K:=J+1
   │         │    │ CALL PUSH (STACK,K,R)
   │         │    │ R:=I-1
   │         │    │ ELSE
   │         │    │    ┌ K:=I-1
   │         │    │    │ CALL PUSH (STACK,L,K)
   │         │    │    └ L:=J+1
   │         │    └ ENDIF
   │         └ ENDIF
   │      ENDIF
   │ IF R< = L THEN
   │ [CALL POP (STACK,L,R)]
   └ ENDIF
UNTIL (R=0) AND (L=0)

END QUICKSORT
```

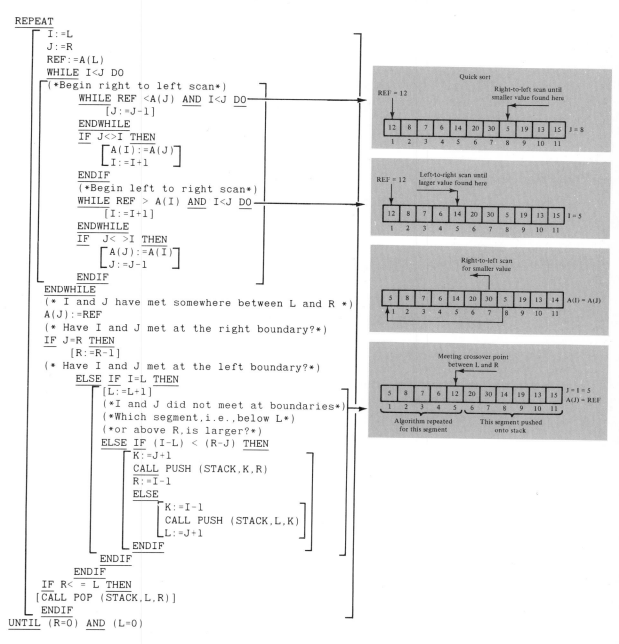

Quick sort

REF = 12   Right-to-left scan until
                  smaller value found here

| 12 | 8 | 7 | 6 | 14 | 20 | 30 | 5 | 19 | 13 | 15 | J = 8
| 1 | 2 | 3 | 4 | 5 | 6 | 7 | 8 | 9 | 10 | 11 |

REF = 12   Left-to-right scan until
             larger value found here

| 12 | 8 | 7 | 6 | 14 | 20 | 30 | 5 | 19 | 13 | 15 | I = 5
| 1 | 2 | 3 | 4 | 5 | 6 | 7 | 8 | 9 | 10 | 11 |

Right-to-left scan
for smaller value

| 5 | 8 | 7 | 6 | 14 | 20 | 30 | 5 | 19 | 13 | 14 | A(I) = A(J)
| 1 | 2 | 3 | 4 | 5 | 6 | 7 | 8 | 9 | 10 | 11 |

Meeting crossover point
between L and R

| 5 | 8 | 7 | 6 | 12 | 20 | 30 | 14 | 19 | 13 | 15 | J = I = 5
| 1 | 2 | 3 | 4 | 5 | 6 | 7 | 8 | 9 | 10 | 11 | A(J) = REF

Algorithm repeated   This segment pushed
for this segment   onto stack

As mentioned earlier, the *average* run time efficiency of the quick sort is $O(n(\log_2 n))$, which is the best that has been achieved for a large array of size n. In the worst case situation, when the array is already sorted, the efficiency of the quick sort may drop down to $O(n^2)$ due to the continuous right to left scan all the way to the last left boundary.[*]

You may wonder how large a stack is needed to sort an array of size n. (Remember that this stack is implicitly created even when you use a language that permits recursion.) Knuth has mathematically estimated that the size of the stack cannot exceed $(1 + \log_2((1/3)(n + 1)))$.[*]

The Heap Sort

The **heap sort** is a sorting algorithm the efficiency of which is roughly equivalent to that of the quick sort; its average efficiency is $O(n(\log_2 n))$ for an array of size n. The method, originally described by Floyd, has 2 phases.[†] In phase 1, the array containing the n data items is viewed as equivalent to a binary tree that is full at all levels except for its rightmost elements (Chapter 6). As an example, suppose we wish to sort the array:

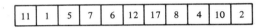

The 1st phase tree appears as shown in Figure 10-4. The goal of phase 1 is now to sort the data elements along each path from leaf node level to the root node. If we wish to sort in ascending order, then the numbers along any path from leaf node to root (except the root) should be in increasing order. To achieve this, we take the following steps:

1. Process the node which is the parent of the rightmost node on the lowest level. If its value is less than the value of its largest child, swap these values, otherwise do nothing.

2. Move left on the same level. Compare the value of the parent node with the values of the child nodes. If the parent is smaller than the largest child, swap them.

3. When the left end of this level is reached, move up a level, and, beginning with the rightmost parent node, repeat step (2). Continue swapping the original parent with the larger of its children until it is larger than its children. In effect, the original parent is being walked down the tree in a fashion that ensures that numbers will be in increasing order along the path.

4. Repeat step (3) until all level 1 nodes have been processed. (Remember that the root is at level 0).

Figure 10-5 shows these steps applied to Figure 10-4.

Phase 2 of the heap sort finds the node with the largest value in the tree and cuts it from the tree. This is then repeated to find the second largest value, which is also removed

---

[*]Knuth, D. E. Op. Cit.

[†]Floyd, R.W. 1964. Algorithm 245: Tree sort 3, *Communications of the Association for Computing Machinery,* 7:701.

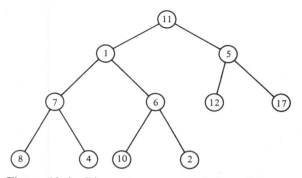

Figure 10-4   Binary tree representation of the array.

from the tree. The process continues until only 2 nodes are left in the tree, which are exchanged if necessary. The precise steps for phase 2 are as follows:

1. Compare the root node with its children, swapping it with the largest child if the largest child is larger than the root.

2. If a swap occurred in step (1), then continue swapping the value which was originally in the root position until it is larger than its children. In effect, this original root node

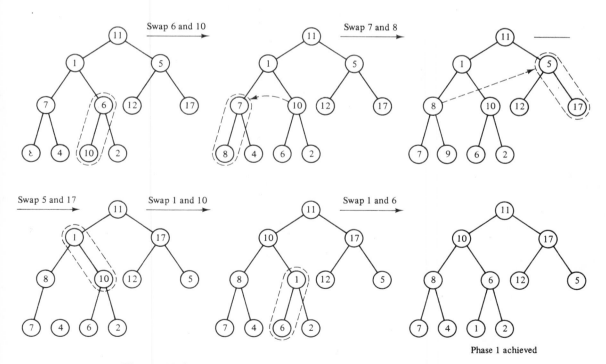

Figure 10-5   Phase 1 of the heap sort applied to binary tree in Figure 10-4.

value is now being walked down a path in the tree to ensure that all paths retain values arranged in ascending order from leaf node to root node.

3. Swap the root node with the bottom rightmost child, sever the new bottom rightmost child from the tree. This is the largest value.

4. Repeat steps (1) through (3) until only two elements are left.

Phase 2 of the heap sort begun in Figure 10-5 is shown for the three highest values in Figure 10-6 on page 244.

   Both phase 1 and phase 2 use the same strategy of walking a parent down a path of the tree via a series of swaps with its children; the PSEUDO HEAPSORT procedure given below calls another procedure, WALKDOWN, which follows.

```
PROCEDURE HEAPSORT (A,N);
VAR P,N,I,A(N),S: INTEGER
(*Both Phase 1 AND Phase 2 call on procedure WALKDOWN*)
(*Begin Phase 1*)
P:=1
I:=N/2+1
WHILE I>2 DO
        ┌I:=I-1
        └CALL WALKDOWN(I,N,A)┘
ENDWHILE
(*Note that N/2 is an integer value and gives the location of
  the last parent in the tree*)
(*Begin Phase 2*)
I:=N+1
WHILE I>2 DO
┌       I:=I-1
        CALL WALKDOWN(A,P,I)
(*Now exchange the root node and the bottom right element*)
        S:=A(P)
        A(P):=A(I)
└       A(I):=S
ENDWHILE
RETURN
END HEAPSORT
```

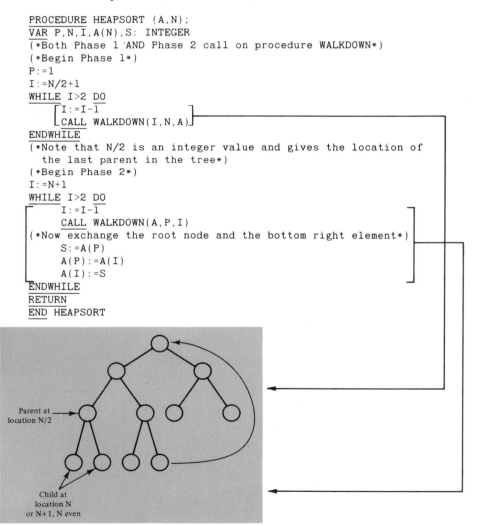

Parent at
location N/2

Child at
location N
or N+1, N even

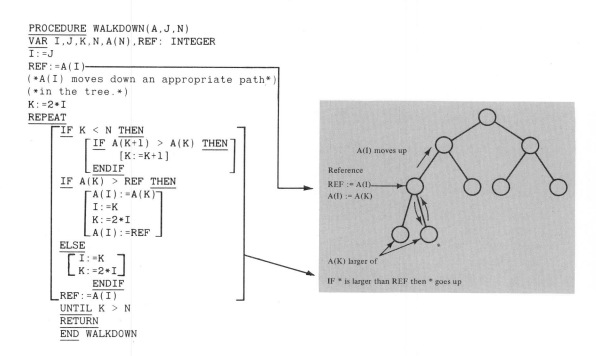

```
PROCEDURE WALKDOWN(A,J,N)
VAR I,J,K,N,A(N),REF: INTEGER
I:=J
REF:=A(I)
(*A(I) moves down an appropriate path*)
(*in the tree.*)
K:=2*I
REPEAT
      ┌IF K < N THEN
      │     ┌IF A(K+1) > A(K) THEN┐
      │     │     [K:=K+1]        │
      │     └ENDIF                ┘
      │ IF A(K) > REF THEN
      │     ┌A(I):=A(K)┐
      │     │I:=K      │
      │     │K:=2*I    │
      │     └A(I):=REF ┘
      │ ELSE
      │     ┌I:=K  ┐
      │     └K:=2*I┘
      │         ENDIF
      └REF:=A(I)
      UNTIL K > N
      RETURN
      END WALKDOWN
```

As mentioned, when *n* is large, the run time efficiency of this sort for both average and worst cases has been calculated to be $O(n(\log_2 n))$.

In general, the heap sort does not perform better than the quick sort. Only when the array is nearly sorted to begin with does the heap sort algorithm gain an advantage. In such a case, the quick sort deteriorates to its worst performance of $O(n^2)$.*

10-3 External Sorting or File Sorting

The sorting algorithms discussed so far apply to arrays that reside in memory. Quite often, voluminous files such as a master file for all the employees in a large corporation must exist on external storage devices because of their size. These on-line storage devices, such as tapes and disks, carry with them specific software and hardware considerations relating to access of stored data.

Only portions of large files can be brought into main memory and sorted. That portion of a file that can reside in main memory is a **segment.** The sorted segment can be sent back to the external storage medium and the next segment brought in. Finally, the partially sorted segments must be merged into a completely sorted file.

Because of the nature of secondary storage devices, bringing a segment of data items into main memory takes longer than does processing it. For instance, it takes time to position the read-write head over the appropriate track of a disk, and more time for the disk to rotate to bring the correct segment to the read-write head. An average input/output operation from and to an auxiliary storage device (not counting processing in memory) may take as long as 200 milliseconds. When you design sort algorithms for files on external media, you must consider this time delay.

*Knuth, D. E. Op. Cit.

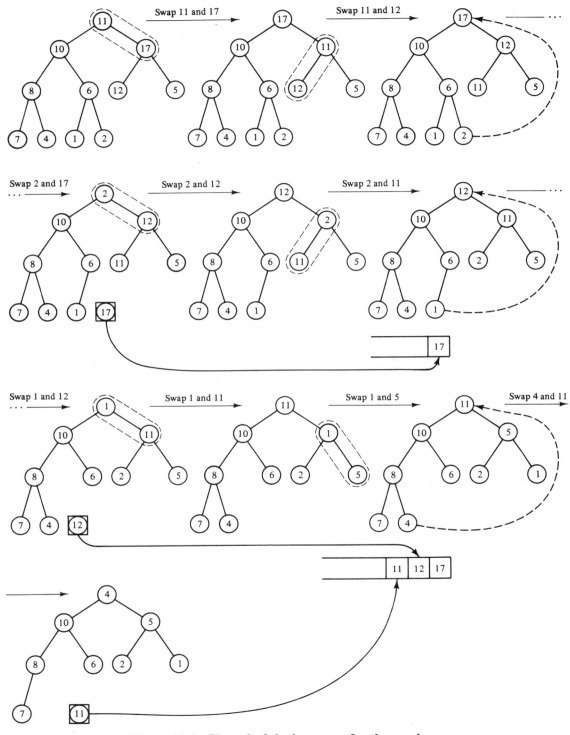

Figure 10-6 Phase 2 of the heap sort for three values.

The Merge Sort

The most common algorithm used in external sorting is the **merge sort.** A file (or subfile) is divided into 2 files, O_1 and O_2. These 2 files are then compared, 1 pair of records at a time, and merged. This is done by writing them on 2 separate new files M_1 and M_2. The elements that do not pair off are simply rewritten into the new files. The records in M_1 and M_2 are now blocked with 2 records in each segment. The 2 blocks (that is, 4 records), 1 from M_1 and 1 from M_2, are merged and written onto the original files O_1 and O_2. The length of the segments in each of O_1 and O_2 is now increased to 4, the merge process applied again, and the new files are written to M_1 and M_2. The process is continued until 1 of the 2 files O_1 or O_2 is empty.

In fact, after r such passes, O_1 and O_2 consist of segments each of which is 2^r records in length. If $2^r \geq n$, then one of the files is empty and the other contains the original file, which is now sorted. Each merge operation requires reading and writing of 2 files, both of which are on the average about $n/2$ records long. Thus, the total number of blocks read or written in a merge operation is approximately $2n/c$, where c is the number of records in a segment. The number of segments accessed for the whole operation is $O((n(\log_2 n))/c)$, which amounts to $O(\log_2 n)$ passes through the entire original file. This is a considerable improvement over the $O(n)$ passes needed in the preceding algorithms.

In order to clarify these concepts, suppose we have an external file containing the data:

$$(2,6,3,1,4,31,23,8,11,19,21,37,14,57,28,45,30,9,35,12,13,18,5,89,77)$$

We divide it into two original files as:

O_1: $(2,6,3,1,4,31,23,8,11,19,21,37)$
O_2: $(14,57,28,45,30,9,35,12,13,18,5,89,77)$

After 1st pass of segments of length 1, we have:

M_1: $((2,14),(3,28),(4,30),(23,35),(11,13),(5,21))$
M_2: $((6,57),(1,45),(9,31),(8,12),(18,19),(37,89),77))$

After the 2nd pass of segments of length 2:

O_1: $((2,6,14,57),(4,9,30,31),(11,13,18,19))$
O_2: $((1,3,28,45),(8,12,23,35),(5,21,37,89),77))$

After the 3rd pass of segments of length 4:

M_1: $((1,2,3,6,14,28,45,57),(5,11,13,18,19,21,37,89))$
M_2: $((4,8,9,12,23,30,31,35),77))$

After the 4th pass of segments of length 8:

O_1: $(1,2,3,4,6,8,9,12,14,23,28,30,31,35,45,57)$
O_2: $(5,11,13,18,19,21,37,77,89)$

After the 5th pass of blocks of length 16:

M_1: $(1,2,3,4,5,6,8,9,11,12,13,14,18,19,21,23,28,30,31,35,37,45,57,77,89)$
M_2: is empty

The algorithm was described beginning with segments of length 1. Substantially larger length segments can be stored in main memory, so the efficiency of the algorithm can be enhanced by taking conveniently larger segments. For example, if an external file has 100,000 records, and a segment of 1000 such records can be stored in main memory, then the entire file can be sorted in 7 passes because $2^7 \times 1000$ is greater than 100,000. The segments in each pass can be ordered by a suitable sorting method such as the quick sort.

The procedure merge sort usually deals with external file media and therefore is system dependent; hence, we have not provided a PSEUDO procedure for it. A specific language implementation of it is considered in the programming problems.

The **polyphase merge sort** is a merge sort with multiple channels. If there is a channel for each of r disk units, then r files $O_1, O_2, \ldots, O_r$ each of block length p, can be merged into $M_1, M_2, \ldots, M_r$ files of blocks of rp length.

SUMMARY

Efficient and reliable data processing depends upon sorted data. The internal and external sorting methods each have their relative efficiencies in different applications. It appears that the quick sort, heap sort, and merge sort can handle arrays of heterogeneous data fairly efficiently. The shell sort is more efficient than the bubble sort, selection sort, and insertion sort. Sorting of larger files that cannot fit in main memory is best accomplished by external sorting techniques such as the merge sort.

The following table compares and comments on the sorting methods discussed in this chapter.

Sorting Method	Run time Proportional to*	Comments
Bubble	n^2	Good for small n ($n \geq 100$)
Selection	n^2	Good for partially sorted data and small n
Insertion	n^2	Good for almost sorted data
Shell	$n^{1.5}$	Good for moderate amounts of data
Quick	$n(\log_2 n)$	Excellent
Heap	$n(\log_2 n)$	Excellent
Merge	$\log_2 n$	Good for external file sorting

*n is the number of data items to be sorted.

KEY TERMS

Ordering
External sorting
Internal sorting
Execution time
Bubble sort
Insertion sort

Selection sort
Shell sort
Diminishing increment sort
Quick sort

Heap sort
Segment
Binary sort
Merge sort
Polyphase merge sort

EXERCISES

1. Why is there a need for sorting?

2. Is it necessary to employ a fancy, most efficient sort routine if the number of data items is no more than 100, and each data item is no more than 80 bytes?

3. Why is the insertion sort called by that name?

4. Why is the bubble sort called by that name?

5. Is the heap sort always better than the quick sort?

6. When is the bubble sort better than the quick sort?

7. Why is the insertion sort most efficient when the original data are in almost sorted order?

8. Using any high-level language, write a procedure shell sort in which the diminishing increments are not relatively prime.

9. Translate the PSEUDO procedure SHELLSORT into a high-level language.

10. Why does the shell sort work for any sequence of diminishing increments as long as the last one is 1?

11. What advantage do the relatively prime values of the increments have over the other values in a shell sort?

12. Under what circumstances would you not use a quick sort?

13. What are the worst case and average case efficiencies of the heap sort?

14. In Chapter 1, POINTER-SORT used an index of pointers to sort data logically without rearranging it. Identify the sort algorithm that was behind the PSEUDO POINTER-SORT procedure. Adapt the POINTER-SORT procedure to each of the other algorithms presented in this chapter.

15. A sorting method is said to be *stable* if two data items of matching value are guaranteed *not* to be rearranged with respect to each other as the algorithm progresses. For example, in the 4 element array:
$$60 \quad 42_1 \quad 80 \quad 42_2$$
a stable sorting method would guarantee a final ordering:
$$42_1 \quad 42_2 \quad 60 \quad 80$$
and not:
$$42_2 \quad 42_1 \quad 60 \quad 80$$
Classify each of the sorting algorithms studied in this chapter by their stability. (To see why stability may be important, consider Programming Problem (6).

PROGRAMMING PROBLEMS

1. Given a sequential file containing an unordered list of passengers and their flight numbers for the Wing and a Prayer Airline Company, produce a listing arranged in flight-number order. Passengers on the same flight should be ordered by last name.

The easy version of this program assumes that all information will fit in main memory, allowing you to use an internal sort. For an added challenge, write the program using an external sort algorithm.

2. Take 1000 randomly generated integers. Apply the bubble sort, shell sort, quick sort, and heap sort. Observe and compare their execution time.

3. Put some hypothetical data on an external file and apply the merge sort to them. Write this program in a high-level language.

4. Write a recursive version of the quick sort procedure given in the text. Implement it in a high-level language that supports recursion.

5. Use a high-level language to create a program that will complete the following steps. Artificially create a file F of 1000 randomly chosen names. Read into a separate file F1 all those names from F whose last names begin with A thru G. Sort this file with heap sort, and store this sorted file in another file LARGE. Now read into F1 all those names from F whose names begin with H thru N, sort it, and append it to the end of LARGE. Repeat this process until all names from F are exhausted. The file LARGE will be the sorted version of the original file F. Observe the execution time of your program.

6. Write a merge sort procedure in Pascal and apply it to the file in Programming Problem (4). Compare its execution time to that obtained with the first program you wrote.

7. Consider a list of records, each containing 4 fields:

   - Name

   - Month of birth

   - Day of birth

   - Year of birth

   Write a program to sort this list in oldest-to-youngest order. People with the same birthdate should be arranged alphabetically. One strategy you could employ would be to concatenate strategically the 4 fields into one, and then just sort that one field. Another strategy would be to sort the list 4 times, each time by a different field. (Think carefully about which field to sort on first.) Which of the strategies would require that you choose a stable sorting algorithm?

If you work in Pascal . . .

The following Pascal program is an exact translation of the PSEUDO SHELLSORT procedure given in (10.2).

```
PROGRAM SHELL (INPUT,OUTPUT);
CONST HUND=100;
TYPE SORTARRAY=ARRAY [1..HUND] OF INTEGER;
VAR ALPHA: SORTARRAY;
VAR P,Q,R: INTEGER;
PROCEDURE SHELLSORT (VAR A:SORTARRAY; VAR N: INTEGER);
VAR I,J,K,S:INTEGER;
    BEGIN
        I:=N DIV 2;
        WHILE I>0 DO
          BEGIN
                J:=I;
                REPEAT
                    J:=J+1;
                    K:=J-I;
                    WHILE K>0 DO
                    BEGIN
                            IF A[K]>A[K+I] THEN
                            BEGIN
                                S:=A[K];
                                A[K]:=A[K+I];
                                A[K+I]:=S;
                                K:=K-I
                            END
                            ELSE
                                K:=0
                    END;
                UNTIL J=N;
                I:=I DIV 2
          END
END;(* THIS THE END OF THE PROCEDURE SHELLSORT *)
BEGIN (* THE MAIN PROGRAM *)
    WRITELN ('   THIS PROCEDURE WILL SORT UP TO 100 INTEGERS');
    WRITELN;
    WRITELN ( ' ENTER HOWMANY (<=100) YOU WANT SORTED');
    READLN (P);
    WRITELN (' NOW ENTER YOUR DATA ONE NUMBER PER LINE');
    FOR Q:= 1 TO P DO
        READLN ( ALPHA[Q]);
    WRITELN (' SORTED DATA FOLLOWS ');
    SHELLSORT (ALPHA,P);
    FOR Q:=1 TO P DO
    BEGIN
        WRITELN;
        WRITELN (ALPHA [Q])
    END;
END.
```

```
C>a:shell
     THIS PROCEDURE WILL SORT UP TO 100 INTEGERS

 ENTER HOWMANY (<=100) YOU WANT SORTED
10
 NOW ENTER YOUR DATA ONE NUMBER PER LINE
45
89
67
12
56
90
345
156
32
56
 SORTED DATA FOLLOWS

        12

        32

        45

        56

        56

        67

        89

        90

       156

       345
```

11

Search Strategies

You always find something the last place you look.

AXIOM OF SEARCHING

11-1 Introductory Considerations

The problem of searching may be likened to a situation that we have all faced in manual record-keeping systems. In such systems, records are typically kept in a metal filing cabinet. Each individual record is kept in a manila folder. The various papers within a folder constitute the **data** associated with that record, whereas the tab on the folder has written on it the **key** by which we identify the record. When we want to pull the folder associated with a particular key, there are several intuitive methods that we may use to find it. If we have been sloppy and have stuffed the folders into the filing cabinet in arbitrary order, we are forced to flip through the folders one by one, comparing the key on each tab to the **target** we are trying to find. In the absence of any **file organization,** such a sequential search is the best that can be done. If we have been more careful in initially organizing the files (for example, by alphabetically ordering the keys), it is clear that we can use more effective search methods. However, these more effective methods require not only a more sophisticated file organization but also one that allows **direct access** to records in the file; that is, we must be able to select a record by its relative position in the file without having to sift through all the records preceding it.

At this point, we shall establish the conventions we will follow for all of the computer-based search procedures developed in this chapter. The procedures will assume two global arrays:

```
GLOBAL VAR N, KEY(N) : INTEGER
GLOBAL VAR DATA(N) : (*Appropriate data type*)
```

The array KEY here contains the key values for all the data we wish to search; it corresponds to what is written on the tabs of our manila filing folders. Each KEY and DATA pair constitute the **fields** within a **record** of our file. The parallel array DATA contains, for each key value, the data corresponding to it; that is, the DATA array corresponds to the contents of the manila folders. This parallel array format is shown in Figure 11-1.

Our algorithms always will use keys of INTEGER data type. As appropriate, we will add remarks concerning modifications that would be necessary if the keys were of a different data type, such as CHARACTER. The parallel structures of Figure 11-1 could exist either in main memory or on a permanent storage medium such as a magnetic disk. This distinction will not affect the PSEUDO versions of the search algorithms. However, the distinction is often important because the efficiency of an algorithm may be influenced by the type of storage media to which it is applied. Where this distinction is important, it always will be noted and discussed thoroughly.

Our calls to a search procedure will always take the form:

```
PROCEDURE SEARCHNAME(TARGET, ITEM, FOUND)
VAR    TARGET : INTEGER
VAR    ITEM : (*Appropriate type, matching that of DATA array.*)
VAR    FOUND : BOOLEAN
       (* Search global KEY array for key value matching TARGET.*)
       (* Return DATA associated with TARGET key in ITEM.*)
       (* FOUND returned as TRUE if search successful, FALSE
          otherwise.*)
```

In those procedures where it is necessary to detect the end of the keys being searched, we will assume the existence of a variable ENDFLAG that has been initially assigned to the final position in the KEY list prior to entering the procedure. In those procedures where it is necessary to know the number of records being searched, we will assume that a global variable NUMBERREC has been similarly initialized outside the search procedure.

11-2   Quantity-Dependent Search Techniques

Sequential Search

The first class of search techniques we shall consider all have efficiencies dependent upon only the numeric quantity of records in the list to be searched. Easiest and least efficient among these techniques is the **sequential search.** This is the technique that must be used when records are stored without any consideration given to order, or when the storage medium lacks any type of direct access facility (for example, magnetic tape). The logic of the PSEUDO procedure SEQUENTIALSEARCH is extremely straightforward; it entails beginning with the first available record and proceeding to the next available record repeatedly until we find the target key or can conclude that it will not be found.

```
PROCEDURE SEQUENTIALSEARCH(TARGET,ITEM,FOUND)
GLOBAL VAR ENDFLAG, N, KEY(N) : INTEGER
GLOBAL VAR DATA(N) : (*Appropriate data type*)
VAR TARGET, I : INTEGER
VAR ITEM : (*Appropriate data type*)
VAR FOUND : BOOLEAN

(* Begin procedure by assuming failure. *)
(* ENDFLAG stores sentinel also found in final KEY position. *)
```

Relative position	KEY	DATA
1	414	JONES
2	437	GARLAND
3	442	SMITH
4	450	ROSEN
⋮	⋮	⋮
	806	RITTER
	913	GARLOCK
NUMBERREC	917	SIMMS

Figure 11-1   General format of data for search algorithms.

```
FOUND := FALSE
I := 1
REPEAT
    IF KEY(I) = TARGET THEN
        FOUND := TRUE
        ITEM := DATA(I)
    ELSE
        [I := I + 1]
    ENDIF
UNTIL KEY(I) = ENDFLAG OR FOUND
RETURN
END SEQUENTIALSEARCH
```

The efficiency of the sequential search is clearly very poor. On the average, it will require NUMBERREC/2 accesses to the list to find a key. In the worst case, the target being sought is not in the list of keys and each record must be accessed. This worst case efficiency can be improved somewhat if the list is ordered (you will do this as an exercise). However, no improvements can change the fact that the efficiency of the sequential search is basically proportional to the number of records in the list. Hence, users searching an external file of 50,000 records for which the average retrieval time per record is 5 milliseconds will have to wait over 2 minutes for responses to their requests. Obviously, that sort of performance will not result in happy users; something better is needed.

Binary Search

By paying what may initially seem like a small price, we can dramatically increase the efficiency of our search effort using a simple technique called the **binary search.** The price we must pay is threefold:

1. The list of keys must be maintained in physical order

2. The number of keys in the list (NUMBERREC) must be maintained

3. There must be direct access by relative position for the keys in the list

Suppose, for example, that the list in Figure 11-2 has the direct access facility cited in (3), and that we wish to locate the data associated with target key 1649. The strategy dictated by the binary search is to begin the search in the middle of the list. In our example of Figure 11-2, we begin the search with the key found at position 5. Because the target we are seeking is greater than the key at position 5, we conclude that the key we want will be found among positions 6 through 10 if it is to be found at all. We split those positions that remain viable candidates by accessing position

$$\frac{6 + 10}{2} = 8$$

Because the key at position 8 is greater than the target, we are able to conclude that the key being sought will be found in position 6 or 7 if it is to be found at all. Notice that, after only 2 accesses into the list, our list of remaining viable candidates for a match has shrunk to 2. (Compare this to the list remaining in a sequential search after 2 accesses into the same list.) We now split the distance between positions 6 and 7, arriving (by integer arithmetic) at position 6. Here we find the key being sought after a mere 3 probes into the list.

Crucial to the entire binary search algorithm are 2 pointers, LOW and HIGH, to the bottom and top of the current list of viable candidates. Should these pointers cross—that is, should HIGH become less than LOW—we conclude that the target does not appear in the list. The entire algorithm is formalized in the PSEUDO procedure BINARYSEARCH:

```
PROCEDURE BINARYSEARCH(TARGET,ITEM,FOUND)
GLOBAL VAR NUMBERREC, N, KEY(N): INTEGER
GLOBAL VAR DATA(N) : (*Appropriate data type*)
VAR TARGET, HIGH, LOW, MID : INTEGER
VAR ITEM : (*Appropriate data type*)
VAR FOUND : BOOLEAN

(* Begin procedure by assuming failure. *)

FOUND := FALSE
LOW := 1
HIGH := NUMBERREC
REPEAT
    MID := (LOW + HIGH) / 2
    IF TARGET < KEY(MID) THEN
        [HIGH := MID-1]
    ELSE IF TARGET > KEY(MID) THEN
        [LOW := MID+1]
    ELSE (*Success!*)
        [ITEM := DATA(MID)]
        [FOUND := TRUE   ]
    ENDIF
    ENDIF
UNTIL FOUND OR (HIGH < LOW)
RETURN
END BINARYSEARCH
```

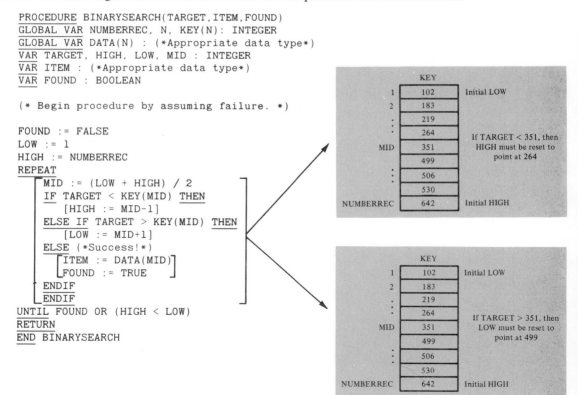

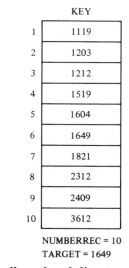

Figure 11-2   Physically ordered direct access key list for binary search.

The effectiveness of the binary search algorithm lies in its continual halving of the list to be searched. When applied to the list of keys in Figure 11-2, the efficiency of the method in the worst case would require 4 accesses. For an ordered list of 50,000 keys the worst case efficiency is a mere 16 accesses. (In case you do not believe this dramatic increase in efficiency as the list gets larger, try plugging "50,000" into a hand-held calculator and count how many times you must halve the displayed number to reduce it to 1.) The same file that would have necessitated an average wait of 2 minutes using a sequential search will permit a virtually instantaneous response when the binary search strategy is used. In more precise algebraic terms, the halving method yields a worst case search efficiency of

```
log₂ NUMBERREC + 1
```

This efficiency at times may be even further enhanced by choosing a technique other than halving to split the remainder of the list into two parts. One such splitting function is to use an interpolative guess as to the most probable position of the key in the list. This is the type of logic used by most humans when searching a phone book for a given name. However, interpolative splitting strategies are dependent upon the the distribution of the keys in the list. Because of the significant effectiveness of the halving strategy, interpolative techniques rarely improve efficiency enough to be worth the added complications involved in their implementation. Moreover, the wrong set of data can actually cause interpolative techniques to become significantly slower than the guaranteed efficiency of halving.

The drawback of the binary search lies not in any consideration of its processing speed but rather in the price that we must pay for being able to use it. What appears on the surface to be a relatively small price is in fact quite steep. We must, for example, continually maintain a count of the number of records in the search list. For a **volatile** list—one undergoing frequent insertions and deletions—this consideration can be a nuisance. But mere nuisances can be endured; what makes the binary search impractical for a volatile list of any size is the requirement that the list of keys be kept in order *physically*. Our discussion of linked lists in Chapter 2 pointed out the enormous amount of data movement involved in such physical ordering. Unfortunately, the linked list structure, although it eliminates the data movement problem, cannot be adapted to the binary search technique because of the direct access requirement. We are seemingly faced with an inescapable quandary.

Binary Tree Search

You should know by this point in your study of data structures that ingenuity can always overcome inescapable quandaries. Actually, the answer to our dilemma has already been presented in Chapters 6 and 7. The order in which the keys of Figure 11-2 would be accessed for a given target can be represented by the full binary tree in Figure 11-3.

In other words, if we are willing to add left and right child pointers to our data records, we can store the list to be searched as a binary tree and duplicate the high efficiency of the binary search *provided* the tree remains full. Notice that as insertions and deletions destroy the fullness of the tree, search efficiency can deteriorate. However, the height-balancing technique described in Chapter 7 will control the processing of insertions and deletions in such a fashion that a given search path in the resulting binary tree will never be more than 45 percent longer than it would be in an optimal full tree.* Hence, the binary tree emerges as the best of both worlds, combining the excellent search efficiency of the binary method with the ability to process quickly insertions and deletions. The binary tree and various derivatives of it will be discussed further in Section 11-4 when we introduce the concept of an index.

11-3   Density-Dependent Search Techniques

In an ideal data processing world, all identifying keys, such as product codes or social security numbers, would start at 1 and follow in sequence thereafter. In any given list, we would merely store the key and its associated data at the position that matched the key. The search efficiency for any key in such a list would be one access to the list, and all data processors could live happily ever after. Unfortunately, in the real world, users desire keys that consist of more meaningful characters, such as names, addresses, or zip codes.

For instance, it may be that in a given inventory control application, product codes are numbered in sequence beginning with 10,000 instead of 1. A moment's reflection should indicate that this is still a highly desirable situation because, given a key, we need merely locate it at position (KEYVALUE − 9999) in the list, and we still have a search efficiency of 1. What we have done here is known as a **key-to-address transformation,** or **hashing function.** A hashing function acts upon a given key to return the relative position in the list where we expect to find the key.

*Knuth, D. 1973. *The Art of Computer Programming: Searching and Sorting*. Menlo Park, CA: Addison-Wesley.

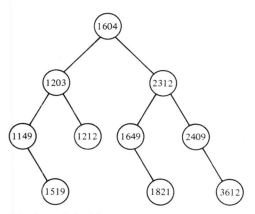

Figure 11-3   Each path in binary tree corresponds to the order in which keys are accessed in a binary search.

Most hashing functions are not as straightforward as the preceding one and present some additional complications that we can quickly illustrate. Let us at this point introduce the hashing function:

```
HASH(KEYVALUE) = (KEYVALUE MOD 4) + 1
```

Then the set of keys 3, 5, 8, and 10 will be loaded into positions 4, 2, 1, and 3, respectively, as illustrated in Figure 11-4. However, if we happen to have 3, 4, 8, and 10 as keys instead of 3, 5, 8, and 10, a problem arises. Namely, 4 and 8 **hash to** the same position. They are said to be **synonyms,** and the result is a **collision.** This dilemma is highlighted in Figure 11-5. Clearly, one of the goals of the hashing functions we develop should be to eliminate such collisions (to the greatest degree possible).

Construction of Hashing Functions

The business of developing hashing functions can be quite intriguing. The essential idea is to build a mathematical black box that will take a key value as input and issue the position in the list where that key value should be located. The position emitted should have as low as possible a probability of conflicting with the position that would be produced for a different key. In addition, the black box we create must also ensure that a given key

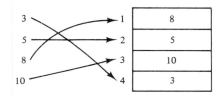

Figure 11-4   Keys 3, 5, 8, and 10 loaded using the hashing function (KEYVALUE MOD 4) + 1.

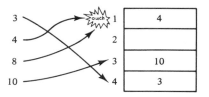

Figure 11-5   If keys 3, 4, 8, and 10 are loaded by hashing function (KEYVALUE MOD 4) + 1, the result is a collision at position 1.

will always produce the same position as output. Those of you who have used a random number generator in past programming projects should begin to note a similarity between some of the properties possessed by a good hashing function and a good random number generator. Indeed, list access via a hashing function is sometimes called **randomized storage,** and the first type of hashing function we discuss below makes direct use of a random number generator.

Use of a Random Number Generator   Many high-level languages provide their users with a random number generator that takes an argument to control how the random numbers generated by it are produced. We use as an example here DEC's FORTRAN, which supplies as a random number generator:

    RAN(I,J)

When calling this function, *I* and *J* act as **seeds,** which are used to produce a real random value between 0 and 1. *I* and *J* are then altered by the random number generator to ensure (with a high degree of probability) that a different random number will be produced the next time the function is called. In traditional applications of such a random number generator, a user will derive the initial seeds by a method that has only a small likelihood of producing the same random sequence twice. For example, many operating systems supply the time, day, month, and year, which could be converted into appropriate initial seeds.

In a hashing application, values of the keys can be supplied as seeds. The random number between 0 and 1 that is correspondingly produced can then be appropriately multiplied, truncated, and shifted to produce a hash value within the desired range of positions. If you are working in a language that does not supply a random number generator, they are not difficult to write. We provide one written in OMSI Pascal-1 in the hashing procedure given in the Pascal supplement at the end of this chapter. Teague* and Maurer and Williams[†] both offer readable discussions on other methods of random number generation.

Folding   In situations where the key to be positioned is not a pure integer, some preliminary work may be required to translate it into a usable form. Take, for instance, the case of a social security number:

---

*Teague, R. 1972. *Computing Problems for FORTRAN Solution*. San Francisco: Canfield.

[†]Maurer, H. A., and Williams, M. R. 1972. *A Collection of Programming Problems and Techniques*. Englewood Cliffs, NJ: Prentice-Hall.

387-58-1505

Viewed as one number, this would cause overflow on many machines. By a method known as **shift folding**, this social security number would be viewed as three separate numbers to be added:

$$
\begin{array}{r}
387 \\
58 \\
+\ 1505 \\
\hline
\end{array}
$$

producing the result 1950. This result could either be regarded as the hash position itself or, more likely, as a pure integer that now could be further acted upon by a hashing technique using a random number generator or division remainder to produce a final hash position in the desired range.

Another folding technique used often is called **boundary folding.** At the boundaries between the numbers making up the key under consideration, every other number is reversed before being added in to the accumulated total. Applying this method to our previous social security number example, we would have:

$$
\begin{array}{rl}
387 & \\
85 & \text{(this number reversed)} \\
+\ 1505 & \\
\hline
\end{array}
$$

yielding a result of 1977. Clearly, the 2 folding methods do not differ by much, and you must often choose between them on the basis of some experimentation as to which will produce more scattered results for a given application.

Regardless of whether shift or boundary folding is used, one of the great advantages of the folding method is its ability to transform noninteger keys into integers suitable for further hashing action. When keys contain alphabetic characters, you can translate them into their ASCII (or other appropriate) codes.

Digit or Character Extraction   In certain situations, a given key value may contain specific characters that are likely to bias any hash value arising from the key. The idea behind extraction is to remove such digits or characters before using the result as a final hash value or passing it on to be further transformed by another method. For instance, a company may choose to identify the various products it manufactures by using a 9 character code that always contains either an A or B in the 1st position and either a 1 or 0 in the 4th position. The rest of the characters in the code tend to occur on a more unpredictable basis. Character extraction would merely dictate the removal of the 1st and 4th characters, leaving a 7 character result to pass on to further processing.

Division Remainder Technique   All hashing presupposes a given range of positions that can be valid outputs of the hash function. In the remainder of this section, we shall assume the existence of a global variable RECORDSPACE that represents the upper limit of our hashing function; that is, the function should produce values between 1 and RECORDSPACE. (Note that RECORDSPACE is not necessarily the same as the dynamic count NUMBERREC.) It should then be evident that:

```
HASH(KEYVALUE) = (KEYVALUE MOD RECORDSPACE) + 1
```

is a valid hashing function for integer KEYVALUE. To begin examining criteria for choosing an appropriate RECORDSPACE, let us load the keys 41, 58, 12, 92, 50, and 91 into a list with RECORDSPACE 15. Figure 11-6 shows the results. In this figure, zeroes are used to denote empty positions, of which there are 9. However, if we keep RECORDSPACE at 15 and try to load the keys 10, 20, 30, 40, 50, 60, and 70, Figure 11-7 shows our result—many collisions. Hence, with this choice of RECORDSPACE, a different set of keys cause disastrous results even though the list seemingly has plenty of room available. On the other hand, if we choose RECORDSPACE 11, we have a list with considerably less room but no collisions. Figure 11-8 on page 262 indicates the hashing postions when the same set of keys is acted upon by 11 instead of 15.

Although these examples are far from conclusive, they suggest that choosing a prime number for RECORDSPACE may produce a more desirable hashing function. In fact, this is true, and Bell has shown that primes of the form $4k + 3$ for some integer k tend to be particularly effective.*

No hashing function can rule out the possibility of collisions; it can only make them less likely. You should be able to detect a key value that will produce a collision for the hashing function used in determining the list of Figure 11-8. Notice that the more full the list becomes, the easier it becomes to produce a collision. Hence, when using hashing as a search strategy, you must be willing to waste some positions in the list; otherwise search efficiency will deteriorate drastically. How much space to waste is an interesting question that we will soon discuss. Another conclusion that emerges is, given that *no* hashing function can eliminate collisions, we must be prepared to handle them when they occur.

Collision Processing

The essential problem in collision processing is to develop an algorithm that will reposition a key in a list when the position dictated by the hashing function itself is already occupied. Ideally, this algorithm should minimize the possibility of future collisions; that is, the problem key should be located at a position that is not likely to be the hashed position of a future key. However, the very nature of hashing makes this criterion difficult to meet with any degree of certainty because a good hashing function does not allow prediction of where future keys are likely to be placed. We will discuss 5 methods of collision processing—linear, quadratic, rehashing, linked, and buckets. In all of the methods, it will be necessary to detect when a given list position is not occupied. To signify this we use a sentinel key value of 0 to distinguish unoccupied positions. As we examine the methods, give some thought to the question of how deletions could be processed from a list accessed by one of these hashing methods: will the zero flag suffice to denote both the *never occupied* and *previously occupied but now vacant* conditions? This question is explored in the exercises at the end of the chapter.

Linear Collision Processing   The **linear collision processing** method is the simplest to implement (and therefore by Murphy's Law the least efficient). It essentially requires that, when a collision occurs, we proceed down the list in sequential order until we find

---

*Bell, J. R. 1970. The quadratic quotient method. *Communication of the Association for Computing Machinery*, 13:107–109.

ARRAY	KEY
1	0
2	91
3	92
4	0
5	0
6	50
7	0
8	0
9	0
10	0
11	0
12	41
13	12
14	58
15	0

**Figure 11-6   Array with RECORDSPACE 15 loaded with keys
41, 58, 12, 92, 50, and 91 using a hashing function.**

a vacant position. The key causing the collision is then placed at this first vacant position. If we come to the physical end of our list in the attempt to place the problem key, we merely wrap around to the top of the list and keep looking for a vacant position. For example, suppose we again use the hashing function:

```
HASH(KEYVALUE) = (KEYVALUE MOD RECORDSPACE) + 1
```

We will use RECORDSPACE 7 and attempt to insert the keys 18, 31, 67, 36, 19, and 34. The sequence of lists in Figure 11-9 on page 263 shows the results of these insertions.

ARRAY	KEY			
1	30	60	(collision)	
2	0			
3	0			
4	0			
5	0			
6	20	50	(collision)	
7	0			
8	0			
9	0			
10	0			
11	10	40	70	(collision)
12	0			
13	0			
14	0			
15	0			

**Figure 11-7   The same array as in Figure 11-6, when loaded with
a different set of keys, shows several collisions.**

ARRAY	KEY
1	0
2	0
3	0
4	0
5	70
6	60
7	50
8	40
9	30
10	20
11	10

Figure 11-8   An array with RECORDSPACE 11 and the same set of keys as Figure 11-6; no collisions result.

The PSEUDO LINEARHASH procedure used to seek a target loaded by the linear method is:

```
PROCEDURE LINEARHASH(TARGET, ITEM, FOUND)
GLOBAL VAR N, RECORDSPACE, KEY(N) : INTEGER
GLOBAL VAR DATA(N) : (*Appropriate data type*)
VAR TARGET, I, J : INTEGER
VAR ITEM : (*Appropriate data type*)
VAR FOUND, WRAPAROUND : BOOLEAN
FOUND := FALSE (*Assume failure*)
WRAPAROUND := FALSE (*Toggled to TRUE when entire list traversed*)
I := HASH(TARGET) (*Call on hashing function*)
J := I
WHILE KEY(J)<>0 AND NOT(WRAPAROUND OR FOUND) DO
  IF TARGET = KEY(J) THEN
      ITEM := DATA(J)
      FOUND := TRUE
  ELSE
      J := (J MOD RECORDSPACE) + 1 (*MOD to insure wraparound*)
      WRAPAROUND := (J=I) (*Has J returned to starting position? *)
  ENDIF
```

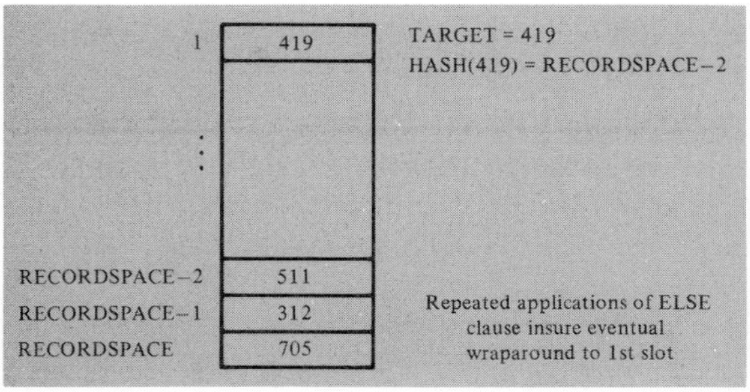

```
ENDWHILE
RETURN
END LINEARHASH
```

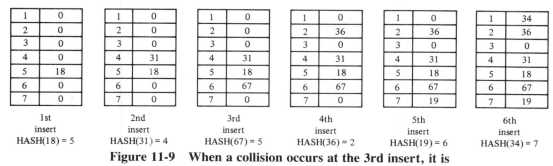

1	0
2	0
3	0
4	0
5	18
6	0
7	0

1st
insert
HASH(18) = 5

1	0
2	0
3	0
4	31
5	18
6	0
7	0

2nd
insert
HASH(31) = 4

1	0
2	0
3	0
4	31
5	18
6	67
7	0

3rd
insert
HASH(67) = 5

1	0
2	36
3	0
4	31
5	18
6	67
7	0

4th
insert
HASH(36) = 2

1	0
2	36
3	0
4	31
5	18
6	67
7	19

5th
insert
HASH(19) = 6

1	34
2	36
3	0
4	31
5	18
6	67
7	19

6th
insert
HASH(34) = 7

Figure 11-9   When a collision occurs at the 3rd insert, it is processed by the linear method; 67 is thus loaded into position 6.

Several remarks are in order concerning this procedure. First, note that the procedure as it stands would not handle list processing in which deletions were required; an additional flagging value would be needed to indicate a list position that had once been occupied and was now vacant because of a deletion. Second, we note that the linear method is not without its flaws. In particular, it is prone to a problem known as **clustering.** Clustering occurs when a hashing function is biased toward the placement of keys into a given region within the storage space. When the linear method is used to resolve collisions, this clustering problem is compounded, because keys that collide are loaded relatively close to the initial collision point. Hence, linear hashing is more likely than the other methods we will discuss to result in the clustering pictured in Figure 11-10.

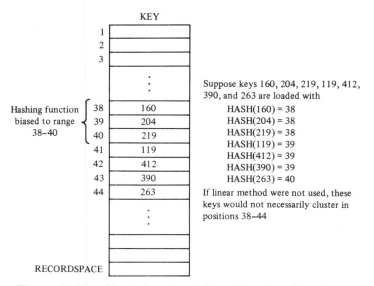

KEY

Suppose keys 160, 204, 219, 119, 412, 390, and 263 are loaded with

HASH(160) = 38
HASH(204) = 38
HASH(219) = 38
HASH(119) = 39
HASH(412) = 39
HASH(390) = 39
HASH(263) = 40

If linear method were not used, these keys would not necessarily cluster in positions 38–44

Figure 11-10   Clustering due to biased hashing function and linear processing.

A final point to note about the linear hashing method is its search efficiency. Knuth has shown that the average number of list accesses for a successful search using the *linear* method is*

```
(1/2) * (1 + 1/(1 - D))
```

where

```
D = NUMBERREC / RECORDSPACE
```

An interesting fact about this search efficiency is that it is *not* dependent solely on the number of records in the list but rather on the density ratio of the number of records currently in the list divided by the total record space available. In other words, no matter how many records there are, a highly efficient result can be obtained if you are willing to waste enough vacant records. This is what is meant by a **density-dependent** search technique. In searches where the target key cannot be found, Knuth's results indicate that the average search efficiency will be:

```
(1/2) * (1 + 1/(1 - D)²)
```

Figure 11-11 illustrates the effectiveness of the linear method by showing the results of computations of the efficiencies for a few strategic values of *D*.

Quadratic and Rehashing Collision Processing   Both **quadratic collision processing** and **rehashing collision processing** attempt to correct the problem of clustering, which occurs with the linear method. They force the problem key to move quickly a considerable distance from the initial collision. By the rehashing method, an entire sequence of hashing functions can be applied to a given key. If a collision results from the 1st hashing function, a 2nd is applied, and if necessary a 3rd and so on until the key can be placed successfully.

The quadratic method has the advantage of not requiring numerous hashing functions for its implementation. Suppose that a key value initially hashes to position *K* and a collision results. On its first attempt to resolve the collision, the quadratic algorithm attempts to place the key at position:

$$K + 1^2$$

If a second attempt is necessary to resolve the collision, position:

$$K + 2^2$$

is probed. In general, the *R*th attempt to resolve the collision probes position

$$K + R^2$$

(with wraparound taken into account). Figure 11-12 illustrates the resulting scattering pattern.

You should verify at this point that, if the hashing function:

```
HASH(KEYVALUE) = (KEYVALUE MOD RECORDSPACE) + 1
```

is used with RECORDSPACE 7, the keys 17, 73, 32, and 80 will be located in positions 4, 5, 6, and 1, respectively.

*Knuth, D. Op. Cit.

D	Efficiency for Successful Search	Efficiency for Unsuccessful Search
0.10	1.06	1.18
0.50	1.50	2.50
0.75	2.50	8.50
0.90	5.50	50.50

Figure 11-11   Efficiency for linear collision processing.

Knuth's results demonstrate the effectiveness of the rehashing and quadratic methods as compared to the linear method. Average search efficiencies improve to:

$$-(1/D) * \log_e(1 - D)$$

for the successful case and:

$$1 / (1 - D)$$

for an unsuccessful search. The numbers presented in Figure 11-13 should be compared to those for the linear method given in Figure 11-11.

The astute reader should have surmised that with the increased efficiency of the quadratic method we must reckon with some drawbacks. First, the computation of a position to be probed when a collision occurs is somewhat more obscure than it was with

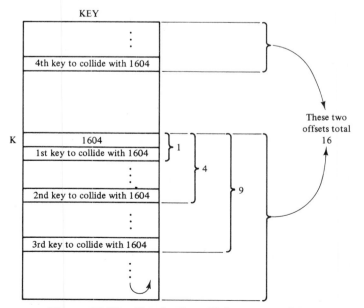

Figure 11-12   Quadratic collision processing.

D	Efficiency for Successful Search	Efficiency for Unsuccessful Search
0.10	1.05	1.11
0.50	1.39	2.00
0.75	1.84	4.00
0.90	2.56	10.00

Figure 11-13   Efficiency for quadratic collision processing.

the linear method. Verify that the position for the *R*th probe after an initial unsuccessful hash to position *K* is given by:

```
((K + R² - 1) MOD RECORDSPACE) + 1
```

A more significant problem, however, is that the quadratic method seemingly offers no guarantee that we will try every position in the list before concluding that a given key cannot be inserted. When the linear method is used, as the list becomes relatively dense with keys, an insertion can fail only if every position in the list is occupied; the linear nature of the search, although inefficient, ensures that every position is checked. However, when the quadratic method is applied to the RECORDSPACE of Figure 11-14, you can confirm that an initial hash to position 4 will lead only to future probing of positions 4, 5, and 8.

A satisfactory answer to the question of what portion of a list will be probed by the quadratic algorithm was fortunately provided by Bell for values of RECORDSPACE that are a prime number of the form $4j + 1$ for some integer *j*.* He showed that, with such a choice of RECORDSPACE, *every* position in the list eventually will be probed by the quadratic method.

Linked Collision Processing   The logic of **linked collision processing** completely eliminates the possibility that one collision could beget another. It requires a storage area divided horizontally into 2 regions—a **prime hash area** and an **overflow area.** Each record requires a LINK field in addition to the KEY and DATA fields. The global variable RECORDSPACE is applicable to the prime hash area only. This storage concept is illustrated in Figure 11-15 on page 268.

Initially, the hashing function translates keys into the prime hashing area. If a collision occurs, the key is inserted into a linked list with its initial node in the prime area and all following nodes in the overflow area (no dummy header is used). Figure 11-16 shows how this method would load the keys 22, 31, 67, 36, 29, and 60 for a RECORDSPACE 7 and hashing function:

```
HASH(KEYVALUE) = (KEYVALUE MOD RECORDSPACE) + 1
```

*Bell, J. R. Op. Cit.

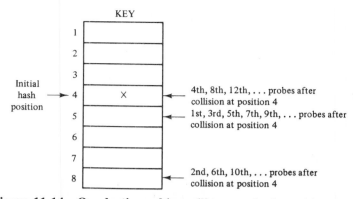

Figure 11-14   Quadratic probing will never check positions 1, 2, 3, 6, 7 after initial hash to 4.

The PSEUDO procedure LINKEDHASH to implement the linked method of collision processing follows. As written, it assumes that all key locations in the prime area have had their corresponding KEY and LINK fields initialized to 0 and NULL, respectively. The assumption is also made that no keys will be deleted.

```
PROCEDURE LINKEDHASH(TARGET, ITEM, FOUND)
GLOBAL VAR N, RECORDSPACE, KEY(N), LINK(N) : INTEGER
GLOBAL VAR DATA(N) : (*Appropriate data type*)
VAR TARGET, I : INTEGER
VAR ITEM : (*Appropriate data type*)
VAR FOUND : BOOLEAN
FOUND := FALSE (*Assume failure*)
I := HASH(TARGET)
REPEAT
     IF TARGET = KEY(I) THEN
          ITEM := DATA(I)
          FOUND := TRUE
     ELSE
          I := LINK(I)
     ENDIF
UNTIL FOUND OR (I = NULL)
RETURN
END LINKEDHASH
```

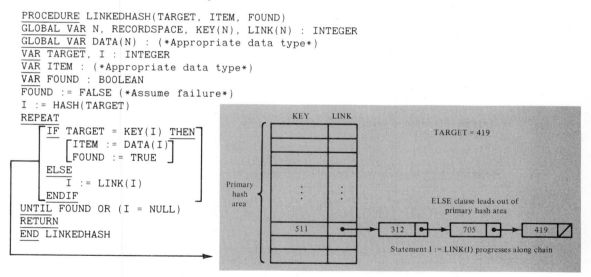

Knuth's efficiency results for the linked hashing method are relative to a density factor (*D*) that is computed using the RECORDSPACE in the prime hashing area only. Hence, unlike the other hashing methods we have discussed, the linked method allows a density factor greater than 1. Given this variation, average search efficiencies for the successful and unsuccessful cases are:

$$1 + D/2 \quad \text{and} \quad D$$

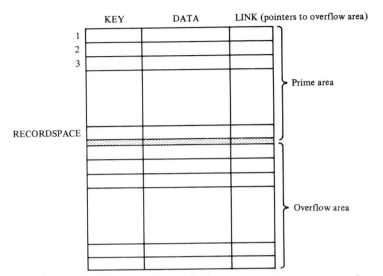

Figure 11-15 Storage allocation for linked collision processing.

respectively. Figure 11-17 shows computations of this search efficiency for selected values of D, and should be compared to the corresponding results for the linear and quadratic methods presented in Figures 11-11 and 11-13, respectively.

Bucket Hashing Collision Processing According to the strategy of **bucket hashing collision processing,** the hashing function transforms a given key to a physically contig-

	KEY	LINK
1	0	NULL
2	22	8
3	0	NULL
4	31	NULL
5	67	10
6	0	NULL
7	0	NULL
8	36	9
9	29	NULL
10	60	NULL
11	0	NULL
12	0	NULL
13	0	NULL
14	0	NULL
15	0	NULL
16	0	NULL
17	0	NULL

Figure 11-16 Loading keys 22, 31, 67, 36, 29, and 60 with KEYVALUE MOD 7 + 1; linked collision processing.

D	Efficiency for Successful Search	Efficiency for Unsuccessful Search
2	2	2
5	3.5	5
10	6	10
20	11	20

Figure 11-17 Search efficiencies for the linked method.

uous region of locations within the list to be searched. This contiguous region is called a *bucket*. Thus, instead of hashing to the *I*th location, a key would hash to the *I*th bucket of locations. The locations encompassed by this bucket would depend upon the bucket size. (We assume that all buckets in a given list are of the same size.) Figure 11-18 illustrates this concept for a list with 7 buckets and a bucket size of 3.

Once we have hashed to a bucket, we must then compare the target in sequential order to all of the keys in that bucket. On the surface, it would seem as if this strategy could do no better than duplicate the efficiency of the linked hash method discussed earlier. Indeed, given that after the initial hash a sequential search is conducted in both cases, the average number of list accesses for a successful or unsuccessful search cannot be improved

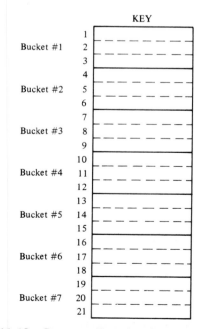

Figure 11-18   Storage allocation for bucket hashing.

by using buckets. Moreover, we must still have provisions for linking to some sort of overflow area in case a series of collisions consume all of the spaces in a given bucket.

What then could be a possible advantage of using buckets? If the list to be searched resides entirely in main memory, there is no advantage. However, if the list resides in a disk file, the bucket method will allow us to take advantage of some of the physical characteristics of the storage medium itself. To see this, let us assume a one-surface disk divided into concentric tracks and pie-shaped sectors as indicated in Figure 11-19.

There are two ways in which the bucket hashing strategy can take advantage of the organization of the data on the disk. First, when records in a contiguous direct access file are stored on a disk, they are generally located in relative record number order along one track, then along an adjacent track. The movement of the read-write head between tracks is generally the cause of the most significant delays in obtaining data from a disk. The further the movement, the greater the delay will be. Hence, if our knowledge of the machine allows us to make a bucket coincide with a track on the disk, then hashing to the beginning of a bucket and proceeding from there using a sequential search within the bucket, and thus within a track, will greatly minimize head movement. A purely linked hashing strategy, on the other hand, will potentially cause the read-write head to move a great deal between tracks. Such consideration of the storage medium itself is an excellent illustration of why you must examine more than the number of list accesses when you measure the efficiency of a program involving disk files.

Another way you can use the bucket hashing algorithm to advantage when disk files are being searched is related to the way records are transferred between the disk and main

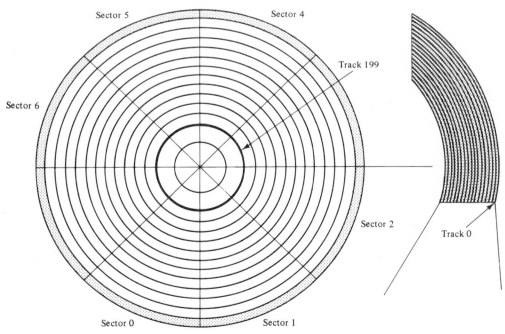

**Figure 11-19 A one-surface disk divided into concentric tracks
and pie-shaped sectors.**

In the world of applications . . .

Suppose you are driving a car with Wisconsin license plates and are stopped for speeding in Illinois. You may notice a brief delay before the officer begins to approach your car. However, according to Daniel and Joan Slotnick in *Computers: Their Structure, Use, and Influence*, the delay will be no longer than 20 seconds.* In that 20 seconds, the following will have occurred. The officer will have radioed your license plate number to Illinois headquarters. From there, it is relayed to the Wisconsin Department of Transportation, where it will be located in the computer file of information on all Wisconsin license plates. If it happens that you are driving a stolen vehicle, the license plate number will be communicated to the National Crime Information Center in Washington, D.C., to obtain further information about the missing car from that agency's massive databank. This information is then routed back to Illinois headquarters and finally to the officer on the scene.

"Armed" with this information, the officer now knows whether she or he should expect trouble when approaching your vehicle. You, on the other hand, assuming you are guilty of nothing but speeding, have not been kept waiting an annoyingly long time— thanks to the efficiency of some computer searching algorithms!

*Slotnik, D., and Slotnick, J. 1979. *Computers: Their Structure, Use, and Influence*. Englewood Cliffs, NJ: Prentice-Hall. p. 239.

---

memory. Frequently, programming languages create the illusion that each record accessed requires a separate disk access. However, records are frequently **blocked;** that is, they are positioned in contiguous regions on a track of the disk so that a fixed number are brought into main memory when a record in that block is requested. This means that, if the record requested already happens to be part of the block presently in main memory, a program statement that requests a record may not require a disk access; only a different mask need be applied to the block already in main memory. With main memory manipulations being orders of magnitude faster than the rate of data transfer to and from a disk, this means that positioning our buckets to coincide with a disk block will necessitate only one disk access each time an entire bucket is sequentially searched. Here again, the more scattered nature of a purely linked hashing algorithm would not allow this disk-oriented efficiency consideration to be taken into account.

11-4 Indexed Search Techniques

Indexed search techniques are especially applicable in searching direct access secondary storage devices. Be sure you understand the last 2 paragraphs of the preceding section before you read this section. The idea behind the use of an **index** is analogous to the way in which we routinely use an address book to find a person. That is, we do not knock on the doors of numerous houses until we find the one where the person we are seeking resides. Instead, we apply a search strategy to an address book. There we use the name of the person as a key to find a pointer, an address, which swiftly leads us to the person. We make only one actual "house access," although our search strategy may require numerous accesses into the address book index.

In computer systems, records (or more precisely blocks) could play the role of houses in the search scenario described above. Data records on disk are (when compared to main memory) terribly slow and awkward creatures to access. One of the reasons for this is that there is often so much data that must be moved from disk to main memory every time a record is accessed. The DATA array we originally presented in Figure 11-1, in many situations, may have thousands of bytes of data associated with each of its positions. Because of this, it can often be advantageous to revise the general picture of Figure 11-1 so that our list of keys is no longer parallel to the data with which they are logically associated, but rather is parallel to a list of pointers that will lead us to those data. This revised picture is presented in Figure 11-20.

Hence, the general strategy of an indexed search is to use the key to search the index, find the relative record position of the associated data, and from there make *only one* access into the data. Because the parallel lists of keys and relative record positions require much less storage than do the data, frequently the entire index can be loaded and permanently held in main memory, necessitating only one disk access for each record being sought. For larger indexes, large blocks of keys and associated pointers at least can be manipulated in main memory, thereby still greatly enhancing search efficiency.

Indexed Sequential Search Technique

The **indexed sequential access method (ISAM)** involves carefully weighing the disk-dependent factors of blocking and track size to build a partial index. The **partial index,** unlike some other index structures we will study, does not reduce to 1 the number of

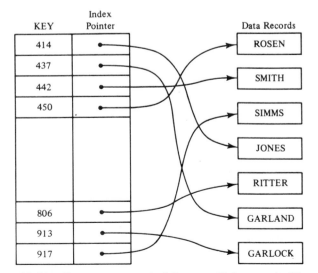

Figure 11-20   Rearrangement of the parallel array in Figure 11-1 to provide a general context for an indexed search.

probes you must make into the data. To continue the analogy between searching for data and searching for a person, ISAM is somewhat like an address book that would lead us to the street on which the person lives, but would leave us to check each of the houses on that street. ISAM correspondingly leads us to an appropriate region (often a track or a **cylinder** containing multiple tracks within a disk pack), and then leaves us to search sequentially within that region.

As an example, let us suppose that we can conveniently fit the partial index, or **directory,** pictured in Figure 11-21 into main memory, and that the organization of our disk file allows 6 records per track. The directory is formed by choosing the highest key value in each track, with a pointer indicating where that track begins. Here our pointers

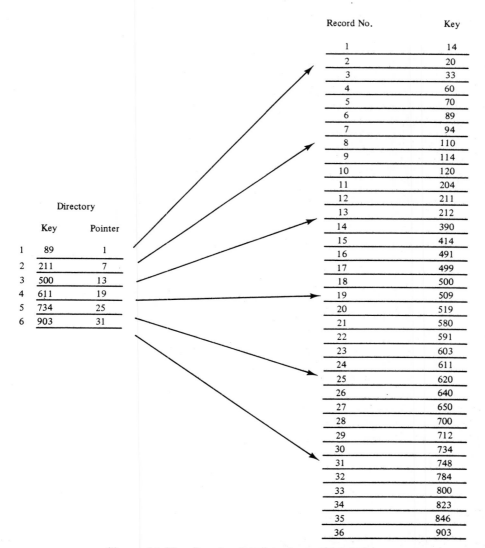

Figure 11-21   One-level indexed sequential file.

are simply relative record numbers; in practice they could well be more disk-dependent. The strategy to conduct an ISAM search is to:

1. Search the main memory directory for a key that is greater than or equal to the target

2. Follow the corresponding pointer out to the disk and there search sequentially until we find a match (success) or the key that the directory maintains as the high key within that particular region (failure)

For the data given in Figure 11-21, the 36 record file would require no more than 6 main memory index accesses plus 6 disk accesses (all of which are located on the same track).

For larger files, it may be advantageous to have more than one level of these directory structures. Consider, for instance, the two-level directory structure for a file with 216 records as given in Figure 11-22. Here we might suppose that storage restrictions allow the entire primary directory to be kept in main memory, the secondary directory to be brought in as a single block of a disk file, and the data records to be stored 6 per track. The primary directory divides the file into regions of 36 records each. The key in the primary directory represents the highest-valued key in a given 36 record region, but the pointer leads us into the subdirectory instead of to the actual file. So, we search the primary directory for a key greater than or equal to the target, and follow the primary directory pointer into the secondary directory. Beginning at the position indicated by the primary directory's pointer, we again search for a key greater than or equal to the target. Notice that the subdirectory has necessitated one disk access in our hypothetical situation. For this price, the 36 record region determined by the primary directory is subdivided into 6 record regions, each of which will lie entirely on 1 track by the time we get out to the disk file. Following the subdirectory's pointer to the actual file, we end up with a relatively short sequential search on the external storage medium.

It should be clear from this discussion that the search efficiency of the indexed sequential technique is dependent upon a variety of factors. Included among them are:

1. To what degree the directory structures are able to subdivide the actual file

2. To what degree the directory structures are able to reside in main memory

3. The relationship of data records to physical characteristics of the disk such as blocking factors, track size, and cylinder size

It should also be clear that the indexed sequential method may not be ideal for a highly volatile file because, as implicitly indicated in Figures 11-21 and 11-22, the data records must be stored in physically increasing (or decreasing) key order. The requirement for physical ordering is obviously not conducive to frequent insertions and deletions. In practice, the solution to this problem is that each file subregion that is ultimately the subject of a sequential search is equipped with a pointer to an overflow area. Insertions are located in this overflow area and linked to the main sequential search area. Hence, as the overflow area builds up, the search efficiency tends to deteriorate. In some applications, this deterioration can be so severe that data processing personnel have been known to refer to ISAM as the Intrinsically Slow Access Method. To avoid this deterioration, you must periodically *reorganize* the file into a new file with no overflow. However, such reorganization cannot be done dynamically. It requires going through the file in key sequential

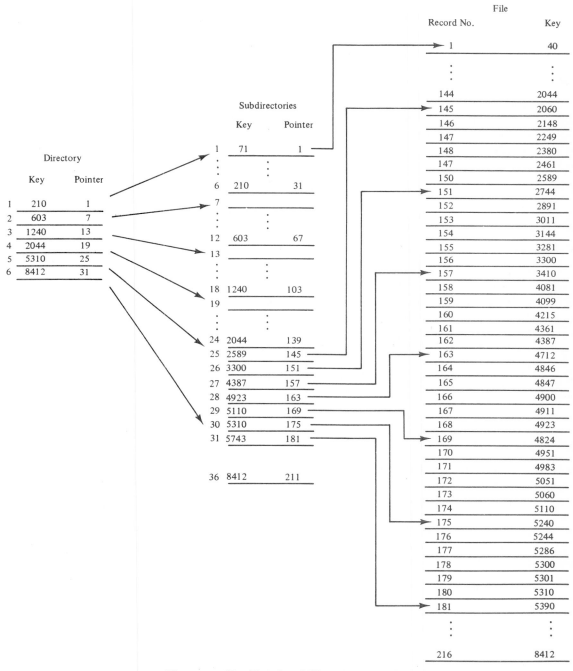

Figure 11-22 Two-level directory structure.

order and copying it into a new one. Along the way, the indexes must be rebuilt, of course. These type of maintenance problems involved with the ISAM structure have led to the development of several more dynamic indexing schemes.

Binary Tree Indexing

The concept of a binary tree search has already been covered in depth in Section 11-2 and in Chapters 6 and 7. The only twist added when the binary tree is an index is that each node of the tree contains a key and a pointer to the record associated with that key in some larger data aggregate. The advantages of using a binary tree as an index structure include:

1. A search efficiency proportional to $\log_2$ NUMBERREC provided the tree is height-balanced

2. The ability to traverse the list indexed by the tree in key order

3. Dynamic insertion and deletion capabilities

These qualities make the binary tree the ideal index structure for situations in which the entire tree can fit in main memory. However, if the data aggregate is so large that the tree index must itself be stored on disk, the efficiency of the structure is less optimal: each node of the index may lie in a disk block separate from the other nodes and hence require a separate disk access. Hence, using the example of 50,000 keys presented in Section 11-2, a search of a binary tree index could require as many as 16 disk accesses. To solve this problem, we would like to cluster those nodes along a given search path into one, or at least relatively few, disk blocks. The B-tree index structure is a variation on the tree index that accomplishes this goal.

B-tree Indexing

Remember that one index entry requires nothing more than a key and a pointer. Moreover, we have been assuming that both the key and the pointer are integers, and we will continue to operate under this assumption during our discussion of **B-trees.** In a B-tree, a given tree node will in fact contain many such key–pointer pairs, because a given B-tree node will coincide with one disk block. The idea behind a B-tree is that we somehow group key–pointer pairs that are related in the search algorithm into a few strategic B-tree nodes; that is, into disk blocks. The following formal definition will be clarified with some some examples.

A B-tree of order n is a structure with the following properties:

1. Every node in the B-tree has sufficient room to store $n - 1$ key–pointer pairs.

2. Additionally, every node has room for n pointers to other nodes in the B-tree (as distinguished from the pointers within key–pointer pairs, which point to the position of a key in the file).

3. Every nonterminal node, except the root node, has at least $n/2$ non-null pointers to other nodes in the B-tree. The root node has at least two non-null pointers to other nodes in the B-tree.

4. All terminal nodes are on the same level.

5. If a node has $m + 1$ non-null pointers to other B-tree nodes, then it must contain m key–pointer pairs for the index itself.

Stipulation (5) says that we can think of a B-tree node as a list

$$P_0, KP_1, P_1, KP_2, P_2, KP_3, \ldots, P_{m-1}, KP_m, P_m$$

where P_i represents the ith pointer to another B-tree node and KP_i represents the ith key–pointer pair.

6. For each B-tree node:
   a. the key value in key–pointer pair KP_{i-1} is less than the key value in key–pointer pair KP_i
   b. all key–pointer pairs in the node pointed to by P_{i-1} contain keys that are less than the key in KP_i
   c. all key–pointer pairs in the node pointed to by P_i contain key values greater than the key in KP_i

A B-tree of order 6 index structure for the 36 record file of Figure 11-21 appears in Figure 11-23. Carefully verify that all 6 defining properties are satisfied. The choice of order 6 for Figure 11-23 on page 279 was made only for the purposes of making the figure fit on a page of text. In practice, the order would be chosen such that it is the maximum number of B-tree pointers and key-pointer pairs that we could fit into one disk block; the choice should be made to force a disk block to coincide with a B-tree node.

Let us now consider what is involved in searching a B-tree for a given key. Within the current node (starting at the root), we must search sequentially through the key values in the node until we come to a match, a key value which is greater than the target, or the end of the key values in that particular node. In the event a match is not made, we have a pointer to an appropriate follow-up node. Verify this algorithm for several of the keys appearing at various levels of Figure 11-23. The sequential search on keys within a given node may at first seem unappealing. However, the key fact to remember here is that each B-tree node is a disk block that is loaded in one move into main memory. Hence, it may be possible to search sequentially on hundreds of keys within a node in the time it would take to load one new node from the disk. Our main concern is to minimize disk accesses, and here we have achieved a worst case search for our 36 entry file in 3 disk accesses.

What in general is the search efficiency for a B-tree index? It should be clear from the nature of the structure that the number of disk accesses for any particular key will be simply the number of levels in the tree. So we must determine the maximum number of levels that the six defining criteria would allow for a B-tree containing NUMBERREC key–pointer pairs; this would be the worst case search efficiency. To determine this value, we use the minimum number of nodes that must be present on any given level. Let L be the smallest integer greater than or equal to $N/2$ where N is the order of the B-tree. Then:

Level 1 contains at least 1 node.
Level 2 contains at least 2 nodes.
Level 3 contains at least $2 \times L$ nodes.
Level 4 contains at least $2 \times L^2$ nodes.

.   .

.   .

.   .

Level m contains at least $2 \times L^{m-2}$ nodes.

Knuth uses this progression to show that the maximum number of levels (and thus the worst case search efficiency) for NUMBERREC key–pointer pairs is*

$$1 + \log_N ((\text{NUMBERREC} + 1)/2)$$

As an example, the index for a file of 50,000 records, which would require on the order of 16 disk accesses using a binary tree structure, could be searched with 3 disk accesses using a B-tree of order 250. Note that the choice of order 250 for this example is not at all unrealistic, given typical block sizes for files.

Unlike ISAM, the B-tree index can handle insertions and deletions dynamically without a resulting deterioration in search efficiency. We will presently discuss how B-tree insertions are performed; the problem of deletions is left for you to examine as an exercise. The essential idea behind a B-tree insertion is that we must first determine which bottom level node should contain the key–pointer pair to be inserted. For instance, suppose that we wanted to insert the key 742 into the B-tree of Figure 11-23. By allowing this key to walk down the B-tree from the root to the bottom level, we could quickly determine that this key belongs in the node presently containing:

$$\left(\text{712/29}\quad \text{734/30}\quad \text{748/31}\quad \text{784/32}\right)$$

By the definition of a B-tree of order 6 this node is not presently full, so no further disk accesses would be necessary to perform the insertion. We would merely need to determine the next available record space in the actual data file (37 in this case) and then add the key–pointer pair 742/37 to this terminal node, resulting in:

$$\left(\text{712/29}\quad \text{734/30}\quad \text{742/37}\quad \text{748/31}\quad \text{784/32}\right)$$

A slightly more difficult situation arises when we find that the key–pointer pair we wish to add should be inserted into a bottom level node that is already full. For instance, this would occur if we attempted to add the key 112 to the B-tree of Figure 11-23. We would load the actual data for this key into file position 38 (given the addition already made in the preceding paragraph) and then determine that the key–pointer pair 112/38 belongs in the bottom level node:

$$\left(\text{94/7}\quad \text{110/8}\quad \text{114/9}\quad \text{120/10}\quad \text{204/11}\right)$$

The stipulation that any given B-tree node have minimally 6/2 = 3 pointers to other B-tree nodes will now allow us to *split* this node, creating one new node with 2 key–pointer pairs and one with 3 key–pointer pairs, and moving 1 of the key–pointer pairs up to the parent of the present node. The resulting B-tree is given in Figure 11-24 on page 280.

*Knuth, D. Op. Cit.

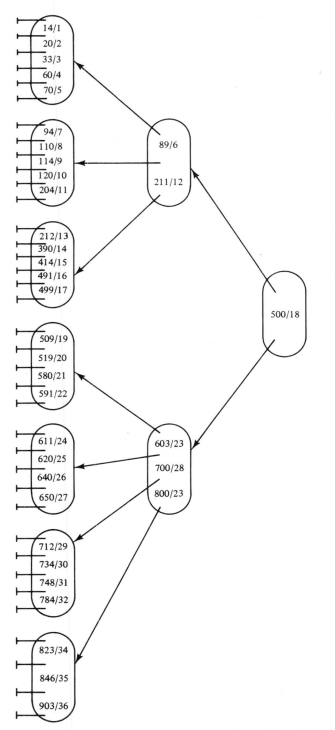

Figure 11-23 **B-tree index of order 6 for file in Figure 11-21.**
A/B denotes key–pointer pair. ⊥denotes null pointer.

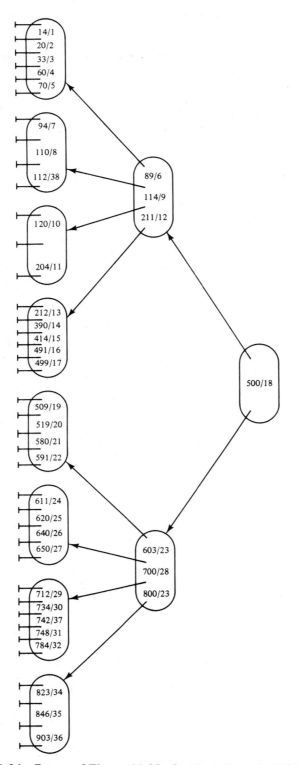

Figure 11-24   B-tree of Figure 11-23 after insertion of 112/38 and 742/37.

Although it does not happen in this particular example, note that it would be entirely possible that the moving of a key–pointer pair up to a parent node that is already full would necessitate a split of this parent node, which would then be handled by the same procedure. Indeed it is possible that key–pointer pairs could be passed all the way up to the root and cause a split of the root node; this is how a new level of the tree would be introduced. Such a split of the root node would force the creation of a new root node, which would have only 1 key–pointer pair and 2 pointers to other B-tree nodes. However, at the root level this is still a sufficient number of pointers to retain the B-tree structure. Because the insertion algorithm for a B-tree requires checking whether a given node is full and potentially moving back up to a parent node, it is convenient to allow space within a node to store:

1. A count of the number of key–pointer pairs in the node

2. A back pointer to the node's parent

Trie Indexing

In all of the indexing applications we have discussed so far, the keys involved have been assumed to be integer. In practice, however, we must be prepared to deal with keys of different types. Perhaps the worst case is that of keys that are variable length character strings. **Trie indexing** was developed as a means of handling this. Let us suppose, for instance, that the strings in the list that follows represent a set of keys. Each string may be thought of as a last name followed by initials and a delimiting "$":

```
ADAMS BT$
COOPER CC$
COOPER PJ$
COWANS DC$
MACGUIRE WH$
MCGUIRE AL$
MEMINGER DD$
SEFTON SD$
SPAN KD$
SPAN LA$
SPANNER DW$
ZARDA JM$
ZARDA PW$
```

An individual node in a trie structure for these keys appears in Figure 11-25. It is essentially a fixed-length array of 28 pointers—1 for each letter of the alphabet, 1 for a blank, and one for the delimiter. Each pointer within 1 of these nodes can lead to 1 of 2 entities—either another node within the trie or the data record for a given key. Hence it may be convenient to embed a flag bit in each pointer indicating the type of entity to

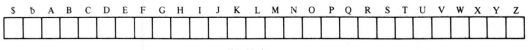

Trie Node

Figure 11-25   Trie node.

which it is pointing. The trie structure for the preceding list of keys is given in Figure 11-26. In this figure, circular nodes are used to represent the destinations of those pointers leading to data records outside the trie structure itself.

The logic behind a trie structure can be best seen by tracing through an example. This search algorithm involves examining the target key on a character by character basis. Let us begin by considering the easy case of finding the data record for ADAMS BT$. We look at A—the first character in the key—and follow the A pointer in the root node to its destination. We know that this destination will be either another node within the trie structure or data record. If it were a node within the trie, it would be a node on the search path for all keys that begin with A. In this case, there is only 1 key in our list that begins with A, so the destination of the A pointer in the root node leads us directly to the data record for ADAMS BT$.

To find the key COOPER CC$ in the trie, we take a somewhat longer search path. We follow the C pointer from the root node down a level to a node shared by all keys starting with C. From there, the O pointer is followed to a trie node shared by all keys which start with CO. This process continues down level by level, following the O pointer to a trie node shared by all keys starting with COO, then the P pointer to a node for all keys starting with COOP, the E pointer to a node for all keys starting with COOPE, the R pointer to a node for all keys starting with COOPER, and the blank (ƀ) pointer to a node shared by all keys starting with COOPERb. Notice that, as each character is read in, we must continue following these pointers from trie node to trie node (instead of from trie node to data record) until the next character uniquely defines the key. At this point, the key in question need no longer share its pointer with other keys. Hence, the pointer now will lead to a data record. This is what happens in our example when we read in the next C to form the uniquely defining substring COOPERƀC.

The search efficiency for the trie index is quite easily determined. The worst case occurs when a key is not uniquely defined until its last character is read in. In this case, we must have potentially as many disk accesses as there are characters in the key before we finally locate the data record. If you are an astute reader however, you will have observed that there is another efficiency consideration—the amount of wasted storage in the trie nodes. In our example using a short list of keys, only a small percentage of the available pointers are ever used. In practice, however, a trie would be used only for an extremely large file; for example, the list represented by a city phone book with names as keys. In such a situation, a much larger number of character combinations occurs and the resulting trie structure is correspondingly much less sparse.

A final point is the ability of the trie index to handle insertions and deletions dynamically. In particular, we will discuss the case for insertions; you will consider deletions as an exercise. Insertion can be broken down into 2 subcases. For both we must begin by reading the key to be inserted on a character-by-character basis and following the appropriate search path in the trie until:

1. We come to a trie node that has a vacant pointer in the character position corresponding to the current character of the insertion key, *or*

2. We come to a data record for a key different than the one being inserted.

The first subcase is illustrated by trying to insert the key COLLINS RT$ into the trie of Figure 11-26. We follow the search path pointers until we come to the trie node shared

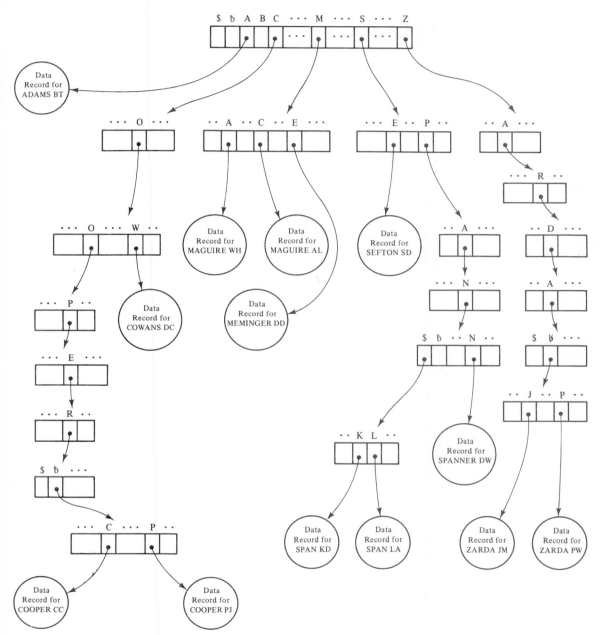

Figure 11-26   Trie index structure.

by all keys starting with CO. At this point, the L pointer is null. The insertion is completed by merely aiming the presently null L pointer to a data record for the key COLLINS RT$.

The second subcase is illustrated by trying to insert the key COOPER PA$ into the trie of Figure 11-26. Here following the search path of the trie eventually leads us to the data record for the key COOPER PJ$. The dynamic solution here is to get a new trie node, aim the P pointer presently leading to the data record for COOPER PJ$ to this new trie node, and use the A and J pointers in the new trie node to lead us to data records for COOPER PA$ and COOPER PJ$ respectively. Both the COLLINS RT$ and COOPER PA$ insertions are shown with the resulting trie in Figure 11-27.

SUMMARY

The following table summarizes the search strategy efficiencies discussed in this chapter.

Summary of Search Efficiencies

Method	Efficiency
Sequential	Worst case: number of records Average: (number of records)/2
Binary	Worst case: $\log_2$ (number of records)
Linear hashing	Average successful: $(1/2) * (1 + 1/(1 - D))$ Average unsuccessful: $(1/2) * (1 + 1/(1 - D)^2)$ where density $D = \dfrac{\text{number of records}}{\text{record space}}$
Quadratic hashing	Average successful: $-(1/D) * \log_e (1 - D)$ Average unsuccessful: $1/(1 - D)$
Chained hashing	Average successful: $1 + D/2$ Average unsuccessful: D (Recordspace used in computation of D is that in primary hash area)

Indexed sequential, one directory level	Worst case:
	   Number of index probes $=$ size of index
	
	   Number of file probes $= \dfrac{\text{number of records}}{\text{size of index}}$

Binary tree index	Worst case:
	   Number of index probes proportional to $\log_2$ (number of records)
	     if height - balanced

B-tree index of order N	Worst case requires
	   $1 + \log_N ((\text{number of records} + 1)/2)$
	   disk accesses for index

Trie index	Worst case requires as many disk accesses to search index as there are characters in target key

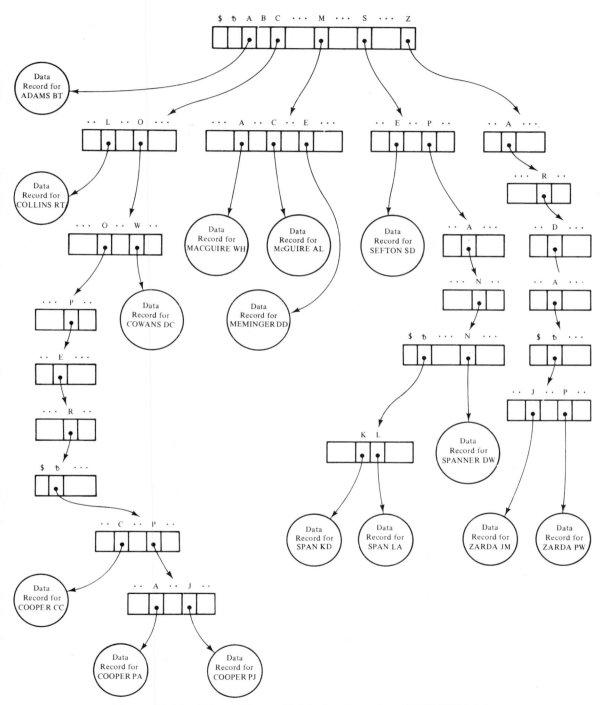

**Figure 11-27   Trie of Figure 11-26 after inserting COLLINS RT\$
and COOPER PA\$.**

KEY TERMS

Key	Synonyms	Clustering
Direct (random) access	Collisions	Track
Field	Randomized storage	Sector
Record	Folding	Blocking
Quantity dependent search	Shift folding	Index
Sequential search	Boundary folding	Indexed sequential
Binary search	Extraction	ISAM
Volatile file	Linear hashing	Directory
Binary tree search	Quadratic hashing	Binary tree index
Density dependent search	Linked hashing	B-tree
Key-to-address transformation	Bucket hashing	Trie
Hashing function		

EXERCISES

1. Suppose you know that the keys in a list are arranged in increasing order. How could the sequential search algorithm presented in this chapter be improved with this knowledge? Rewrite the PSEUDO procedure to incorporate this improvement.

2. Rewrite the binary search algorithm presented in this chapter with a list-splitting function other than halving. One possibility here would be to use an interpolation strategy that would examine the target's relative distance between the current low and high. Test run your program against a pure binary search and accumulate statistics to determine whether there is any significant difference in efficiency between the techniques.

3. Write the PSEUDO form of the algorithm for the binary tree search.

4. Suppose you are given a list of data in increasing order of keys. Develop a PSEUDO algorithm that will load this list into an *optimal* binary search tree.

5. Write the PSEUDO algorithm to insert a key into a B-tree.

6. Discuss a key deletion strategy for B-trees. Write a PSEUDO procedure that implements your strategy.

7. Write the PSEUDO algorithm to insert a key and its data record into a trie.

8. Discuss a key deletion strategy for trie indexes. Write a PSEUDO procedure to implement your strategy.

9. Write PSEUDO procedures to insert a key into a list to be searched by

   a. Linear hashing

   b. Quadratic hashing

   c. Linked hashing

   d. Bucket hashing

10. Write PSEUDO procedures to search for a key using

a. The quadratic hashing method

b. The bucket hashing method

11. Devise strategies to delete keys from a list being maintained by each of the 4 hashing strategies in Exercise (9). Write PSEUDO versions for each of these algorithms. Given your deletion strategy, what modifications would need to be made in the various search and insertion procedures of Exercises (9) and (10)?

12. Develop a PSEUDO procedure to search a list using ISAM. Initially assume just one directory. Then alter the procedure so that it would work with one subdirectory.

13. Devise PSEUDO procedures to handle insertions into and deletions from a list maintained by ISAM. Do the strategies reflected by these procedures require any modifications in your answers to Exercise (12)?

14. Carefully read your system reference material concerning the specifics of how disk file records are blocked. Then explain how this knowledge would influence your decisions in the construction of:

a. An ISAM index structure

b. A B-tree index structure

c. A trie index structure

d. A bucket hashing structure

15. If you are familiar with probability and statistics, try to answer this: Given a table with 400 slots, what is the probability that a hashing function will produce a collision before the table is 10% full?

PROGRAMMING PROBLEMS

1. The Wing and a Prayer Airline Company has the records of all its customers stored in the following form:

- Last Name

- First Name

- Address

- Arbitrarily long list of flights on which reservations have been booked

Using a trie index, write a search and retrieval program that will allow input of a customer's last name (and, if necessary, the first name and address to resolve conflicts created by matching last names) and then output all flights on which that customer has booked reservations.

2. Using a large collection of randomly generated keys, write a series of programs that will test various hashing functions you develop. In particular, your programs should report statistics on the number of collisions generated by each hashing function. This information could be valuable in guiding future decisions about which hashing functions and techniques are most effective for your particular system.

3. Consider a student data record which consists of:

   - Student identification number

   - Student name

   - State of residence

   - Sex

   Choose an index structure to process a file of such records. Then write an ACID program to maintain such a file. ACID is a commonly used acronym meaning your program should have the capability to

   - Add a record

   - Change a record

   - Inspect a record

   - Delete a record

4. Suppose that data records for a phone book file consist of a key field containing both name and address and a field containing the phone number for that key. Devise an appropriate index for such a file. Then write a program that calls for input of:

   a. Ideally, a complete key, *or*

   b. As much of the initial portion of a key as the inquirer is able to provide

   In the case of (a), your program should output the phone number corresponding to the unique key. In the case of (b), have your program output all keys (and their phone numbers) that match the initial portion provided.

5. Consider the following problem faced in the development of a compiler. The source program contains many character string symbols such as variable names and procedure names. Each of these character string symbols has associated with it various attributes such as memory location and data type. However, it would be too time-consuming and awkward for a compiler actually to manipulate character strings. Instead, each string should be identified with an integer that is viewed as an equivalent to the string for the purpose of compiler manipulation. In addition to serving as a compact equivalent form of a string symbol within the source program, this integer can also serve as a direct pointer into a table of attributes for that symbol. Devise a transformation procedure that associates a string with an integer, which in turn serves as a pointer into a table of attributes. Test the structure(s) you develop by using them in a program that scans a source program written in a language like Pascal. You will in effect have written the symbol table modules for a compiler.

6. The Pascal supplement at the end of the chapter presents a hashing program capable of adding records to a direct access file and then searching for these records by their integer identification number key. Modify this program in any or all of the following ways:

a. Alter the hashing function so that it accepts an alphabetic key

b. Add an error trap to the program that will catch an attempt to add a record for which a key already exists in the file

c. Add the capability to change a record that already exists in the file

d. Add the capability to delete a record in the file

7. Hashing can be used effectively to solve the sparse matrix problem presented in Chapter 8. Use the row–column coordinates of a sparse matrix entry as arguments to a hashing function that determines that entry's position in a linear list. Apply this method in implementing one of the sparse matrix programming problems from Chapter 8.

If you work in Pascal . . .

The following Pascal program uses hashing to add records to a file and then search for them using the program's *Inspect* option. Two aspects of the program need to be more fully explained because their implementation in Pascal will be machine-dependent.

First the hashing function used in the program makes use of a random number generator, which is designed to take advantage of integer overflow on a 16 bit machine. This would have to be suitably adjusted for machines with a larger word size.

Second, the program uses the direct access file command *SEEK(F,N)* to bring the *N*th record from the file *F* into the main memory buffer area for that file. Standard Pascal makes no provisions for direct access files; the SEEK statement is an extension provided in OMSI Pascal-1. Your local system reference manuals should be consulted to determine how direct access files are implemented in your version of Pascal.

```
        program hashfile(input,output,f);
        (* Demonstrate hashing as file search technique *)

    CONST
        recordspace = 200;

    TYPE
        biginteger = 0..65535;
        recordposition = 1..recordspace;
        employeerecord = RECORD
                            idno : biginteger;
                            initials : ARRAY [1..2] OF char;
                            lastname : ARRAY [1..9] OF char;
                            salary : real
                         END;

    VAR
        f : FILE OF employeerecord;
        command : char;
        workingcopy : employeerecord;

    FUNCTION hash(id:biginteger):recordposition;

        FUNCTION random(seed:biginteger):real;
        BEGIN (* RANDOM *)
            seed:=(seed*13077+6925)MOD 32768;
            random:=seed/32768.0
        END (* RANDOM *);

    BEGIN
        hash :=trunc(recordspace*random(id)) + 1
        END;
        (* hash *)

    PROCEDURE addrec;
        (* Add record to the file.  What's missing here? *)
```

```
VAR
   pos, origpos : recordposition;
   emptyslot : boolean;

BEGIN
   write('Enter ID number-->');
   readln(workingcopy.idno);
   write('Enter initials-->');
   readln(workingcopy.initials);
   write('Enter last name-->');
   readln(workingcopy.lastname);
   write('Enter salary-->');
   readln(workingcopy.salary);
   pos := hash(workingcopy.idno);
   origpos := pos;
   emptyslot := false;
    REPEAT
      seek(f,pos);
      IF f^.idno = 0
        THEN
          BEGIN
            f^ := workingcopy;
            put(f);
            emptyslot := true
          END
        ELSE
          pos := pos MOD recordspace + 1
    UNTIL (pos = origpos) OR emptyslot;
   IF emptyslot
     THEN
     writeln('Record has been added.')
     ELSE
     writeln('No room for record in file.')
 END;
(* addrec *)


PROCEDURE inspect;
  (* Search for and display record *)

VAR
   pos, origpos, target : recordposition;
   found : boolean;
BEGIN
   write('ID number to inspect-->');
   readln(target);
   pos := hash(target);
   origpos := pos;
   found := false;
   seek(f,pos);
    REPEAT
      workingcopy := f^;
      IF workingcopy.idno = target
```

```
              THEN
              BEGIN
                found := true;
                writeln(workingcopy.idno);
                writeln(workingcopy.initials, workingcopy.lastname);
                writeln(workingcopy.salary);
                writeln
              END
            ELSE
              BEGIN
                pos := pos MOD recordspace + 1;
                seek(f,pos)
              END
          UNTIL (origpos = pos) OR found OR (workingcopy.idno = 0);
          IF NOT found
          THEN
            writeln('Record ', target, ' cannot be found.')
      END;
    (* inspect *)

  BEGIN (* main *)
    reset(f,'rfile2.dat/SEEK');
     REPEAT
       write('Command — A)dd record, I)nspect, or Q)uit --->');
       readln(command);
       CASE command OF
          'A' : addrec;
          'I' : inspect;
          'Q' :
           BEGIN
           END;
          ELSE writeln('Invalid command')
        END (* CASE *)
      UNTIL command = 'Q'
    close(f)
  END.
```

Sample Run:

```
Command — A)dd record, I)nspect, or Q)uit --->A
Enter ID number--->1094
Enter initials--->BD
Enter last name--->CUMMINGS
Enter salary--->4.5
Record has been added.
Command — A)dd record, I)nspect, or Q)uit --->A
Enter ID number--->7783
Enter initials--->FG
Enter last name--->MINTON
Enter salary--->6.5
Record has been added.
Command — A)dd record, I)nspect, or Q)uit --->I
```

```
ID number to inspect--->1094
   1094
BDCUMMINGS
 4.500000E+00

Command - A)dd record, I)nspect, or Q)uit --->I
ID number to inspect--->7783
   7783
FGMINTON
 6.500000E+00

Command - A)dd record, I)nspect, or Q)uit --->Q

Ready
```

12

Data Structures and Data Management

From each according to his ability, to each according to his need.

KARL MARX (1818–1883)

12-1   Introductory Considerations

Any application of data structures has as a general goal the management of data within a computer system. **Computer system** in this context refers to the integrated whole consisting of central processing unit, main memory, and associated peripheral devices. In this concluding chapter, we shall not introduce any new data structures; rather, we will explore how combinations of the data structures we have already studied can be applied in 2 rather broad data management areas.

The first of these occurs typically in the writing of operating systems for multiuser machines and is called **garbage collection.** As used in this chapter, garbage collection is effectively recovering memory allocated to a user who no longer needs it. There is a hint of socialism to garbage collection algorithms. Each system user should get precisely what she or he needs at any given instant, but no more than is needed. As soon as a user's needs partially or completely vanish, the resources which were so generously doled out should be greedily reclaimed by the operating system in its big brother role.

The other general area we shall explore is the more file-oriented problem known as **database management.** A database is a collection of logically related files. Managing information in such a collection is database management, techniques which have arisen as solutions to the following types of problems:

1. In a large organization, each department maintains its own files. As a consequence, updates such as address changes frequently are made in one file but not in another.

The database solution is to store the data only once and give each department a pointer to that part of the data which it needs.

2. In an application such as a student records keeping system, the proverbial professional student takes more courses than allowed by the fixed length records that were thought to allow ample space when the system was originally designed. The database solution is to view records as dynamic entities.

3. A customer file is organized to search effectively by social security number. Unfortunately, the names of all customers who live in California are needed. The database solution is to plan ahead and realize that the organization of a file may in fact require efficient access by more than just one **primary key.**

Such problems still arise far too often in data processing applications. The database approach is not only to consider the relationships between the records within a given file but also to consider relationships between various files.

The problems of garbage collection and database management taken up in this chapter are meant to serve as illustrations of how data structures can be applied. Definitive treatment of these problems are the subject matter for advanced courses, which have as their prerequisite a thorough knowledge of data structures. Our intention here is to give the curious reader a hint of what lies ahead.

12-2 Garbage Collection

We have briefly touched upon the problem of allocation and recovery of memory resources in Chapters 2 and 3. In Chapter 2, we developed the PSEUDO procedures GETNODE and RETURNNODE for the purpose of allocating and recovering **fixed-size memory nodes** to be used in list processing. In Chapter 3, we discussed a process called **compaction** which could be called upon at periodic intervals to relocate character strings in memory, thereby reorganizing memory in such a fashion that all free space is shifted to one large contiguous memory area. Prior to the compaction process, such free space obtained from the deallocation of string storage is likely to be scattered in small **fragments** of various sizes throughout memory. Indeed, the problem solved by the compaction process is often called the **fragmentation problem.**

The fragmentation problem occurs on a larger and more complicated scale in multiuser operating systems. Consider, for instance the sequence of user requests portrayed in Figure 12-1. The complications presented by a multiuser environment will not allow this fragmentation problem to be solved by either of our earlier strategies. The GETNODE/ RETURNNODE scheme will fail because it deals with fixed-size nodes, and clearly user requests to such an operating system will be for memory allocations of varying sizes. The compaction technique, on the other hand, would require user activity to stop while memory is reorganized in a way requiring large scale data movement. Hence compaction would not be dynamic enough to be used on the scale required by a multiuser operating system.

An initial approach to solving this problem is to generalize the algorithm behind the GETNODE/RETURNNODE procedures of Chapter 2, enabling them to handle variable-length records. For instance, the free blocks pictured in the last memory snapshot of Figure 12-1 could be linked into an **available block list** by allocating 2 words in each block to store the size of the block and a pointer to the next available block. This concept

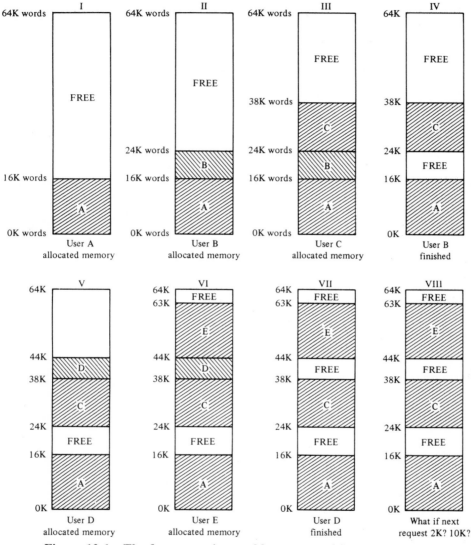

Figure 12-1 The fragmentation problem on a multiuser system.

is highlighted in Figure 12-2. When a new user request is made of the list in Figure 12-2, the list can be searched for the first block whose size meets the request (or for the block whose size comes closest to meeting the request). Having determined the block to allocate for the user request, it would be wise to next check whether or not the user actually requires the entire block. If not, it could be split—giving the user what is requested and keeping what remains of the block in the available block list. This strategy, applied to the available block list of Figure 12-2 for a request of 2K memory, yields the result displayed in Figure 12-3.

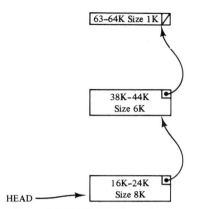

Figure 12-2   Available block list derived from snapshot VIII of Figure 12-2.

Unfortunately, this scheme will lead to only another problem when it comes time to garbage collect the memory blocks no longer needed by users. Consider, for instance, what happens if the 2K memory block allocated in Figure 12-3 is returned by its user prior to any other changes being made in the available space structure. The new available space list now contains one additional 2K block as indicated in Figure 12-4.

Clearly, as more and more of these relatively small blocks are returned the available list will have an inordinate number of very small blocks. This is not desirable; eventually it will be impossible to fill the legitimate request of a user needing one large memory

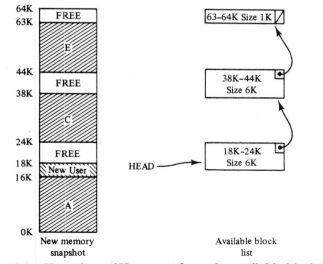

Figure 12-3   Honoring a 2K request from the available block list of Figure 12-2.

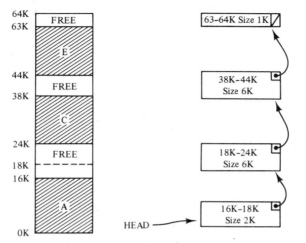

Figure 12-4   Available block list after returning the 2K block.

block. We will have small neighboring blocks the sum of whose sizes may collectively surpass the total memory needed by the large request. However, because they are partitioned into many small blocks instead of relatively few large blocks, it will be impossible to fill the request. To remedy this problem, we must devise a method that will allow a block being returned to the available list to be **coalesced** with the other block(s) in the list that are the physical neighbor(s) of the returning block.

Buddy Systems

A common method for doing this is to designate for each potential block 1 or 2 **buddy** blocks. A buddy must reside next to its corresponding block in memory. When a block is ready to be returned, we check the available space list for its buddy. If the buddy is also available, we coalesce the 2 before returning them as one block to available space. This is not quite as easy as it sounds, however. To determine the buddy of a given block, it will be necessary to impose certain restrictions upon block sizes and/or to store a fair amount of bookkeeping data in each block. We shall examine 3 buddy schemes:

1. Binary buddies

2. Fibonacci buddies

3. Boundary tag buddies.

They differ in the data structures used for their implementation. After stating the general algorithms, we shall devote more detailed attention to a discussion of these data structures.

```
PROCEDURE ALLOCATE(S,P)

(* Given a request for a memory block of size S, return a pointer P to *)
(* a memory block that meets the request with a minimum amount of *)
(* waste *)
```

```
CALL A SEARCH PROCEDURE TO SEARCH THE AVAILABLE BLOCK LIST(S) AND
     FIND A BLOCK WHICH SURPASSES THE SIZE REQUESTED WITH THE LEAST
     POSSIBLE AMOUNT OF EXCESS.
IF NO SUCH BLOCK CAN BE FOUND THEN
        [CALL INSUFFICIENT-MEMORY]
ELSE IF THE BLOCK FOUND CANNOT BE SPLIT INTO BUDDIES (ONE OF WHICH
     WOULD SATISFY THE SIZE REQUESTED) THEN
        [RETURN THE POINTER FROM THE SEARCH PROCEDURE AS P]
ELSE (* THE BUDDY SYSTEM BEING USED ALLOWS SPLITTING *)
       ⎡SPLIT THE BLOCK INTO TWO BUDDIES                          ⎤
       ⎢RETURN ONE BUDDY APPROPRIATELY TO AVAILABLE BLOCK LIST(S) ⎥
       ⎣RETURN P AS THE POINTER TO THE OTHER BUDDY                ⎦
ENDIF
RETURN
END ALLOCATE
```

The search procedure called upon to find a block in this procedure would be dependent upon the data structure used by a particular buddy system to store available blocks. Whether a block, once found, can be further split is determined by the restrictions the given buddy system imposes on block sizes.

A similar generic algorithm to perform garbage collection on a returning memory block is presented below in recursive form. The recursion expresses the fact that, once a returning block has been coalesced with its buddy on the left or right, we have a larger block that may itself be a candidate for coalescing with another buddy.

```
PROCEDURE GARBAGECOLLECT(P,AVAIL)

(* Perform garbage collection on memory block being pointed to by P. *)
(* AVAIL represents the available space structure used by the buddy *)
(* system in question. *)
(* Begin by recursively coalescing P with its buddies. *)

CALL COALESCE(P,AVAIL)    (* See procedure COALESCE below *)

(* Upon return from COALESCE, P may well be pointing to a much larger *)
(* block than it was before. The final step is now to attach this *)
(* potentially larger block to the available space structure. *)

CALL ATTACH(P,AVAIL)
RETURN
END GARBAGECOLLECT

PROCEDURE COALESCE(P,AVAIL)

(* This procedure will coalesce block pointed to by P with a buddy *)
(* on its left or right. AVAIL represents the available block *)
(* structure used by this particular buddy method. *)
(* The call to CHECK-BUDDIES below represents a call to a procedure *)
(* that will determine whether buddies of P exist in the available *)
(* space structure. If a left buddy of P is available, then a pointer *)
(* to it is returned in LBUDDY. Otherwise LBUDDY is returned as NULL. *)
(* A similar convention is followed for the pointer RBUDDY. *)
```

```
CALL CHECK—BUDDIES(P,AVAIL,LBUDDY,RBUDDY)

(* If both LBUDDY and RBUDDY come back as NULL, both of the *)
(* conditional tests that follow will fail and an immediate *)
(* return will result. Otherwise coalescing must occur on left *)
(* and/or right. *)

IF RBUDDY <> NULL THEN
     ┌ REMOVE RBUDDY FROM AVAIL STRUCTURE                                ┐
     │ CHANGE APPROPRIATE FIELDS IN P TO COALESCE P WITH RBUDDY          │
     │    (* Fields dependent upon buddy system being used *)            │
     │ CALL COALESCE(P, AVAIL)                                           │
     │       (* Recursively attempt to coalesce the new, larger P        │
     └         with its buddies *)                                      ┘
ENDIF
IF LBUDDY <> NULL THEN
     ┌ REMOVE LBUDDY FROM AVAIL STRUCTURE                               ┐
     │ CHANGE APPROPRIATE FIELDS IN LBUDDY TO COALESCE P & LBUDDY       │
     │    (* Fields depending upon buddy system being used *)           │
     │ SET P TO LBUDDY (* P points at new, larger block *)              │
     │ CALL COALESCE(P,AVAIL)                                           │
     │       (* Recursively attempt to coalesce the new, larger P        │
     └         with its buddies *)                                      ┘
ENDIF

RETURN
END COALESCE
```

A discussion of the 3 buddy systems follows. From the generic procedures ALLO-CATE and GARBAGECOLLECT given above, it is clear that a detailed exposition must entail a description both of the data structure used to store available blocks and of the bookkeeping data that must be stored within and about each memory block.

Binary Buddy System   The logic of the **binary buddy** system requires that all blocks be of size 2^i for some i. Whenever a block is split, the resulting 2 buddies must be of equal size. That is, if a block of size 2^i is split, then the resulting buddies will each be of size 2^{i-1}. As an example, let us suppose that we have 2^{16} ($= 64$K) words of memory to manage and that we wish to allocate no blocks smaller than 2^{10} ($= 1$K) words. Then, at any given time, we could potentially have free blocks of size 2 raised to the 10th, 11th, 12th, 13th, 14th, 15th, and 16th powers. The available space structure in this case will consist of a *doubly linked* list of free blocks for each of the 7 potential block sizes. Hence we would need head pointers:

```
AVAIL(1) ---> Head of list for blocks of size 2¹⁰
AVAIL(2) ---> Head of list for blocks of size 2¹¹
AVAIL(3) ---> Head of list for blocks of size 2¹²
          .                    .
          .                    .
          .                    .
AVAIL(7) ---> Head of list for blocks of size 2¹⁶
```

Any given block would need to contain the following bookkeeping information:

- A Boolean flag to indicate whether or not it is free

- An integer field to store its size

- Left and right links used when it is a node in an AVAIL list

A graphic illustration of such a node is given in Figure 12-5.

Initially, all 2^{16} words of memory would be viewed as one free block; that is, AVAIL(7) would point to the beginning of memory and all other AVAIL pointers would be null. Now let us suppose that a sequence of user requests come in the order:

a. Request for memory block of size 2^{14}

b. Request for memory block of size 2^{13}

c. Request for memory block of size 2^{14}

d. Request for memory block of size 2^{14}

e. Block from (a) no longer needed.

f. Block from (b) no longer needed.

The dynamic fashion in which these requests would be processed can be best described in a pictorial fashion. In Figure 12-6 on pages 302–304, we have used tree diagrams to highlight the splitting and coalescing that would occur as (a) through (f) are processed. Memory addresses in this figure are given as $0, 1, 2, \ldots, i, \ldots, 62, 63$ where i represents the beginning of the $(i + 1)$st 1K memory block (of which there are 64 in all).

Three comments are needed to explain more fully the actions highlighted in Figure 12-6. First, we note that the moral of coalescing is that one available block of size $2N$ is always preferred to two available blocks of size N: the whole is greater than the sum of its parts. This is why, in returning the block from (b) in Figure 12-6, we coalesce two 8K blocks into a 16K block and then immediately take advantage of an available 16K left buddy to coalesce further into a 32K block.

Second, the binary nature of the splitting scheme means that, when a block is returned, the address of its buddy can be determined immediately. For instance, the block of size 2^{14} that begins at address 0 (relative to 1K blocks) has a right buddy of the same size that begins at address 16 (relative to 1K blocks). The location of this block's buddy is purely a function of the block's own size and location. In absolute terms, a block of size 2^i with starting address $n \times 2^i$ will have a right buddy with starting address $(n + 1) \times 2^i$ if n is even and a left buddy starting at address $(n - 1) \times 2^i$ if n is odd. This means that, as a block is being returned, a simple computation allows us to find its buddy whose free

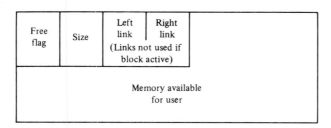

Figure 12-5   Bookkeeping information in block for binary buddy system.

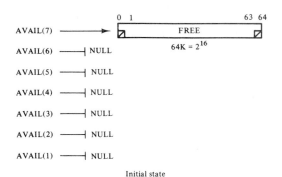

Initial state

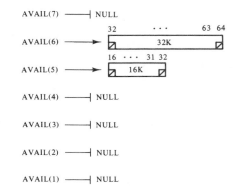

Request (a) processed

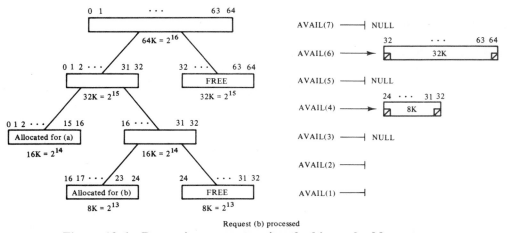

Request (b) processed

Figure 12-6 Processing requests using the binary buddy system.

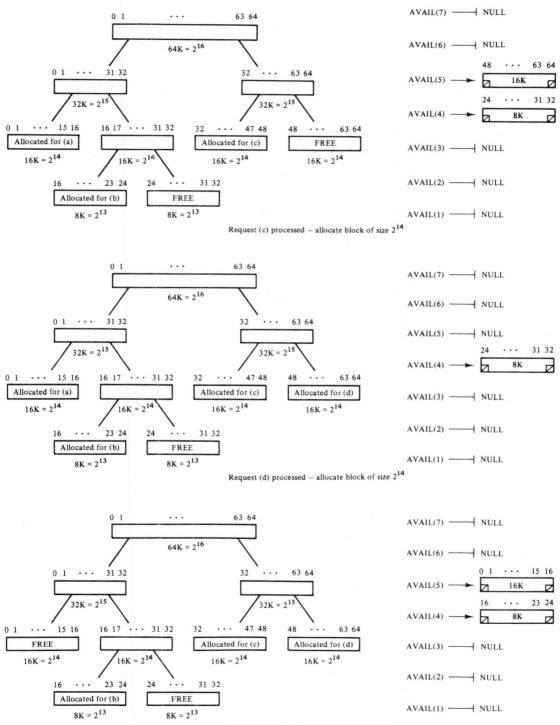

Request (c) processed – allocate block of size 2^{14}

Request (d) processed – allocate block of size 2^{14}

Block from (a) returned – no coalescing occurs

Figure 12-6 Continued.

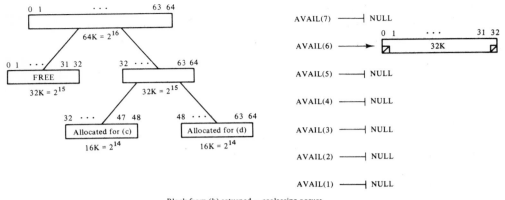

Block from (b) returned – coalescing occurs

Figure 12-6   Continued.

flag would then be checked to determine whether or not coalescing is possible. Notice that, in a binary buddy system, a given block has either a left or right buddy but not both.

Third, if the buddy of the block returned is free, the doubly linked nature of the available block lists becomes crucial. This is because we have essentially jumped into the middle of an available space list in accessing the buddy of the block to be returned. Consequently, without the double linking, we would not have the prior pointer necessary to remove this buddy from the available list of which it is presently a part. Of course, once a returning block has been coalesced with its buddy, we now have a new returning block that may recursively undergo further coalescing as indicated in our generic COALESCE procedure.

Fibonacci Buddy System   Let us begin a consideration of the **Fibonacci buddy** system by analyzing the binary buddy system. Contradictory as this may seem, the rationale is that we must seek to define the relationships between block sizes that must exist in a buddy system of this type. Examining the sequence of possible block sizes in the binary system,

$$2^1, 2^2, 2^3, \ldots, 2^{10}, 2^{11}, \ldots$$

we notice that every member of the sequence except the first is the sum of adding the previous member to itself. Because any block size (except the smallest possible) must potentially result from coalescing 2 smaller blocks, any sequence of possible block sizes for a buddy system of this variety must have the property that any size within the sequence must be the sum of 2 preceding members of the sequence. In the binary buddy system, this sum always is obtained by adding the size of the immediately prior member of the sequence to itself. However, the binary system is a special case; all that is required is that any size can be represented as the sum of 2 smaller sizes.

Perhaps the most famous sequence of numbers having this property is the Fibonacci sequence. The ith member of the Fibonacci sequence can be recursively defined as:

$$F_1 = 1$$

$$F_2 = 1$$

$$F_i = F_{i-1} + F_{i-2} \quad \text{for} \quad i > 2$$

Hence, the initial members of the Fibonacci sequence are:

$$1, 1, 2, 3, 5, 8, 13, 21, 34, \ldots$$

Suppose, for instance, that we were managing 21K memory and were faced with the following requests for storage:

a. Request for 7K

b. Request for 7K

c. Request for 2K

d. 7K from (b) no longer needed

e. 2K from (c) no longer needed

f. 7K from (a) no longer needed

Figure 12-7 on pages 306–308 highlights the allocation, deallocation, and resulting coalescing that would occur as these requests were processed.

Note that some additional overhead is required when the Fibonacci buddy system is used. Depending on the implementation scheme, it may be necessary to store the Fibonacci numbers themselves in an array to allow quick access to data necessary to allocate, split, and coalesce blocks. The alternative to this would be to recompute the sequence each time it is needed. Second, unlike the binary system, it is not clear from a block's size and location whether it is the left buddy or right buddy of another block. Consequently, it becomes necessary to store some additional bookkeeping data within each block. These data take the form of a **left buddy count** field as indicated in Figure 12-8 on page 309. This left buddy count maintains a record of how deep a given block is nested as the left buddy of other blocks. In Figure 12-7, the left buddy count is indicated by the circled digit appearing above each block. The algorithm for maintaining this left buddy count involves:

1. As a block is split, the resulting left buddy has its left buddy count field increased by 1. The resulting right buddy has its left buddy count field set to 0.

2. As coalescing occurs, the left buddy must always have its left buddy count field decreased by 1.

Given the increase in overhead involved in the Fibonacci system, it is certainly a valid question to ask whether it offers any advantage over the binary system. Its primary advantage lies in the fact that it allows for a greater variety of possible block sizes in a given amount of memory than does its binary counterpart. For instance, in 64K words of memory the binary system would allow block sizes of 1K, 2K, 4K, 8K, 16K, 32K, and 64K—7 possibilities in all. The Fibonacci method would yield potential block sizes of 1K, 2K, 3K, 5K, 8K, 13K, 21K, 34K, and 55K—9 sizes in all. Clearly a greater variety of sizes will allow us to allocate memory in a fashion that minimizes the difference between what the user actually needs and what our block sizes force us to give. In fact, if we use a more generalized *kth Fibonacci sequence* defined by:

$$F_j = 1 \quad \text{for} \quad j = 1, 2, \ldots, k$$

$$F_j = F_{j-1} + F_{j-k} \quad \text{for} \quad j > k$$

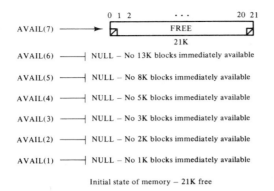

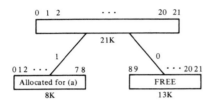

Initial state of memory – 21K free

Request (a) processed – 8K allocated for 7K request

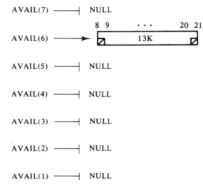

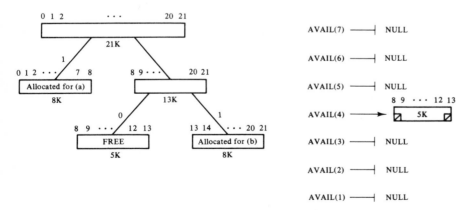

Request (b) processed – 8K allocated for 7K request

**Figure 12-7   Processing requests using the Fibonacci buddy
system. Circled digits represent left buddy counts.**

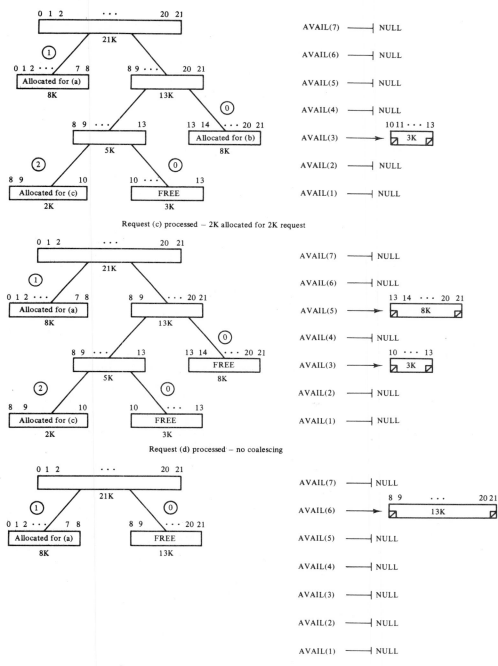

Request (c) processed – 2K allocated for 2K request

Request (d) processed – no coalescing

Request (e) processed – coalescing occurs up to 13K block

Figure 12-7 Continued.

Request (f) processed – coalescing occurs – one free 21K block results

Figure 12-7   Continued.

then we can readily see that the larger k becomes, the finer our partitioning of block sizes will be. (Notice that, by this definition, the binary buddy system is generated by the 1st Fibonacci sequence.) Of course, with each increase in k comes a corresponding increase in the overhead of bookkeeping information that must be balanced against the greater selection of block sizes. Refer to Hinds for a more theoretical discussion of which k may be appropriate to choose in a given situation.*

Boundary Tag Buddy System   Both the binary and Fibonacci systems have the disadvantage of not allowing an arbitrary selection of block sizes and thereby forcing the waste of some memory each time a user's request does not precisely match one of the specified block sizes. The **boundary tag** method overcomes this drawback but only at the expense of requiring even more bookkeeping data than either of the other methods. The reason why the binary and Fibonacci schemes limit us to a finite number of block sizes and splitting possibilities is that, without such a limitation, it would be impossible to determine where a block's buddy begins. For instance, suppose that we were using the Fibonacci buddy system and were about to return a block of size 13K whose left buddy count field was checked and found to be zero. Because of the limitations on the sizes into which a block may be split when using the Fibonacci method, we know that this block must have a left buddy of size 8K with which it could possibly coalesce. Using the starting address of the block to be returned and the fact that it has a left buddy of size 8K, the starting address of the left buddy can thereby be obtained. Note that this problem of determining the size and starting location of a returning block's buddy is less complicated if the returning buddy has a right buddy instead of a left buddy. In this situation, the starting location and size of the returning block would tell us the starting address of the right buddy. Then, provided we have stored the bookkeeping information for that right buddy precisely at its starting location, the size field and free flag are immediately available for our inspection. This distinction between finding the size and starting location of left and right buddies in the binary and Fibonacci systems is highlighted in Figure 12-9.

Figure 12-9 should make it apparent that if we were willing to store duplicate copies of a block's size and free flag at its right boundary as well as its left boundary, then the

*Hinds, J. A. 1973. A design for the buddy system with arbitrary sequences of block sizes. *Technical Report No. 74*, Buffalo, NY: SUNY Buffalo.

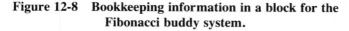

Figure 12-8   **Bookkeeping information in a block for the Fibonacci buddy system.**

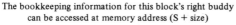

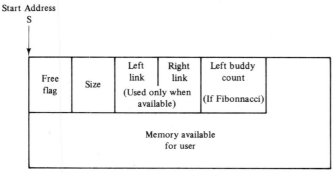

The bookkeeping information for this block's right buddy
can be accessed at memory address (S + size)

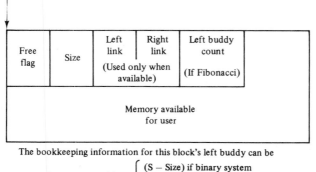

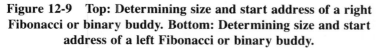

The bookkeeping information for this block's left buddy can be

accessed at memory address $\begin{cases} (S - \text{Size}) \text{ if binary system} \\ (S - \text{Fibonacci number preceding size}) \\ \quad \text{if Fibonacci system} \end{cases}$

Figure 12-9   Top: Determining size and start address of a right Fibonacci or binary buddy. Bottom: Determining size and start address of a left Fibonacci or binary buddy.

problem of determining the starting address of a left buddy would not require *a priori* knowledge of what its size must be. Its size could be determined by checking the bookkeeping information along the right boundary. The effect is to allow sizes to be chosen arbitrarily to meet a user's specific request. No longer is it necessary to allocate 13K to meet an 11K request because the available choices of potential block sizes demand it. This is the primary motivation behind the boundary tag buddy system. A block and the bookkeeping information within it would now appear as shown in Figure 12-10.

As is always the case, the boundary tag technique has advantages and disadvantages that you must consider carefully before concluding that it is the method to use in a particular context. Of course, the major advantage is that it allows a user's request to be granted *precisely,* with no excess memory being allocated and therefore wasted. The logic of the method also determines that a given block is not a left or right buddy per se. Rather any block except one starting or ending at a memory boundary has *both* a left and a right buddy with which it can potentially coalesce. The primary disadvantages of the boundary tag method are that additional bookkeeping information must be stored and maintained within each block and that the available space structure now must be stored as one long doubly linked list instead of as a sequence of doubly linked lists for each of the respective block sizes allowed. This latter point means that, in determining whether a user's request can be met, the boundary tag method requires sequentially searching a single available space list—a slower process than is required for either the binary or Fibonacci schemes. At this point, we encourage you to trace through the actions diagrammed in Figure 12-11 on pages 311–313, showing the allocation and deallocation of memory as the following requests are processed:

a. Initially all memory, 64K, is free

b. User requests 7K

c. User requests 9K

d. User requests 4K

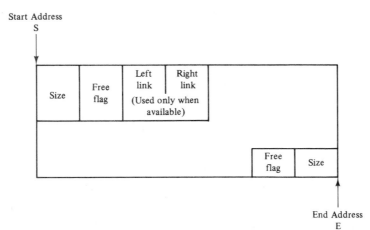

Figure 12-10   Block and bookkeeping information for the boundary tag method.

e. Memory requested in (c) no longer needed

f. Memory requested in (b) no longer needed

g. Memory requested in (d) no longer needed

The 3 memory management methods discussed in this section provide an excellent illustration of the application of data structures at the operating system level. We note in particular that all 3 methods require the use of one or more doubly linked lists to store available memory blocks. The elegance of this relatively simple data structure allows us

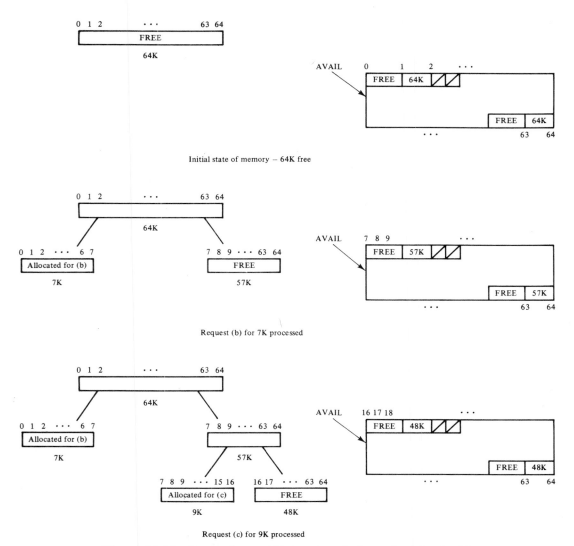

Figure 12-11   Processing requests using the boundary tag buddy system.

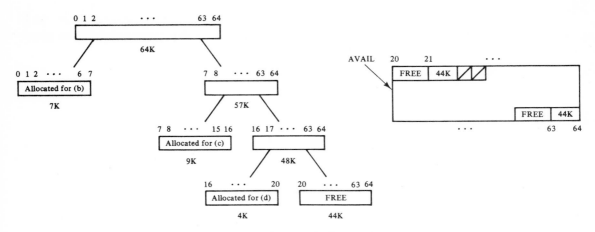

Request (d) for 4K processed

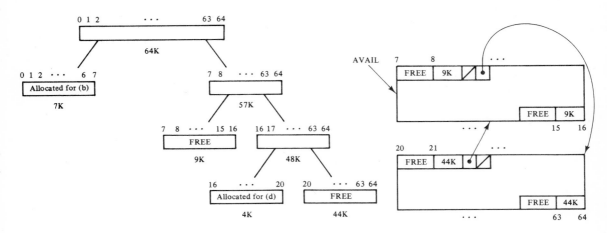

(e) Processed — no coalescing

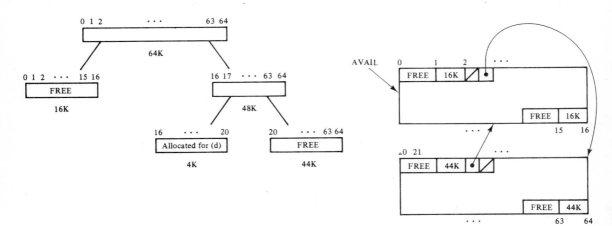

(f) Processed — returning block coalesces with right buddy

Figure 12-11   Continued.

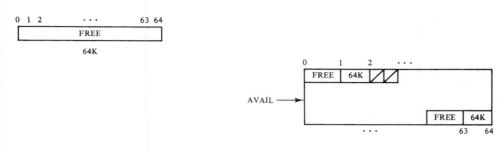

(g) Processed — coalescing occurs on both sides

Figure 12-11 Continued.

to delete a given block from the middle of an available list without having to traverse the entire list to find a prior pointer as we would be forced to do with a singly linked list. In the next section we shall consider how a broad knowledge of data structures can be applied in the management of files.

12-3 Database Management

In general we may think of a file as a collection of parallel lists. For example, Figure 12-12 pictures the file of employee records for a hypothetical company. The vertical lines in this figure divide the file into separate lists, or **fields,** whereas the horizontal lines divide the file into separate occurrences of complete employee **records.**

A **database** can be defined as a collection of logically **related** files. As an easy example of a database and the advantages it offers in comparison to normal file processing, consider the following **data duplication** problem. Suppose that our hypothetical company decides that, for privacy considerations, the accounting department should not have access to an employee's EDUCATIONAL-LEVEL or SPOUSE-NAME. Similarly, the company's Committee on Planning Social Events should not have access to an employee's SALARY-RATE or TAX-CATEGORY. The nondatabase approach to this problem would be to create 2 separate, unrelated files—one containing the information needed by accounting department and the other containing the data needed by the social planning committee. However,

EMPLOYEE-NAME	ADDRESS	SALARY-RATE	TAX-CATEGORY	EDUCATIONAL-LEVEL	SPOUSE-NAME
Cowans, P.	N. 4th St.	9.34	A	12	Joyce
Jones, D.	E. 9th St.	8.45	B	16	Bert
Hiller, B.	S. 8th St.	7.09	A	14	Grace
Miller, S.	W. 3rd St.	6.45	C	12	Ernie
Smith, W.	E. 1st St.	9.12	A	16	Bertha

Figure 12-12 Employee record file for hypothetical company.

this approach leads to the storage of the EMPLOYEE-NAME and ADDRESS fields in 2 separate files. The problems involved with such data duplication go well beyond the amount of disk space that is consumed in storing certain data items more than once. Just as serious is the problem of accurately updating information that is stored in such a duplicate fashion. For instance, if an employee should move, the change of address would have to be made in 2 separate places and potentially by 2 separate individuals. Clearly there is the danger that this approach may result in one employee being listed as living at 2 different addresses— one for payroll and one for social planning.

The database approach to solving this data duplication problem would be to divide the file presented in Figure 12-12 into 3 *related* files as indicated in Figure 12-13. Note that 3 files replace the single file that appeared in Figure 12-12. One file, containing the EMPLOYEE-NAME and TAX-CATEGORY fields, is open to accounting department access only. A third file, containing the fields needed by social planning, is open only to access by those users. The relationship between records in the files of this database is extremely straightforward; records in the same relative position in different files are related to each other. Hence, a social planning committee member could use a search routine to find an employee's name in the common access file and then access the same position in the file limited to social planning access to determine the employee's EDUCATIONAL-LEVEL and SPOUSE-NAME. Note that any information updates, such as an address change, would have to be made only once and would be immediately known to all users entitled to that information.

The Variable Length Records Problem

Let us now consider a situation that arises in systems maintaining student records at a university. Each student's name must be related to a variable number of courses that the student has taken. Viewed from the perspective of storing all the data in one file, we are faced with the variable length records that appear in Figure 12-14.

Clearly, the jagged edge traced on the right of the data in Figure 12-14 presents some data storage problems. How much storage do we allocate for each student's record to

Accounting Department Access Only		Common Access		Social Planing Access Only	
SALARY-RATE	TAX-CATEGORY	EMPLOYEE-NAME	ADDRESS	EDUCATIONAL-LEVEL	SPOUSE-NAME
9.34	A	Cowans, P.	N. 4th St.	12	Joyce
8.45	B	Jones, D.	E. 9th St.	16	Bert
7.09	A	Hiller, B.	S. 8th St.	14	Grace
6.45	C	Miller, S.	W. 3rd St.	12	Ernie
9.12	A	Smith, W.	E. 1st St.	16	Bertha

Figure 12-13   Employee database derived from Figure 12-12.

STUDENT	COURSE1	COURSE2	COURSE3	COURSE4	COURSE5	COURSE6
Egghead, I.	BOT422 A	MAT444 B	PHI309 A	CPS110B		
Kopf, D.	MAT111 C	ENG201 D				
Smart, B.	PHI723 B	PSY388 A	ZOO910 A	CPS310 B	ENG222 B	MAT311 A

Figure 12-14   Variable length student records.

ensure that we do not run out of course space for the professional student? At the same time, how do we hold wasted course space to a minimum? The answers conflict. The professional student may require 100 course fields, but such allocation will be a tremendous waste for most of our students.

A database perspective, on the other hand, would be to view these data as 2 separate files—a student name file and a course grade record file—with relationships existing between the records in each file. Here the relationship between student name records and course grade records would be **one-to-many** as opposed to the **one-to-one** type of relationship that existed in our previous example of an employee database. That is, each student is related to many course grade records, whereas each employee was related to only one accounting record and one social planning record. The added complexity of the one-to-many relationship would require pointers to maintain the relationship between student and course grade files, as indicated in Figure 12-15, which shows the courses taken by each student as a linked list with the head pointer being stored in the student name file.

The one-to-many relationship exemplified between the student and course grade files in the student database system of Figure 12-15 is an integral consideration in nearly all database management problems. In fact, as we shall see, more complex database relationships usually are implemented by decomposing them into several one-to-many relationships. A convenient way of representing such a one-to-many relationship appears in

	Student Name File			Course Record File		
	STUDENT	LINK		COURSE	GRADE	LINK
1	Egghead, I.	1		1 BOT422	A	4
2	Kopf, D.	2		2 MAT111	C	5
3	Smart, B.	3		3 PHI723	B	6
				4 MAT444	B	8
				5 ENG201	D	NULL
				6 PSY388	A	7
				7 ZOO910	A	9
				8 PHI309	A	10
				9 CPS310	B	11
				10 CPS110	B	NULL
				11 ENG222	B	12
				12 MAT311	A	NULL

Figure 12-15   Student records database derived from Figure 12-14.

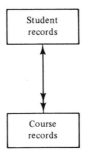

Figure 12-16   Notation for a one-to-many relationship.

Kroehnke and is illustrated for our student records database in Figure 12-16.* In this figure, the double arrows pointing at the course file indicate that there may be more than one course grade record for each student record. The single arrow pointing towards the student file indicates that there is only one student record associated with each course grade record.

Note that a one-to-many database relationship is just a special example of the general tree that we have already studied in Chapters 6 and 7. To see this, note the essentially equivalent information stored in the database in Figure 12-15 and the general tree of Figure 12-17.

Secondary Key Processing

As another example of how a one-to-many relationship may arise in database processing, consider the file of student records which appears in Figure 12-18 on page 318. In this example, we have what seems to be a rather ordinary fixed-size record file in which each student record consists of that student's

1. Identification number

2. Name

3. Sex

4. Class—FReshman, SOphomore, JUnior, or SEnior

Assume that the file is organized so that we may use one of the search procedures described in Chapter 11 to locate a student quickly by using his or her identification number as a key.

The organization of the student records file in Figure 12-18 is adequate if all user requests are of the form "Find the data for the student who has ID number XXXXX." However, users are notorious for coming up with requests that the organization of the file was not designed to handle. Examples of such requests for the file of Figure 12-18 would include:

1. Find all female students

*Kroehnke, D. 1977. *Database Processing*. Chicago: Science Research Associates.

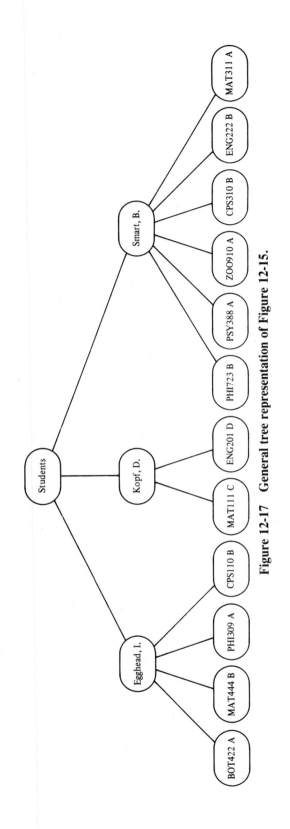

Figure 12-17 General tree representation of Figure 12-15.

	IDNUMBER	NAME	SEX	CLASS
1	34762	JONES,T.	M	JU
2	37938	GARNER,D.	M	SE
3	12387	EVANS,K.	F	FR
4	27127	HOYT,L.	F	SO
5	93791	HAYES,P.	M	JU
6	35261	MURPHY,G.	F	SO
7	59795	ZEMAN,G.	F	SO
8	23719	MILLER,B.	M	FR
9	64272	DAVIS,K.	M	SE
10	48262	AARON,H.	M	FR
11	58799	RUTH,B.	F	JU
12	97271	GEHRIG,L.	M	SO
13	59143	COSELL,H.	F	FR
14	87927	BURKE,J.	F	SE
15	28098	SMITH,P.	M	JU
16	47819	WOLF,B.	F	SE

Figure 12-18   Student records organized by IDNUMBER field.

2. Find all sophomore students

3. Find all students who are male *and* juniors

4. Find all students who are female *or* seniors

These requests represent attempts to access the records in the file by a **nonunique secondary key.** That is, each of the preceding requests view a field (or fields) other than the usual **primary key** of IDNUMBER as the key by which records are to be accessed. Moreover, the access being requested is via secondary key fields, for which many records may share the same value (they are *nonunique*). The nonunique nature of these key fields means that each secondary key in effect defines a one-to-many relationship between the records in the file. For example, the one-to-many relationships existing in the file of Figure 12-18 are shown in Figure 12-19.

Implementing One-to-Many Relationships

Given the organization of the file in Figure 12-18, the only strategy that can be used to handle secondary key requests is to plod through the file sequentially, checking each record to see if it meets the criteria specified. However, in databases with large numbers of records, this sequential plodding approach may well be too slow to be practical. Users want their requests handled immediately; forcing them to wait minutes for a response from the system is a good way to become unemployed. The key to effective database management is to:

1. Plan ahead: foresee the types of secondary key requests that are likely to be made for a given database.

2. Build the one-to-many relationships represented by these secondary keys into the structure of the files that make up the database.

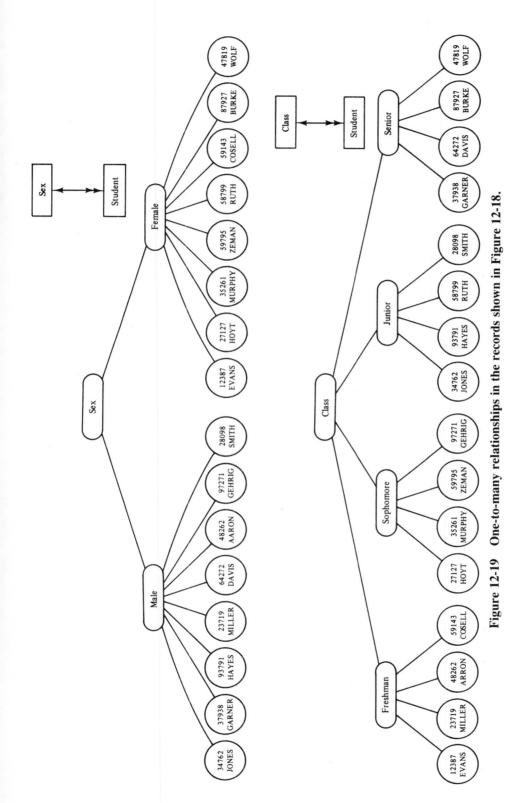

Figure 12-19   One-to-many relationships in the records shown in Figure 12-18.

We will concentrate on the second of these 2 steps. This is not to say that the 1st step is less important. However, the analysis of what users may want from a system is not per se a data structures consideration and is more appropriately taken up in systems analysis study. The second question of how to build one-to-many relationships into the files that compose a database is most commonly approached using one of 2 strategies—multilink or inverted files.

Multilink Files   The **multilink file** strategy requires that, for each secondary key field by which we anticipate accessing the file, a link field be established in the record structure of the file. This link field is then used to link together all those records that share a given value for the secondary key in question. Essentially this means that each secondary key gives rise to multiple linked lists—one such list for each value that the key may take on. These linked lists weave their way through the database, allowing users to access efficiently only those records in which they are interested. There is no need to sift through and discard records that have a secondary key value other than the one being sought, because such records are not included in the linked list that is being followed through the file. A multilink implementation for the student database of Figures 12-18 and 12-19 is given in Figure 12-20. In database terminology, such a multilink implementation strategy is also called a **chained pointer** database. (Refer back to Figure 1-1 on page 3.)

Some comments are in order concerning the relative advantages and disadvantages of a multilink file viewed from the perspective of what we already know about its underlying data structure—the linked list. First, we have extremely efficient sequential processing of those records satisfying a single secondary key value; we need merely traverse the corresponding linked list. The number of file accesses required is merely the number of records that satisfy that particular key value. Second, although in the example of Figure 12-20 we have not maintained the multiple lists in any particular order, such ordering (for example, alphabetically by student name) would not be difficult to maintain given the ease and efficiency by which insertions and deletions are handled with a linked list. One consideration would be to maintain the various one-to-many relationships as doubly linked lists. Otherwise, a deletion would require accessing the record to be deleted by its primary key and then removing it from all the one-to-many relationships in which it participates. If each one-to-many relationship is a linked list, we are potentially deleting from the middle of a linked list without having traversed the entire list up to that point. This is precisely the situation in which a doubly linked list gives us the necessary previous pointer without requiring the list traversal necessitated by a singly linked list. Third, changes in a secondary key value for a record are merely a matter of a deletion from one list followed by an insertion into another list. Hence, a sex change for COSELL,H. in Figure 12-20, though an ordeal from a biological viewpoint, would prove to be quite trivial for our multilink database.

The advantages of a multilink file, as with any data structure, are offset by disadvantages that must be carefully considered on an application-by-application basis. The first of these disadvantages for a multilink file is that the storage of links within the record itself makes it quite difficult to add a new one-to-many relationship after the database has been built. This would be a problem, for example, if we maintained a STATE-OF-RESIDENCE field in the student database of Figure 12-20 but did not build the corresponding 50 linked lists for states into the original database. If the administration of the university belatedly decided that they now wanted to process students by STATE-OF-RESIDENCE,

	ID NUMBER	NAME	SEX	SEXLINK	CLASS	CLASSLINK
1	34762	JONES,T.	M	2	JU	5
2	37938	GARNER,D.	M	5	SE	9
3	12387	EVANS,K.	F	4	FR	8
4	27127	HOYT,L.	F	6	SO	6
5	93791	HAYES,P.	M	8	JU	11
6	35261	MURPHY,G.	F	7	SO	7
7	59795	ZEMAN,G.	F	11	SO	12
8	23719	MILLER,B.	M	9	FR	10
9	64272	DAVIS,K.	M	10	SE	14
10	48262	AARON,H.	M	12	FR	13
11	58799	RUTH,B.	F	13	JU	15
12	97271	GEHRIG,L.	M	15	SO	NULL
13	59143	COSELL,H.	F	14	FR	NULL
14	87927	BURKE,J.	F	16	SE	16
15	28098	SMITH,P.	M	NULL	JU	NULL
16	47819	WOLF,B.	F	NULL	SE	NULL

MALE-HEAD-POINTER = 1   SO-HEAD-POINTER = 4
FEMALE-HEAD-POINTER = 3   JU-HEAD-POINTER = 1
FR-HEAD-POINTER = 3   SE-HEAD-POINTER = 2

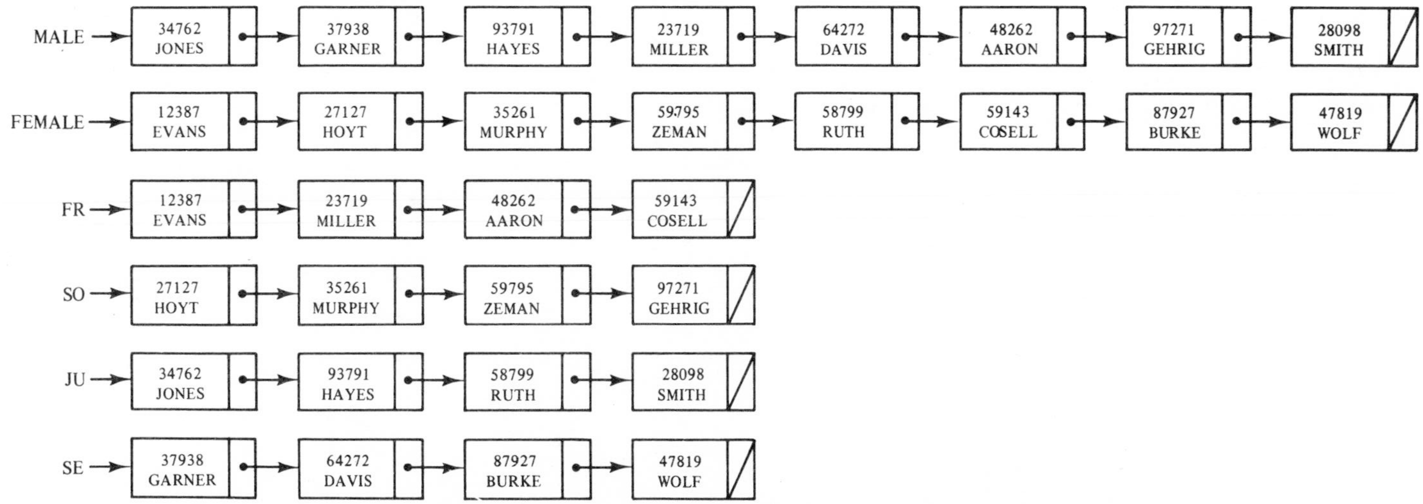

Figure 12-20 Top: physical representation of multilink student database from Figure 12-18. Bottom: logical representation of multilink student database.

the database would have to be rebuilt from scratch instead of being dynamically altered to reflect this new one-to-many relationship. In practice, because users frequently make such after the fact requests, this disadvantage can be very serious, again emphasizing the need for careful pre-implementation planning in database design.

Another disadvantage of the multilink method involves the fashion in which queries involving Boolean combinations of secondary key values must be processed. For example, suppose the database of Figure 12-20 were to be queried for all students who were FEMALE or SENIORS. Any algorithm to process this request, given an underlying multilist structure, would require a complete traversal of both the FEMALE *and* the SENIOR lists. The records of those students who are *both* FEMALE *and* SENIOR would be accessed twice using such an algorithm. In the worst possible case, in which the N members of the SENIOR class coincided with the N FEMALE students at our hypothetical university, we would actually require $2 \times N$ disk accesses to determine this N member set.

The 2 disadvantages cited above should be kept in mind as we begin the following discussion of inverted files. In particular, inverted file implementations of one-to-many relationships are able to circumvent both of these drawbacks at the expense of using a structure that is slightly more difficult to maintain.

Inverted Files   The essential idea behind the **inverted file** strategy is *not* to place in the data records themselves the bookkeeping information necessary for efficient secondary key processing. Note that it was the placement of such bookkeeping information in the data records of a multilink file that led to both of its inefficiencies. Instead, the inverted file method locates these data about data in small files that are maintained apart from the actual data records. These small inverted files, in effect, are indexes that contain the relative record positions of those records sharing identical values for a given secondary key. For instance, inverted files for the database of Figure 12-18 are given in Figure 12-21.

INVERTED FILE FOR SEX FIELD

VALUE	POSITIONS OF RECORDS HAVING THIS VALUE
M	1 2 5 8 9 10 12 15
F	3 4 6 7 11 13 14 16

INVERTED FILE FOR CLASS FIELD

VALUE	POSITIONS OF RECORDS HAVING THIS VALUE
FR	3 8 10 13
SO	4 6 7 12
JU	1 5 11 15
SE	2 9 14 16

Figure 12-21   Inverted files for database of Figure 12-18.

Given a secondary key query, we would have to search the appropriate inverted file for that particular secondary key value. Once found, we have at our disposal the list of all positions in the data file where we will find records satisfying the query. Hence, inverted files invert a problem such as searching for all students who are JUNIORS into the problem of searching a much smaller file for the key value JU and then merely accessing all of the records we find associated with that key value. Searching the inverted file for a particular key value is highly efficient, because the file contains only relative record positions and no real data. Hence the inverted files themselves are small, allowing large portions to reside in main memory at any given time. Moreover, the lists of relative record positions pictured in Figure 12-21 could be stored by any of the list storage techniques that we have discussed in earlier chapters of this book: dense linear arrays, linked lists, or trees. The decision as to what type of list implementation you should use to maintain the relative record positions would involve such considerations as the frequency with which insertions and deletions occur and whether or not it is important to traverse the records satisfying a query in a particular order (for example, alphabetically by student name).

Both of the inefficiencies cited in our previous discussion of multilink files are resolved by the inverted file approach. First, should we wish to add an inverted file for a many-to-one relationship after a database is already built, it requires just one sequential pass through the data records to build the appropriate inverted file. Because the data records themselves contain no bookkeeping information, they do not need to be reconstructed as they would in the multilink implementation. Second, the problem of accessing certain records twice for some Boolean queries of the database is alleviated by the fact that the set of records meeting such a Boolean query may be determined by looking solely at the inverted files. Moreover, this determination occurs at main memory speeds, because large portions of the inverted files can be brought into main memory for efficient processing.

The disadvantages of the inverted file approach lie primarily in the added algorithmic complexity it introduces. Each inverted file adds another file to the overall database. This file may be another physical file, in which case there are the problems typically associated with file input and output such as finding available buffer space in main memory and minimizing the number of times which the file must be opened and closed. On the other hand, if the inverted file merely represents a logical remapping of a small portion of the same file that stores the data records, then extreme care must be taken to ensure that you do not confuse bookkeeping data and actual data. Moreover, inverted files are more difficult to maintain than their multilink counterparts. Consider, for instance, the problem of deleting a record whose primary key equals a specified input. To do this, we must:

1. Search the actual data file for the primary key

2. Determine the values this record takes on for various secondary key fields

3. Remember these values and the record position of the actual data record

4. For each inverted file, search for the key value and record position in (3) and appropriately delete this record position from the list of record positions

Clearly, although this process could occur at a high rate of speed if search strategies and list representation techniques are wisely chosen, it is still considerably more complex than deletion from multilink lists.

More Complex Database Relationships and Their Implementation

Two relationships in addition to the one-to-many relationship are recognized in database terminology—the simple network and the complex network. The term *network* in this context is only loosely affiliated with the concept of networks covered in Chapter 9. A **simple network** is nothing more than a restricted graph consisting of several one-to-many relationships, and a **complex network** is equivalent to a full-blown, directed graph. When implemented, both simple and complex networks are decomposed into multiple one-to-many relationships, which are then implemented by one of the techniques already discussed. This process of decomposing a graph into a spanning forest of trees (that is, one-to-many relationships) was covered in 9-3; you may wish to review that section.

Simple Networks   As an example of a simple network relationship, let us again consider a university records system in which course records are classified both by their level (FReshman, SOphomore, JUnior, or SEnior) and by the department in which they are offered. We will assume that the university has only 3 departments (designated as departments 1, 2, and 3) and 8 courses (designated as A, B, C, D, E, F, G, and H). The 2 one-to-many relationships in this database—those of course-level-to-course and department-to-course—are represented in Figure 12-22. Notice that the structure in Figure 12-22 is a graph that is not quite a tree. Rather, each course node has, in a sense, 2 parents: one course level parent and one department parent.

Formally, we would say that a simple network is a collection of several one-to-many relationships whose resulting representation as a graph is *acyclic* in the sense defined in Chapter 9. Working more intuitively from the picture presented in Figure 12-22, we could say that a simple network is a near-tree in which a child may have multiple parents but only one parent of any given type. This intuitive definition should make it immediately evident how the simple network of Figure 12-22 could be implemented as a spanning forest of trees. Such a spanning forest is given in Figure 12-23. Notice that, in the spanning forest of Figure 12-23, all course nodes actually appear twice. It should be clear from what we have already said about avoiding data duplication that these course nodes would not actually be stored in 2 separate physical locations. For example, the fact that course B appears as subordinate to both course level JU and department 3 in Figure 12-23 merely indicates that both the course level JU node and the department 1 node have associated with them logical pointers to the actual physical location of the data for course B.

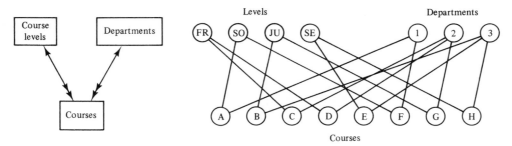

Figure 12-22   Simple network relationship among course levels, departments, and courses.

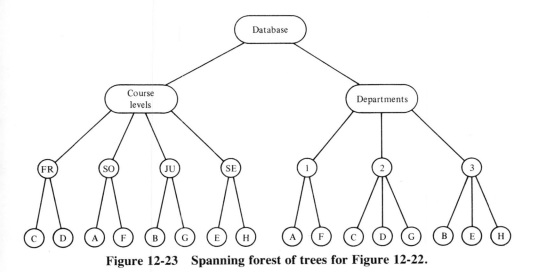

Figure 12-23   Spanning forest of trees for Figure 12-22.

Complex Networks   In contrast to a simple network, a complex network corresponds to what we have previously described as a (potentially cyclic) directed graph in Chapter 9. For example, consider the relationship that would exist between students and current course offerings in our university records system. Each student is enrolled in one or more courses; we have a one-to-many relationship running from student records to current course offering records. Conversely, each current offering is enrolled by many students; there is also a one-to-many relationship running from current course offering records to student records. A situation such as this, where we have one-to-many relationships running in both directions, is called a many-to-many relationship, or complex network. An example of such a complex network for a university offering courses A, B, and C and with students SMITH, JONES, MURRAY, BACH, and LEWIS is given in Figure 12-24. The double-headed arrows running in both directions in this figure indicate the one-to-many relationships in both directions.

Note that the complex network of Figure 12-24 could be represented by the adjacency matrix of Figure 12-25. However, the current trends in database terminology generally avoid any direct reference to the notion of adjacency matrices. Instead, the database

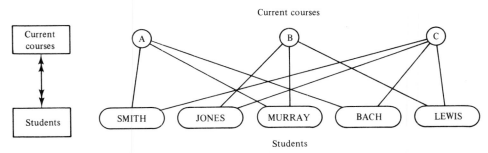

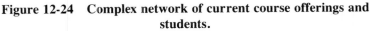

Figure 12-24   Complex network of current course offerings and students.

	SMITH	JONES	MURRAY	BACH	LEWIS
A	1	0	1	1	0
B	0	1	1	0	1
C	1	1	0	1	1

Figure 12-25   Adjacency matrix for complex network of Figure 12-24.

approach to representing a complex network such as that appearing in Figure 12-24 is first to decompose it into its spanning forest of trees. One such decomposition for the complex network of Figure 12-24 is given in Figure 12-26. Once decomposed, the spanning forest of trees is essentially nothing more than a collection of one-to-many relationships, each of which may be represented using the techniques already discussed in this chapter.

Two remarks are in order concerning the spanning forest in Figure 12-26. The first is merely a reiteration: you should not assume, because a particular course offering or student name appears at more than one node in a spanning forest, that that course number or student name is actually stored more than once in the database. The spanning forest represents only the logical arrangement of data in the database, not the physical arrangement. Second, note that, although the database environment avoids direct mention and use of adjacency matrices such as that appearing in Figure 12-25, the implementation of a spanning forest of trees using multilink or inverted file techniques is functionally equivalent to a sparse matrix representation of an adjacency matrix that allows direct access by both row and column. Hence, in many ways, database management is just an application of the data structures we have already studied, hidden under a veneer of slightly different terminology.

12-4   Database Management Systems

A **database management system (DBMS)** consists of software that establishes and maintains the relationships between the records and files in a database and allows users to make queries of the database based on the relationships that are represented therein. Up to this point, the emphasis of this chapter has been to describe how the authors of a DBMS might go about implementing the various relationships within a database. However, the current trends in database technology indicate that an increasingly smaller percentage of the people involved with database will be authoring such systems. This is because of the emergence of a large number of general purpose DBMS's that will in fact build the implementation of a database for the user provided the user can accurately describe the database in the language accepted by the DBMS. This means that there are 3 groups of people involved with the development and usage of general purpose DBMS's:

1. The authors of the system. This group is involved in the development of algorithms to build and maintain the multilink and inverted files that underlie the entire database.

2. The naive end users of the system. This group simply makes queries of the system and then watches it all happen with little understanding of why it is happening.

3. The sophisticated end users of the system. Perhaps a better term to describe this group would be **database designers.** They are concerned with communicating to the general-purpose DBMS a description of their desired database so that the DBMS can build the necessary structures to maintain the system.

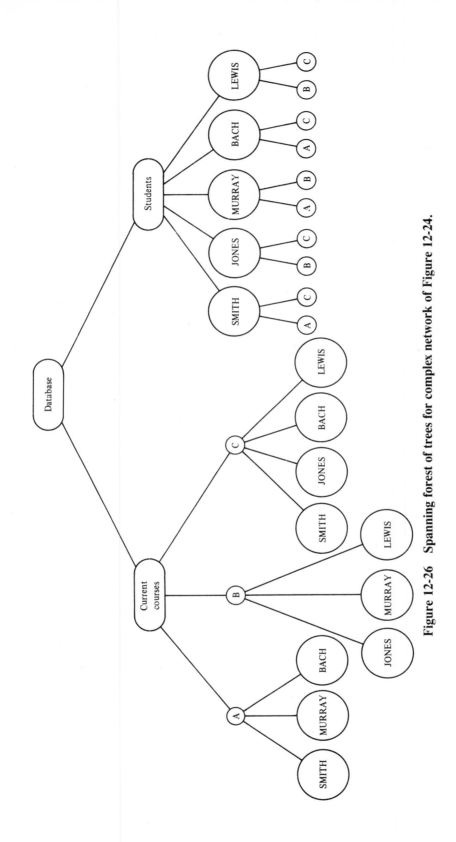

Figure 12-26 Spanning forest of trees for complex network of Figure 12-24.

It is to this last group that our remarks in the closing portion of this chapter are directed. The database designer must thoroughly understand the structures upon which a general purpose DBMS is based. She or he need not be concerned with the actual implementation of such structures, because the DBMS will do that. Instead, based upon a knowledge of the capabilities and limitations of the structures used by the DBMS, the database designer can use the DBMS effectively to build and maintain a variety of databases.

Three primary database models exist—the hierarchical model, the CODASYL model, and the relational model. We give a brief description of how a database designer could use each of these models to represent the types of database relationships described in the previous section: the one-to-many relationship, the simple network, and the complex network. There are complete books written about each of the 3 models, cited in the bibliography at the end of the chapter. We provide an introduction that could serve as the basis for further study.

The Hierarchical Model

The **hierarchical model** represents the earliest of the 3 database models. Hence, as one might expect, it is also the most limited. Its best-known implementation is in the IMS (Information Management System) marketed by IBM. The basic building block made available to the database designer using the hierarchical model is the tree, the one-to-many relationship. This means that the language of the particular hierarchical DBMS being used allows the designer to specify the one-to-many relationships that he or she wants in the database. Automatically, the necessary links or inverted files are built and maintained by the DBMS; this is no longer a concern of the designer.

However, should the designer using the hierarchical model wish to build more complex database relationships, such as simple and complex networks, into the database, it is the responsibility of the designer to decompose such relationships into several one-to-many relationships—just as we did in Figures 12-23 and 12-26. The designer is additionally able to specify which of the multiple occurrences of an item in such a decomposition are to be physical occurrences and which are to be logical pointers.

The crucial limitation of the hierarchical model is that, as a model, it is too tightly tied to the implementation schemes for databases. That is, because multilink files and inverted files are the 2 primary implementation schemes for DBMSs and because they directly represent only one-to-many relationships, the hierarchical model forces its designer to work solely in terms of that relationship. In a sense, the only real independence between the hierarchical model and its underlying implementation is that it is inconsequential to the model whether multilink or inverted files are used.

The CODASYL Model

Developed under the auspices of the Data Base Task Group of the Conference on Data Systems Languages, the CODASYL model offers the designer a slightly more general-purpose modeling tool.* The CODASYL model uses the notion of a **set** to describe one-to-many and simple network relationships. The analogy between CODASYL sets and trees as we have described them is quite straightforward. Each set has an owner (the parent) and

---

*CODASYL Data Base Task Group Report. 1971. New York: Association for Computing Machinery.

members (the children). By declaring sets in the language of the CODASYL model, the designer is able to specify one-to-many relationships that the DBMS should build and maintain. For instance, with a declaration of the form:

```
SET IS COURSELEVEL-COURSE
    OWNER IS COURSELEVEL
    MEMBER IS COURSE
```

and:

```
SET IS DEPT-COURSE
    OWNER IS DEPT
    MEMBER IS COURSE
```

the designer could establish the simple network relationship given in Figure 12-22. Notice that, conceptually, the CODASYL model and the hierarchical model are very similar. That is, although different terminology is used, a CODASYL set is still essentially a hierarchical tree. The primary conceptual difference between them is that the CODASYL model does not force the designer to view members as existing twice within the database (either physically or logically) when a simple network relationship is specified. In graphic terms, it could be said that the hierarchical model forces the designer to specify a simple network in terms of its spanning forest, as in Figure 12-23. The CODASYL model, on the other hand, allows the designer who is defining a simple network to work directly from her or his perception of what a simple network really is—not a spanning forest, but rather what appears in Figure 12-22.

Like the hierarchical model, the CODASYL model gives no means for directly defining a complex network. The method used by the CODASYL model designer to implement such a network, however, is somewhat different from the decomposition into trees forced upon the designer using the hierarchical model. Instead, the CODASYL model allows the designer to define (sometimes artificially) **intersection records** to act as a pseudolink between the records in a many-to-many relationship. As an example of such intersection records, let us consider how the CODASYL designer might define the complex network of Figure 12-24. He or she would look for some data item that the current course records and the student records share in their respective one-to-many relationships. Such an item could be TIME. For courses, TIME would mean the time(s) at which sections of the course are offered. For a student's records, TIME would mean the time(s) at which *that student* is in class. By this definition of TIME, it is an item that is shared in a one-to-many relationship by both course offering records and student records. It therefore could be used to go from a given student to the many courses being taken by the student and, conversely, from a given course to the many students in that course. This method of defining a complex network in terms of an intersection record is illustrated in Figure 12-27. Note that the multiple occurrences of certain items in Figure 12-27 represent logical occurrences only.

The Relational Model

First formulated by Codd, the relational model is a radical departure from the hierarchical and CODASYL models in that it is *completely* abstracted from the underlying implementation scheme.* The designer using the relational model describes her or his database in terms

---

*Codd, E. F. 1970. A relational model of data for large shared databanks. *Communication of the Association for Computing Machinery* 13 (6).

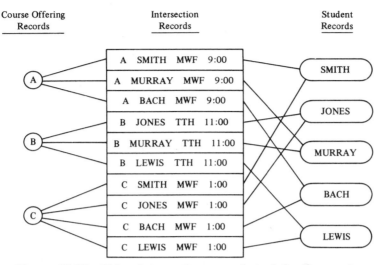

Course Offering Records   Intersection Records   Student Records

Figure 12-27   Using intersection records to define a complex network.

of relations. A **relation** is simply a table of rows and columns. To a certain degree, a relation looks like a file. Each column corresponds to a field name and each row to a record. Figure 12-28 gives a relation in which each row represents a student record, and the columns represent NAME, SEX, and CLASS.

Initially, it may seem contradictory that something as simple as a relation allowing no variable length rows could in fact lead to the most general, flexible database model yet developed, but this is indeed the case. The power of the method is that the database designer is free to define virtually any relation that is needed to specify a particular relationship within a database. Moreover, Codd has supplied a collection of general purpose operations upon relations (called the *relational algebra* and *relational calculus*), which allow the designer to build a variety of new relations from existing old ones. As an example of how a relation can be used to reflect a one-to-many relationship in a database, consider the STUDENT-to-COURSE relation appearing in Figure 12-29. This is the relational model embodiment of the one-to-many relationship that initially appeared in Figure 12-14. Codd's relational algebra would then allow us to draw from the relation of Figure 12-29 new relations that, for example, could isolate all the rows of the relation belonging to one particular student. Note that the multiple occurrences of NAMEs within

NAME	SEX	CLASS
Egghead, I.	M	FR
Kopf, D.	F	SO
Smart, B.	M	SO

Figure 12-28   Student record relation.

NAME	COURSE
Egghead, I.	BOT422 A
Egghead, I.	MAT444 B
Egghead, I.	PHI309 A
Egghead, I.	CPS110 B
Kopf, D.	MAT111 C
Kopf, D.	ENG201 D
Smart, B.	PHI723 B
Smart, B.	PSY388 A
Smart, B.	ZOO910 A
Smart, B.	CPS310 B
Smart, B.	ENG222 B
Smart, B.	MAT311 A

**Figure 12-29   Relation for one-to-many STUDENT-to-COURSE
relationship of Figure 12-14.**

the relation of Figure 12-29 is of no concern at the database *design* level. The occurrences represent logical occurrences only; their physical placement in the database is an *implementation* concern.

As examples of how relations can similarly be used to define simple and complex networks, Figure 12-30 shows relations for the simple and complex networks that originally appeared in Figures 12-22 and 12-24, respectively. Note again the difference between the relations of Figure 12-30 and their implementations. As relations consisting of rows and columns, they unambiguously contain all of the necessary information to describe a simple or complex network. Consequently, they are ideal from the database design perspective. Underneath the elegant simplicity of being able to describe a database in terms of relations must still lie an implementation scheme that relies on a collection of data structure techniques to ensure that the designer's perception of rows and columns can in fact be represented in a fashion resulting in a tolerable efficiency.

The relational model would seem to represent the ultimate in a DBMS, completely unshackling the designer from any considerations or limitations derived from the underlying implementation scheme. This evolution toward complete generality is not a trivial matter. Codd first proposed his model in 1970; only recently have practical relational DBMS's become available in the marketplace. There seems to be little doubt, however, that it is the DBMS of the future.

SUMMARY

In this chapter we have attempted to give an overview of how a general knowledge of data structures may be applied in 2 specific areas—memory management and database management. The problem of memory management is typically encountered by an oper-

COURSE LEVEL	COURSE	DEPT
FR	C	2
FR	D	2
SO	A	1
SO	F	1
JU	B	3
JU	G	2
SE	E	3
SE	E	3

COURSE	STUDENT
A	SMITH
A	MURRAY
A	BACH
B	JONES
B	MURRAY
B	LEWIS
C	SMITH
C	JONES
C	BACH
C	LEWIS

**Figure 12-30   Top: relation for the simple network of Figure 12-22.
Bottom: relation for the complex network of Figure 12-24.**

ating system that must allocate and then reclaim or **garbage collect** appropriately sized blocks of memory among its many users. Three memory management techniques were discussed: the binary buddy system, the Fibonacci buddy system, and the boundary tag buddy system. The database management problem more typically applies to huge amounts of data stored in various related files. Three general database models exist—the hierarchical model, the CODASYL model, and the relational model. Underlying the conceptual framework of the model, there are two primary implementation techniques: multilink or inverted files. Most commercially available database management systems use one or potentially a combination of these techniques.

In the world of applications . . .

An article entitled *R(elational)DBMS: Is Now the Time?*, which appeared in the March, 1984 issue of *Datamation*, gives an excellent profile of the impact that relational database management systems are about to have. According to Michael Stonebreaker of Relational Technologies, Inc., "Relational database is an answer. Now what is the question?" Perhaps the question is how to design user-oriented DBMS's that hide the complexities of the data structures behind the scenes from those users who have absolutely no desire to deal with them. This idea of *data abstraction* has been the goal of the relational model since it was first put forth by Ted Codd of IBM more than 10 years ago—to allow the user to view the data as a simple table of records divided into fields.

What kept the relational model from having anything more than a theoretical effect until the 1980s? The answer is that the simplicity of the data organization as seen by the naive user must be correspondingly matched by a detailed complexity in the underlying data structures when the system is designed. This complexity means that relational systems have tended to be slow—particularly on small computers. However, Peter Tierney of Relational Technologies sees much progress being made. The article quotes Tierney as saying, "There are no technical barriers (to increasing speed). We know we can increase the speed by a factor of 2 in the next 6 months."

KEY TERMS

Garbage collection
Database management
Primary key
Compaction
Fragmentation
Available list
Binary buddy system
Fibonacci buddy system
Boundary tag buddy
    system
Left buddy count

Kth Fibonacci sequence
Field
Record
Data duplication problem
Variable length records
    problem
One-to-many relationship
Secondary key
Multilink files
Chained pointer database
Inverted files

Simple network
Complex network
Spanning forest
Acyclic graph
DBMS
Hierarchical model
CODASYL model
Intersection records
Relational model
Relations

GENERAL DBMS BIBLIOGRAPHY

Atre, S. 1980. *Database: Structured Techniques*. New York: Wiley.

Auerbach Publishers, Inc., (ed.) 1981. *Practical Database Management*. Reston, VA: Reston.

Date, C. J. 1974. *An Introduction to Database Systems*. Reading, MA: Addison-Wesley.

Ellzey, R. S. 1982. *Data Structures for Computer Information Systems*. Chicago: Science Research Associates.

Flores, I. 1977. *Data Structure and Management*. Englewood Cliffs, NJ: Prentice-Hall.

Johnson, L., and Cooper, R. 1981. *File Techniques for Database Organization in COBOL*. Englewood Cliffs, NJ: Prentice-Hall.

Katzan, H. 1975. *Computer Data Management and Database Technology*. New York: Van Nostrand, Reinhold.

Martin, J. 1975. *Computer Database Organization*. Englewood Cliffs, NJ: Prentice-Hall.

Martin, J. 1976. *Principles of Database Management*. Englewood Cliffs, NJ: Prentice-Hall.

Sprowles, C. R. 1976. *Management Data Bases*. Santa Barbara, CA: Wiley/Hamilton.

EXERCISES

1. Write PSEUDO algorithms ALLOCATE and GARBAGECOLLECT specifically for the binary buddy system.

2. Write PSEUDO algorithms ALLOCATE and GARBAGECOLLECT specifically for the Fibonacci buddy system.

3. Write PSEUDO algorithms ALLOCATE and GARBAGECOLLECT specifically for the boundary tag buddy system.

4. In processing secondary keys via the multilink and inverted file methods, is it possible not to store the actual data for each secondary key in each record? That is, the potential secondary key values could be stored once in a separate table instead of being stored repeatedly in each individual record. Discuss the pros and cons of doing this.

5. What are the advantages of double linking in multilink files?

6. What are the relative advantages and disadvantages of multilink files versus inverted files?

7. Develop a general PSEUDO algorithm for record deletion in an inverted file database.

8. What are the relative advantages and disadvantages of the 3 buddy systems discussed in this chapter?

9. If you are familiar with Pascal, discuss what sort of memory management algorithms and structures you would use to implement its NEW and DISPOSE procedures.

10. In the boundary tag buddy system, one long doubly linked list of available blocks is maintained. When a user request is received, this list must be searched for a suitable block. A question arises whether this search should continue until the first block which meets the user's request is encountered (a *first fit* strategy) or until it is certain that the block to be allocated for the user is the one that comes closest to meeting the request (a *best fit* strategy). Discuss the relative advantages and disadvantages of the first fit and best fit methods.

11. For each of the following diagrams:

    a. determine whether it represents a simple or complex network

    b. decompose it into a spanning forest of trees.

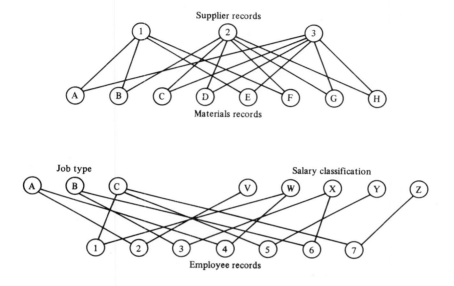

PROGRAMMING PROBLEMS

1. Passenger records for the Wing and a Prayer Airline Company consist of

        Last name
        First name
        Street address
        State of residence
        ZIP code
        Phone number
        First class or tourist class preference
        Smoker or nonsmoker seating preference

A passenger's last name is the primary key to his or her record, with first name and street address potentially used to ensure uniqueness. State of residence, first class or tourist class preference, and smoker or nonsmoker seating preference are to be regarded as secondary keys. Additionally, each passenger possesses arbitrarily many:

a. Records of flights taken during the past year, with the mileage for each of these flights

b. Records of future flights on which reservations have been booked

Design a database organization and then write a program that will allow a Wing and a Prayer agent to:

a. Add a passenger record to the database

b. Add a future flight reservation record for a specified passenger

c. Cancel a future flight reservation for a specified passenger

d. Change a passenger record or future flight reservation for a specified passenger

e. Inspect all future flight reservations for a specified passenger

f. Determine whether a specified passenger qualifies for a "frequent flyer" discount; that is, whether she or he has flown more than 3000 miles during the past year

g. Purge from the database records of all flights that occurred more than one year ago

h. Search for passengers having a specified secondary key value (such as all passengers living in Utah)

i. Allow secondary key searches to be built out of Boolean combinations of secondary key values (such as all passengers who prefer to travel first class AND in a non-smoking section)

2. Simulate a multiuser operating system environment for each of the 3 buddy systems discussed in this chapter by declaring a large array and randomly generating user requests for pieces of this array. Have your program accumulate statistics as to how each of the methods performs relative to percentage of requests that could be met, average amount of memory not in use, average amount of wasted memory (that is, space given to a user in excess of the amount requested), average time to process a request, and so on.

3. Suppose that a student record at a university contains fields for that student's identification number, name, sex, class, and state of residence. Sex, class, and state of residence are to be regarded as secondary keys. Additionally, each student possesses arbitrarily many grade records, each consisting of the name of the course taken and the grade received. Design a database organization and then write a program that will allow a user to:

a. Add a student record to the student database

b. Add a course record for a specified student

c. Change a student record or course record for a specified student

d. Delete a specified student from the database, with all associated course records

e. Inspect the record of a given student

f. Search for those students having a specified secondary key value

g. Allow secondary key searches to be built out of Boolean combinations of secondary key values (such as all female juniors from New York)

PSEUDO/Pascal
Syntax Considerations

General Goals

PSEUDO	Pascal
1. To facilitate the expression of algorithms that can be easily translated into a variety of languages.	To provide a language capable of representing structured algorithms.
2. To avoid the use of specialized tools unique to certain languages; for example, presupposing the existence of a NEW and DISPOSE function as provided in Pascal.	To provide certain specialized tools, such as NEW and DISPOSE, which can greatly increase programmer productivity provided they are thoroughly understood.
3. To avoid syntactical considerations and emphasize algorithmic concepts using graphic aids such as brackets and diagrammatic documentation.	To allow automatic machine translation (compilation) into object code; must have formal enough syntax and graphic enhancements must be avoided.

Stylistic Conventions

PSEUDO	Pascal
1. One statement per physical line. If more than one line is needed, indicate continuation by → and appropriate indentation of secondary line.	Statements separated by semicolons.
2. A block of statements is: ■ Enclosed by a keyword pair WHILE-ENDWHILE IF-ENDIF FOR-ENDFOR REPEAT-UNTIL ■ Indented under its leading keyword ■ Bracketed to highlight it graphically	A block of statements is: ■ Enclosed by a keyword pair BEGIN-END REPEAT-UNTIL
3. Commentary may be written, enclosed by (* · · · *), or graphic in the form of diagrams that clarify what a given block of code does.	Commentary must be written, enclosed by (* · · · *) or {. . .}.

Control Constructs

PSEUDO	*Pascal*

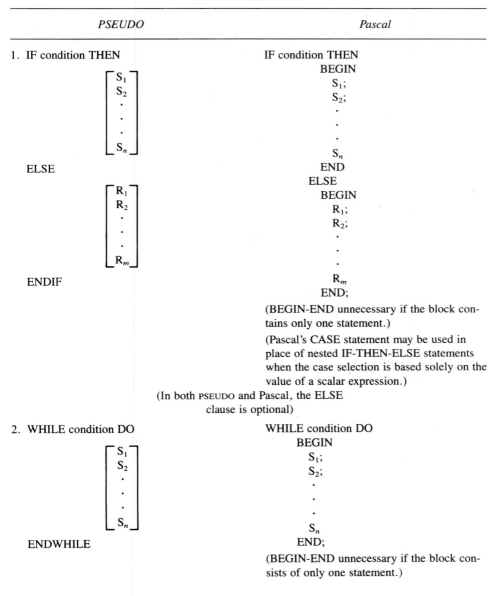

1. IF condition THEN

$$\begin{bmatrix} S_1 \\ S_2 \\ \cdot \\ \cdot \\ \cdot \\ S_n \end{bmatrix}$$

ELSE

$$\begin{bmatrix} R_1 \\ R_2 \\ \cdot \\ \cdot \\ \cdot \\ R_m \end{bmatrix}$$

ENDIF

```
IF condition THEN
    BEGIN
        S₁;
        S₂;
        .
        .
        .
        Sₙ
    END
ELSE
    BEGIN
        R₁;
        R₂;
        .
        .
        .
        Rₘ
    END;
```

(BEGIN-END unnecessary if the block contains only one statement.)

(Pascal's CASE statement may be used in place of nested IF-THEN-ELSE statements when the case selection is based solely on the value of a scalar expression.)

(In both PSEUDO and Pascal, the ELSE clause is optional)

2. WHILE condition DO

$$\begin{bmatrix} S_1 \\ S_2 \\ \cdot \\ \cdot \\ \cdot \\ S_n \end{bmatrix}$$

ENDWHILE

```
WHILE condition DO
    BEGIN
        S₁;
        S₂;
        .
        .
        .
        Sₙ
    END;
```

(BEGIN-END unnecessary if the block consists of only one statement.)

PSEUDO	*Pascal*
3. REPEAT	REPEAT

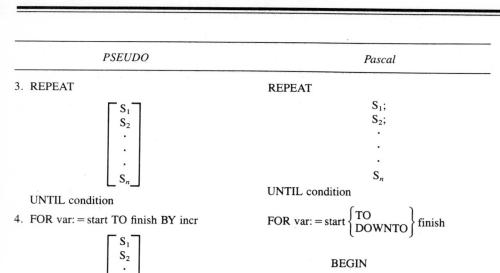

3. REPEAT

$$\begin{bmatrix} S_1 \\ S_2 \\ \cdot \\ \cdot \\ \cdot \\ S_n \end{bmatrix}$$

UNTIL condition

4. FOR var: = start TO finish BY incr

$$\begin{bmatrix} S_1 \\ S_2 \\ \cdot \\ \cdot \\ \cdot \\ S_n \end{bmatrix}$$

ENDFOR

(If "BY incr" is omitted, an increment of 1 is assumed.)

REPEAT

S_1;
S_2;
.
.
.
S_n

UNTIL condition

FOR var: = start $\begin{Bmatrix} \text{TO} \\ \text{DOWNTO} \end{Bmatrix}$ finish

BEGIN
S_1
S_2
.
.
.
S_r
END

(Only increments of 1 and -1 are allowed in Pascal.)

Declaration of Variables

PSEUDO	*Pascal*
1. Five basic types of elementary data: • INTEGER • REAL • CHARACTER • BOOLEAN • LABEL LABEL's are used to "tag" program statements, usually because they are potentially branching destinations	Four basic types of elementary data: • INTEGER • REAL • CHAR • BOOLEAN In Pascal, labels are not declared as a data type. Rather, they have their own LABEL declaration section. Moreover, in Pascal, labels must be numbers. That is, 123 is a valid label for a program statement but L1 is not.
2. The VAR statement is used to declare procedure parameters and other variables local to a procedure. The GLOBAL VAR statement is used to declare variables that must be accessed by all procedures relating to a specific task.	The VAR statement is used to declare variables local to a procedure. Procedure parameters are declared within the procedure's argument list. The Pascal standard does not specify how an isolated external procedure is to declare global variables. Because this is implementor-dependent, you must consult your local reference manuals for details.
3. Arrays of single or multiple dimensions can be declared using the VAR statement. *Example*: VAR M(14):INTEGER Individual array data elements can be INTEGER, REAL, CHARACTER, or BOOLEAN.	Arrays of single or multiple dimensions can be declared using an appropriate combination of VAR and TYPE statements. *Example*: TYPE CT =ARRAY[1..14] 　　　　　OF INTEGER; ． ． ． VAR COUNT:CT; Individual array data elements can be INTEGER, REAL, CHAR, BOOLEAN, or any previously defined types
4. Subscript ranges always begin at 1.	Subscript ranges may be declared in a variety of ways. However, the most common choice is to have them begin at 1.
5. Arrays passed as parameters to a procedure may have a variable dimension. *Example*: PROCEDURE EX(AR,N) VAR N,AR(N):INTEGER	Any array passed to a procedure as a parameter must be dimensioned to the size expected by the procedure. The only exception to this rule is in those isolated Pascal implementations that allow "conformant" array parameters.

PSEUDO	*Pascal*
6. Record declarations do not exist. A group of records is implemented by parallel arrays, with one array for each field in the record. See the implementation of the link and data field for a linked list node in Chapter 2.	Records can be declared to group together heterogeneous fields under a common name. See the implementation of linked list nodes in the Pascal supplement for Chapter 2.
7. Arrays are directly accessible memory locations. PSEUDO itself does not make a distinction between main memory and secondary memory devices such as magnetic disks. In most algorithms throughout the book arrays may be thought of as existing in main memory. However, in some chapters (particularly 11 and 12), the implications of magnetic disk storage are discussed extensively.	In Pascal, arrays are strictly main memory structures. Standard Pascal makes no provision for direct-access files. However, most implementations of Pascal offer some type of direct-access capability. The Pascal supplement for Chapter 11 gives an illustration. Consult your local reference material.
8. Dynamic memory allocation is the responsibility of the programmer. See the GETNODE and RETURNNODE procedures described in Chapter 2.	Dynamic memory allocation is handled by the supplied NEW and DISPOSE procedures. See the Pascal supplement for Chapter 2 for information on how to use these procedures.

Program Modules—Procedures and Functions

PSEUDO	*Pascal*

1. Defining a procedure/function:

$\begin{Bmatrix} \text{PROCEDURE} \\ \text{FUNCTION} \end{Bmatrix}$ `NAME(argument list)`

.
.
.

`END NAME`

Defining a procedure/function:

$\begin{Bmatrix} \text{PROCEDURE} \\ \text{FUNCTION} \end{Bmatrix}$ `NAME(argument list)`

.
.
.

`END;`

2. The order in which procedures appear is not relevant.

   A procedure cannot be called by another until it has been defined. Thus, in the physical listing of a Pascal program, the procedure definition must appear prior to its invocation. The only way to avoid this restriction is to use Pascal's FORWARD declaration.

3. Function values are returned by assigning the appropriate value to the name of the function.

   Function values are returned by assigning the appropriate value to the name of the function.

4. A procedure is invoked by the CALL statement.

   A procedure is invoked by the occurrence of its name within the calling program unit.

5. Control is transferred back to the calling program by the RETURN statement.

   Control is transferred back to the calling program by reaching the delimiting END for the procedure function. If a conditional test inside the procedure dictates a return action, this aspect of Pascal may necessitate using a GOTO to transfer to the END of the procedure or introducing a Boolean variable to avoid the use of the GOTO. See the Pascal supplement for Chapter 1 for an illustration.

6. In general, you can assume that a procedure receives the address of the parameters it is passed. Hence it is actually working on the calling program unit's variable and may alter them. That is, in general, parameters are passed by reference. There are, however, three exceptions to this general rule:

   - Parameters that are constants
   - Parameters that are expressions
   - Parameters for a procedure that is called recursively.

   In each exception, you can assume that the procedure receives a local copy of the value of the calling unit's variable. For a discussion of why this is necessary in recursion, see Chapter 5.

   Whether a parameter is passed by reference or by value is determined by whether the programmer uses a VAR declaration in the parameter list for the procedure.

B

Hints and Solutions

Chapter 1 Solutions

1.
```
PROCEDURE  LARGE—SMALL (A,N)
VAR  A(N),N,I,LARGE,SMALL:INTEGER
LARGE:=A(1)
SMALL:=A(1)
FOR I:= 2 TO N DO

        ┌IF LARGE < A(I) THEN┐
        │        [LARGE:=A(I)]│
        │ENDIF                │
        │IF SMALL > A(I) THEN │
        │        [SMALL:=A(I)]│
        └ENDIF                ┘

ENDFOR
WRITE 'LARGEST IN THE ARRAY =', LARGE
WRITE 'SMALLEST IN THE ARRAY =', SMALL
RETURN
END LARGE—SMALL
```

3.
```
PROCEDURE REVERSE;
GLOBAL VAR A(N),N:INTEGER
VAR B(N),N,I:INTEGER
FOR I:=1 TO N DO
    [ B(I):=A(I)   ]
ENDFOR
FOR I:=1 TO N DO
    [A(I):=B(N+1-I)]
ENDFOR
```

Chapter 2 Solutions

1. The POINTER-SORT in Chapter 1 is essentially a bubble sort applied to the indices of an array. There is therefore movement of data. In a linked list, there is no movement of the stored data.

3. Initialize a linked list as suggested in this chapter. As you read a data item compare it to every other data item while walking through the list from the beginning, and insert it into its correct place into the list. When you are done entering data, simply walk through the linked list printing every node.

5. For the Pascal version; consider a linked list pointed to by HEAD in which each node is recorded with its link field LINK. Then the following code deletes the last node:

```
HOLD:=HEAD;
PREV:=HEAD;
IF HEAD <> NIL THEN
BEGIN
    WHILE HOLD ↑ LINK <> 0 DO
        BEGIN
            PREV.=HOLD;
            HOLD:=HOLD.LINK
        END;
    PREV ↑ LINK:=NIL
END;
```

7. First modify INSERTNODE and DELETENODE, given in the text, so that the corresponding linked list has a dummy header pointed to by the head of the list. Call this dummy header PREFIRST. Add 1 to the count in PREFIRST at the end of INSERTNODE. Similarly subtract 1 from PREFIRST at the end of DELETENODE.

9. The linked list suggested in (3) can be made into a doubly linked list containing ordered data. If a particular node pointed to by some pointer POINT1 is to be deleted, then the procedure DELETE-NODE-DOUBLE in the text can be inserted as is.

11. Adapt the procedure DELETE-NODE-DOUBLE given in the text. Only minor changes are needed.

13. Because there is no null link in a circular list, the ELSE portion of the procedure DELETE-NODE given in the text for a singly linked list is all that is needed.

Chapter 3 Solutions

1. Pascal version:

```
(*GLOBAL DECLARATIONS*)
CONST N=100;
VAR LENGTH:ARRAY[1..N] OF INTEGER;
    INDEX:ARRAY[1..N] OF INTEGER;
    WORK:ARRAY[1..1000] OF CHAR;
PROCEDURE  ASSIGN_WORKSPACE(VAR I,J: INTEGER);
(* Assign a string J beginning at the position INDEX[J]in*)
(*the workspace WORK to another string I. The length of the*)
(*J string is LENGTH[J] *)
BEGIN
          INDEX[I]:=INDEX[J];
          LENGTH[I]:=LENGTH[J]
END(*ASSIGN_WORKSPACE*);
```

3. Pascal version:

```
PROCEDURE WORKCONCATENATE (VAR I,J,M,NEW : INTEGER);
(*This procedure concatenates two strings presently*)
(*existing in the work space WORK and stores the concatenated*)
(*string beginning at the free portion of the work space. The*)
(*free portion of the work space begins at the position M. As*)
(*in the solution of (1), LENGTH, INDEX and WORK are suitable*)
(*arrays declared in the calling program. LENGTH[T],*)
(*INDEX[T] give respectively the length and the starting*)
(*position of the string T in the work space WORK*)
(*Assume that WORK is large enough to hold I,J and I+J*)
(*strings*)
(*String NEW= String I + String J*)

VAR L,N : INTEGER;
BEGIN    (*First copy the string I*)
    FOR L:=INDEX[I] TO LENGTH[I] DO
        WORK[M+L-1]:=WORK[L];
    (*Now copy the J string*)
    FOR N:=INDEX[J] TO LENGTH[J] DO
        WORK[M+INDEX[I]+N-1]:=WORK[N];
    INDEX[NEW]:=M;
    LENGTH[NEW]:=LENGTH[I] + LENGTH[J]
END (*WORKCONCATENATE*)
```

5. PSEUDO version:

```
PROCEDURE FINDPAT(MAINSTR,PATSTR,L,M,FOUND)
    VAR   MAINSTR(L),PATSTR(M):CHARACTER(1)
    VAR   FLAG,FOUND,CONTINUE:BOOLEAN
    VAR   I,J : INTEGER
    (*This procedure finds the first occurrence of*)
    (*the pattern string PATSTR of length M inside*)
    (*of the main string MAINSTR of length L*)
    (*If the string is found, the boolean flag FOUND*)
    (*is returned as TRUE. Otherwise FOUND is*)
    (*returned as FALSE*)
```

```
FLAG:=TRUE
FOUND:=FALSE
CONTINUE:=TRUE
IF L > M THEN (*PATSTR too long*)

      ┌FOUND:=FALSE┐
      └RETURN      ┘

ENDIF
I:=0
WHILE FLAG AND I(I <=M-L) DO

      ┌I:=I+1                                              ┐
      │J:=I                                                │
      │WHILE J <=L AND CONTINUE DO                         │
      │                                                    │
      │      ┌IF PATSTR[J]<>MAINSTR[J] THEN┐               │
      │      │        [CONTINUE:=FALSE]    │               │
      │      │ENDIF                        │               │
      │      │IF CONTINUE THEN             │               │
      │      │        [J:=J+1]             │               │
      │      └ENDIF                        ┘               │
      │                                                    │
      │ENDWHILE                                            │
      │(*IF J=L+1 the match is found*)                     │
      │IF J=L+1 THEN                                       │
      │                                                    │
      │      ┌FOUND:=TRUE ┐                                │
      │      └FLAG:=FALSE ┘                                │
      │                                                    │
      └ENDIF                                               ┘

ENDWHILE
RETURN
END FINDPAT
```

7. PSEUDO version:

```
PROCEDURE FINDPAT(MAINH,LINKM,PATH,LINKP,L,N,FOUND,
 →DATAM,DATAP)
(*This procedure searches a linked string maintained by*)
(*LINK P and headed by PATH inside another linked string*)
(*whose head is MAINH and which is maintained by*)
(*LINKM. DATAM contains the data for the main*)
(*string while DATAP carries the data for the*)
(*string to be searched. N is the length (in the*)
(*prefirst node) of the main string. L is the length*)
(*of the pattern string. Both lists are taken to be*)
(*singly linked list*)

VAR   MAINH,PATH,LINKM(N), LINKP(L),L,N:INTEGER
VAR   DATAM(N), DATAP(L) : CHARACTER(1)
VAR   FOUND,FLAG : BOOLEAN
VAR   M1,P1,P2,NULL : INTEGER
```

```
FOUND:=FALSE
NULL:=0
FLAG:=TRUE

IF L > N THEN
     [RETURN]
ENDIF
P1:=LINKM[MAINH]
P2:=LINKP[PATH]
WHILE FLAG AND P1 <> NULL DO

    P2:=LINKP(PATH)
    M1:=P1
    WHILE DATAM(M1)=DATAP(P2) AND P2 <> NULL AND P1 <>
→       NULL DO
            [M1:=LINKM(M1)]
            [P2:=LINKP(P2)]
    ENDWHILE
            IF P2=NULL THEN    (*String found*)

                [FOUND:=TRUE ]
                [FLAG:=FALSE ]
            ENDIF
            P1:=LINKM(P1)
    ENDWHILE
    RETURN
    END FINDPAT
```

9. Solution to (5) with minor modifications can be adapted.

11. Use the solution to (5) to first find the substring PATSTR of length L inside of the main string MAINSTR of length N. If $L > N$, no deletion occurs. Suppose therefore, $L \leq N$. Now if $L = N$, then the whole string is deleted. If $L < N$, and PATSTR is found beginning at position J in MAINSTR then the following coding of the BASIC version can be used to finish the problem:

```
10   FOR M=J TO N-L : MAINSTR(M)=MAINSTR(L+J) : NEXT M
20   FOR M=N-L+1 TO N : MAINSTR(M)=" ": NEXT M
```

13. In a manner of the solution of (7), first find where inside the mainstring (MAINSTR) the substring (PATSTR) begins. Suppose the substring PATSTR begins at node J of the mainstring MAINSTR. Reassign the pointers so that the node (in MAINSTR) that points to J now points to the node $J + L + 1$ in MAINSTR.

Chapter 4 Solutions

1. The following PSEUDO procedure removes a processed node from a *N*-priority queue:

```
PROCEDURE REMOVEFROMPRIORITYQUEUE(L,AVAIL,ITEM)
    GLOBAL VAR HEAD(N),REAR(N),LINK(N),N:INTEGER
    GLOBAL VAR DATA(N):CHARACTER
    VAR ITEM:CHARACTER
    VAR L,AVAIL:INTEGER
    (*Remove a processed item from a queue of priority L*)
    (*HEAD(I) is the pointer to the front of queue of priority I*)
    (*REAR(I) is the pointer to the rear of the queue of priority I*)
    (*Linked List is maintained via LINK*)
    IF LINK(HEAD(L)) = REAR(L) THEN

        ⎡WRITE   'EMPTY QUEUE'⎤
        ⎣RETURN               ⎦

    ELSE
        ⎡P:=LINK(HEAD(L))      ⎤
        ⎢ITEM:=DATA(P)         ⎥
        ⎣LINK(HEAD(L))=LINK(P) ⎦
    ENDIF
    IF REAR(L)=P THEN
        [REAR(L):=HEAD(L)] (*Removed from one entry queue*)
    ENDIF
    CALL RETURNNODE(AVAIL,P)
    RETURN
    END REMOVEFROMPRIORITYQUEUE
```

Calling Convention: CALL REMOVEFROMPRIORITYQUEUE(L,AVAIL,ITEM)

3. The following PSUEDO procedure pushes an item onto a stack implemented with a linked list.

```
PROCEDURE PUSH(HEAD,TOP,N,LINK,AVAIL,ITEM,DATA)
    (*HEAD points to the top of the STACK*)
    (*TOP points to the first data item on the stack*)
    (*ITEM is pushed on top of the stack*)
    (*Linked list maintained via LINK*)
VAR  HEAD,TOP,N,LINK(N),AVAIL,P : INTEGER
VAR  DATA(N),ITEM:CHARACTER
    (*First get an empty node pointed to by P*)
    CALL GETNODE(LINK,AVAIL,N,P)
    DATA(P):=ITEM
    LINK(P):=TOP
    TOP:=P
    LINK(HEAD):=TOP
(*Now update the count in the prefirst node*)
    DATA(HEAD):=DATA(HEAD)+1
RETURN
END PUSH
```

5. When implementing a circular queue of maximum size MAX, one location must be sacrificed. At the expense of one memory location, we now have the following stipulations:

```
FRONT=REAR                → one-entry queue
(REAR MOD MAX)+1 = FRONT  → empty queue
(REAR MOD MAX)+2=FRONT     → full queue
```

7.
```
PROCEDURE REMOVEFROMCIRCULAR(QUEUE,ARRAYSIZE,FRONT,REAR,
 →ITEM,EMPTY)
   (*This procedure removes an item from a circular queue*)
   (*The boolean flag EMPTY is returned as TRUE if the*)
   (*QUEUE is empty, and FALSE if the operation is successful*)
VAR   QUEUE(ARRAYSIZE),ITEM:CHARACTER
VAR   FRONT,REAR,ARRAYSIZE:INTEGER
VAR   EMPTY:BOOLEAN
        IF (REAR MOD ARRAYSIZE)+1 = FRONT THEN
            [EMPTY:=TRUE] (*Empty Queue*)
        ELSE IF FRONT=REAR THEN

        ┌ ┌EMPTY:=FALSE          ┐ ┐  (*Removal from*)
        │ │ITEM:=QUEUE(FRONT)    │ │  (*a nonempty queue*)
        │ └FRONT:=FRONT+1        ┘ │
        │                         │
        │         ENDIF           │
        └                         ┘
        ENDIF
        RETURN
END REMOVEFROMCIRCULAR
```

Chapter 5 Solutions

1. A *stack* is a data structure with the storage scheme that the last data item in is first one out. The acronym LIFO (last-in-first-out) applies to a stack.

3. Stack priority table:

Character	*	/	+	−	(	)	#
Stack Priority	2	2	1	1	0	undefined or infinity	0

5. A recursive procedure calls on itself, just as an image of you standing between two parallel mirrors duplicates itself infinitely often.

Chapter 6 Solutions

1.

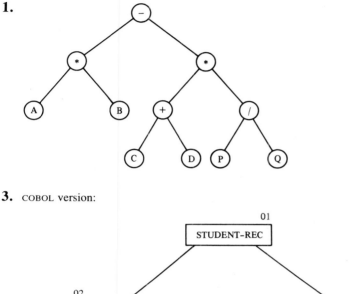

3. COBOL version:

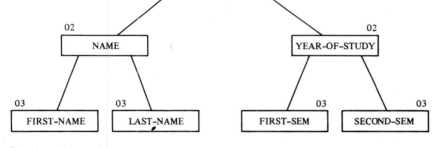

Pascal version is similar.

5. If the data being entered into the tree are uniformly heterogeneous, the tree can be expected to have just about an equal number of left and right subtrees each with almost equal number of nodes. This is the best situation as far as the fullness of the tree is concerned. If, however, the data are almost sorted, then in the worst case situation there may not be any left subtree (as would occur for an alphabetized data item) or any right subtree (as would occur in a numerical data item sorted in a decreasing order).

7.
```
PROCEDURE DELETEBINTREE (LLINK,RLINK,BLINK,P,ROOT,N)
  (*This procedure deletes a node pointed to by P*)
  (*from a binary tree pointed to by ROOT.*)
  (*The tree represents an ordered list in its inorder*)
  (*traversal fashion. The tree is implemented via*)
  (*LLINK and RLINK pointers where LLINK(I) and*)
  (*RLINK(I) represent the left child and right child*)
  (*pointers for the node pointed to by I in the tree*)
  (*BLINK(I) points to the parent of I.*)
    VAR Q,LLINK(N),RLINK(N),BLINK(N),N,P,X, ROOT:INTEGER
    VAR  NULL:INTEGER
```

```
NULL:=0
IF  (RLINK(LLINK(P) = NULL) AND LLINK(P) <> NULL THEN

    ┌X:=P                  (*case 1*)                      ┐
    │P:=LLINK(X)                                           │
    │RLINK(P):=RLINK(X)                                    │
    └CALL  RETURNNODE(X) (*as per chapter 2*)              ┘
  ELSE
  IF (RLINK(LLINK(P))<>NULL) AND (LLINK(P)<>NULL) THEN

    ┌       X:=P                                                   ┐
    │       Q:=RLINK(LLINK(X))                                     │
    │       BLINK(Q):=LLINK(X)                                     │
    │       WHILE RLINK(Q) <> NULL DO                              │
    │           ┌Q:=RLINK(Q)                      ┐                │
    │           └BLINK(Q):=RLINK(BLINK(Q))        ┘                │
    │       ENDWHILE                                               │
    │           (*Having found node Q to replace P*)              │
    │           (*adjust pointers to appropriately link*)         │
    │           (*it into the tree.*)                             │
    │       RLINK(Q):=RLINK(X)                                     │
    │       P:=Q                                                   │
    │       RLINK(BLINK(Q)):=LLINK(Q)                              │
    │       LLINK(Q):=LLINK(X)                                     │
    └       CALL RETURNNODE(X)                                     ┘
  ENDIF
          ELSE IF (LLINK(P)=NULL) AND (RLINK(P)<>NULL) THEN
              ┌X:=P                    (*Node pointed to*)      ┐
              │P:=RLINK(X)             (*by P has no left*)     │
              └CALL  RETURNNODE(X)(*child but has a right child*)┘
                  ELSE (*Node pointed to by P has no children*)

                      ┌X:=P               ┐
                      │P:=NULL            │
                      └CALL RETURNNODE(X) ┘

              ENDIF

ENDIF
RETURN
END DELETEBINTREE
```

Chapter 7 Solutions

1. Preorder scheme:

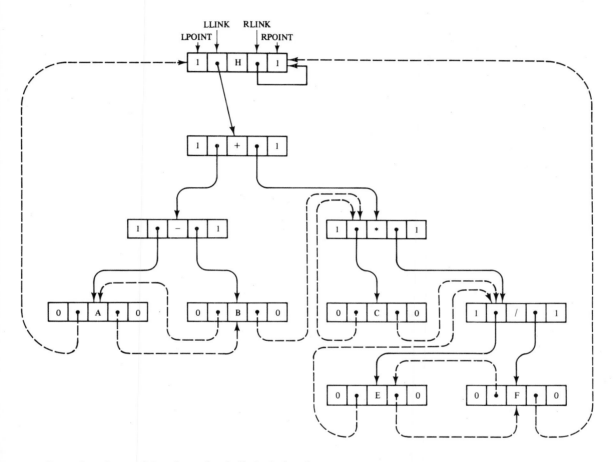

Postorder scheme of threads can be similarly designed.

3.
```
PROCEDURE THREAD-PREORDER(ROOT)
(*Performs a threaded preorder traversal of the tree with*)
(*dummy root node pointed to by ROOT.*)
(*Global variables are used to maintain the links, threads*)
(*and data portions of the tree structure.*)
GLOBAL VAR N,LLINK(N),RLINK(N):INTEGER
GLOBAL VAR DATA(N) : CHARACTER
GLOBAL VAR TLPOINT(N),TRPOINT(N):BOOLEAN
VAR ROOT,P:INTEGER
P:=ROOT
REPEAT
        (*The following IF statement alters P to point to*)
        (*its preorder successor according to the diagram.*)
```

```
IF TRPOINT(P) THEN
      [P:=RLINK(P)]
ELSE

   ┌ P:=LLINK(P)
   │ WHILE NOT TLPOINT(P) DO
   │    ┌ IF  P<>ROOT THEN
   │    │        [WRITE DATA(P)]
   │    │ ENDIF
   │    └    P:=LLINK(P)
   │ ENDWHILE
   └

ENDIF
UNTIL P=ROOT
RETURN
END THREAD-PREORDER
```

5. The inorder traversal of a general tree is not possible because the order of precedence of the parent node in relation to children is not defined.

7.
```
PROCEDURE REVERSEINORD(ROOT)
(*This procedure traverses a threaded binary tree in reverse*)
(*order*)
GLOBAL VAR LLINK(N),RLINK(N),TR(N),TL(N),N,ROOT:INTEGER
GLOBAL VAR FLAG(N):BOOLEAN
GLOBAL VAR TR(N),TL(N):INTEGER
(*Threaded tree in inorder fashion is maintained by global*)
(*LLINK,RLINK,TR,TL,FLAG. IF TR(P)=1 it means the RLINK(P)*)
(*is a thread. Similarly if TL(P)=1 then the left link of*)
(*the node pointed to by P is a thread. If FLAG(P) is true,*)
(*then the node pointed to by P has been processed*)
VAR P:INTEGER
  P:=ROOT
  FLAG(P):=FALSE
  REPEAT

     ┌ WHILE (TR(P)=0 AND (NOT FLAG(P) DO
     │          [P:=RLINK(P)]
     │ ENDWHILE
     │ IF NOT FLAG(P) THEN
     │
     │         ┌WRITE DATA(P)
     │         └FLAG(P):=TRUE
     │ ENDIF
     │ IF TL(P)=1 AND LLINK(P)<> ROOT THEN
     │         ┌WRITE DATA(LLINK(P)
     │         └FLAG(LLINK(P)):=TRUE
     │ ENDIF
     └ P:=LLINK(P)


UNTIL (P=ROOT)
RETURN
END REVERSEINORDER
```

9. Deletion of a node from an AVL tree. The following steps outline the algorithm that can be written in any high level language.

Case 1: *The node* N *to be deleted has two children.* This can be reduced to the case when *N* has at most one child. To do that, first find the inorder predecessor *M* of *N*. *M* is now guaranteed to have no children because of the way it was found. Rotate *M* into the position of *N* with the same parent, left and right children, and the balance factor as that of *N*. Now delete *M* from its original position.

Case 2: *The node* N *to be deleted has at the most one child.* Delete *N* by linking the parent of *N* to the child of *N* (or reducing the link to NULL if no child exists). The height of the subtree of *N* is reduced by 1. To trace the effects of this change on the height of all subtrees from *N* back to the root of the tree, use a boolean variable FLAG. The value of FLAG, the BF (balance factor) of a node, and so on dictate the action to be taken. The following list explains the necessary steps for such an action. Set the FLAG to true for changes to be made, and false if no changes are to be made, in which case the algorithm stops.

- A. *The BF of* N *is zero.* The BF of *N* is adjusted depending on whether the left or right subtree of *N* has been shortened. The FLAG becomes false.

- B. *The BF of* N *is not zero and the taller subtree was shortened.* Make BF of *N* as 0, and leave FLAG as true.

- C. *The BF of* N *is not zero, and the shorter subtree was further shortened.* Because height violation of the AVL tree has occurred, we apply appropriate rotation to restore height balance. In this case let *R* be the root of the taller subtree. Now we have three subcases:

  - (a) *The BF of* R *is zero.* A single proper rotation (discussed in the text) restores height balance, and the FLAG becomes false.

  - (b) *The BF of* R *= BF of* N. Apply rotation, set the BF of *R* equal to BF of *N*, and make FLAG true.

  - (c) *The BF of* R *and BF of* N *are opposite* (as 2 and −2 or −2 and 2). Apply the double rotation first around *R* and then around *N*, set the BF of the new root to zero, and set other BFs appropriately.

11.
```
PROCEDURE RIGHT-OF-RIGHT(PIVOT)
   (*Perform AVL-rotation for case 2 on subtree pointed to*)
   (*by PIVOT*)
   (*GLOBAL LLINK,RLINK,DATA are defined as in Chapter 6*)
   (*GLOBAL BF array is additional field for a node. It is used to store*)
   (*the balance factor*)
GLOBAL VAR N,LLINK(N),RLINK(N),BF(N):INTEGER
GLOBAL VAR DATA(N):CHARACTER
VAR P,Q,PIVOT:INTEGER
   (*Begin by altering the necessary pointers*)
   P:=RLINK(PIVOT)
   Q:=LLINK(P)
   RLINK(PIVOT):=Q
   LLINK(P):=PIVOT
   PIVOT:=P
   (*Now adjust the balance factor BF*)
```

```
BF(PIVOT):=0
  BF(LLINK(PIVOT)):=0
RETURN
END RIGHT-OF-RIGHT
```

In a similar manner, follow the guidlines of the procedure RIGHT-OF-LEFT in the text for writing the procedure LEFT-OF-RIGHT. Only minor changes are needed.

13.

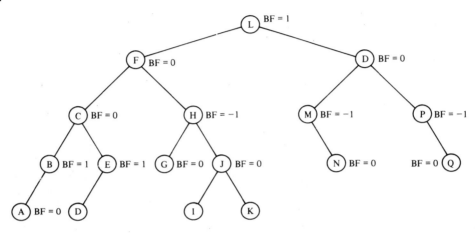

Chapter 8 Solutions

1. For a two-dimensional array, storage in row-major form implies that, in the actual linear storage allocated for the array, all the elements within a row are stored contiguously. That is, the mapping of two-dimensional array elements to linear storage would appear as:

Column major implies that the elements of a column would be stored contiguously. For higher dimensioned arrays, left subscript major storage is the analogue of row major storage; that is, all entries for a fixed setting of the leftmost subscript are grouped contiguously. Similarly, right subscript major is the analogue of column major.

3. The term *sparse* in relation to a multidimensional array refers to a relatively high percentage of zeroes being stored in the array. The sparse matrix problem is the problem of representing such an array in computer memory without having to store all of these zeroes.

5. The linear list is:

19   64   23   61   71   17   99   90   44   84   81   8   8   36   57   18   32   12
10   12   61   96   15   34

7. Picture a three-dimensional array as multiple occurrences of a two-dimensional array. Each row with each occurrence has a nonzero band of entries, just as each row of an ordinary two-dimensional array has a nonzero band.

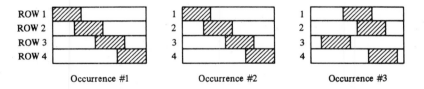

Shaded regions represent nonzero band

The entries within the nonzero bands must be stored in one long linear list. The nonzero band in the first row of the first occurrence would be stored first, then the nonzero band in the second row of the first occurrence, and so on. The arrays FIRSTNONZERO, LASTNONZERO, and SUM described in the text's treatment of the generalized dope vector method would now be two-dimensional arrays instead of one-dimensional arrays. Hence the bookkeeping data about the new three-dimensional structure now must be stored in two-dimensional structures with the following interpretations

FIRSTNONZERO(I,J) = the column position of the first nonzero entry in the Jth row of the Ith occurrence

LASTNONZERO(I,J) = the column position of the last nonzero entry in the Jth row of the Ith occurrence

SUM(I,J) = the total number of entries in nonzero bands that are stored prior to the band in the Jth row of the Ith occurrence.

Under these considerations, the procedures SPARSE(I,J) and PUT(V,I,J) in Chapter 8 can be easily converted to procedures SPARSE(I,J,K) and PUT(V,I,J,K), which will apply in the three-dimensional case.

9. Given the solution described for 8, the efficiency ratio would be:

$$\frac{\text{NROW} + \text{NCOL} + \text{N}*5}{\text{NROW} * \text{NCOL}}$$

11. An arbitrary range of ordinal values such as

$$-4 \quad . \quad . \quad . \quad 4$$

would have to be mapped into the range

$$1 \quad . \quad . \quad . \quad 9$$

by adding 5 before applying the translation techniques discussed in this chapter.

13. No, because an entry in the LASTNONZERO vector may be computed from entries in the FIRSTNONZERO and SUM vectors via:

```
LASTNONZERO(I) = FIRSTNONZERO(I) + (SUM(I+1) - SUM(I)+1)
```

Chapter 9 Solutions

1. A tree.

3. 0 (zero).

5. A spanning forest is the decomposition of a graph (or network) into a collection of disjoint trees according to a particular traversal scheme for visiting the nodes of the graph. Depth-first search and breadth-first search yield respectively depth-first spanning forest and breadth-first spanning forest.

7. A spanning tree is a tree associated with a network. All the nodes of the graph appear on the tree once. A minimum spanning tree is a spanning tree organized so that the total edgeweight between nodes is minimized.

9.

Node	Indegree	Outdegree
A	1	2
B	2	1
C	1	1

11. The program is a trivial matter. The sum in each row represents the outdegree of the corresponding node. There are 2 paths of length 3 between A and B. These are A→C→D→B and A→B→A→B.

13. FORTRAN version

```
        SUBROUTINE  FINDP(MAT,N,L1,L2,,FLAG)
C       Determine if there is a path between L1 and L2 of
C       a graph whose adjacency matrix is MAT. If a
C       path exists return FLAG as true
        INTEGER  MAT(N,N), POWER(N,N), WORK(N,N)
        LOGICAL FLAG
C       Transfer MAT into POWER and WORK
        DO 10 J=1,N
        DO 10 K=1,N
        POWER(J,K) = MAT(J,K)
        WORK(J,K) = MAT(J,K)
10      CONTINUE
        DO 20 MAN=1,N
           IF (POWER(L1,L2).NE.0) GOTO 300
C       Clean up POWER
           DO 30 LAMP=1,N
           DO 30 KLAMP=1,N
              POWER(LAMP,KLAMP)=0
30         CONTINUE
C          Compute POWER
           DO 40 I=1,N
              DO 50 J=1,N
                 DO 60 K=1,N
                 POWER(I,J)=POWER(I,J)+WORK(I,K)*MAT(K,J)
60               CONTINUE
50            CONTINUE
40         CONTINUE
```

```
      C       Transfer POWER TO WORK
                DO 70 L=1,N
                DO 70 M=1,N
                  WORK(L,M)=POWER(L,M)
      70      CONTINUE
      20      CONTINUE
              FLAG=.FALSE.
              GOTO 400.
     300      FLAG=.TRUE.
     400      RETURN
              END
```

15.
```
     PROCEDURE  FINDMIN(I,J)
       (*Find a node J not on the tree having minimum*)
       (*edgeweight with a node I already on the tree*)
       (*Adjacency matrix of the graph is global MAT(N,N)*)
       (*ROW(K) holds the minimum of nonzero entries of*)
       (*the Kth row. Global INCLUDED(K) is a boolean*)
       (*variable which is FALSE for K not on the tree*)
     GLOBAL VAR   MAT(N,N) N, MAXINT,I,J:INTEGER
     GLOBAL VAR   INCLUDED(N):BOOLEAN
     VAR  FLAG : BOOLEAN
     VAR  SUB(N),LO,K,I1,I2,COL,ROW(N):INTEGER
     FLAG:=FALSE
     FOR I2:=1 TO N DO

        ⎡ROW(I2):=0⎤
        ⎣SUB(I2):=0⎦

     ENDFOR
     K:=1
     WHILE INCLUDED(K) DO

        ⎡FLAG:=TRUE
        ⎢LO:=MAXINT
        ⎢    FOR I1:=1 TO N DO
        ⎢        IF LO > MAT(K,I1) AND MAT(K,I1) <> 0 THEN
        ⎢            ⎡LO:=MAT(K,I1)⎤
        ⎢            ⎣COL:=I1       ⎦
        ⎢        ENDIF
        ⎢        ENDFOR
        ⎢    SUB(COL):=LO  (*Keeps track of what COL LO is*)
        ⎢    ROW(K):=LO   (*Keeps track of what row it belongs to*)
        ⎣    K:=K+1

     ENDWHILE
       (*Now find nonzero minimum in SUB and its position in SUB.*)
       (*The position of minimum in SUB pinpoints J*)
     WHILE FLAG DO
```

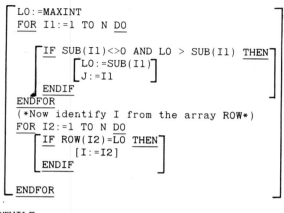

```
LO:=MAXINT
FOR I1:=1 TO N DO

        IF SUB(I1)<>0 AND LO > SUB(I1) THEN
              LO:=SUB(I1)
              J:=I1
        ENDIF
ENDFOR
(*Now identify I from the array ROW*)
FOR I2:=1 TO N DO
        IF ROW(I2)=LO THEN
              [I:=I2]
        ENDIF

   ENDFOR
```

```
ENDWHILE
RETURN
END FINDMIN
```

17. No.

19. This coding is almost entirely contained in the innermost loop of the procedure MIN-PATH-FLOYD given in the text.

21. Follow the guidelines of the procedure DF-SEARCH. The logic and the code for breadth-first search steps are mirror images of DF-SEARCH.

23. Both these cases have been explained in detail in the text to build their respective proofs by induction.

25. The only procedure that can conceivably present some challenge is FINDMIN; refer to the solution of (15).

Chapter 10 Solutions

1. All practical data processing requires accessing records quickly and efficiently. Search algorithms are most efficient only when the records are sorted according to some specified keys. If the records in a file were not sorted, searching for a particular record would require checking every record until the match is made. This is unnecessary wastefulness of precious computer time, especially if the file to be searched is very large.

   Consider, for example, a file consisting of 1000 unsorted records. To find a record in this file we may, in the worst case, need to make 1000 comparisons. If the same file is sorted on some key, then a binary search algorithm can pinpoint the record in less than 10 comparisons.

3. The insertion sort derives its name from the fact that in its *i*th iteration it inserts the *i*th record in its correct place among the first *i* records.

5. No.

7. Data exchange in insertion sort is minimal when the array to be sorted is in almost sorted order.

9. See the Pascal procedure in the text at the end of this chapter.

11. There is no special magic about the relatively prime values of the increments. Other choices would work also. Choosing values of the increments as powers of 2, such as 16, 8, 4, 2, 1 would not be advisable because the keys compared on one pass would be compared again. Keeping increments relatively prime avoids this problem.

13. If n is the size of the array to be sorted, then the average and worst case efficiency of the heap sort is $0(n \log_2 n)$.

15. Bubble sort, insertion sort, selection sort, and the merge sort are stable. Quick sort, shell sort, and heap sort are not stable.

Chapter 11 Solutions

1. In the case where the TARGET is not to be found in the list, the search could be terminated as soon as a KEY greater than the TARGET is encountered.

3.
```
PROCEDURE BINARYTREESEARCH(TARGET,ITEM,FOUND)
GLOBAL VAR   N,LCHILD(N),KEY(N),RCHILD(N),ROOT:INTEGER
GLOBAL VAR   DATA(N): (*Appropriate data type*)
VAR   TARGET,P:INTEGER
VAR   ITEM: (*Appropriate data type*)
VAR   FOUND:BOOLEAN
FOUND:=FALSE
P:=ROOT
REPEAT
    IF TARGET < KEY(P) THEN
        [P:=LCHILD(P)]
    ELSE IF TARGET > KEY(P) THEN
        [P:=RCHILD(P)]
    ELSE
        ITEM:=DATA(P)
        FOUND:=TRUE
    ENDIF
    ENDIF
UNTIL FOUND OR P=NULL
RETURN
END BINARYTREESEARCH
```

5. The general sketch of a solution in PSEUDO follows. Because a B-tree index presupposes a file-oriented system, the specific implementation would depend on the intricacies of the file-handling statements in the high-level language selected. Note that the solution assumes (as indicated in the text) that each B-tree node includes:

- A count of the number of key-pointer pairs in the node

- A back-pointer to the node's parent

```
PROCEDURE INSERT—B—TREE(NEWKEY)
GLOBAL VAR N:INTEGER   (*Represents order of B—tree*)

(*The call to SEARCH returns a pointer P to the bottom*)
(*level node in which NEWKEY belongs.*)

CALL SEARCH(NEWKEY,P)

(*The next call, depending upon the list structure in the*)
(*node pointed to by P, is responsible for inserting the*)
(*key—pointer pair for NEWKEY into the B—tree node*)
(*indicated by P.*)

CALL INSERT(NEWKEY,P)

(*Finally, if the preceding insert caused the B—tree node*)
(*to overflow, we must, perhaps repeatedly, split a node*)
(*and pass a key up to the parent node.*)
```

```
WHILE COUNT(P) > N-1 DO
      ┌ CALL SPLIT(P)   (*Split node P into 2*)                    ┐
      │ CALL INSERT(SPLITKEY,PARENT) (*Pass splitting key to*)     │
      │                                      (*parent*)            │
      └ P:=PARENT                                                  ┘
ENDWHILE
RETURN
END INSERT-B-TREE
```

7. The general sketch of a solution in PSEUDO follows. Because a trie index presupposes a file-oriented system, a specific implementation would depend on the intricacies of the file-handling statements in the chosen language.

```
PROCEDURE INSERT-TRIE(NEWKEY)
GLOBAL VAR  N,M,ROOT:INTEGER
GLOBAL VAR   TRIENODE(N,28):CHARACTER
          (*TRIENODE represents an array of nodes as*)
          (*pictured in Figure 11-25.*)
VAR NEWKEY(M),KEY(M):CHARACTER
VAR P,Q,R,I:INTEGER
I:=1
P:=ROOT
WHILE (TRIENODE(P,POS(NEWKEY(I))) <> NULL) AND --->
            (TRIENODE(P,POS(NEWKEY(I))) > 0 DO

    ┌ (*The preceding WHILE assumes existence of function*)┐
    │ (*POS which returns ordinal position of character*)  │
    │ (*NEWKEY(I) relative to indexing of TRIENODE and*)   │
    │ (*that negative values are used to point to actual*) │
    │ (*data records.*)                                    │
    │ P:=TRIENODE(P,POS(NEWKEY(I)))                        │
    └ I:=I+1                                               ┘

ENDWHILE
IF TRIENODE(P,POS(NEWKEY(I))) = NULL THEN
    ┌ TRIENODE(P,POS(NEWKEY(I))):=(*Data record position for*)┐
    └                                      (*NEWKEY*)          ┘
ELSE

    ┌ R:=TRIENODE(P,POS(NEWKEY(I)))                           ┐
    │ (*Fetch KEY pointed at by R from data record file*)     │
    │ WHILE KEY(I+1) = NEWKEY(I+1)                             │
    │       ┌ CALL GETNODE(Q)                           ┐      │
    │       │ TRIENODE(P,POS(NEWKEY(I))):=Q DO          │      │
    │       │ P:=Q                                      │      │
    │       └ I:=I+1                                    ┘      │
    │ ENDWHILE                                                │
    │ CALL GETNODE(Q)                                         │
    │ TRIENODE(Q,POS(KEY(I+1))):=R                            │
    │ TRIENODE(Q,POS(NEWKEY(I+1))):=(*Data record position*)  │
    └                                      (*for NEWKEY*)      ┘

ENDIF
RETURN
END INSERT-TRIE
```

9.
```
PROCEDURE INSERTLINEARHASH(NEWKEY,ITEM)
     (*Insert NEWKEY and associated DATA in ITEM*)
     (*into linearly hashed structure.*)
GLOBAL VAR N,RECORDSPACE,KEY(N):INTEGER
GLOBAL VAR DATA(N): (*Appropriate type*)
VAR   NEWKEY,J:INTEGER
VAR   ITEM:(*Appropriate type*)
J:=HASH(NEWKEY)
WHILE KEY(J) <> 0
   [ J;=(J MOD RECORDSPACE) + 1 ]
ENDWHILE
KEY(J):=NEWKEY
DATA(J):=ITEM
RETURN
END INSERTLINEARHASH
```

The insertion procedures for the other methods would be similarly handled, with appropriate modifications made in the WHILE loop to take care of collision processing.

11. The key in any deletion strategy for a hashed file is to use separate flags to distinguish locations that are:

EMPTY AND NEVER ACTIVE

versus

EMPTY BUT PREVIOUSLY ACTIVE

Without such a distinction, the search procedure cannot determine whether or not it should stop upon coming to an empty record.

13. The key to these procedures is to keep the file itself physically ordered by key values. As an insertion into a sequential search block overflows that block, the final item in the block must be moved out to an overflow area. As this occurs, a pointer to that overflow area must be inserted within the block itself. In this regard, the method is similar to linked hashing and the resolution of a full bucket in bucket hashing. Deletions may be handled simply by inserting an empty flag in the area occupied by the key to be deleted. As the file is periodically rebuilt, these flagged records may be physically removed from the file.

Chapter 12 Solutions

1. Follow the guide given by the generic PROCEDURE ALLOCATE(S,P) and PROCEDURE GARBAGECOLLECT(P,AVAIL) in the text. In particular note that, for the binary buddy system, whether a returning block has a left or right buddy (clearly it cannot have both) is simply a function of the block's starting address.

3. Follow the general strategy of the generic procedures given in the text. In particular, note that for the boundary tag method:

   - There are no limitations on block sizes that may be allocated.

   - When coalescing occurs, this is the only 1 of the 3 methods in which a given block can have *both* left and right buddies.

5. If a record to be deleted is accessed directly without a list traversal, deletion is *immediately* possible because of the back pointer.

7. Four steps are involved—search for the key to be deleted, determine the secondary key values of the record associated with this key, store these secondary key values with the position of the record to be deleted, and finally delete this record position from the list associated with each of the secondary key values.

9. Because Pascal's NEW and DISPOSE procedures must handle requests for blocks of greatly varying yet precise sizes, aspects of the boundary tag method could be applied. The binary and Fibonacci systems would not apply because of the precise block sizes that are needed. Another strategy might be to maintain multiple linked lists of blocks for each type of record in the Pascal program. By this strategy, a generalization of the GETNODE and RETURN-NODE procedures from Chapter 2 could be used.

11. The first is a complex network; the second is a simple network.

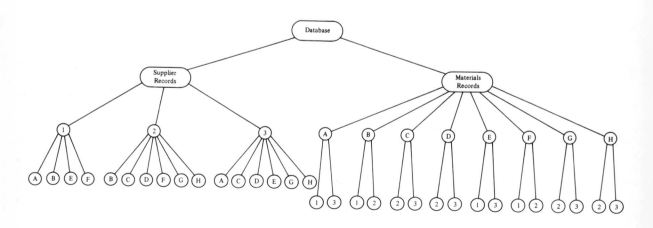

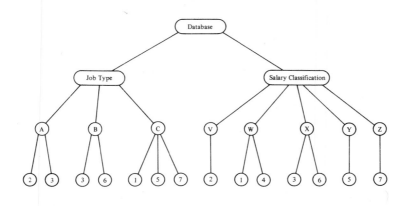

C

Local System Notes

Local System Notes

Local System Notes

Local System Notes

Local System Notes

Local System Notes

Local System Notes

Local System Notes

Local System Notes

Local System Notes

Local System Notes

Local System Notes

Local System Notes

Local System Notes

Glossary
of Terms*

*Numbers in brackets at the end of each entry refer to the chapter in which the term is first discussed.

acyclic graph   A directed graph in which there are no paths from any one node back to itself. [9]

adjacency matrix   A way to represent the physical structure of a graph by a matrix that holds locational information about the graph. [9]

algorithm   The concise instructions that manipulate related data items. A collection of steps that solve a specified problem in a finite number of steps. [1]

arc   A directed path between two nodes of a graph. [9]

array   A collection of a specific number of variable data elements, individual members of which may be accessed by specifying numeric coordinates. [1]

assignment   The copying of one variable into another. [3]

available list   A linked list containing nodes that are presently not in use for active data storage. [2], [12]

AVL-rotation   A process by which a tree is maintained in a form close to full, thereby ensuring rapid insertions and searches. Developed by Adelson-Velskii and Landis. See also height-balanced tree. [7]

backward arc   Indicates that it is possible to follow arcs through a graph to arrive at one's origin. [9]

band matrices: Matrices in which the nonzero entries tend to cluster around the middle of each row. [8]

binary buddy system   A memory allocation system is which all blocks are of a size 2^i for some i. When a block is split, the resulting blocks must be equal in size. Available space is kept track of using a doubly linked list. [12]

binary search   A method used to search an ordered list. The search begins in the middle of a table and determines whether the argument is in the upper or lower half of the table, and then continues to divide that portion of the table in which the argument being sought is located until the argument is found. [11]

binary tree   A finite set of elements arranged into a structure consisting of a root and two disjoint subtrees. [6]

binary tree index   Stores nodes containing a key and a pointer to a record associated with that key in a binary tree. [11]

binary tree representation of a general tree   Requires that each node have only two pointer fields. The first pointer indicates the leftmost child of the node, and the second pointer identifies the next sibling of the node. [7]

binary tree search   Implements the binary search method through use of a binary tree structure. [11]

blocking   The positioning of records into contiguous regions on a track of a disk so that a fixed number are brought into main memory when a record in that block is requested. [11]

boundary folding   When producing a hash position, every other number in a key is reversed before being added into the total. [11]

boundary tag buddy system   A garbage collection scheme that allows arbitrary selection of block sizes, thereby saving memory from being wasted. [12]

B-tree   A generalized tree that can dynamically handle insertions and deletions without a deterioration in search efficiency. Its main application is as an index into a file. [11]

bubble sort   Compares the top element of an array with its successor, swapping the two if they are not in the proper order. [10]

bucket hashing   Transforms a key to a position representing a physically contiguous region of locations. After having hashed to the bucket, records are accessed sequentially. [11]

chained pointer database   A database relationship in which the use of a secondary key is handled by linking together all those records that share a given value for the secondary key. [12]

child   A descendant of a preceding node in a tree. [6]

circular linked list   A linked list in which the last node of the list points to the first node in the list, eliminating the need for null pointers. [2]

CODASYL model   A database management system that uses the notion of a set to describe one-to-many and simple network relationships. [12]

column major   A method by which multidimensional arrays are stored in a linear sequence in memory by columns. [8]

concatenation   The joining together of two character strings. [3]

clustering   A problem arising when a hashing function is biased toward placement of keys into a single region within a storage space. [11]

collisions   A problem arising in hashing when two items hash to the same position. [11]

compaction   A process by which character strings are relocated in memory resulting in a shift of available free space to one large contiguous memory region. [12]

complex network   A directed graph where there are many-to-many relationships between records. [12]

cross arc   Uses the depth-first search to connect various nodes on different trees within the spanning forest of a graph. [9]

cycle   A path in a directed graph of length at least 1 that originates and terminates at the same node in the graph. [9]

database   A collection of logically related data files on which operations are performed. [12]

database management   The problem of managing a collection of logically related files. [12]

data duplication problem   A problem arising in database management that occurs when the same information is stored more than once in separate files. [12]

data structure   A way of organizing data that considers not only the items stored but also their relationships to each other. Requires efficient algorithms for accessing the data both in main memory and on secondary storage devices. Efficiency is intrinsically linked to the structure of data being processed. [1]

DBMS   Database management system [12]

deletion   A procedure that removes a designated portion of a string from a larger string. [3]

density-dependent search   A search method that is dependent on the ratio of the number of records currently in the list divided by the total record space available. [11]

depth of a tree   The maximum level of any node in a tree. [6]

digraph   A graph in which an edge between two nodes is directionally oriented. [9]

diminishing return sort   A synonym for shell sort. [10]

direct (random) access   The ability to access any location in a storage medium without first having to access prior locations. [11]

directory   The index that stores file locations. [11]

dope vector   Contains information that helps to interpret the actual data in an array. [8]

doubly linked list   A linked list containing two pointers, one to its predecessor and another to its successor, thus allowing traversal of the list both backwards and forwards. [2]

dummy header   A node in a linked list that points to the first node that contains valid data. It is used to simplify code for insertions and deletions at the beginning of a linked list. [2]

edge   A directed path between two nodes of a graph. [9]

execution time   A measure of the efficiency of an algorithm determined by the number of operations that must be performed. [1], [10]

external sorting   The sorting of data that resides on secondary storage device. [10]

extraction   Removing any digits or characters that are likely to bias a hash value of a key before hashing. [11]

Fibonnaci buddy system   A garbage collection scheme that allows for a large variety of possible block size within a given memory space by allocating blocks of a size in the Fibonnaci sequence. [12]

Fibonnaci numbers   Numbers that are the sum of the preceding two numbers in a sequence. For example, 1, 1, 2, 3, 5, 8, 13 . . . [12]

field   A subdivision of a record that contains an elementary data item. [11]

fixed length method   String variables are allocated to handle the maximum possible string length that is envisioned for an application. [3]

folding   A hashing method by which noninteger keys are transformed into integers suitable for further hashing action. [11]

fragmentation   A problem that occurs when allocation and deallocation of memory breaks free space up into smaller, less useful portions. [12]

garbage collection   The effective recovery of memory that is no longer in use. [12]

generalized dope vector method   A method of efficiently representing sparse band matrices. [8]

general tree   A tree in which each node may have any number of descendant nodes. [7]

graph   A many-to-many relationship between objects in a database. [9]

graph traversal   An algorithm that determines the possible ways of visiting the nodes of a graph. [9]

hashing function   Acts upon a given key in such a way as to return a position in a list where the key can be placed. [11]

heap sort   A two-phase sort procedure that uses a full binary tree structure. [10]

height-balanced tree   Maximizes the speed with which insertions and searches are handled by decreasing the depth to which one must search for an item in a tree. It involves maintaining full trees. See AVL-rotation. [7]

hierarchical model   A database model that limits its users to specifying one-to-many relationships. Many-to-many relationships can be implemented only by decomposition into one-to-many relations.

incidence matrix   A way the physical structure of a graph can be represented by a matrix that holds locational information about the nodes in the graph. [9]

indegree   The number of arcs entering a node. [9]

index   A list of keys and locational information around which a file is organized. [11]

indexed sequential access method   A partial index is built that leads to an appropriate region, where a sequential search is then undertaken. [11]

infix   In the determination of an arithmetic expression the arithmetic operator appears between the two operands to which it is being applied. Infix notation often requires parentheses to specify a desired order of operation. [5]

inorder predecessor   The node that, in an ordered list, comes before a node being examined. [7]

inorder successor   The node that, in an ordered list, follows a node being examined. [7]

inorder traversal   An algorithm that moves through a tree in such a fashion that an ordered list results. [6]

insertion   The procedure by which a given string is added into the middle of another string. [3]

insertion sort   Inserts in the ith pass the ith element in its correct place. [10]

internal sorting   Retains all the data to be sorted in main memory. [10]

intersection record   A record used to link one-to-many relationships having that record in common into a many-to-many relationship. [12]

ISAM   Indexed sequential access method [11]

inverted files   Locates information about the data in small files that are maintained apart from the actual data records. These files are indices containing relative record positions of those records sharing identical values for a given secondary key. [12]

key   A data item that identifies a record. [11]

key-to-address transformation   An algorithm that acts on a given key in such a way as to return a position in a list where the key can be placed. A synonym for hashing. [11]

LABEL   A statement position identifier that can be referenced by other statements. [1]

left buddy count   Maintains a record of how deep a given block is nested as the left buddy of other blocks. [12]

iinear hashing   When a collision occurs while hashing, proceed down a list in sequential order until a vacant position is found. [11]

linked hashing   Requires a storage area divided into two parts—a prime hash area and an overflow area. Initially, a hashing function translates keys into the prime area. Collisions are resolved by linking into the overflow area. [11]

linked list   A structure that contains not only a data field but also one pointer to other nodes in the list. The pointer system in the linked list structure eliminates the need for a lot of movement of data. Thus, insertions and deletions become more economical in terms of processing time. [2]

linked list method   Allows for dynamic string allocation with no limit on string length and also for efficient insertions and deletions. [3]

many-to-many relationship   Each node or record in a database may be related to many other nodes or records without any limitation on the type of relationship. The relationship need not be hierarchical. See one-to-many relationship. [12]

matrix   A two-dimensional array in which the position of a data element must be specified by giving two coordinates. [8], [9]

merge sort   Most commonly used in external sorting. A file is divided into two subfiles. These files are compared, one pair of records at a time, and merged by writing them to other files for further comparisons. [10]

minimum spanning tree   A subcollection of the nodes and edges of a network that results in a tree of minimum edge weight. [9]

mod   The remainder of dividing two numbers P and Q. For example, 5 mod 2 = 1. [4]

multidimensional array   An array of rank higher than one. Each data element must be specified by giving one coordinate for each dimension. [8]

multilink files   A database relationship in which the use of a secondary key is handled by linking together all those records that share a given value for a secondary key. [12]

multilinked list   A linked list structure that has links for each of several orders in which the list is to be traversed. [2]

network   A graph with a value placed on the path between two nodes. For example, a distance between two places. [9]

one-dimensional array   A specific number of consecutive memory locations. This number is the size of the vector. [2]

one-to-many relationship   Each node or record in a file is hierarchically related to many other nodes or records in a database. [12]

outdegree   The number of arcs exiting a node of a digraph. [9]

parsing   The process of collapsing different expressions into one unique form, which simplifies its eventual evaluation. [5]

path   A sequence of arcs connecting two nodes of a digraph. [9]

pattern matching   The procedure by which one can search a given string for an occurrence of another string. [3]

polyphase merge sort   A merge sort using multiple channels. [10]

pop   Removing the top entry from a stack. [4]

postfix   In the determination of an arithmetic expression the need for parentheses is eliminated because the operator is placed directly after the two operands to which it applies. Also called reverse Polish notation. [5]

postorder traversal A recursive tree traversal in which the root is processed after its children. [6]

prefix In the determination of an arithmetic statement, the operator is placed directly before the two operands to which it applies. [5]

preorder traversal A recursive tree traversal in which the root is processed before its children. [6]

primary key The field on which a file is most commonly accessed. Usually primary keys are unique. [12]

push Adding a new entry onto a stack. [4]

quadratic hashing Resolves collisions by proceeding to locations HASH(KEY) + 1^2, HASH(KEY) + 2^2, HASH(KEY) + 3^2, . . . until an available position is found. [11]

quantity dependent search A search method the efficiency of which is dependent on the quantity of data stored. [11]

queue A first-in-first-out (FIFO) list structure in which insertions are limited to one end of the list, whereas deletions may occur only at the other end. [4], [5]

quick sort A pivotal item near the middle of the array is chosen, then moves are made such that items on one side of the pivot are smaller than the pivot and those on the other side are larger. This procedure is applied recursively until the whole array is sorted. [10]

randomized storage Sorting and accessing elements in a list by the use of a hashing function. [11]

rank The number of dimensions of an array. [8]

record A group of related data items. [11]

recursion A conditional call by a procedure or function to itself. [5]

relational model A database management system that describes the database in terms of tables called *relations*. [12]

relations A table of rows and columns in which each row corresponds to a record and each column to a field name. [12]

reverse Polish notation See postfix. [5]

root The highest level of a tree. It is the only node in the tree to which a direct pointer exists. [6]

row major The method by which multidimensional arrays are stored in a linear sequence in memory by allocating consecutive positions in a list for each new row. [8]

secondary key A key other than the primary key on which one may sort a file or search for an item. [12]

sector A predefined pie-shaped slice on a circular magnetic disk. [11]

selection sort Successive elements are selected from a file or array and placed in their proper position. [10]

sequential search Involves beginning with the first record in a list and examining each subsequent record until the record being sought is found. [11]

shell sort   An array is divided into smaller segments that are then separately sorted using insertion sort. [10]

shift folding   A hashing method by which noninteger keys are broken up and added into a total, which is used as the hash key. [11]

shortest path   An algorithm used in graph structures that proceeds by obtaining from nodes not yet selected that node closest to the source node and keeping track of these in an array. On completion of the algorithm, the data in the array determine the shortest path from a given node to all other nodes. [9]

simple network   A collection of several one-to-many relationships whose resulting representation as a graph is acyclic. [12]

singly linked list   A linked list in which each node contains only one link field pointing to the next node in the list. [2]

sink node   A node that has no arcs exiting from it. [9]

source node   A node that has no arcs entering it. [9]

spanning forest   A set of trees obtained by decomposing a graph with a depth-first search. [9]

sparse matrix   An array with a low percentage of nonzero entries. [8]

stack   A last-in-first-out (LIFO) list structure in which both insertions and deletions occur at only one end of the list. [4], [5]

string length   The length of a string is the number of characters in the string with all trailing blanks removed. For example, "TOOTbb" takes up 6 spaces. Its actual length is 4. [3]

strongly connected   A digraph in which there exists, for any two nodes, a bidirectional path between them. [9]

substring operations   A procedure that allows a user to examine a portion of a string. [3]

subtree   A subset of a tree that is itself a tree. [6]

symmetric matrix   A matrix in which the ith row and ith column always are identical. An incidence matrix for an undirected graph is an example. [9]

synonyms   Describes two keys that hash to the same position. [11]

ternary tree representation of general tree   Requires that each node of a general tree have three pointer fields; one for the left sibling, one for children, and one for a right sibling. [7]

threaded tree   Eliminates the need for recursive traversal through a tree by making use of null pointers to point to preceding or succeeding nodes. [7]

topological sort   An algorithm to establish an ordered relationship among the nodes of graph that ensures that its adjacency matrix has only zeros below the main diagonal. [10]

track   One of the concentric circles of storage into which a magnetic disk is divided. [11]

tree   A data structure that represents a hierarchical order of precedence between two related items. [6]

trie   A method of handling keys that are variable length strings. Each node of the trie consists of an array of pointers (one for each possible character) that point either to another node in the trie or to the actual data record for the key. [11]

upper triangular matrix   A matrix in which all entries below the main diagonal are zeros. [10]

variable length records problem   A database storage allocation problem that occurs when the length of a particular record is not fixed. [12]

vector   A one-dimensional array. [2]

volatile file   A file that undergoes frequent insertions and deletions. [11]

weakly connected   A digraph in which there exists between any two nodes a unidirectional path. [9]

workspace/index table method   One large memory workspace is allocated, and all strings are stored in it. Information about this string storage is kept in a separate index table. [3]

Index